This fascinating study in the sociology of knowledge documents the refutation of scientific foundations for racism in Britain and the United States between the two world wars, when racial differences were no longer attributed to biology but to culture. Dr Barkan considers the social significance of this transformation, particularly its effect on race relations in the modern world. Discussing the work of the leading biologists and anthropologists who wrote about race between the wars, he argues that the impetus for the shift in ideologies of race came from the inclusion of outsiders (women, Jews, and leftists) who infused greater egalitarianism into scientific discourse. But even though the emerging view of race was constrained by a scientific language, modern theorists were as much influenced by social and political events as were their predecessors.

THE RETREAT OF SCIENTIFIC RACISM

THE RETREAT OF SCIENTIFIC RACISM

Changing concepts of race in Britain and the United States between the world wars

ELAZAR BARKAN

CAMBRIDGE
UNIVERSITY PRESS

Published by the Press Syndicate of the University of Cambridge
The Pitt Building, Trumpington Street, Cambridge CB2 1RP
40 West 20th Street, New York NY 10011 4211, USA
10 Stamford Road, Oakleigh, Melbourne 3166, Australia

First published 1992
Reprinted 1996

Printed in Great Britain by Athenæum Press Ltd, Gateshead, Tyne & Wear

British Library cataloguing in publication data

Barkan, Elazar.
The retreat of scientific racism: changing concepts of race in Britain and the
United States between the world wars.
1. Race. Theories, history
I. Title
305.8001

Library of Congress cataloguing in publication data

Barkan, Elazar.
The retreat of scientific racism: changing concepts of race in Britain and the
United States between the world wars / Elazar Barkan.
p.   cm.
Includes Index.
ISBN 0 521 39193 8
1. Race. 2. Physical anthropology. 3. Eugenics – Great Britain – History. 4.
Eugenics – United States – History. 5. Racism – Great Britain – History. 6. Racism –
United States – History. 7. Great Britain – Race relations. 8. United States – Race
relations.
I. Title.
GN269.B368   1992
305.8 – dc20   90–20129   CIP

ISBN 0 521 391938 hardback

Transferred to digital reprinting 2000
Printed in the United States of America

In Memory of
Shmuel Benkler

Contents

ix

Preface

Racism is a universal affliction, but its representation as an oppressive and dogmatic ideology captured center stage only during the years between the World Wars. Prior to that time, social differentiation based upon real or assumed racial distinctions was thought to be part of the natural order. Hence, the principal retreat of racism conveyed the recognition that racial terminology is not value free, and that social organization based on a racial hierarchy is repugnant. To describe this change, I have reconstructed the scientific discourse on race among British and American anthropologists and biologists, whom I believe to have been pivotal in this shift. The actors in the story below were scientists of a very mixed bag, personally and professionally. Yet they all shared a belief that the centrality of race for cultural and political discourse depended largely on its scientific legitimacy. For various subjective motives – that is, sociological variables – they chose to address the topic of race, which was consequently transformed from a scientific fact into a political hot potato. Racism did not disappear but racial ideologies ceased to command respectability.

Despite the long-standing ambivalence about causality in the human sciences and although exclusionary explanatory claims have gradually diminished, the belief persists that affinities, long-term structural changes, and *mentalité*, provide the motives and rationale for historical changes. Admissions of contingency, indeterminism, and open-endedness often disguise a fundamental belief in causal relationships which cannot, however, be substantiated epistemologically. Therefore, I would like to make my belief explicit: within the social, economic and political constraints, the discourse on race enjoyed a certain degree of autonomy, and was shaped by the experts and intellectuals who appear in the following pages. Perhaps the prevalent conviction that racism is determined by social and

political factors is the best proof that the retreat I speak of has
become the dominating view.

"Making a difference" is the subject of this book. The repudiation of racism by scientists was a crucial step in the growth of
global egalitarianism. Disparities between the West and the rest –
as well as within Western democracies, together with the ever
present ethnic and racial animosities – may provide a sound basis
for skepticism regarding the retreat of racism. Yet, the shift has
occurred. Racial differences are viewed in cultural terms, not biological, xenophobia has become more egalitarian, and the strife is
no longer waged in the name of superiority. This transformation
has been the retreat of racism.

I have incurred many debts of genuine gratitude on the road
towards the final version of this book. My understanding of the
intellectual and political milieu of the period studied was enriched
by the personal memories and vignettes provided by Sir Raymond
Firth, Otto Klineberg, Robert K. Merton, Harry Shapiro, Dirk
Struik, and Lord Zuckerman, for whose time and generosity I am
grateful.

My intellectual apprenticeship owes much to Shulamit Volkov,
Saul Friedländer, and Yehuda Elkana, who introduced me to
important issues in cultural history during my early studies at Tel
Aviv University. Rudi Binion, Eugene Black, Sam Schweber and
Everett Mendelssohn provided guidance and encouragement
through the steps towards my dissertation at Brandeis University. I
am particularly indebted to I. Bernard Cohen, Daniel Kevles, and
George W. Stocking Jr. for their constructive comments on the
manuscript.

While writing this book I have been affiliated with Brandeis
University; the History of Science Department, the Center for
European Studies, and the Social Studies Program at Harvard
University; and the California Institute of Technology. Many col-
leagues have provided advice, support and friendship. Among them
I am especially grateful to Garland Allen, Peter Baldwin, Allan
Brandt, Nathan Glazer, Leigh Hafrey, Gerald Holton, the late
Nathan Huggins, Andy Markovits, Diane Paul, Barbara Gutmann-
Rosenkrantz, and Bernard Wasserstein, who have willingly read
and commented on my work at various stages. I would like to thank
Mary Lee and William Bossert, the Masters of Lowell House at
Harvard University, for their kindness and unmatched hospitality.

I am happy to acknowledge financial support for research from the Sachar International Fellowship, the Tauber Institute, the Memorial Foundation for Jewish Culture, and the Rockefeller Foundation. For assistance and permission to quote from unpublished archival sources I would like to thank Rear-Admiral J. A. L. Myres (J. L. Myres), Naomi Mitchison (J. B. S. Haldane), and the librarians of the Bodleian Library, Oxford; the Eugenics Society Records, Wellcome Institute for the History of Medicine, London; King's College, London; London School of Economics; University College, London; the University Library, Manuscript Division, Cambridge; the American Philosophical Society, Philadelphia; the National Anthropology Archives, Smithsonian Institute, Washington; the American Jewish Committee Archives, New York; the Library of Congress, Washington; the Woodson Research Center, Rice University, Houston; and in particular the Tozzer and Widener Libraries at Harvard University.

I am highly indebted to my editors, Jessica Kuper and Con Coroneos, for their patient and skillful suggestions which have greatly improved the quality of the manuscript.

My wife, Diana Barkan, has helped and encouraged me throughout. Many thanks.

Pasadena, 1990.

Abbreviations for manuscript collections

ACHP	A. C. Haddon, Cambridge, England
AES	American Eugenics Society Papers at the American Philosophical Society
AHP	A. Hrdlicka, National Anthropology Archives, Smithsonian Institute
AJC	American Jewish Committee Archives, New York
BMP	Bronislaw Malinowski, London School of Economics
CBDP	C. B. Davenport, American Philosophical Society
CPB	C. P. Blacker, in EUG/SA
CSP	C. S. Seligman, London School of Economics
EAHP	E. A. Hooton, Peabody Museum, Harvard University
EUG/SA	Eugenics Society Records, Wellcome Institute for the History of Medicine, London
FBP	Franz Boas, American Philosophical Society
FSP	Frederick Osborn, American Philosophical Society
HSJP	H. S. Jennings, American Philosophical Society
JBSHP	J. B. S. Haldane, University College, London
JCM	J. C. Merriam, Library of Congress
JLMP	John Linton Myres, Bodleian Library, Oxford
JMCP	J. M. Cattell Papers, Library of Congress
JSHP	J. S. Huxley, Rice University, Houston
KPP	Karl Pearson, University College, London
LLP	Lionel Penrose, University College, London
RPP	Raymond Pearl, American Philosophical Society
RRGP	R. R. Gates, King's College, London

Introduction

The Nazi regime has compelled us all to recognize the lethal
potential of the concept of race and the horrendous consequences of
its misuse. After World War II the painful recognition of what had
been inflicted in the name of race led to the discrediting of racism in
international politics and contributed to the decline and repudiation
of scientific racism in intellectual discourse. In charting the rise and
fall of racial thought and racism, the growing body of historical
literature has tended to focus on racist ideologues from the early
part of the twentieth century, ignoring the actual process of the
repudiation of racism.[1] Because racism nowadays is perceived as
irrational and unscientific, its elimination from culture and science
is deemed, at least implicitly, to have been inevitable: once Nazi
atrocities had been revealed, racism was rejected. An extension of
this view is the historical misconception that Nazi racism was
renounced as early as the 1930s. In fact, the response in both the
United States and Britain was neither immediate nor of sufficient
strength to discredit theories of racial superiority. By 1938 only a
small segment of the educated public had reformulated its attitude
on the question of race in response to the Nazi menace.

This book examines the scientific repudiation of racism by
reconstructing the discourse on race in Britain and the United
States between the world wars. During this period, race was
perceived primarily as a scientific concept, a perception which was

---

[1] Leon Poliakov in *The Aryan Myth: A History of Racist and Nationalist Ideas in Europe* (New York;
New American Library, 1971) places the myth at the center of Western culture, but does not
devote any space to its decline. Standard works include: Thomas F. Gosset, *Race, The History
of an Idea in America* (1963; New York: Schocken Books, 1965); Nancy Stepan, *The Idea of Race
in Science* (Hamden, Conn: Archon Books, 1982); Michael Banton, *Racial and Ethnic
Competition*, Comparative Ethnic and Race Relations Series (Cambridge: Cambridge
University Press, 1983), and *Racial Theories* (Cambridge: Cambridge University Press,
1987); Hamilton Cravens, *The Triumph of Evolution, American Scientists and the Heredity –
Environment Controversy, 1900–1941* (Philadelphia: University of Pennsylvania Press, 1978).

itself a legacy of the nineteenth century. By the turn of the century, racial theories which constructed a hierarchy of races with the Nordic at the top were considered factual, free of prejudice and generally pertinent to social and political analysis. Scientists were entrusted with the tasks of discriminating between fact and opinion and defining the social and political discourses of race. Accordingly, the focus of this study is upon the scientific community, in particular biologists and anthropologists. It compares national beliefs with professional ideas, demonstrating that the initial scientific repudiation of racism *preceded* the rise of Nazism and thus discredited a crucial source of high-brow racism. While the defeat of Nazism undoubtedly helped in disseminating the rejection of racist ideas, the rebuff of Nazi racism itself was not a *sui generis* response. The decline of scientific racism was due to changes in the sciences and of the scientists themselves, and was closely related to the politics of race in Britain and the United States.

RACE AND RACISM

At the beginning of the twentieth century, the term "race" had a far wider meaning than at present, being used to refer to any geographical, religious, class-based or color-based grouping. Although sanctioned by science, its scientific usage was multiple, ambiguous and at times self-contradictory. The inherent confusion of the term has been recognized by The Oxford English Dictionary which notes its imprecise usage "even among anthropologists," the lack of a "generally accepted classification or terminology" and the resultant "almost unlimited attributes and combinations."[2] Despite the confusion, race was a respectable scientific category. Typologies and hierarchies of race were presented as self-evidently appropriate at the beginning of the century, and cultural analysis along racial lines conveyed no particular stigma. Although "racialism" denoting prejudice based on race difference, was introduced into the language at the turn of the century, there was little use for the term because racial differences were regarded as matters of fact, not of prejudice. Race was perceived to be a biological category, a natural phenomenon unaffected by social forces. The major social thinkers of the second half of the nineteenth century did not articulate any critique of racial theories; even for self-proclaimed egalitarians, the

[2] OED, Supplement vol. 3, 1972.

inferiority of certain races was no more to be contested than the law of gravity to be regarded as immoral. Before any social critique of racial thinking was possible, the belief in the biological validity of race as a concept had to be undermined. This occurred in the twentieth century during the interwar years, although doubts about the validity of race were present much earlier. While the OED included such derivatives as "racism" and "racial" for the first time only in 1972, it notes that the term "racial" began to be used frequently at the end of the nineteenth century. The use of "racism" as a derogatory neologism was first recorded in English in the 1930s but again the appearance of a neologism to denote racial prejudice suggests that the debunking of race theories and their crude political analogies began sometime earlier. Certainly, little more than a decade after the end of World War I the situation changed dramatically. Among leading scientific circles in the United States and Britain, race typology as an element of causal cultural explanation became largely discredited, racial differentiation began to be limited to physical characteristics, and prejudicial action based on racial discrimination came to be viewed as racism.

One reason for this decline was a lack of epistemological foundations for racial classification, a lack which led to endless irresolvable inconsistencies and contradictions. For example, a popular anthropological method for delineating races was the measurement of skulls and other bodily features. Despite visible exterior physical differences among, say, Orientals, Whites, Blacks, and Amerindians, it became apparent to anthropologists that racial typology was incapable of any consistent demarcations, and the classification quandary made formal taxonomy impossible. Furthermore, numerous distinct populations did not conform to accepted categories, and any classification became hopelessly entangled with themes of ethnicity and nationality, encouraging many scholars to deny the possibility of a "science of race."[3] In addition to the unresolved dispute over the relative impact of heredity versus environment and the proliferation of disciplinary approaches, ethnicity and culture further obscured the subject of race. Thus, as a social category which refers to a supposedly recognizable entity based on primordial biological properties, notions of race sustained its popular appeal

---

[3] An early version and a classic is Ashley M. F. Montagu, *Man's Most Dangerous Myth; The Fallacy of Race*, foreword by Aldous Huxley (New York: Columbia University Press, 1942; fifth edn, New York: Oxford University Press, 1974).

and is still widely invoked. It is for this reason that one can talk about attitudes towards race, even at a time when scientific opinion rejects the usefulness of race as a classificatory tool. While intuitively the present role of racial ideas in society may counter the sense that scientifically race has declined, the distinction between race as a scientific idea and as a social category needs to be borne in mind.

The decline during the 1920s in the scientific respectability of applying racial-biological perspectives to cultural questions left the field open to commentators who were interested in the subject for broadly defined political motives and not merely for intrinsically scientific reasons. The competing disciplinary attitudes – including a scientific rejection of the validity of racial typology – collided with a rise in political prejudice within Europe. This polarized the debate over race, and facilitated the debunking of what came to be viewed as racism. The discrediting of race prejudice was a result of the conscious efforts and commitment of a minority of scientists who pursued their goal through scientific research and writing, as well as through academic politics. In most respects, these scientists belonged to the core of the scientific establishment, but to some extent they remained social and political outsiders. This duality and tension particularly explains their relative sensitivity to race.

THE PROFESSIONALIZATION OF THE STUDY OF RACE

Traditionally, the science of race belonged to physical anthropology which became popular in the mid nineteenth century, reached its zenith at the turn of the century, and its nadir in the years before World War II. With physical anthropology losing ground during the first half of the twentieth century, race came to be addressed by scientists from a number of new fields – genetics, social and cultural anthropology, sociology and psychology. Many were involved in the eugenics movement, which was much concerned with racial questions. By the 1930s, however, fewer scientists were devoting their career solely to the scientific study of race: "raciology" was a vanishing vocation. Despite the growing stature of genetics as the science of heredity, human genetics offered no explanation of the physical distinctions vital to racial classifications. Physical anthropologists accumulated data which had no epistemological justification, nor did their data yield results that could sanction comparisons meaningful beyond local variations. Sociologists, for professional reasons, were only too happy to avoid reducing social differences to racial taxonomy, but had to leave the critique of the biological foundation of race to biologists and anthropologists. Psychologists seized on the professional quandary over race rather early, and by the mid-twenties began to discredit the notion of inherent mental differences between racial groups. In none of these areas was the study of race part of the disciplinary canon. Typically, while the scientists and scholars I discuss in the book were central to the discussion on race, for most of them the study of race was not their main endeavor.

My comparison between the American and British scientific communities suggests that historial and geographical conditions, more than internal scientific considerations, determined their specific views on race. The degree of racial sensibility – lesser in Britain than in the United States – affected ideas about race. Scientists addressed the concept of race in relation to their social and institutional traditions. This may seem self-evident to the reader because the topic of race nowadays is viewed as overtly political. Yet, the central role of politics to the concept of race in this study should not lead to a reductionist conclusion that science determined politics, nor the reverse, that politics determined science. Rather the two were strongly intertwined. The scientific "base," "structure," "*longue durée*," was inexorably compounded with the political "superstructure," and "events."

In the long run the need for scientific validation constrained both racists and egalitarians. Developments in science helped more to discredit unfounded claims than to clarify the idea of race. For example, according to a theory popular in the first two decades of the century, physical and social characteristics, such as height, intelligence, color, or behavior, are inherited through a single gene. However, laboratory work in genetics at the time distinguished between phenotype and genotype, and indicated that heredity was much more complex. A physical characteristic was shown to be generated by numerous genes with greatly varied consequences. Within a scientifically accepted spectrum, individual scientists opted for certain versions of the numerous coexisting explanations and claims. But, once a theory was categorically proved wrong, no political commitment in an open society could sustain it. Falsification was thus important in closing off opinions. But non-falsification was not a proof, it merely left the theory as a tool in the political field.

In the following pages, I investigate this construction of scientific conventions of race within the social context of the professional community. In this reconstruction, I explore how individual scientists integrated science and politics in the formulation of the concept of race. It was scientists as individuals who elected whether or not to participate in public debate, and to adopt one perspective over another. There were no strict conventions of behavior, rather there were various accepted professional positions from egalitarianism to racism. The scientists discussed in this book were selected because they actively participated in the debate on race, and their positions on the issue are examined in part through their biographies. In considering how formative experience contributed and shaped the individual scholar's attitude to race, I look at age, professional and social aspirations (and rivalry), ideological commitments, chosen medium, and idiosyncrasies. These factors have all proved to be significant in suggesting an explanation as to why one scientist chose a certain perspective in preference to another in the debate over race.

Yet, while dealing with individuals, my focus remains on the scientific community. Ideas or individuals exist only as part of a discourse. I examine individual contributors to the discussion in an attempt to show the disparate viable scientific options. In this manner, a number of scientists may emerge as heroes in the fight against racism, but stardom depended upon an individual's professional standing, not merely on the adoption of a substantive position. The impact of each scientist on the evolution of the concept of race was determined by social criteria – the scientist's professional position and exposure. Left-wing circles in England and intellectuals in New York provided a congenial atmosphere to scientists who debunked scientific theories which supported racism as a response to contemporary politics. Hence these are discussed in greater detail, especially in the third part of the book. In these sub-cultures, scientists nurtured their new egalitarian positions even before they reached out to their peers and the public.

While either anthropology or biology could have served as a focal sub-discourse to explore the shift against racism, many members of these disciplines never participated in the discussion on race. My comparison of two scientific disciplines in two countries therefore enables me to examine those factors which transcend the specific features of each community. Anthropologists in the United States and biologists in Britain provided the leadership in discrediting racism. This suggests that neither the national nor the disciplinary discourse was sufficient to determine a scientist's position on race. Thus, in addition to the intrinsic interest of the biographical details of individual scholars, it is of methodological importance to understand the individual positions on the issue of race not only in the communal context, but also from a personal perspective.

Through analyzing the work and lives of the protagonists, it is possible to separate the scientifically acceptable and culturally respectable from claims that were being gradually discredited as racism. Scientists, however, are not always eager to elucidate publicly, nor to probe for themselves, the non-scientific motives involved in a certain research theme. It is necessary, then, to set the image of "scientific objectivity," projected by biologists and anthropologists against their personal commitments and political views. I focus on centers and elites within the scientific community, but at the same time seek to avoid whiggish or synoptic treatment: I do not present science in terms of preordained progress, nor do I build an edifice of a coherent body of knowledge about race as elucidated by scientists who were at the forefront of their discipline and held similar opinions. None the less, "pure" science swayed the racial views of its practitioners. This approach of reconstructing the discourse on race led me to include various contemporary participants, whose long term contributions have vanished, while leaving out a number of major anthropologists and biologists who were silent on the issue of race.[4]

In the last hundred years scientists are primarily "specific" professional intellectuals: that is, their credentials stem from knowledge of their discipline which at times they use in the political arena. Thus, their political status (both within and outside academia) depends on their professional standing. There are, however, few scientists who retain the status of intellectuals, that is they constitute a "universal" breed and are "acknowledged the

---

[4] T. H. Morgan and Sewell Wright are conspicuously absent. Both supported the eugenics movement in the early twenties but had no specific or unique view. Thus while their racial and eugenic views are of interest in a study of their own science, they are less so in a study of race. Bronislaw Malinowski played a minor role in the refutation of racism relative to his contributions to anthropology; hence, the minimal attention he receives despite his centrality to the discipline.

right of speaking in the capacity of master of truth and justice,"
even on topics where their credentials are not pertinent.[5] During
the interwar years a number of scientists enjoyed wide popularity
and played the role of universal intellectuals, but the status of most
scientists depended upon their professional position, with a great
diversity within each generation in their approach to politics,
especially among scientists who constituted the "center."

The distinction between scientists who are considered experts –
scientific intellectuals – and those who are viewed as universal
savants depends in part upon their degree of involvement. The
least engaged were those who commented on the subject only
occasionally. Those who opposed race dogmatism recognized the
dominance of culture in explanations of racial differences, but they
did not devote any special effort towards criticizing the pervasive
use of racial typology in general discourse. Instead they provided
tacit support for attempts to undermine the connection between
science and race dogmatism. A second group consisted of those
who participated in some professional anti-racist activities, may
have published in professional journals, but did not assume the role
of leaders of public opinion. The third group, the hard core,
included those who published in the popular/political press, a
number of whom devoted monographs to the refutation of racism.
All of them became politically committed to the fight against
scientific racism.

The last group, which combined a professional with a general
appeal, comprises most of the academicians examined in this book.
They were not necessarily the most important contemporary
scientists in their field (though many were), nor were their contributions in the long term the most substantial. Rather, their significance stems from the special needs of addressing professional
and general audiences simultaneously. This proved most effective
in shaping the scientific discourse on race, and their writing
became authoritative. At their best they combined the status of a
universal intellectual with that of the scientist, the expert.[6] With
the growing turmoil and increasing political stakes surrounding
racism, a larger number of scientists resorted, under the guise of

[5] Foucault separates the professional from the intellectual along generational lines. Michel
Foucault, *Power/Knowledge; Selected Interviews and Other Writings 1972–1977*, edited by Colin
Gordon (New York: Pantheon Books, 1980), pp. 126–133.
[6] Foucault's term (*Power/Knowledge*, pp. 126–133) for the scientist is the "absolute savant."

science, to political propaganda. Fighting racism was a glorious use of scientific credentials, but was none the less political.

The common denominator for those involved scientists who discredited racism was that while they belonged to the establishment, they were also outsiders. This group, mostly university teachers belong to a homogeneous genteel milieu, was differentiated, however, along lines of ethnic marginality, gender, geography, politics and ideology.[7] In these scientific elites, humble background was not a formal hurdle, but affiliation with the intellectual aristocracy in England, such as J. B. S. Haldane or Julian Huxley, proved a distinct advantage. Both Haldane and Huxley were insiders on account of their social professional position, while their politics placed them outside the mainstream. The status of partial outsider encouraged a greater sensitivity to racial attributes, and led to active criticism of racism. The United States had neither a comparable aristocracy nor politically radical scientists. Instead, the core of the discipline was determined largely by geographical proximity to major academic centers. Distance and lack of communication continuously frustrated close interaction. Geography in and of itself was important; New York was the center of racial discourse in the United States. California was too far away from the center for even the most prominent of its scientists to participate in the national scientific-intellectual discourse on race.

While biology was relatively homogeneous socially and politically, the presence of Jews and women in anthropology was significant. Gender and ethnicity played an important part in sorting out convictions on race. While Jews, the single most eminent minority in the scientific community, were institutionally and scientifically – though not so much socially – insiders, they were discredited on the question of race for having a subjective, minority, agenda. There was a general distrust in intellectual discourse for "special interests." This served to delegitimize Jewish authorities in the fight against racism.[8] Black social scientists produced distin-

---

[7] Edward Shils, *The Intellectuals and the Powers* (Chicago: University of Chicago Press, 1972), the theoretical parts and especially "British Intellectuals in the Mid Twentieth Century," pp. 135–153, and his "Center and Periphery" in *The Constitution of Society* (Chicago: University of Chicago Press, 1982), pp. 93–109; Joseph Ben-David, *The Scientists' Role in Society*, with a new introduction (Chicago: The University of Chicago Press, 1971, 1984), especially the introduction and chapter I; Robert K. Merton, "The Perspective of Insiders and Outsiders," in *The Sociology of Science* (Chicago: University of Chicago Press, 1973).

[8] Merton, "The Perspective of Insiders and Outsiders," *The Sociology of Science*; for comparison with later views on subjectivity, see also George De Vos and Lola Romanucci-Ross,

guished work, but their unique influence was felt primarily within black sociology. Before World War II, their impact on the black community was greater than on the wider society and negligible within the scientific community. Among the few women who belonged to the scientific establishment, the most renowned were anthropologists. Within the dominant group – upper class Englishmen and Wasps, the crucial factor in determining a position on race were ideology and political affinity, but the rule of thumb that left-of-center scientists were more likely to renounce racism applied only since the 1930s.

The role of scientists as intellectuals was evident first of all within the scientific community. Their impact on public opinion was largely indirect and at times enigmatic. It is possible to think of the transformation of the concept of race within sub-discourses. The initial construction took place within a relatively cohesive group of scientists based upon "tacit knowledge" and social "intuitions" which shaped relations within the community – it was then disseminated to a wider public.[9] Intermediate stages between the public discourse and the internal disciplinary discussion were within the educated public and among scientists in general. The group of scientists within each discipline, subdiscipline or speciality, represented different sub-discourses. However, individuals belonged concurrently to several groups according to sociological classifications which included ethnicity, class and geography. Hence, for an idea to receive legitimacy, it first had to be accepted within a peer group, and then disseminated by its members to other spheres. The ideas which eventually led to the shift in the concept of race originated at several different levels, and, depending on the circumstances, were then relayed to other groups.

This book describes the rejection of racism in science by focusing in the first part on the growth of skepticism concerning the validity of racial theories that developed initially among anthropologists. This skepticism resulted from their recognition that study of the biological fundamentals of racial heredity was beyond the range of

Ethnic Identity, Cultural Continuities and Change (Chicago: University of Chicago Press, 1982); Joyce Lander (ed), The Death of White Sociology (New York; Vintage Books, 1973); Talal Asad (ed), Anthropology and the Colonial Encounter (London: Ithaca Press, 1973).

[9] T. S. Kuhn, The Structure of Scientific Revolutions, 2nd edn (Chicago: University of Chicago Press, 1970), p. 195. The switch from race to ethnicity could correspond to a shift in paradigms in Kuhn's sense of "the entire constellation of beliefs, values ... shared by the members of a given community" (p. 175), but this terminology can not be sustained since there was no science of race, and raciology even in its hey-day was not an academic discipline.

their discipline. It led anthropologists to pursue cultural and social studies of race, while they hoped biologists would explicate the mechanism of racial heredity and the relation between genetics and social characteristics.

The biologists' attitudes are examined in the second part, which explores the way in which they faced the challenge of studying the social significance of racial heredity while lacking pertinent knowledge. Fruit flies and paramecia enabled biologists to elucidate a more sophisticated view of the process of heredity and its interaction with the environment, and to illuminate the distinctions between phenotype and genotype. However, this research did not provide data on such racial characteristics as color or physiognomy. The growth of biological knowledge enabled false racial claims made in the name of science to be refuted; it closed off options of what came to be viewed as pseudo-science. But biologists were unable to provide an assertive statement about the nature and significance of race.

Following the discrediting of assumed knowledge of racial characteristics, a number of scientists explicitly rejected racial typology as racism, and popularized anti-racist ideas in both interpretive and theoretical work. The third part of the book describes the declining appeal of race during the 1930s, particularly in its manifestly political aspects. It focuses on the scientists who accepted the responsibility of opposing racism as it was advanced in the name of science. These scientists became political activists and leading intellectuals ready to address the issue of race even though it had become politically anathema for most of their peers.

PART I

Anthropology

CHAPTER I

Constructing a British identity

COLORS INTO RACES

The modern meaning of race[1] originated in eighteenth-century zoology, and was later applied to humans by Johann Friedrich Blumenbach, who formulated a terminology of physical anthropology and classified humankind into the now all-too-familiar color categories: black, brown, yellow, red and white. Blumenbach, influenced by the relatively open-minded and non-xenophobic ideology of the Enlightenment, stressed both the continuity of racial varieties as part of a great human unity, and the impossibility of drawing exact demarcations.[2] Similarly his compatriot, Johann Herder, in locating race within the social sciences, saw it as the result more of the "physico-geographical history of man" than of a "systematic natural history."[3] The scientific interest in racial classification was deepened by European exposure to a greater variety of previously unknown human "types" in the expeditions of the late eighteenth century, as well as by Europe's increasing intercontinental trade with, and economic dependency upon, non-European resources – especially the African slave trade.

During the nineteenth century scientists reified the concept of race and endowed it with explanatory powers beyond its initial taxonomic purpose. In the first half of the century, polygenism became popular and the perceived distinctions among races sharply widened. Physical differences were correlated with cultural and

[1] For an earlier usage of race to describe the alien, see John Block Friedman, *The Monstrous Races in Medieval Art and Thought* (Cambridge, Mass.: Harvard University Press, 1981).

[2] J. F. Blumenbach, "On the Natural Variety of Mankind" (1775), in *Anthropological Treatise*, trans. T. Bendyshe (London: Anthropological Society, 1865), pp. 98–99, 100.

[3] Johann Herder, *Outlines of a Philosophy of the History of Man*, trans. T. Churchill (Riga, 1784; London: J. Johnson, 1803), I, p. 298.

social status through biological justification. Whether or not this was the purpose of all race theorists,[4] political domination buttressed by biological rationalization proliferated during the second half of the nineteenth century – one result of the growing reputation enjoyed by biology in the aftermath of the *Origins of Species*. The theory of evolution inherently illuminates changes. None the less, the acceptance of evolution did not mitigate the belief in the permanence of racial type, and although race maintained its status as a biological entity, its characterization became more complicated.

Color differentiation alone was no longer adequate as a method for explicating racial variety. Several alternative methods were used to supplement it. The most important physical taxonomy was based on head or skull shape, a feature presumed to be stable over numerous generations. The measurement represented averages which were supposed to describe real racial divisions according to broad and long heads.[5] Other popular indexes included hair and eye color, and nose shape. A different taxonomy dealt with linguistic divisions, and of the various possibilities here the tracing of the racial heredity of the Aryans in Europe became the most popular pursuit.

Count Gobineau, the "father of racist ideology," mixed aristocratic pessimism, romanticism, theology together with biology, all of which became part of a shared European value system based on racial differentiation. Gobineau's views on race were a culmination of pre-Darwinian ideas: a description of permanent types aimed at a moral genealogy, classified into epochs which were separated by catastrophes. His focus was on civilization, not on physical anthropology, but he viewed hybridization as both the source of civilization and of degeneracy, the latter accounting for his pessimism.[6]

---

[4] It has been argued that race was a concept invented by the ruling classes in order to maintain privileges. Ashley Montagu, *Man's Most Dangerous Myth: The Fallacy of Race*, (1942; fifth edn, New York: Oxford University Press, 1974), pp. 38–39.

[5] The cephalic index as a tool of racial classification originated with Anders Retzius, a Swedish anatomist, who in 1842 applied the system to Europe. The index represented the ratio of width to length (width × 100/length). The technical term for the elongated skull was dolicocephalic (below 75), the broader skull was called brachycephalic (above 80) and mesocephalic was located in between. This division became the focal point of racial studies, producing the tripartite European division of Nordic, Alpine, and Mediterranean. Retzius attempted to fit the socio-linguistic units in Europe to the biological morphologies, but he was pre-evolutionist and never came to appreciate the taxonomic limitations. See Earl W. Count (ed.), *This Is Race. An Anthology Selected From the International Literature on Races of Man* (New York: Schuman, 1950), pp. 75–89, 709–710; Nancy Stepan, *The Idea of Race in Science* (Hamden, Conn: Archon Books, 1982), p. 97.

[6] Arthur De Gobineau, *The Inequality of Human Races* (1853; New York: Howard Fertig, 1967); Michael D. Biddiss, *Father of Racist Ideology: The Social and Political Thought of Count Gobineau*

The survival of the idea of a permanent type within the new evolutionary framework enhanced Gobineau's appeal for the new generation of thinkers.

The search for racial antiquity stimulated developments in Teutonic anthropology and Aryan linguistics – fields which were always very closely related. Whether the time scale was to be historical or zoological, however, was never established, and two related disciplines, classical archaeology and paleontology, were often utilized indiscriminately. Not surprisingly the different questions raised in these disciplines led to disparate results and perplexing racial descriptions. As Thomas Henry Huxley had shown, there was no necessary correlation between race and language, but his caution was heeded by few.[7] The driving force behind racial differentiation was nationalism, which demanded of its followers total commitment, even at the expense of internal logic and incoherence. The intensification of national rivalry in Europe in the latter part of the century stimulated the pursuit of still greater racial differentiation. The increasing number of racial categories around this time reflected an eagerness to use primordial affinities as modes of justification for nationalism sanctioned by the growing repute of biology and evolution theory.

The flood of racial systems obfuscated the nature of race irreversibly. Concurrently, the study of race was becoming institutionalized through the establishment of anthropological societies in Paris, London, New York, Moscow, Florence, Berlin and Vienna. These societies testified to – and provided the locus for – the growing interest in the scientific study of race, which reinforced notions of the hierarchy, antiquity, and immutability of human races. Anthropologists disagreed over whether the different human groups constituted a species division or merely a racial one. The main difference was between the polygenists who did not believe in evolution and therefore judged the different species to be a result of different creation, and the monogenists who believed in a single species. When Darwin addressed the question in the *Descent of Man*, he pointed to the disagreements "among capable judges" (who divided humans into groups varying in number from 2 to 63) and empha-

(New York: Weybright and Talley, 1970); Banton, *The Idea of Race* (London: Tavistock, 1977), pp. 41–46.

[7] T. H. Huxley, "Ethics and Evolution" (1893), in *Evolution and Ethics and Other Essays* (London: Macmillan, 1894), pp. 1–45.

sized that races "graduate into each other, and that it is hardly possible to discover clear distinctive characters between them." His conclusion that racial differences were not of great evolutionary importance was mostly ignored by his contemporaries, and the enigma of the mechanism of heredity and the riddle of functionalism versus sexual selection in racial adaptation remained.

Consequently, the proliferation of data failed to answer the problem of how to discriminate between alternative methodologies. The general purpose was to define and delineate the original pure races and to look for the unity behind the great variety. The search was for real primordial races, not abstractions, and the oft-quoted definition by Paul Topinard of race as "an abstract conception, a notion of continuity in discontinuity," should not be misunderstood to be questioning the existence of race. Topinard pointed to the shortcoming of physical anthropology in describing these ancestral races in the hope of salvaging the principle of taxonomy.[8] Increased data aggravated methodological problems but this situation did not turn into an epistemological dilemma until after World War I.

Race theories and racism have been presented as an almost natural outcome of the power relationships between various groups. This is supposedly most evident in the case of the blacks' enslavement in the United States. Yet, the South American experience suggests that it was not an inevitable outcome. There, the freed black was accorded a substantial degree of social equality. In the United States in contrast, race outlived slavery and became an independent ingredient "fatally united with the physical and permanent fact of color."[9] Race perceptions were greatly influenced by race relations, but the precise reciprocity was not predetermined.

During the nineteenth century racism as a derogatory term to denote disapproval of racial classification did not exist. From a later twentieth century hindsight the beliefs of most Europeans in their own racial superiority could be labeled racist. Yet, such lumping may be misleading, because even within the reified hierarchical perception of race in the 19th century, there existed a spectrum of

---

[8] P. Topinard, *Anthropology* (London: Chapman and Hall).

[9] A. de Tocqueville, *Democracy in America*, trans. George Lawrence, ed. J. P. Mayer (Garden City, NY: Doubleday, 1969), I, pp. 355–363. Recent scholarship, especially from Brazil, has maintained the dichotomy between North and South America, while suggesting a more sophisticated view and a less clear opposition. For historiographical and historical perspective, see Carl Degler, *Neither Black nor White. Slavery and Race Relations in Brazil and the United States* (Wisconsin: The University of Wisconsin Press, 1986).

opinions from vicious xenophobia and aggressive racism to bene-
volent self-exaltation. Disregarding this differentiation may testify
to a high moral stand, but it is still important to recognize the
contextual contemporary differentiation in the perceptions of the
nature of race because these created later nuances which facilitated
a rejection of racism.

The "Aryan Myth" was central at the turn of the century not only
in Germany but also in Britain and the United States. It was
seductive to the European mind because it posited a high-brow
racism underwritten by an increasingly reputable science. But if
science legitimized racism, it also made it vulnerable to changes in
scientific outlook. To the degree that science was subject to its own
internal dynamics, scientific developments served eventually to
discredit racist claims. It led to questioning and later the disappearance of a primordial race of mythical ancestors and an
inevitable decline in the appeal of race: the greater the popularity of
the science of race became, the more data were available and the
more elusive turned the primordial ancestors. Even beliefs in
progress and decline were couched in racial terminology.

At the beginning of the twentieth century anthropologists
centered their investigations on race, but professional identity was
sufficiently diffuse for many practitioners to have no institutional
bond with the discipline. The discourse was thematic rather than
disciplinary. Anthropological societies continued to provide a local
forum, but academic appointments became the most prestigious
professional form of legitimation. A broad division along subject
matter separated paleontology from ethnology: paleontologists with
mostly medical training searched for primordial human ancestors
and the "missing link." The ethnologists studied the primitives[10] as
a living testimony for the prehistory of civilization. The archaeologists and classicists who focused on the immediate pre- and early
history were chronologically sandwiched. Despite a shared interest
in physical anthropology and racial classification, the disparate
approaches led to conflicting answers. The early belief that race,
culture and language were different manifestations of the one inherent entity enabled the use of cultural and linguistic data to delineate
racial taxonomy. Later, the separation of these disciplines from
each other and the growing independence of culture, language, and

[10] The word "primitive" denotes a historical use, and obviously neither carries value
judgment nor presents an ontological statement.

racial ancestry diminished the centrality of racial studies and created space for a new anthropology.

In order to reconstruct the anthropological discourse on race with its great disciplinary fragmentation, one has to follow the clues of various institutional settings and to situate the major archaeologists, paleontologists, linguists and ethnologists. The following story first traces the developments in Britain as traditional ethnology became professionalized and incorporated into Oxford and Cambridge. It then explores the input of scientists with medical expertise, mostly in London, who commented on the nature of race by reconstructing the antiquity of humankind. After pausing briefly on race relations in Britain, the discussion moves to the American scene. American anthropology was divided in its attitude to race: on the one hand, there were the egalitarians – Boas, his students and supporters – and on the other, the racists. The British story is more diffuse, but two experiences in particular helped shape the discipline early in the twentieth century; the move of the anthropologist from the armchair into the field, and the Piltdown affair.

A TRANSITION TO MODERN BRITISH ANTHROPOLOGY

The first British anthropological expedition reached the Torres Straits in April 1898. The six anthropologists landed on Thursday Island, and during the next several months they surveyed the volcanic Murray Islands and Papua New Guinea, whose native Papuans had by then become partially civilized by missionaries. Between the first discovery of the straits in the early seventeenth century and Captain Cook's visit at the end of the eighteenth century when he claimed the Islands for Britain, the islanders were left mostly to themselves. Much had changed, however, by the second half of the nineteenth century, when pearls and religion caused greater Western intervention. By the end of the century, island traditions were remembered only by the old men whose numbers were fast declining. The new breed of anthropologists embarked upon studying these primitives. Faced with a different task from their older peers – the armchair anthropologists – the younger group studied their subjects directly in the field, and did not rely on second-hand sources such as stories by travelers or missionaries. In addition to resurrecting European prehistory by analogy, of speculating from contemporary primitives into Europeans of bygone days, these modern anthropologists sought to record vanishing traditions of vanishing peoples. The new interest in the primitives for their own sake was a novelty that shaped a dramatically innovative discipline, one which was potentially empathetic with its subject matter. The older prominent anthropologists of the day had never before met primitives, nor had they any desire to do so. Their writings relied on testimonies by explorers and travelers, whose imaginations, experience and credibility varied greatly. In contrast, the young members of the expedition addressed their subjects of study in close proximity, relied upon their own experience and in some cases even moderated their sense of cultural superiority with sympathy. A new type of anthropology was born.[11]

In the second half of the nineteenth century, the remains of early man were excavated in Europe. A number of the findings achieved wide recognition: Neanderthal and Cro-Magnon became household names. The evolutionary story of humankind was extended in time, supplemented with evidence and numerous conjectures. The race to antiquity was conducted against the background of intense national rivalry in Europe, which Britain was losing to France and Germany. Partly for this reason, the presentation in 1912 of a Piltdown man – which reputedly, "at least," matched the antiquity of man on the Continent – was widely celebrated by British scientists. Outsiders were more skeptical of what indeed turned out to be one of the most notorious scientific frauds ever. But that lay in the future. In the meantime, for four decades and despite skepticism, Piltdown sustained partial scientific credibility and notwithstanding the lack of a reliable specimen, Piltdown was referred to as representing an ancient "race." While mistaken interpretations were later attributed to an initial fraud, contemporary disagreements caused intense scientific and personal rivalry, and influenced physical anthropology and the study of race in Britain for decades.

The Torres Straits Expedition and the Piltdown affair had critical impacts on British anthropology at the turn of the century. The results influenced long-term attitudes and predispositions, but did not lead to a major theoretical reformation or an institutional restructuring. This period was still characterized by the congenial symbiosis between amateurs and professionals, the highly speculative nature of anthropology and the lack of any theoretical bond.

[11] A. C. Haddon (ed.), *Reports of the Cambridge Anthropological Expedition to the Torres Straits*, 6 vols. (Cambridge: Cambridge University Press, 1901–1935).

"Gentleman" status still served as an important professional qualification, perhaps more so than in other disciplines.

The gentlemen who populated the anthropological societies were
still in 1900 part of the ruling classes of the most powerful empire.
Their subordinates were the natives around the globe, and the poor
at home, all of whom were classified and characterized in terms of
race. One of the most prominent representatives of this type of
anthropologist was John Beddoe who was a popular authority on
the subject of races in Britain. This was well illustrated in his
conclusion to an essay on the "Anthropological History of Europe"
where he used race as a category to differentiate along class and
national lines, and to claim that progress and civilization were a
result of the physical superiority of the upper classes. His views were
unabashedly naive and blissfully ignorant of the possibility that such
claims might be questionable or constitute racism. Illustrative of
this type of inquiry, Beddoe addressed the European class struggle
and the superiority of the rich over poor, and the city dweller over
the person from the provinces. Explaining the increase of size in the
heads of Parisians, "a change not accompanied apparently by any
increase in maximum breadth, but depending purely on an enlar-
gement of the frontal lobe," Beddoe assigned it to the process of
selection where "the cleverer people in all ranks ... have been
attracted to the center of progress and the goal of ambition." Once
the racial competition was transferred to the New World, the French
were relegated to an intermediate stage compared with the Anglo-
Americans, whose superiority kept them apart from the natives:

There is in the colonists plenty of size, of vigour, of beauty, and of
intellectual power; nevertheless, there are signs which lead some to doubt
whether all these will be permanent. The birth-rate tends to decrease
among the pure Anglo-Americans, while the French Canadians, strongly
crossed with native Indian blood, are multiplying with alarming rapidity;
and the American military statistics seem *prima facie*, to indicate that the
climate is less suitable to the blond than to the brunette.[12]

This however, did not adversely affect Beddoe's commitment to
the concept of superiority, and it is therefore not surprising that
Beddoe quoted favorably the notorious G. Vacher de Lapouge, who
assigned the majority of "men of genius, or originality, men who

[12] John Beddoe, "Anthropological History of Europe" (1891), quoted in Count (ed.), *This Is
Race*, pp. 162–170.

have made their mark in history, or literature, or science," to "the longheaded blonds," whom most people incorrectly call "Aryans."

Beddoe's views suggest a great fluidity in the use of the term race, and the fact that no clear demarcation existed between the nature of the anthropological concept and commonplace bigotry. In following the discourse on race it should be remembered that in Britain it was often studied as part of another issue, the antiquity of man or class relations, presumably because race had no direct political implication, in contrast, for instance, to the United States or Germany. The British attitudes to racial questions before World War II were based in part on the imperial experience, but mainly on ignorance. Thus, colored people lacked any specific identity and were all simply characterized as "natives."[13] This practice was in stark contrast to the keen awareness of "racial," namely ethnic, plurality in British history – of Saxons, Celts, Normans, Irish, Welsh, Scots and English, with numerous sub-divisions. The British recognized racial distinctions concerning whites, which applied primarily to England and secondarily to Europe and America, but blurred the racial specificity of the colored population, most of whom lived in the colonies, with but a few representatives in Britain. This awareness of ethnic complexity in their own past encouraged the British to stress the benefits of racial and cultural mixture among Europeans, and hence they were generally reluctant to attribute national success to racial or cultural purity, as did many Germans.[14] This traditional relativist approach to race was limited to internal divisions among whites; it did not apply to intermixture between whites and blacks which most of the British people regarded as "biologically as well as socially disastrous."[15] Despite the polarized approaches, the term race had been used to denote subdivisions among Europeans as well as the divisions between whites and blacks.

Racism in England has been ascribed to British imperialism, and a recent study has concluded that "the golden age of the British

---

[13] A 1948 investigation concluded that about 95 percent of the British-held views on colored people were "based entirely on some stereotyped idea rather than on first-hand personal knowledge." The result of the study "Race Relations and the Schools" was published by the League of Coloured Peoples and conducted by educationalists, of which Little was the Honorary Secretary. K. L. Little, *Negroes in Britain, A Study of Racial Relations in English Society* (London: Kegan Paul, 1948), p. 218.

[14] See, for example, G. B. Trigger, *Gordon Childe: Revolutions in Archaeology* (New York: Columbia University Press, 1980), p. 26.

[15] See Little, *Negroes in Britain*, p. 236.

Empire was the golden age of British racism too.''[16] Racial insensitivity was prevalent across the political spectrum, and it was not until
after World War II that humanitarians and liberals displayed
greater awareness of the issue of racial offensiveness. A striking
demonstration of the prevalence of this type of racism even after
World War I is found in the response of the British Left in 1920 to
the French occupation of the Rhine. The British Left, in support of
Germany, campaigned against France for employing black occupation troops. Edmond Dean Morel, the British socialist and
humanitarian orchestrated the attacks with the help of the *Daily
Herald*, the leading left-wing daily in Britain. He received wide
cooperation and encountered little opposition to the inflammatory
language he used to describe alleged rapes and sexual crimes by the
colored French soldiers on the Rhine, referring to them as oversexed
syphilitic rapists, "primitive African barbarians" who terrorized
the German countryside and are an "abominable outrage upon
womanhood." Embellishing his accusation with pseudo-physiology,
he called the Africans "the most developed sexually of any" race.
"For well-known physiological reasons," he added, "the raping of a
white woman by a negro [sic] is nearly always accompanied by
serious injury and not infrequently has fatal results."[17] Such was the
language of a paper which claimed to be a "champion" of "the
rights of the African native *in his own home*."[18] This sinister use of
racism resulted precisely from the highbrow respectability of racial
animosity. It was done in the name of supporting the young Weimar
Republic and its socialist government. Most Europeans who
opposed the occupation did not object to this racist abuse as a
tool for political pressure to remove the French from the Rhine.
Therefore anti-imperialists and colonialists found refuge in racist
propaganda. The American left was, however, more aware of the
wickedness of such a racist argument. Racism constituted a more
significant political issue in the United States than in Britain.
Differentiating between political and human atrocities, the *Nation*

[16] Peter Fryer, *Staying Power, the History of Black People in Britain* (London: Pluto, 1984), p. 165.
[17] Morel was a secretary and co-founder of the Union of Democratic Control and editor of its
influential journal *Foreign Affairs*, a member of the Independent Labour Party and later of
the Labour Party. His father was French and his full name was Georges Edmond Pierre
Achille Morel de Ville. He had founded the Congo Reform Association, which was largely
responsible for ending the infamous reign of King Leopold I over the Congo. See the *Daily
Herald*, April 10, 1920, 1,4, and Robert C. Reinders, "Racism on the Left: E. D. Morel and
the 'Black Horror on the Rhine'," *International Review of Social History*, 13 (1968), 111–126.
[18] Quoted in Reinders, "Racism," pp. 2, 17 (emphasis added).

concluded: "There is a black horror on the Rhine, but it is not a Negro horror."[19] Race was clearly not subject to political divisions in Britain at the end of World War I. Differences of opinion were in the final analysis subject to factual confirmation, not to ideological conflict. The views the liberal Morel and the anthropologist Beddoe displayed were racist speculations based on supposedly scientific foundations. Within the congenial coexistence of the homogeneous British ruling class, there was no source to initiate a critique of racism.

British anthropologists belonged to the upper middle class, and as a group displayed an urge to contribute to the success of the Empire, to participate, often directly, in the colonial enterprise, and to receive the approval of social and professional peers. The misfortune of anthropology from the practitioners' perspective was its rejection by the ruling class. An initial minimal interaction between the government and academic anthropology led slowly to a more active interest by civil servants in the young discipline, especially at Oxford and Cambridge, which even led at times to consultation with anthropologists or the seeking of concrete help, such as in translation. As a result, there was embedded tension in anthropologists' approach to race; their audience included civil servants, missionaries and others who were involved professionally with the peoples of the Empire, and they hoped the discipline would prosper by participating in the formulation of imperial policies. Yet at the same time the anthropologists molded the opinions of their audience by outlaying new facts, which they believed to be based on objective scientific investigation, according to the best positivist tradition. The anthropologists' position was caught between satisfying the needs of the Empire as understood by the civil servants and perhaps achieving a higher social status, and their growing empathy with the peoples of the Empire. The participants were often unconscious of this tension and believed themselves to be motivated solely by scientific objectivity.

THE FOUNDING FATHERS

I regret the diminution of the old blond lympho-sanguine stock, which has hitherto served England well in many ways, but is apparently

[19] *Nation* 62 (1921), 366, 733–734; 63 (1922), 264. And the *New Republic*, 26 (March 9, 1921), 29–30. Quoted in Reinders, "Racism," p. 20.

doomed to give way to a darker and more mobile type, largely the offspring of the proletariat, and more adapted to the atmosphere of great cities.[20]

This note is taken from a past President of the Royal Anthropological Institute who was lecturing to the most prestigious anthropological forum, bemoaning in a familiar tone the racial decline of Britain: from the creative aristocratic nordic race to a new undistinguished darker race. John Beddoe's career had begun before British anthropologists embarked on field trips, when he wrote extensively on *The Races of Britain*,[21] from historical perspectives with contemporary concerns. The industrial revolution and growing democracy had definitely changed Britain, and at the turn of the century this was perceived in racial terms. Such pessimism couched in racial concepts displayed what in hindsight can be judged as racist sentiments, but at the time was considered factual and non-controversial bio-social commentary. From this Victorian framework, modern anthropology emerged at the end of the century to explicate its views on race.

Edward Burnett Tylor who coined the anthropological term "culture," established anthropology at Oxford in 1875. Tylor made his way to a professorship literally single-handed, for he had no students, no department and, some said, only his wife as audience. In Cambridge, in the meantime, the legacy of Thomas Henry Huxley and the presence of James Frazer constituted the prehistory of anthropology. The institutional foundations developed slowly from 1895 on, when the discipline became synonymous with Alfred C. Haddon, who converted from zoology to physical anthropology as a result of a five months stay in 1888 at the Torres Straits studying marine biology. Friendly contacts with the islanders and awareness of their disappearing tradition led him ten years later to organize a successful expedition which marked the inception of modern anthropology. A hero's welcome at Cambridge upon the return of the expedition led to a petition on Haddon's behalf for a chair in

[20] John Beddoe, "Colour and Race," Huxley Memorial Lecture, 1905, *Journal, Royal Anthropological Institute of Great Britain and Ireland (JRAI)*, 219–250 (quote 237).

[21] John Beddoe, *The Races of Britain: A Contribution to the Anthropology of Western Europe* (Bristol: Arrowsmith, 1885).

anthropology: the attempt failed, and Haddon had to settle in 1900 for a lectureship.[22]

The Torres Straits Expedition turned out to be Haddon's most successful field trip, and brought him together with William Halse Rivers Rivers, William McDougall, Charles S. Myres, Charles G. Seligman, Anthony Wilkin and Sidney H. Ray. Friendship and a search for adventure provided some of the expeditioners with a stronger motivation than scientific curiosity, much like other British exploits, including Darwin's voyage on the Beagle. The Cambridge anthropologists were trained in medicine and biology and had a psychological orientation. By the 1920s, the five leading veterans of the Torres Straits had gone their separate ways. As a result of the expedition, Rivers, who had had little previous interest in anthropology, became one of its most influential theorists in England. He adopted diffusionism, but due to his early death in 1922, he became more of a legacy than a factor in British anthropology. McDougall who developed his own theory of racial instinct, emigrated to the United States, where his influence was especially important during the early 1920s among immigration restrictionists. Charles Myres continued to work in psychology, but did not address the question of race in any significant way. The other two, Haddon and Seligman, became pillars of British anthropology during the period and largely steered its course in the first three decades of the century.

Haddon, politically a mild nonconformist, generally avoided public controversy and refrained from direct professional confrontations. His success was due less to ingenuity than to hard work and persistence. Before the outbreak of World War I, his progressivism had brought him in contact with correspondents who addressed him as a fighter "on behalf of the [racially] oppressed." Although he closely followed the question of blacks in the United States, he rarely involved himself directly in political issues. One of these rare occasions was the Universal Race Congress of 1911 in London. Haddon pioneered and led the old school of anthropology; his career was distinguished by his influence in gaining recognition for the discipline in British science. Nevertheless, he was unable to

---

[22] It took another nine years to turn the lectureship into a readership, and in Haddon's time it never became a professorship. A. Hingston Quiggin, *Haddon, The Head Hunter* (Cambridge: Cambridge University Press, 1942), and Haddon's papers at the Cambridge University Library (ACHP).

strengthen anthropology at Cambridge, where he always remained somewhat of an outsider.[23]

Haddon came to Cambridge as a student in 1875, and was to spend most of the next sixty-five years there. Truly a man of his times, he entertained all the prejudices held by his generation. Although he did not concur with the tendency to speak of the lower races as closer to the simian stage, he did not doubt that "on the whole, the white race has progressed beyond the black race," in physical, mental, and moral traits. Haddon accepted a recapitulation form of phylogeny whereby the child "repeats in its growth" the features of the savages "from which civilized man has so recently emerged." According to this view, child psychology reflected that of the savage, for example, "in the singing games of children [which is] a persistence of savage and barbaric practice."[24] But Haddon also saw that the gap between civilized and primitive resulted in part from the environment. The pleasant South Sea, lacking "example and stimulus to exertion," was Haddon's reason for the Murray Islanders having remained uncivilized. Their backwardness did not interfere with Haddon's esteem for them as "very creditable specimens of savage humanity." The anthropologist looking at the local population from a western perspective was beginning to empathize with his subjects: "The truth is, we call them lazy because they won't work for the white man more than they care to. Why should they?"[25] Such was the cradle of egalitarianism.

Very gradually this potential equality among the races was explicated, and the gap between savage and civilized diminished. By the twenties, the distinction became one of degree, not of substance. Talking about progress among primitives, a novelty in itself, Haddon pleaded with "those who regard such savages as being 'simple'" for a new, more sophisticated approach: "backward peoples have a mentality of pretty much the same nature, though not so trained, as that of civilized peoples." Method and pro-

---

[23] ACHP, 5406, 5368. This is evident in many obituaries, memoirs and historical studies which refer to Haddon. One recent evaluation states that "In 1900, physical anthropology was the area of anthropology in which professionalization was most advanced, and Haddon was one of the few 'professionals' competent in physical anthropology who showed great keenness for collecting materials on folklore and other customs." James Urry, "Englishmen, Celts and Iberians: The Ethnographic Survey of the United Kingdom, 1892–1899," in G. Stocking (ed.), Functionalism Historicized. Essays on British Social Anthropology (Madison: University of Wisconsin Press, 1984), p. 98.

[24] A. C. Haddon, The Study of Man (London: Bliss, Sands, & Co. 1898), pp. xxii–xxiv.

[25] A. C. Haddon, Head Hunters, Black, White and Brown (London: Methuen, 1901), p. 19.

fessionalism became important for the evaluation of non-Western people; field researchers showed empathy to the societies they studied. Haddon, the seventy-two-year-old (grand)father of British fieldwork anthropology, continuously adjusted his egalitarianism, and came to criticize explicitly the "well-read library students who maintain that backward peoples have a 'prelogical mind'; as a matter of fact, in the ordinary concerns of life they are as rational and logical as the rest of mankind, but 'magic-suffused psychology' intercepts the process of reason in them to a greater extent than with us."[26]

Similarly, in teaching anthropology, social methodology and substance replaced taxonomy at center stage. In Cambridge, anthropology was studied as part of the geographical tripos. Examinations from 1915 to 1928 illustrate this transformation. Earlier versions consisted of nine questions, five of them on racial taxonomy and four on social descriptions: five questions had to be answered in all. The new format consisted of two sections, but only one question was an absolute requirement from each section, one of which was on racial topics. While both formats demanded at least one response on racial classification, the earlier allowed a student to answer only questions on racial description and the latter showed a clear preference for social anthropology.[27]

Haddon published *The Races of Man and Their Distribution* in 1909, updating it in 1925. The earlier version already contained an incipient critique of racial taxonomy as a concept for which it "really seems impossible to frame a satisfactory definition." Alternative terms for races were suggested, such as "people" to account for a variety of communities including those with racial mixture. But none achieved any meaningful success. Despite Haddon's persistent use of racial terminology, he was alert to epistemological and linguistic difficulties and hence more receptive to alternatives.[28] In the 1925 edition, Haddon expressed the tentativeness of taxonomic definitions in no uncertain terms. They were "a matter of individual opinion," and "with more complete knowledge it becomes increasingly difficult to define race." Likewise "generalizations ... of large

26 A. C. Haddon, "Environment and Culture Progress Among Primitive Peoples," The Herbertson Memorial Lecture, delivered in London, October 26, 1927, Newtown [pamphlet], pp. 7, 6.
27 See ACHP, 4009.
28 A. C. Haddon, *The Races of Man and Their Distribution* (London: Milner & Company, 1909), p. 6.

areas tend to mark the real ethnic diversity ... and to produce a
fictitious appearance of uniformity."[29] "It is very doubtful,"
Haddon concluded, "whether there are at the present time any races
that can be termed 'pure.'"[30]

Haddon stumbled over all the epistemological difficulties presented by the study of races. Stability versus change posed a special
problem since races were by definition static, but then how did one
account for progress? Haddon settled for discrepancy between his
argument and its substantiation. Despite the migrations in Europe,
the distribution of "the main racial elements," as he put it, is the
same as it had been in late Neolithic times. But when he compared
the plasticity of human groups, he concluded that "certain races are
more static than others, and this may perhaps be granted for what
are termed the lower races." Similarly to other anthropologists,
Haddon interpreted the static component of racial typology according to whether he referred to civilized or to primitive races.
Population mixture in Europe enabled the advent of civilization but
did not interfere with its positive stable racial division. Conversely,
the isolation of many of the lower races until their encounter with
the white man meant that this static situation implied lack of
progress.[31]

Charles G. Seligman, Haddon's colleague on the Torres Straits
Expedition, also addressed the psychological dichotomy between
civilized and primitive races. He became a prominent anthropologist and exemplified the ambivalence of the older generation
towards race. Until the 1930s, he headed the anthropology department of the London School of Economics, overseeing the transition
to functional social anthropology. He counted among his students
Bronislaw Malinowski, E. E. Evans-Pritchard, Raymond Firth and
many of the other social anthropologists who were educated at the
school before 1934. His contributions varied, but perhaps none had
greater impact than *Races of Africa*, first published in 1930 and
reissued in a fourth edition by Oxford University Press in 1979.[32]

---

[29] Haddon's views on the balance between diversity and uniformity became outmoded after
   World War I. See, for example, Fleure's criticism in his letter to Haddon, Dec. 7, 1918, "I
   have given a good deal of thought to the matter and am inclined to think you go too far in
   accepting old views based purely on averages." ACHP 4039.

[30] Haddon, *The Races of Man and Their Distribution* (New York: Macmillan, 1925), pp. 1–2.

[31] *Races of Man*, pp. 64, 159.

[32] Recognizing that the book's thesis was no longer accepted by most anthropologists, the
   Oxford University Press hailed it as a "classic statement." But the excuse for republication
   was much more prosaic: it "remains ... the only book of its size that deals with all the

This reflects more on the state of scholarship on Africa than on Seligman, yet it is remarkable that a text written at a time of general ignorance about Africa sustained its position for so long.

While officially at London, Seligman shared much with the Oxbridge anthropologists, and he even lived at Oxford for many years. A descendant on his maternal side of Emanuel Mendez da Costa, who in 1747 had become the second Jewish Fellow of the Royal Society, Charles Gabriel Seligman was born into a middle class wine merchant's family. He trained in medicine at St. Thomas's Hospital, and was to embark on an uneventful career. A series of coincidences coupled with his devout interest in research led to his participation in the Torres Straits Expedition, despite Haddon's lack of initial enthusiasm about his recruitment. In 1905, Seligman married Brenda Z. Salaman, who came from a scholarly family, and had an anthropological career in her own right: together the Seligmans became part of the core of British anthropology.

Seligman specialized in the application of psychoanalysis to anthropology, but felt at home in many other areas on which he published much.[33] His views on race represented the mainstream thought in the profession, but gain additional historical significance in that Seligman was one of the scientists most actively involved in combating Nazi racism during the thirties. None the less, a recent study of Social Darwinism in England claims that Seligman exemplified "attitudes which expressed a belief in the racial superiority of the white man."[34] This commonplace incoherence of racial views in Seligman's case is amplified because, while he was prone to accept many racialist arguments uncritically, he came to reject racism for ethnic and socio-political reasons.

Seligman was primarily a collector: he devoted most of his time to assembling data, explicitly refraining from a theoretical framework. "Theories will be out of date in ten years," he is quoted as saying.

peoples of the African continent," and the distinguished Press judged it to be a suitable statement on Africa for the 1980s. C. S. Seligman, *Races of Africa*, fourth edn (Oxford: Oxford University Press, 1979), publisher's note.

[33] For information about Seligman, see A. C. Haddon, "Appreciation," in E. E. Evans Pritchard *et al.*, *Essays Presented to C. G. Seligman, 1873–1940*, Man, 41 (1941), 1–6; M. J. Herskovits, "Charles Gabriel Seligman," *American Anthropologist*, 43 (1941), 437–439; Fortes, "Seligman, C. G.," *International Encyclopedia of the Social Sciences* (New York: Crowell Collier and Macmillan, 1968).

[34] Greta Jones, *Social Darwinism and English Thought: The Interaction Between Biological and Social Theory* (New Jersey: Humanities Press, 1980), p. 171.

"It is the facts on which they are based that will always be of use."[35] Indeed, his *Races of Africa* underscored his reluctance for theory, though in this case the book maintained its appeal even when the facts in it were recognized as inaccurate. Yet, despite this commitment to facts, in his Presidential Address to the Royal Anthropological Institute in 1924 he preferred to speak on the contact between anthropology and psychology rather than to describe ethnological data the "Seligs," as they were nicknamed, had recently collected east of the White Nile. In this address, Seligman adopted Jung's extrovert and introvert ideal types as tools to analyze the psychological distinction between civilized and primitives as understood in racial terms. Significantly, he chose to speak about differences in degree rather than kind. He evaluated most Europeans as introverts and most savages as extroverts. The introvert was presented as a rational man of principles and systems who transcends the limitations of experience by abstract reasoning. The extrovert "regards only matters of fact. Experience is his master, his exclusive guide and inspiration ... Thought is merely a reaction to external experience." The distinction suggested itself to Seligman because in "certain reactions" the primitives "resembled hysterics" at least superficially. But Seligman candidly admitted: "it would hardly be convincing to bring forward the claim that the great majority of individuals among savage peoples were normally in a condition brought about among a minority of ourselves by conditions of stress and conflict." Yet, thanks to Jung, Seligman could reinforce the distinction between the civilized and primitive, attributing to the latter a state of irrationality without its pathological aspects. In order for the division into types to have a racial meaning, Seligman had to show that it was innate and hereditary. Since no studies had been done to support the claim, Seligman invoked Jung himself who obligingly informed Seligman "that in four out of five of his own children he made his diagnosis in the first month of life." Savages had to be extroverts, Seligman assumed, since "no savage community containing a preponderant number of introverts would long survive." This was accentuated among the leadership, because the "chiefs appear to be even more extrovert than the mass of their commoners." As to Europeans, Seligman followed the German anthropologist Fritz Lenz, accepting with only mild criticism the claimed Nordic superiority and the suitability of the Alpine races

[35] Herskovits, "Seligman," p. 438.

"to village life" as against their "little tendency to adventure and colonization." This unventuresome rustic breed "failed to yield any outstanding personalities in science," but luckily it did produce "a number of the greatest musicians."[36] Seligman was trained as a typologist, but his interest in the substance of classification shifted from physical anthropology to psychology and culture, while maintaining the reified status of races. It was during the twenties that the confusion over the relation between racial taxonomy and culture was most prevalent; the traditional formal classification was sustained, while its epistemology and consequently content were rapidly changing.

Essentially, Seligman did not change his opinions in the following years. Conflicting evidence makes it that much harder to evaluate his racialist views. He accepted diffusionism, with the straightforward claim that "the history of Africa South of the Sahara is no more than the story of the permeation through the ages, in different degrees and at various times, of the Negro and Bushman aborigines by Hamitic blood and culture. The Hamites were, in fact, the great civilizing force of black Africa."[37] This statement scarcely points to ethnological egalitarianism, yet Seligman advanced other suggestions in 1924 which by 1932 he transformed to convey explicit egalitarian implications. Dream interpretation and sense perceptions both suggested to him that, while there were differences between individuals, these did not correspond to racial typology, "being in the main personal, not racial." Seligman recognized one "exception ... with regard to [the] threshold of pain."[38]

He found it "absurd to maintain that the primitive adult is childish in his mental capacities and powers of action," and the same applied to the neurotic. Nevertheless, he found "similarities in structure and manner, though not degree and functioning."[39] The implications for Seligman were that "if it is found that savage

[36] C. G. Seligman, "Anthropology and Psychology: A Study of Some Points of Contact," *JRAI*, 54 (1924), 14–15, 23, 26, 46, 28–30. On the racist aspects of Lenz, see Erwin Baur, Eugen Fischer, and Fritz Lenz, *Menschliche Erblichkeitslehre* (Munich, 1923), translated as *Human Heredity* (New York: Eden and Cedar Paul, 1931).
[37] Seligman, *Races of Africa* (1930), p. 19. Also quoted in Henrika Kuklick, ("Tribal Exemplars: Images of Political Authority in British Anthropology, 1885–1945," in Stocking [ed.], *Functionalism Historicized*, pp. 70–71,) who claims that Seligman was the most important anthropologist who continued to equate race and culture during the thirties. Seligman's position was not clear, nor was his ambivalence unique.
[38] C. G. Seligman, "Anthropological Perspective and Psychological Theory," The Huxley Memorial Lecture for 1932, *JRAI*, 62 (1932), 196.
[39] "Anthropological Perspective," p. 206.

dreams conform in constitution and function to the theoretical explanations offered by psychologists working on the dreams of folk of Western race and culture" it is a proof "that the savage mind and the mind of Western civilized man are essentially alike."[40]

Seligman no doubt thought in terms of racial taxonomies, but his attitude to the work of the social anthropologists at the London School of Economics enabled him to make the transformation and to reverse his earlier rigid conventions. The shift occurred in two stages: at first Seligman replaced the dichotomy of civilized-savage by a hierarchy of an endless number of races, and then minimized the differences along the scale. Equality was still a long way off, and other components in Seligman's thought only increased the confusion.[41] Yet being among the few anthropologists with a training in psychology, Seligman took important steps in discrediting psychological racism.

In contrast to Cambridge or London, Oxford had no field ethnologists before 1936. But, by the first decade of the twentieth century anthropology at Oxford had made some advances since Tylor days: there was a committee, a program, and, within a few years, even a handful of students. The original members remained unchanged until the 1930s, and included John Linton Myres (Classics) and R. R. Marett (Philosophy, Religion).[42]

John Linton Myres, a classicist, was concerned mainly with Greece, its archaeology, history and ancient geography. His main impact on anthropology, between the late 1880s and his retirement in 1939, was in British academic political circles.[43] He held official positions in many societies, serving as President of the Royal Anthropological Institute from 1928 to 1931 and as General Secretary of the British Association from 1919 to 1932. He was the first editor of *Man* in 1901–3, and in 1931 returned to edit it for an additional fifteen years. His willingness to be involved in adminis-

[40] "Anthropological Perspective," p. 219.
[41] For his mixing of the terms ethnic and subspecies in the 1930s, see ch. 6 below.
[42] Since 1908, and for twenty years, Marett coordinated the committee: "In the creation of a new School much more was involved than drawing up a programme. In particular, one had to find pupils." Robert R. Marett, *A Jerseyman at Oxford* (London: Oxford University Press, 1941), pp. 167–169. Other members of the committee were Arthur Thompson (Anatomy) and Henry Balfour (Technology.)
[43] For biographical information, see J. Boardman "Myres, Sir John Linton" in *Dictionary of National Biography, 1951–1960*, pp. 762–763; Myres papers, Bodleian (JLMP); on his role in politics, see also his various reports published in *Man*, and *JRAI*. His stay in Oxford excluded a short three-year spell in Liverpool (1907–10).

trative matters and university politics made him a powerful member of the anthropology community, which lacked support from the establishment. He represented British science for many years in international diplomacy, making notable efforts to arrange the Congrès International des Sciences Anthropologiques et Ethnologiques. The congress was originally planned before World War I, but because of national rivalry was finally convened only in 1934, when the question of race had once again become an overtly divisive issue of international politics. Myres was interested in the broader applications of anthropology, and in its possible benefits to the colonial administration. His were represented as the most knowledgeable and well-informed views, even though they were not the result of original research.

In 1922, he opened a discussion at the British Association on the correlation between mental and physical characteristics aimed at constructing a psychological racial taxonomy, basing his argument on personal impressionistic observation. Myres concurred with the view that these characteristics "are sufficiently widespread over large areas as to claim provisional acceptance as racial qualities." The characteristics included, for instance, "the plodding, detail-loving industry of the mid-European 'Alpine' strain ..." while others such as red-pigmentation "seem to result from disturbance of physiological and psychological make-up by cross-breeding." Myres bolstered his argument by an analogy with animal breeding, declaring that "the hypothesis that mental characters are correlated with physical and transmissible in such correlation, stands the test of experiment among the higher mammals." Myres suspended judgment on the ethical superiority of one race over another but testified that in the offsprings in mixed marriages of British and Greek, "the temperament closely followed the breed."[44]

His views reflected the conventions of racial thought at the time, but he also echoed crucial epistemological questions. He recognized how susceptible anthropology was to political influence when he characterized polygeny – the belief in the multiple origin of humankind – as "a controversial comedy in which it is difficult to say whether anthropology or politics did more ... to misguide and

[44] J. L. Myres, "Correlation of Mental and Physical Characteristics in Man: Being a summary of the opening address in a discussion which took place in Section H, at the meeting of the British Association at Hull in September, 1922," *Man*, 23 (1923), 116–119.

deform the other."[45] Perhaps more important, however, was his analysis of different time scales.

The concept of time is crucial to the understanding of the chaos which existed in anthropological theory. Anthropologists often compounded geological, zoological, and historical time scales and Myres demonstrated this when, for example, he argued that a certain group such as "the North Mongol" had gone through a marked change "within the historical period." He asked the anthropologists to reflect upon whether that meant a psychological as well as physical evolution. If the latter, how could it have taken place in such a short zoological time period? The alternative, unacceptable premise at the time, would have been that there was no correlation between physical and psychological racial characteristics.[46] Myres broke no new ground, yet as commentator from within the discipline he underscored the contradiction and paradox in contemporary evolution theories of anthropology, according to which a constant racial type was set within a dynamically developing world. The problem was not easy to resolve, but that it was rarely even addressed is testimony to discrepancies in the application of Darwinian evolution to anthropology.

The other leading Oxford anthropologist, Robert Randolph Marett, had trained in philosophy and sociology. Marett's colleagues viewed anthropology as a peculiar activity, unworthy of a scholar: "a man of your talents seems rather wasted on the habits of backward races," wrote a friend. Myres was a classicist, and therefore at the heart of the academic establishment. Unlike Myres, whose anthropology was part of the more respectable classics, Marett's closer engagement with the primitive accentuated his outsider status. As in the case of Haddon, who was never promoted beyond a junior appointment at Cambridge, Marett felt his engagement with traditional societies was perceived as somewhat eccentric, a minor "scandal," despite the fact that he never did any field work. Years later he commented: "as it was, I divided my attention impartially between the beliefs of the savage and those of the Oxford undergraduate." It was his personal attitudes rather than any specific theory which, early on, had determined his

---

[45] J. L. Myres, *The Influence of Politics on the Course of Political Science* (Berkeley: University of California Press, 1916), p. 68.
[46] Myres, "Correlation", p. 118.

egalitarian views on the racial question. A humanitarian with a good sense of humor, this Jerseyman was an outsider at the very center of British academia.[47]

Marett's first public venture into the field of anthropology was an attack on Tylor's animism, which equated ritual and belief. Marett argued for a comparable analysis of savage and civilized societies and opposed the reduction of anthropology to barbarology. Cooperation with colonialism is now judged in hindsight as a sign of reactionary and exploitative attitudes on the part of anthropologists.[48] This was perceived differently at a time when political judgment viewed colonialism – if not all of its implications – as a positive and modernizing force. For anthropologists the question was not whether their cooperation would facilitate colonialism, but rather whether given colonialism, their cooperation would be beneficial to the subjugated peoples of the Empire. Marett took great pride in the fact that his students applied his teaching to their colonial administration as civil servants. He concluded that "the lot of the people under their charge is bettered by the sympathetic understanding with which they are treated." Even were Marett substantially wrong, his concern for the benefit of the indigenous population ahead of efficient administration is significant.[49] Marett never did any field studies, and spent most of his life teaching. Despite this characteristically remote perception of non-Europeans during the twenties, Oxford scholars by virtue of institutional prestige sustained their impact on the intellectual formulation of the concept of race. In the meantime, physical anthropologists, from a variety of backgrounds, were debating the nature of race and the antiquity of humankind.

---

[47] Marett, *A Jerseyman At Oxford*, p. 164.

[48] Talal Asad (ed.), *Anthropology and the Colonial Encounter* (London: Ithaca Press, 1975); Gerrit Huizer and Bruce Mannheim, *The Politics of Anthropology, From Colonialism and Sexism Toward a View From Below* (The Hague: Mouton, 1979).

[49] Marett, *A Jerseyman at Oxford*, pp. 163, 171. Altruism was not the sole motivation; Marett was just as proud of his little contribution to the strengthening of the Empire by force when he recalled in the same work that "in 1903, there arrived from Somaliland a mass of linguistic jottings mostly on the back of envelopes, and he [my brother-in-law] bid me somehow to convert it *instantly* into a manual for the use of the troops in their forthcoming campaign against the Dervishes. I could get hold of nobody who knew a word of Somali, and my only German authority was sketchy. Yet the Clarendon Press duly sent off my version neatly bound in Khaki, and they won the war on that, even if my brother-in-law in his later and more elaborate work implies that the real language was somewhat different" (p.179).

MUMMIES, BONES AND STONES

Prehistory had been a focal interest in the study of race. The excavation of Piltdown man generated excitement and heated debates even among the supporters of the theory, both for the critical dilemmas it presented concerning human evolution and for its implication for racial typology. Anatomists and archaeologists participated in a quest for the earliest ancestors, a competition which involved national and individual glory, and one that even today periodically engages public opinion and is headlined in the daily press. Hence, expertise provided a temptation and an opportunity for scientists to act as universal intellectuals and to pontificate on racial development in general. In addition, scientists were able to participate in and contribute to the nation's cultural development and to its competition with rivals. The several disparate reconstructions of the brain and jaw of Piltdown man endowed even the most idiosyncratic political and cultural interpretation with professional and scientific legitimacy.

In this section I investigate the contribution of paleontology and archaeology to the formulation of the concept of race. I begin by following the career of Arthur Keith and G. Elliot Smith, the two most prominent scientists who supported the validity of the Piltdown findings, but who nevertheless disagreed with each other on the interpretation of the findings, in a dispute which eventually was to reflect their conflicting views on the role of race in modern society. The focus is then shifted to Gordon Childe, who investigated the racial composition of British ancestry by addressing a shorter chronological scale – from the earliest times of European civilization – and who had the greatest impact between the wars on British archaeology. All three scientists were highly regarded by their contemporaries and used their prestigious professional position to popularize their own unique and peculiar racial theories.

The debate over race, however, did not deal with bones *per se* but revolved around cultural interpretations and psychological speculations concerning human nature and abilities. These were related to – but not determined by – the paleontological and archaeological findings. The mutual influence between their racial theories and their specific scientific positions was highly idiosyncratic: Keith maintained his staunch racial views regardless of the changing circumstances; Smith evolved gradually to advocate a non-racist position; and Childe transformed his views abruptly in an anti-racist direction during the mid-twenties. As such, this trio provides an illuminating test-case for the ambiguity of the "specific intellectual," who applied his (not directly related) expertise to the general question of race, while maintaining a facade that his scientific credentials were indeed pertinent. Oscillating between the biological and the cultural, all three argued that cultural theories were founded upon biological taxonomies. Historically, intellectual interest in biological determinism diminished previously to racial typology. Initially when universal cultural theories became popular they were based on general racial classification; only later were they replaced by diversified theories and historical particularism.

One of the first cultural holistic schools was diffusionism, and its most vocal and uncompromising prophet in England was Grafton Elliot Smith. Diffusionists argued that culture and technology were invented once and were later transmitted throughout the globe. They were vehemently opposed to the notion of multiple inventions. During the twenties, the diffusionists were locked in a bitter controversy with functionalists who accused diffusionism of a fragmentary understanding of culture, or treating each part of it as autonomous. The functionalists, in contract, investigated the idea and function of social components. It has been suggested, however, that diffusionists did see culture as complexes – that their emphasis on tracing various elements separately was a research program, not a theory. In practice, this distinction was blurred as diffusionists studied isolated cultural elements, paying no attention to their transfer and reception as part of a complex whole. In this, they gave scientific legitimation to the notion of the white man's burden in bringing "culture" to the "natives": civilization could be transplanted with little concern for local conditions. If all cultures had traveled and disseminated similarly ever since the fourth millennium B.C., then there was nothing especially sinister about Western colonialism.

Yet, diffusionism was innovative in its focus on culture, not race. In practice, diffusionists did not look for universal laws, but rather used artifacts to follow and reconstruct processes and trace a path by which cultural elements were transmitted. The idea of diffusion was accepted by various schools, and its eventual rejection during the thirties was the result more of its combative and exclusionary approach than of its principal tenets, for its supporters aroused hostility by rejecting the very possibility of multiple inventions. While this limited the impact of diffusionism, primarily to ethnology, it none the less provided an important force in the opposition to racial typologies.

Sir Grafton Elliot Smith, prominent in the world of anatomy in the first three decades of the century, is remembered foremost for his anthropological theories and the polemics over diffusionism. In 1938, a year after his death, partly as a statement in a waning controversy, Elliot Smith's close associates published a commemorative volume in which almost for the last time his diffusionism was viewed sympathetically. This was an obituary: a political statement in a long-standing theoretical and personal conflict. In 1972 the Anatomical Society of Great Britain and Ireland together with the Zoological Society of London held a centennial symposium in his honor. The organizer, Lord Zuckerman, regretted Smith's diversion to man's physical and social evolution, suggesting that had he devoted himself entirely to comparative neurology his "fame would have been ensured."[50]

The history of anthropology lends itself to many conflicting interpretations, primarily because of inconsistency in anthropologists' writings. The work of many leading theorists is self-contradictory and shows affinity to competing schools. Paradigms held at best for only one section of the profession and were replaced each generation. Elliot Smith exemplifies these vicissitudes in their extreme. He was prominent in the scientific community and among his other distinctions he served as Vice President of the Royal Society. He received honors in England and abroad and his position in the academic establishment transcended disciplinary boundaries.

Elliot Smith was born in New South Wales in 1871, where he began his medical career. At the age of twenty five he traveled to England with few plans for what turned out to be a permanent migration. Smith was a successful anatomist. He researched and taught at Cambridge and London, and in 1900 accepted the professorship of anatomy in the Government School of Medicine in Cairo. While still in Egypt his prominence was attested to by his

[50] Warren R. Dawson (ed.), *Sir Grafton Elliot Smith, A Biographical Record by His Colleagues* (London: Jonathan Cape, 1938). J. T. Wilson, "G. E. Smith," *Obituary Notices of Fellows of the Royal Society* (1938), 323–333; S. Zuckerman (ed.), *The Concepts of Human Evolution* (London: The Zoological Society of London, 1973), p. 5. Another participant, E. Leach was unusually blunt in his evaluation of Smith's legacy: "What [Elliot Smith] taught us as regards ethnology was absolute rubbish" (p. 436).

election to the Royal Society (1907), and following a decade at Manchester University, he opened the new anatomy department at University College London (1919). By then he had reached the pinnacle of British academic prestige. His credentials went further than medicine, and in 1923 his anthropological expertise led the Rockefeller Foundation to ask him to draft a plan for the development of Australian anthropology. During the 1920s his success received wide public recognition. His fame grew, his semi-popular books and articles were widely read, and he was in demand as a speaker on topics that ranged from mummies – especially after the discovery of the tomb of Tutankhamen – to an overall description of the origin of man. In 1930, he published *Human History*, which became his most popular book.[51]

Elliot Smith's publication on the diffusion of culture and his professional standing made him a central figure in the formulation of the concept of race in British anthropology in the early twenties. Perhaps most important from this perspective was his reluctance to address the question of race-mixture, or to distinguish between race and culture. Essentially he held a favorable view of the peaceful human nature in its pre-civilization stage, and believed that diffusionism was possible because the structure of the brain was similar among all humans. Yet, he compared contemporary primitive races to the man-like apes in their limited innate ability to invent civilization, a view which although it reflected general pessimism and the belief in the conservative nature of humankind, was more condescending to the "uncivilized." This addressed the larger debate over the antiquity of man, and brought Elliot Smith into conflict with Arthur Keith. Both had been trained as anatomists, and both were interested in archaeology and the origins of man, yet their views on humankind and race were diametrically opposed.

[51] Dawson (ed.), *Sir Grafton Elliot Smith*, p. 80–87. Elliot Smith transferred from Manchester to University College London, in 1919, despite attempts by Cambridge to attract him to St. Johns College. His main reason for preferring London over Cambridge were the grand plans for a medical center larger than any before. The plans were enhanced by a grant from the Rockefeller Foundation of £370,000 to Smith's anatomy department, and £835,000 to the medical school and hospital of University College London. (See H. A. Harris, in Dawson [ed.], *Sir Grafton Elliot Smith*, p. 173.) In 1930, after the discovery of Sinanthropus, the Rockefeller Foundation asked Smith to check the finding *in situ* (Perry, in Dawson [ed.], *Sir Grafton Elliot Smith*, p. 98). He was a main speaker at the British Association in 1923, the Galton Lecturer in 1924, taught anthropology at the University of California and in 1925 taught at the École de Médecine in Paris. One honor Smith was denied until (almost too) late in life was the Huxley Medal from the Royal Anthropology Institute which he finally received in 1935, when he was already too ill to read his lecture to the Institute.

Keith was born in Scotland, the son of a farmer, and received his Bachelor's degree at nearby Aberdeen. His first interest was collecting botanical specimens, and he later moved into anatomy, concentrating on primates, and enlarging his scope to comparative anatomy and finally physical anthropology and the evolution of man. His distinction was earned in cardiology due to his discovery of the heart's pacemaker (sinoatrial node) in 1906. While this would assume a much greater importance forty years later with the development of heart surgery, Keith's prominence in English science reached its peak during the twenties. In 1908 he was elected to the conservatorship of the Royal College of Surgeons, where he focused the collection of the Hunterian Museum on the history of the human body. For the next quarter of a century his prominent standing at the College provided him with a professional base from which to disseminate his views on nationalism and race.[52]

The debate over Piltdown Man led Keith and Elliot Smith into a controversy and animosity that never subsided. The conflict was manifested in the use each made of the findings to enhance a different theory of evolution and of racial differentiation. Keith advocated a greater antiquity to match his theory of an early divergent racial evolution followed by a long period of racial stability. Hence his efforts to increase the brain size of Piltdown Man to equal modern man, implied that the modern races have existed for a longer period than was generally assumed. Elliot Smith emphasized, in contrast, that the structure of the brain in Piltdown Man resembled that of modern Homo sapiens, but was of a much smaller size, which would have corroborated his own claim that human evolution resulted from the initial potentiality of the brain which evolved earlier, followed by physical changes and a recognition of the advantages of upright posture. The moral and public

[52] Biographical information is based on W. LeFanu, "Keith, Arthur," in *Dictionary of Scientific Biography*, vol. 8, pp. 278–279; Le Gros Clark, "Keith, Sir Arthur" in *Dictionary of National Biography*, 1951–1960, pp. 565–566; *Who was Who*, 1960; and *Sir A. Keith, An Autobiography* (London: Watts & Co., 1950). In 1946, E. Hooton wrote in the preface to Keith, *Evolution and Ethics*: "The name of Sir Arthur Keith deserves to be associated with those of Charles Darwin and Thomas Huxley in the study of the evolution of man." Hooton was prone to exaggeration, but even for him this was uniquely laudatory. This was how Keith was introduced to the American public by the most important physical anthropologist of the country. Others who were not so positive in their evaluation of his scientific achievements, none the less recognized his widespread impact. S. Zuckerman, for example, considered Keith "a superficial scientist" and argued that his "scientific qualities I usually felt were almost in inverse proportion to his widespread influence and charm." S. Zuckerman (ed.), *The Concepts of Human Evolution*, pp. 11, 5.

message of Piltdown as conveyed by Keith and Smith was even more polarized.

National pride played a major role in the acceptance of Piltdown. Elliot Smith was explicitly proud of the ancient lineage of the human species as evidenced by the fossil records. He rejoiced in both the "*antiquity* and *diversity* of the human family" (emphasis added). Long after the discovery of Piltdown he wrote:

> If the introduction of a hitherto unknown and exotic relative into the family circle increases our pride in the length of our ancestry and the variety of our kinsmen, it is also a useful discipline in humility in reminding us what strange and uncouth cousins of ours once roamed the world, unknown to us and to our immediate predecessors.[53]

None of those involved in the dispute received much credit. Several of the protagonists were blamed for falsifying the evidence and charged with the overall responsibility for the fraud. These included Elliot Smith, and more recently, Arthur Keith.[54]

By the 1920s, Elliot Smith was quite convinced that his version of the course of human evolution was correct, and he turned from investigation to preaching. His religion was hyperdiffusionism, which he publicized mainly through rewritten earlier papers which now included some additional contributions from Dawson and others. Smith began writing on cultural anthropology as a lighter side of his work, especially in Manchester, where he felt in relative isolation. According to Daryll Forde, Smith told him that "these were … recreational activities" for a man with a very heavy schedule.[55] What began as a part-time occupation turned Elliot Smith into an anthropologist, a discipline for which he became a major spokesman. In this respect Elliot Smith belonged to a group of outsiders who, like many other anthropologists of his period, were

[53] G. Elliot Smith *et al.*, *Man, His Origin, Development and Culture* (London: Ernest Benn, 1931), p. 14. S. J. Gould, "Piltdown Revisited," *The Panda's Thumb* (New York: Norton, 1980), pp. 108–125.
[54] Roland Miller, *The Piltdown Men* (London: Gollanz, 1972). This charge is probably unfounded, as both Zuckerman and Weiner have argued. Though the counter arguments may have been based on emotions, (for example Zuckerman: "Elliot Smith would never have falsified in order to refute those who may have differed from him," Zuckerman [ed.], *The Concepts of Human Evolution*, p. 20) the evidence presented by the two seemed convincing. See Zuckerman and Weiner in the above collection. The evidence against Keith is forthcoming in a book by Spencer (Oxford University Press) and has been previewed in the *New York Times* in a front-page article. No smoking gun is found, and the search continues.
[55] Forde, in S. Zuckerman, (ed.), *The Concepts of Human Evolution*, pp. 424–425.

distinguished from insiders by having primary affiliation with other
disciplines, in particular medicine.

Elliot Smith viewed anthropology as part of the medical sciences.
His innovation in anatomy at University College London was based
on his broad perception of human biology, which included
expanding the number of sub-disciplines taught, such as the introduction of radiography into the medical training, and more con-
troversially the creation of a readership in anthropology and a
lectureship in the history of medicine.[56] Among Smith's students
were Raymond A. Dart, whom he sent to South Africa, where he
discovered Australopithecus, and Davidson Black, who discovered
Sinanthropus.

In 1926 Smith outlined his perception of what constituted the
school of anthropology at University College London, and what
directions it should take: "In the first place we have been endeavor-
ing to rescue physical anthropology from the thraldom of anthro-
pometrists, to integrate the subject more definitely with biological
work in close co-operation with work in general biology and
embryology, physiology and psychology." Taking this unique
approach, "we have found ... a most fruitful and stimulating line ...
not merely from the point of view of mere teaching and interesting
students, but in provoking serious investigation."

This biological approach did not blind Smith to the importance of
the cultural and psychological factors which led to mass migrations,
bringing about the integration of cultural anthropology with
medical sciences in the anatomy department.[57] The Smith enigma
concerns why such a comprehensive attitude turned into an extreme
hyperdiffusionism and how "a man famous as a physical anthropologist ... [could] become notorious as a cultural anthropologist."
Why, if his social anthropology was unacceptable, was it taken so
seriously?[58] The paradox was that the diffusionists were accustomed
to analytical thinking in the laboratory, while their ethnology was

[56] The position in anthropology was planned to be offered to W. H. R. Rivers, but eventually
went to W. J. Perry, Elliot Smith's disciple from Manchester. Charles Singer was
appointed by Smith to lecturer (later professor) of the history of medicine. H. A. Harris, in
Dawson (ed.), *Sir Grafton Elliot Smith.*
[57] "An ideal Institute of Anthropology should be associated with a School of Anatomy where
particular attention is being paid to neurology and the evolution of the brain, with a School
of Experimental Psychology," and a detailed analysis of their interaction. Elliot Smith to
C. M. Hincks, Jan. 1926. In Dawson (ed.), *Sir Grafton Elliot Smith,* pp. 89–95.
[58] Glyn Daniel "Elliot Smith, Egypt and Diffusionism," in Zuckerman (ed.), *The Concepts of
Human Evolution,* p. 407.

"credulously obsessed with a pseudo-historical dogma."[59] This was an example of a scientist stepping out of the laboratory but maintaining the professional credentials while lacking the necessary knowledge. Part of the explanation was Smith's intense commitment. He had given up ethnological research for pseudo-religion. His closest disciple appropriately described his methodology in terms of revelations rather than experiments. Addressing Smith's "greatest" achievement – the theory that discoveries and inventions are made only once – W. J. Perry claimed it most "remarkable since he perceived its truth, not by laborious induction from vast and detailed studies, but by virtue of a profound insight which enabled him to recognize the essential connections between diverse phenomena more or less remote in time and place." His egyptocentrism was so extreme that when asked what was "the development of culture in the rest of the world when Egypt was laying the foundation of our civilization, the answer came at once: 'Nothing'." One should remember that this was related by Smith's most loyal follower, supplemented with a comment that the accumulation of evidence since Elliot Smith made that claim "tended to confirm the essential accuracy of what was then *an astonishing generalization*" (emphasis added).[60] Part of the growing commitment to hyperdiffusionism was a result of public exposure. From 1911, when Smith's alleged conversion to diffusionism occurred under the influence of Rivers, through the twenties, when he turned into its most vocal prophet, and to the end of his life when his views were almost totally rejected, he never retracted them, nor accepted any contradictory evidence.

Did Elliot Smith ever really distinguish between race and culture? There is much confusion on that score in his writings. He discussed races as if they were hierarchical "separate subspecies." Although he recognized the existence of interfertility of the human races, he was reluctant to discuss racial mixture. He spoke about the capacity of cultural innovation as a special characteristic of the Mediterranean race, initially acquired incidentally and later passed on. In differentiating among races, as in other ethnological questions, he resorted to common sense as the ultimate arbiter, enabling him to come up with an easy clear and inflexible division:

---

[59] Fortes (on Elliot Smith and Rivers,) in Zuckerman (ed.), *The Concepts of Human Evolution*, pp. 427–428.
[60] W. J. Perry, in Dawson (ed.), *Sir Grafton Elliot Smith*, pp. 212, 214.

Whatever criteria may be adopted as racial distinctions ... there are certain outstanding features, which the man in the street is competent to recognize, without any special training, for differentiating six well-defined types of mankind: The aboriginal Australian, the Negro, the Mongol, the Mediterranean, the Alpine and the Nordic races.

His main interest in racial classification lay in the European differentiation, for which Elliot Smith accepted the tripartite conventional division. The rest of mankind was also divided three ways: the dichotomy is clear; the white man *contra mundo*.[61]

Keith's perception of human nature stood in direct opposition to Elliot Smith's conception of the peaceful savage. For Keith, humanity had a combative aggressive personality which was at the source of racial and national development. He viewed race and nationality as interchangeable: new races were formed as new groups were amalgamated into new nationalities. This he explained by a theory according to which hormones create the physical changes characterizing the different races – this at a time of scientific ignorance about hormones. Keith also considered isolation as another crucial factor of racial separation. Although his theory was first publicized in the second decade of the century, he did not mention genes, but rather spoke about heredity through hormones. Within its distorted logic, the theory emphasized the biological instability of races, and therefore could have contained an anti-racial element. Keith's indiscriminate use of time scales confused biological evolution through isolation (the zoological time scale) with cultural changes which created new nationalities (the historical time scale), as though both related to comparable periods. This perception, which Keith shared with many of his peers, led inevitably to contradictions which Keith resolved by drawing with great faith upon the theory of racial typology. The systems presented by both Smith and Keith contained elements which could have been interpreted in either a racist or an egalitarian manner. During the thirties, the political implications resulted in their choosing very different directions.

Elliot Smith is an unlikely hero in the story of the transition away from formal racial typology. Despite what has been said so far, he was one of the more important early anti-racists. His egalitarianism, if his attitude can be so termed,[62] stemmed from deep

[61] G. Elliot Smith *et al.*, *Early Man, His Origin, Development and Culture* (London: Ernest Benn, 1931), p. 15.
[62] Compare to the Harvard physical anthropologist Earnest Hooton, pp. 101–108 below.

pessimism and a general disappointment with Homo Sapiens, especially as manifested under civilized circumstances. Arguing that conservatism was the strongest driving force in societies, he rejected and opposed the notion of innovations, and concluded that the acquisition of violence was the main result of progress. In 1927 Elliot Smith delivered a sermon on the innate peacefulness of human beings, ascribing pacifism to savages:

Man is by nature a kindly and considerate creature, with an instinctive tendency to monogamy and the formation of a happy family group bound together by mutual affection and consideration. This is the basis of all social organization. The old theories of primitive promiscuity and lack of sexual restraint are now shown to be devoid of any foundation and to be the very reverse of truth.[63]

It is easy to maintain that Elliot Smith projected English middle-class values on the world and to read cultural imperialism into this attitude. Such an argument overlooks his foremost emphasis on the unity of mankind. He argued that only by chance was civilization developed by one group rather than another. The primitive world provided a romantic alternative to the evils of modernity. It was endowed with pacifism, honesty and decency, highlighting the psychic unity of humankind.

In contrast, the mechanism of Keith's evolutionary theory turned it into a racist exposition, which in the thirties was exploited as such by war-mongers and racists alike. For Keith, isolation was primarily mental, that is, a matter of alienation and antagonism. Physical barriers such as oceans were insufficient: evolution required racial-national rivalry: namely, war. Keith's debate was conducted more with Darwin than with his contemporaries. He disagreed with Darwin's concept of sexual selection of racial evolution as past phenomena, arguing that it was alive and kicking. Keith emphasized inborn reaction or prejudice – race feeling – "as part of the evolutionary machinery which safeguards the purity of the race. Human prejudices have usually a biological significance."[64] Seeing mental predisposition as instrumental in achieving isolation, Keith felt he had embarked on a new evolutionary theory: "inborn human nature as a factor in securing isolation was a new idea."[65]

[63] May 17, 1927, the Conway Memorial Lecture, published in Elliot Smith, *Human History*, p. 41.
[64] Keith, "The Evolution of the Human Races," Huxley Memorial Lecture, 1928, *JRAI*, 58 (1928), 316.
[65] *Autobiography*, p. 396.

Keith's empiricism was sanctioned by his own personal experience. He described a family he knew "in which the effects of an over-action of a pituitary hormone were very evident. If this family were to become a nucleus of a new race, then it must be kept separated from other families." But the opposite had taken place: "What I actually saw happening was that the members of the family scattered as they married, and with the dispersion the characteristics of the family seemed to disappear." Hence "a machinery of group isolation" was needed which was not physical.[66] All that remained was for him to collect data which would prove his hypothesis, and that he did.

The reception to the theory was mixed. It was widespread and at the very least did not encounter great opposition. Keith's standing in the scientific community certainly legitimized his views in the eyes of the public, and he continued to promulgate these views into the 1930s when confusion over racial matters was the rule, not the exception. Although Keith expected public enthusiasm to mount, and was disappointed with the reception to his theory – "it seemed to be a case of still birth" – his view none the less commanded a great deal of attention. His advocacy of war as an evolutionary, positive, force, was a strong antidote to the pacifism in England during the thirties. World War I encouraged his formulation of the theory. The prevalent view was that war was unconnected to race; after all, the Japanese and the English were fighting on the same side. But Keith concluded that in the history of mankind "war had been born in the process of human evolution. Its *germ lay in the spirit* of animosity which kept neighboring tribes apart."[67] This confusion between a physical, material interpretation and idealism was evident in his mixed metaphors, and its importance lay in the support it gave to blatant racism during the thirties.

In presenting a critical appraisal of Elliot Smith's views on race and anthropology, the risk is that a distorted and ridiculous portrait might result when the intention is exactly the opposite. Elliot Smith was a very articulate scientist and a sharp critic of others' work (excluding diffusionism). Though his own theory of race was self-contradictory, it was important in the present context for its egalitarian components, which were not part of the mainstream, scientific and cultural discourse. In 1924, Elliot Smith delivered the Galton Lecture entitled "The Problem of Race." Much in his text

[66] *Autobiography*, pp. 394–395.   [67] *Autobiography*, p. 396 (emphasis added).

supported the notion that, despite inner contradictions, he was on balance an egalitarian. Yet it is only fair to say that an opposite reading of the text is possible, and that this reading is as much a result of the context of the lecture as of its textual analysis. The Eugenic Society was probably the most sympathetic audience in the British Isles for a racist exposition. But Elliot Smith attacked much of the nonsense prevalent in academic circles on the question of race,[68] and testified in the name of an unknown ex-professor of zoology to the impossible task of classifying human races. He went on to emphasize the role of the environment and "a special series of events [which] presented the opportunities" for those who "in fact became the inventors of civilization." Above all, he argued that there were "abundant facts" "to dissociate the idea of race and culture." A decade later, Elliot Smith became part of a committee which tried to give that divorce official sanction, but failed. In his argument for the unity of humankind he looked to the power of speech, that is the universal ability to talk rather than at the hierarchy of literacy among different groups. His commitment for human unity stopped short of allowing a critique of diffusionism. He rejected the concept of unity as "utterly misleading" and "preposterous pretense" when it was advanced to argue multiple inventions of folklore stories.[69]

For Keith, both nationality and race implied physical differentiation. He viewed the progeny of racial mixture to be "so grouped with either," while a national mixture "gives rise to a progeny which may pass as a member of either parent nationality."[70] This dichotomy was clearest in the United States, where "we see a machinery at work which maintains racial frontiers but breaks down all national barriers." This system, was opposed to that of South America, which resolved racial antagonism by the fusion of blood and "has given the world a jangling series of small people, not any of which is equal, either in body or in mind to the pioneer Iberian stock." Keith's choice between the two Americas was presented as a scientific conclusion: "From the anthropologist's point of view, the Northern experiment is a successful one."[71] Keith viewed nation-

---

[68] In the lecture he attacked two unnamed writers (Karl Pearson and Ronald Dixon) for disseminating nonsense disguised as scientific theory.

[69] Elliot Smith, "Problems of Race," *Eugenics Review*, 60, 1 (1968), 26–30.

[70] Keith, *Nationality and Race, From an Anthropologist's Point of View*, Robert Boyle Lecture, Nov. 17, 1919 (Oxford: Oxford University Press, 1919), p. 9.

[71] Keith, *Nationality and Race*, pp. 11–12.

alism as the modern expression of man's deepest feeling: tribalism. Against the background of the European theater of World War I, he found it easy to rebuff idealistic internationalism. "Many writers believe that class or sectional tribal organizations can actually be made to cut across national and even racial frontiers. We have seen, however, that at the declaration of war, all such sectional bonds snap, for war is the match which fires the tribal spirit, exalts it to a national flame, and destroys intertribal schisms." To many, the widespread popular support for the war came as a surprise, for Keith, in retrospect, it proved a healthy sign that the mechanism of evolution was still at work.[72]

Despite his scientific claims, Keith's definitions of race and nationality were based on contemporary common sense, but as it turned out, the theory was confused and incoherent. Keith described the intermediate races as "stages of an evolutionary scale" from 100 percent to zero differentiation.[73] He agreed that hybridization contributes to race formation, but argued that it played a minor role compared with nationality: "a human race may be at any stage of differentiation; a nation may be an incipient race, however mixed may be the derivation of its original population."[74] Evidently, the dichotomy between races and nationalities made little sense even to Keith.

More illuminating were his analyses of the "racial" components of the British Isles done in a different mood each time. In 1919, proud of the achievement of the British tribe in the European war, Keith rallied anthropological justification to conclude:

I do not think there is an anthropologist in Europe who by mere inspection could tell the Irish from the English group. From a physical point of view the Celts and the Saxons are one; whatever be the source of their mutual antagonism, it does not lie in a difference of race. It is often said that we British are a mixed and mongrel collection of types and breeds; the truth is that as regards physical type the inhabitants of the British Isles are the most uniform of all the large nationalities of Europe.[75]

---

[72] *Nationality and Race*, p. 37.

[73] Keith does not explain what constitutes total or no differentiation; it is easier to imagine intermediate positions, but what does it mean that two groups are 100 percent different on an evolutionary scale?

[74] Keith, "The Evolution of the Human Races." *JRAI*, 58 (1928), pp. 317–318.

[75] Keith, *Nationality and Race*, pp. 23–24. The reviewer in *Man* (April 1920), p. 61, F. G. Parson, contested Keith's assertion that no anthropologist could distinguish among the "races" of Britain. From this perspective Keith could suddenly be perceived as non-racialist.

A decade later he changed his position unannounced and unawares: "The nationalities of Britain I regard as partly differentiated races." For this belief Keith blithely cited no evidence:

I believe, but I have never put my belief to the test of actual proof, that in a mixed crowd composed of individuals drawn from our four nationalities I could identify, from physical appearance, 15 percent. of the men of Wales, about the same percentage from the Irish Free State, and about ten percent. of Scotch and English. Our nationalities are real races.

Random choices could presumably have scored better.[76] As time passed Keith became more adamant about the similarity of race and nationality. By 1931, he included in a paper on "The Evolution of Human Races, Past and Present," headings such as "Patriotism as a Factor in Race-Building," and "Nation and Race are the Same Thing." The racial division among the British was drawn even more sharply, with Wales carrying the banner: "No matter what racial mixtures have entered into the composition of the Welsh people in the past, that mixture is being welded into a new race under the working of a common national spirit." The Scottish question presented a harder dilemma for Keith. He had to implement his view that "the manifestations of a young nationality are not willful perversions of human nature, but have a deep significance." At the same time he refused to join the Scottish nationalists. "At heart I am still a ... Scotsman," he declared, whereupon racial cooperation unexpectedly became a constructive force. Instead of racial antagonism, Scotland's "national spirit can be developed more fully and more completely as a member of a great confederation of peoples." "National spirit" triumphed over racial instincts, both towards the larger group, Britain, and within "the distinctive nationality of Scotland," which had incorporated "the diverse races ... that are and have inherited the spirit of her nationality."[77] Keith's scientific convictions were overwhelmed by his conservative politics as was the case when he declined to join the Eugenics

[76] Keith, "The Evolution of the Human Races," *JRAI*, 58 (1928), 320. The form, the annual distinguished lecture of the Anthropological Institute, reflected on the state of the discipline as much as on Keith himself. But not all of his audience agreed. Lord Raglan ridiculed the recognition: "he could also no doubt identify from physical appearance a considerable proportion of lawyers, and soldiers," and added that "the fact [is] that language, religion and training all leave their traces on physiognomy, and it is often possible to diagnose a man's 'race' from his physical appearance although he exhibits no true racial characteristics whatsoever." *Man*, 29 (1929), 96.
[77] Arthur Keith, "The Evolution of Human Races, Past and Present," in G. Elliot Smith *et al.*, *Early Man, His Origin, Development and Culture*, pp. 51, 55, 59–60.

Society, preferring the status quo over intervention: "I could not make up my mind as to the kind of people my country might be in need of fifty years hence; the kind that would not be needed – the undesirable – presented an easier problem."[78]

An extraordinary example of the tolerance, or perhaps chaos, which characterized British science is the lecture Keith delivered in May 1924 on "Phrenological Studies of the Skull and Brain of Sir Thomas Browne of Norwich." Phrenology had been outdated for almost three quarters of a century, and Keith was aware that it had "to be abandoned." He nevertheless believed "that some day Gall's dream of a science of phrenology must come true." His language conveys the sense that phrenology had been rejected by mistake and ignored the fact that it was dismissed because proven wrong. Keith gave two reasons for his belief in the future of phrenology. First, the physical dimensions of the brain had grown apace with mental abilities. Secondly, regions in the brain were devoted to specific tasks. These correct, if unsophisticated, observations led to an astonishing conclusion: "When our knowledge of the human nervous system is perfected, it will be possible by a mere inspection of a brain to assess the mental potentialities of its owner. This is the ultimate goal of the scientific phrenologist." Short of this phrenological fantasy, Keith avowed: "We cannot discuss the cranial characters ... unless we bring to our task a knowledge of the workings of [the] mind."[79] In hindsight, one could presume that this could have potentially meant that contemporary physical anthropology and the biological sciences were unable to address cultural issues – a similar position was guiding the egalitarian argument. Instead, Keith's approach was to expand the domain of conjectures from the crania to the inner working of the brain. The skulls of Piltdown Man and Thomas Browne of Norwich provided Keith with two of the best opportunities to pursue his most unfounded cultural conjectures. The present allegation that Keith have masterminded the Piltdown

[78] *Autobiography*, p. 400. Most eugenicists agreed on "negative" and not on "positive" policies, and Keith definitely would not have felt out of place professionally or socially on account of his views.

[79] A. Keith, "Phrenological Studies of the Skull and Brain of Sir Thomas Browne of Norwich," *The Henderson Trust Lectures*, No. 3 (May 9, 1924) (London: Oliver and Boyd, 1924), pp. 3–5. Keith admitted that by "present knowledge" it was impossible to explain the "peculiar abilities" of the individual, and limited himself to the "grosser features of the brain." But the hope was there that with the help of X-rays it would be possible to form "an accurate estimate of the development of the brain ... and ... infer the abilities of the child" (p. 30).

fraud would turn him into a Dickensian villain: a racist and a con. All of this did not detract from Keith's contemporary standing in the scientific community; there was little connection between the eventual rejection of the substance of his theories and his continued distinguished position in the scientific community. Three years after he published his phrenological work, in 1927, Keith was elected to the presidency of the British Association for the Advancement of Science.

THE SHIFT IN BRITISH ARCHAEOLOGY

As well as being medical experts, Arthur Keith and Grafton Elliot Smith were also part-time archaeologists and paleontologists. But in the growing specialization of the post World War I period, a new professional school of archaeology was emerging and by the late 1920s the attention of archaeologists was beginning to turn away from racial classification. Gordon Childe personified this shift: his legacy dominates the history of the interwar years in British archaeology. An Australian, a Marxist and a theoretician, this outsider embodied the establishment of Scottish archaeology, holding at Edinburgh University the only chair in prehistory in Scotland. His eccentricity rivalled his professional reputation, which was founded upon his comparative approach and analysis of European prehistory. Among the ideas he introduced into archaeology was the concept of culture, the result of his close association with other facets of anthropology, which he no doubt encountered while working as the librarian of the Royal Anthropological Institute in London between his earlier political career and his appointment to the chair of archaeology in Edinburgh.[80]

Biographical retrospectives underscore his erudition and his pleasure at displaying it as a source of professional status. This was manifested especially in his attempts to impress colleagues with his mastery of languages, which could at times backfire, as it did once in Norway, when he was brought two dozen beers instead of raspberries.[81] There was better reason to be impressed with his mastery of

[80] B. McNairn, *The Method and Theory of V. Gordon Childe: Economic Social and Cultural Interpretations of Prehistory* (Edinburgh: Edinburgh University Press, 1980); G. B. Trigger, *Gordon Childe: Revolutions in Archaeology* (New York: Columbia University Press, 1980); Sally Green, *Prehistorian: A Biography of V. Gordon Childe* (Bradford-on-Avon: Moonraker Press, 1981).

[81] Green, *V. Gordon Childe*, p. 76.

European and Near Eastern archaeology. Nevertheless, Childe's eccentricity meant that when he was not interested in an issue, he made a point of not knowing anything about it. America was a case in point. He claimed to have "never got around to reading" about American archaeology, but his references in lectures to the American way of life and to Americans as "loathsome fascist hyenas" displayed more than lack of interest.[82] This did not prevent Harvard from inviting him to speak about prehistory at the Tercentenary celebration in 1936, nor did he decline that or other American invitations. Appropriately enough, his support for the Soviet Union was professional and political; ranging from his interest in Soviet archaeology to political support of the Hitler-Stalin pact, to subleasing a place in London in "Moscow Mansions," chosen for its name.[83] Against such background, it is not surprising to learn that Childe was more explicit than his contemporaries in admitting that his political views and his historical writing were correlated. Childe did not hesitate to advance his political views in public. Such was the case with his criticism of Nazi race theories early in 1933. His shift was especially acute from the mid-twenties, when his scientific and theoretical work supported the superiority of the Aryans, to the thirties, when he became a leader among anti-racists.

Only a few years earlier, in 1926, Childe published *The Aryans*, a complementary volume to his earlier work, *The Dawn of European Civilization* (1925) which concentrated on philology and Indo-European origins. He accepted much of the self proclaimed Aryan superiority, and showed how the Europeans were able to transform the Oriental culture into a unique Western civilization. *The Aryans* never needed a second edition, and was disregarded in later years by the author.[84] Yet the question remains; what was the significance of the work? And what did Childe try to achieve in the book?

Partial motivation for Childe was his search for professional recognition. The two books were a result of four years of work in which he could devote only part of his time to writing. In the controversy between the Orientalists and the Occidentalists, who claimed priority in civilization for the East and West respectively,

[82] Green, *V. Gordon Childe*, p. 86.
[83] Green, *V. Gordon Childe*, pp. 73, 76–77, 103–104, 135–136.
[84] Trigger, *Gordon Childe*, p. 37; Green, *V. Gordon Childe*, p. 53. The book was reprinted in 1987, by Dorset.

Childe came down on the side of compromise. Both sides agreed that diffusionism explained the spread of culture. Gustav Kossina, a German archaeologist and Occidentalist, who later became a national hero in Nazi Germany, located the source of European culture with the Aryans rather than in the Near East.[85] Childe's synthesis took Kossina's work a step further to show how the Europeans were able to adopt the culture of the East to form a distinct new civilization. *The Aryans* shows that Childe tended to accept the conventional contemporary racism in a modified form. In his attempt to present a new theory, conditioned by his Marxism, he came out strongly against linking the Nordics with imperialism and anti-semitism, and criticized the misuse of Aryanism which had led Indo-European philology into disrepute.[86] More specifically, he challenged Kossina's claim that the archaeological remains of tall dolichocephalics (with elongated skulls) in Northern Germany were to be equated with the modern population of Germany. Childe argued that the dolichocephalic were short, that the findings could not be dated, and that the race was more likely to have come from Eastern Europe.[87] Yet, a captive of prevalent prejudice, Childe praised the progressiveness of the north European countries in prehistoric times, employing the distinction of creative races, meaning the Greeks and the Nordics (which included Britain and Germany) as separate from the passive French and Iberians.[88] He rejected the more egregious aspects of German superiority, but shared the belief that innate characteristics of race explained the progress of history.[89]

Much in *The Aryans* suggests that Childe's perceptions were indeed racist, but in a peculiar way. Childe conceded that the original Aryans belonged to the Nordic race, the modern population of northern Europe. Within the conventional wisdom that judged race and culture to be synonymous, Childe argued that the

---

[85] Trigger, *Gordon Childe*, p. 26. In the context of Imperial rivalry, this made Kossina unpopular in Britain already in the pre-war years.

[86] V. Gordon Childe, *The Aryans: A Study of Indo-European Origins* (London: K. Paul, Trench and Trunber, 1926), p. 164.

[87] *The Aryans*, p. 179.

[88] *The Dawn*, pp. 108, 151, 242, 259, 302; Quoted in Trigger, *Gordon Childe*, p. 50.

[89] This should be viewed in light of the argument that the dominance of philology over ethnology was outdated by over half a century, which by then was predominantly influenced by archaeology, physical anthropology and folklore. Childe's position suggests that the impact was not one-sided nor was it forgotten. Cf. George W. Stocking, Jr., "From Chronology to Ethnology: James Cowles Prichard and British Anthropology, 1800–1850," in J. C. Prichard, *Researches into the Physical History of Man*, pp. ix–cx.

"Nordics' superiority in physique fitted them to be the vehicles of a superior language." Yet he denied that Aryan superiority was vested in material culture, a meaningful category to a Marxist: "the lasting gift bequeathed by Aryans to the conquered peoples was neither a higher material culture nor a superior physique, but ... a more excellent language and the mentality it generated."[90] That Childe attributed a limited importance to material culture as compared with language suggests that his Marxism was only partially integrated in his scientific work.

In 1933, Childe enrolled in the anti-fascist campaign with anti-racist articles which not only combated Nazi theories, but also reoriented his archaeological thinking. Childe, who from 1930 had begun to concentrate on material diffusionism, recanted the political implications of his earlier interpretation of Nordic superiority to the extent that he tipped the balance in favor of the Oriental and against the Occidental school.[91] Recognizing the difficulties involved in defining living races, he emphasized the greater speculative component in reconstructing the physical unity of prehistoric groups. Pointing out that only head-form and possibly stature and the shape of the nose were available to the archaeologist, he contested that the nominalist classification of skulls into specific groups would conceal the true diversity within populations. Replacing the term "race" with "people," Childe found it politically advisable to emphasize the "three distinct layers" of the prehistoric invaders of Britain, and the contemporary tripartite division of the Jewish people. The implicit message was the underlying unity of the English and the Jews in their opposition to racism. But this adherence to a terminology of "distinct" (biological), sub-groups within a modern population, suggests that his interpretation still echoed conventional racial typology. The meaningful sub-divisions, however, were the political, cultural and social: none of these corresponded to the racial division, which Childe none the less implied was still traceable.[92] Employing archaeology to support his politics, Childe argued in the fall of 1933 that it proved racism and fascism wrong and emphasized that the independence of culture from physical race existed already in prehistoric times. Despite his

[90] *The Aryans*, pp. 159–164, 211–212.
[91] For his earlier emphasis on material diffusionism, see *The Bronze Age* (New York: Macmillan, 1930). Also Green, *V. Gordon Childe*, p. 55.
[92] V. Gordon Childe, "Races, People and Cultures in Prehistoric Europe," *History*, 18 (1933), 193–203.

criticism of the ignorance and imprecise use of the term race among race theorists, he fell victim to similar errors. He spoke of race as a biological term yet criticized the "false analogy" between man and poultry and his simplified substitution of "race" by "people" was based on a false assumption of an undisputed biological definition of race.[93] Scientifically, Childe was on shaky ground, but because the critique was primarily political, it proved a sound tactic. He never attempted to write a major work against racial interpretation, nor was he an active intellectual leader in the movement against racism. He did associate, however, with leftist academicians, members of the "Invisible College" sharing with them cuisine and spirits in their "club" Tots and Quots.[94] Occasionally he voiced his opposition to racism, especially against its pretense to scientific respectability.[95] In the process he distanced himself from his earlier contention that Aryans constituted a physical unit and instead urged that the term be used only in its linguistic meaning. When published, in 1942, the idea was not novel, but it signified Childe's (and archaeology's) rejection of racial typology.[96]

A BRITISH GLIMPSE AT RACE RELATIONS

British attitudes to race touched very little on race relations. The scientists were primarily Classics scholars or had medical training, with interests in the origins of humankind and the peoples of the Empire. They approached the question of race on a more theoretical level than did their American counterparts. Their prejudices were a result of interest in a remote problem and not a direct response to racial conflicts. Britain had little racial strife, except for antagonism encountered by the small non-European population residing in port towns. The post World War I demobilization had increased Liverpool's black population to a figure estimated variously from 2,000 to 5,000, a large proportion of which was unemployed. Blacks faced growing animosity and by May 1919, were attacked repeatedly in the streets. Liverpool had more pronounced ethnic

93 For a reference to his outdated ethnography, see Trigger, *Gordon Childe*, pp. 75, 99. The argument was presented in a lecture to his students, published as Gordon V. Childe, "Is Prehistory Practical?' *Antiquity*, 7 (1933), 410–418.

94 Zuckerman, *From Apes to Warlords*, p. 393. Werskey, *"Invisible College"*.

95 In 1936 he opposed (in a letter to *Nature*, 137 [1936], 1,074) the preparations for a new International Association of Ethnology which was to take place in Edinburgh in 1937, and was financed by the German Research Institute. See Green, *V. Gordon Childe*, p. 86.

96 V. Gordon Childe, *What Happened in History* (London: Harmondsworth, 1942), p. 150.

neighborhoods than any other city in England and the editor of the *Liverpool Echo* was able to distinguish "Chinatown," "dark town," and "other alien quarters." Segregation positively enabled the authorities, he felt, to exercise social control over the undesirable elements among the mainly "quiet and law abiding Negroes."[97] Nevertheless, these subdued citizens were subject to increasing harassment.

Liverpool attracted black sailors because they were paid much better compared with signing on a ship at a colonial port. Though they were discriminated against in English ports and were refused work as long as there were any white sailors available (prejudice being shared by Trade Unions and employers alike), some did try their luck in Britain.[98] Intercommunual relations worsened and one riot ended in the lynching and killing of a black veteran. A major source of conflict was attributed to the social interaction between the groups. In the words of a police officer, "The negroes would not have been touched but for their relations with white women."[99] Sexual relations between black men and white women were, as has so often been the case an explosive source of racial animosity. The *Times* explained that "In the post war situation many [blacks] married Liverpool women and while it is admitted that some of them made good husbands the intermarriage of black men and white women, not to mention other relationships, has excited much feeling." Sir Ralph Williams, a former colonial administrator, relied on his previous experience to support his prejudice:

Every one of us has, probably, many friends among the coloured people, whom we bear in our kindliest remembrance ... [hostility] does not, either, I think, arise from any feeling of social superiority. The cause is far deeper. It is an instinctive certainty that sexual relations between white women and coloured men revolt our very nature.[100]

By the early 1920s, the interracial relations improved and ceased to capture the headlines. They nevertheless remained part of the social structure of the city, and attracted anthropologists to study racial mixture, a rare topic in England. In the midtwenties the Eugenic Society sponsored a "race crossing" investigation in

[97] Quoted in Fryer, *Staying Power*, p. 299.
[98] Roy May and Robin Cohen, "The Interaction Between Race and Colonialism: A Case Study of the Liverpool Race Riots of 1919," *Race and Class*, 16 (1974–5), 117–118.
[99] Fryer, *Staying Power*, pp. 299–302.
[100] *The Times*, June 10 and June 16, 1919, quoted in May and Cohen, "The Interaction Between Race and Colonialism," pp. 115–116.

Liverpool. Centered on the progeny of English and Chinese, it covered fifteen families and forty-five children. The initiative for the study was local, but when the Liverpudlians recognized that their university was unable to provide an experienced investigator, they approached the Eugenics Society.[101] Mrs. C. B. S. Hodson, the secretary of the society, became very quickly the driving force for the survey and solicited Herbert John Fleure, who had just published on the *Races of England and Wales*, to undertake the project.[102]

Fleure was at the time a geographer working at University College, Aberystwyth, Wales. In 1904 he had been appointed as lecturer in the established fields of geology, zoology and botany, since at the time geography was largely a non-academic discipline struggling to achieve recognition. Yet he was able to devote most of his time to geography and anthropology, which were finally recognized academically when, in 1917, he was endowed a chair in the two disciplines. H. J. Fleure was born in Guernsey, where he spent his first twenty years and acquired in addition to his "Englishness," strong affinities to France, and religiously was affiliated with the Methodist Church, a combination which later influenced his scientific and socialist creed. Fleure viewed humanistic and scientific studies as part of a greater whole: "Scientific work leads to the satisfaction of our desire for unity, and this desire is for me, an artistic desire."[103] Fleure's views were shaped by his romantic picture of Guernsey, an intimate, industrious community dominated by the values of autonomy, cooperation, and egalitarianism. This peaceful nature led him to interpret humankind's instincts as pacifist and cooperative and to view with pessimism progress through antagonism and war. Scientific studies provided a second component of his suggestion at the turn of the century that "Biological Socialism" may provide a viable alternative to Spencerism and that evolution often results from cooperation as well as competition. A Darwinian by conviction, he did not equate evolution with progress, and was closer to T. H. Huxley than to Spencer. Biology taught him "that great steps forward in the evolution of

---

[101] See pp. 151–152, 190, on eugenics.

[102] H. J. Fleure, *The Races of England and Wales, A Study of Recent Research* (London: Benn, 1923).

[103] H. J. Fleure "On the Artistic Side of Science," *The Dragon*, 27 (1905), 123. Quoted in J. A, Campbell, "Some Sources of the Humanism of H. J. Fleure," *Research Papers, School of Geography, Oxford University* (1972), p. 5.

animal structure have been taken not so much by successes of an epoch as by its failures" (1919).[104]

As a geographer and an anthropologist very much in the traditional style, Fleure accepted the reality of racial differentiation even in Europe, where all the populations exhibit types of diverse origins living and maintaining those type characters side by side in spite of intermarriage and of absence of any consciousness of diversity. These various types, each with mental aptitudes and limitations that are in some degree correlated with their physique, make diverse contributions to the life of each people.

Nevertheless, he rejected from early on the political misuse of racial terminology. His erroneous interpretation of races, which described racial characteristics as having an autonomous existence and remaining stable in a mixed population, was the foundation upon which his critique against the 'folly' of mistaking language for race was built: he attributed common descent to peoples who speak a common language such as "Latin, Anglo-Saxon, Teutonic, Slavonic and other groups." While such criticism was meant to reject the political terms most abused in support of racism, at this earlier stage Fleure did not question the reality and stability of racial taxonomy.[105]

Fleure had occasional contacts with the Eugenics Society. He supported its ideals, but criticized opinions reported from its meetings, most of which he missed on account primarily of his distance from London. His opposition to the Society stemmed from, his socialism and was directed mostly against its class prejudice and belief that the improvement of the race is synonymous with the preservation of the social order: "so long as we have a society aiming at maximum aggregate monetary resources, we are thereby necessarily committed to have an ill bred people," namely "people the majority of whom have a bad or a poor heredity." His criticism emphasized a methodological fallacy prevalent in discussions of race: the "disposition to disregard differences of kind, to treat all ... English people as essentially homologous." He did not oppose a biological racial taxonomy, rather its indiscriminate application. In his opposition to the reductionism of a mechanical and statistical

---

[104] Campbell, *Fleure*, p. 15.

[105] In his analysis of the reshaping of Europe in the post-World War I period, Fleure preferred to speak of nations and languages and avoided altogether the term race, but for one short criticism. H. J. Fleure, *The Treaty Settlement of Europe* (London: Oxford University Press, 1921), pp. 18–19.

approach, Fleure emphasized "the morphological outlook with its appreciation of differences of kind, in body and mind, that will go farthest towards saving and developing and multiplying the best."[106]

When Hodson approached Fleure with a request to conduct a study of racial crossing in Liverpool, she thought to include "simple physical data" as well as "all the usual social data" and hoped that Fleure or his assistant could work through local volunteers who would then conduct the actual survey. Hodson also solicited advice across the ocean, from the American eugenicist Charles Davenport, who supplied her with a Chinese contact man to advise on a relatively detailed questionnaire, which he advanced merely tentatively, since few previous studies had been conducted on "the offspring of Chinese-Caucasian intermarriages." The American impact was evident also in her perhaps not so "usual" suggestion that a psychologist would join the team to conduct I.Q. tests, the most fashionable device of racial studies in the United States for some years. Fleure was not enthusiastic:

The Mental Test people have not yet got hold of adequate ways of testing people who are not fully familiar with the language in which the tests are given and this is responsible for the ridiculous & rather disgraceful statements that are so widely exported from U.S.A. about the various elements of the U.S.A. & its population. I am watching keenly for improvements in M.T. methods but until they come I should not like to have a real bit of scientific work, such as that which we are trying to do, mixed up with what is in danger of being a mere political stand. I don't by any means suggest that Mental Tests in England have that sinister aspect as yet, but I do feel we should be careful not to promote unconsciously, such a painful possibility.

Hodson quickly apologized implying she did not expect the minorities to perform worse, or castigate them through the use of psychology: "I gather ... that the little hybrid children seemed rather precocious."[107]

Fleure's opposition resulted from skepticism of methodological innovations, primarily those that came from the United States, rather than from any dislike of racial implications of the results of I.Q. testing – after all he did believe in the physical and mental

---

[106] Fleure's lecture to the Eugenics Society, probably late spring 1921. SA/EUG/C.109. Also Fleure to Leonard Darwin, April 15, 1921.
[107] Hodson to Fleure, Sept. 8, 1924; Hodson to Fleure, May 8, 1925; Fleure to Hodson, May 12, 1925; Hodson to Fleure, May 13, 1925. SA/EUG/D.179.

permanence of races. These methodological doubts were manifested
even more in his opposition to the results Boas achieved in a study of
immigrants' skulls, which pointed to the opposite conclusion,
namely that immigrants were quick to adapt to the new environment even in the shape of their skulls.[108] He advocated a middle
ground "so we may hope to be preserved from the pitfalls into which
tumble so many of the worshipers and some of the haters of the type
so often discussed as either the Noble Nord or the Blonde Beast."[109]

Investigating racial mixture was a sensitive topic and not always
popular, as Hodson, who continued to sponsor similar studies, was
well aware. These studies included physiological and psychological
research, and the field workers were volunteers from women's
organizations and the health and education authorities. To overcome opposition, Hodson proceeded where she encountered least
resistance. In instructing the volunteers, she explained: "my plan is
always to go to work gently, and withdraw if any objections appear
to be aroused. One never can tell in research of this kind on what
point obstacles may arise, and one always begins with the
consciousness that the talk may only proceed a little way." In some
cases the enthusiasm of the volunteers aroused contention among
prospective candidates for the study, not least because of their
amateurism in presenting the proposed investigation.[110]

These studies were mostly done by Fleure's assistant, R. M.
Fleming who became involved in the question of human hybridization in England, leading her to initiate a study of its social
implications. This resulted in designating a committee "for the
Welfare of Half Caste Children" which studied the "color problem"
in Liverpool. It concluded that the colored children were brought up
in "deplorable" conditions but also recognized the difficulty of
achieving "real amelioration" in their situation. Perhaps most
revealing of the general attitude of the population to the minority
question was that a committee formed out of sympathy for this
minority had reached pessimistic conclusions. The committee suggested a stricter control over non-European immigration, a principle Britain was to adopt thirty-five years later, and under different
circumstances. A leftist critique of the condition of the minority
population in Liverpool could only advocate segregation as a

---

[108] See below, pp. 83–85.
[109] Fleure's lecture to the Eugenics Society, n.d. SA/EUG/C.179.
[110] Hodson to Cowlen, Nov. 4, 1924. Hodson to Fleming, May 3, 1927. SA/EUG/D.179.

solution. This did not stem from a racist attitude, nor would the people involved have seen it as an ideological statement in any sense. In the tradition of English empiricism, the committee presumed to advance the best practical solution. The reviewer of the report for *Man* was Fleure, still the mentor and supervisor of Fleming. His words testify to the liberal position:

It is interesting that Miss Fleming does not find the children of mixed race to be notably inferior in inherent qualities; in the case of Anglo-Chinese crosses, indeed, they seem to be almost superior. Nevertheless, the conditions of upbringing are such that the continuation of the birth of numbers of these children in our midst is a serious social danger.[111]

Fleure's surprise that persons of mixed race were not inferior, as well as his perception that their very existence in England constituted a "serious social danger," presents the intellectual context in which the critique of racial typology was shaping up. Over the decade, Fleure was closely involved with the question of racial mixture in England, yet he minimized the problem numerically and socially by limiting the origin of the mixed population to maritime commerce: in reality many had lived in England for a long time, and some were the offspring of people who had served the Crown and had earned citizenship in combat or other service. Significantly, no reliable data on the number of persons in this category exist. The language used by Fleure suggests that though he was anti-racist, he certainly accepted a strict racial taxonomy, as well as sharing the stereotypical attitude of his time that the mere existence of racial minorities implied social trouble.

Fleure approached the question of race in 1926 still very much along the positivist, reductionist tradition, displaying a measure of determinism mixed with anti-racist reformist language. Addressing the Anthropology Section at the British Association, Fleure rehearsed all the arguments of the stability of racial types, exhorting the "masterly fashion" in which Elliot Smith had written on the early stages of the evolution of man and the diffusion of culture. Pleading ignorance on the origin of humankind, but recognizing that people had "gone through a long history before they came to Europe," Fleure speculated about the climatic conditions that facilitated the

[111] H. J. F[leure] review of M. E. Fletcher, "Report on an Investigation into the Colour Problem in Liverpool and Other Ports," with a foreword by Prof. P. M. Roxby. Issued by the Liverpool Association for the Welfare of Half-Caste Children, Liverpool 1930, in *Man*, 30, 162 (Dec. 1930), 229.

vigor and alertness characteristic of *Homo sapiens*. Though he refrained from saying so outright, Fleure implied that the European climate was the ideal, even the only possible, environment for evolution.[112] He believed anthropology to be approaching "a stage at which it is possible to outline something of the process of race development." Since such a view necessitated a traditional interpretation of heredity, Fleure reserved his criticism for Boas's opinions of the "rapid modifiability of type."[113] This emphasis on the importance of heredity did not stem from any insight into its mechanism. In fact, Fleure displayed an error typical of contemporary anthropologists who were uncertain about the validity of inherited characteristics: "I should be sorry to give the impression that I was either blind to the problems [of heredity] or disposed either to extreme Lamarckism or to pure anti-Lamarckism."[114] In his eugenic prophesy, Fleure predicted "that a Racial Study will develop great practical value for education, for the fight against tuberculosis and other diseases, and for race improvement." This use of the term race – as a synonym for humankind or nation – had no racist overtones, although such indiscriminate use was a source of confusion and lent mistaken respectability to the racist arguments of others. Fleure himself was using the same podium to speak against "race arrogance" and for "an enrichment of public opinion on social questions" and "a check on schemes that do not sufficiently allow for the mutual adaptations between diverse human stocks and diverse environments."[115]

Methodologically, Fleure was careful to clarify the terms he was using and to avoid reification of statistical abstracts such as the cephalic index, central to the conventional classification of European races: "these groupings are purely artificial," he argued, stressing "the importance of study of individual heads rather than of averages of numbers of measurements." He explained the complexity of characters such as stature, which statistically can convey a wrong impression ("we get the appearance of blended inheritance"), and was quick to highlight the racist implications ("the reader will at once be put on his guard against the common political statements about the Latin race, Teutonic race ..."). In the thirties,

---

[112] H. J. Fleure, "The Regional Balance of Racial Evolution" (pamphlet), *Address Section H, British Association for the Advancement of Science* (Oxford, 1926), p. 5.
[113] Fleure, "Regional Balance," p. 25.   [114] Fleure, "Regional Balance."
[115] Fleure, "Regional Balance," pp. 26–27.

this methodological skepticism enhanced his political criticism of the multiple and confusing meanings of race, and Fleure took part in reshaping the concept. But this was done primarily within the frame of his earlier work, without developing new theoretical constructs.[116]

Traditional British anthropology in its various sub-disciplines, was experiencing a growing confusion about the ontological status of race, which resulted in widespread skepticism, but concurrently enabled racist theories and attitudes to flourish. The ensuing theoretical chaos left the door open to the explicit rejection of racism, once the issue climbed higher on the political/social agenda. The inability of anthropologists to define race, according to the new biology, especially populations genetics, resulted in their deferring to biologists, who became the foremost scientific speakers on the issue of race during the 1930s. Concurrently, the emphasis of British anthropology shifted from ethnology and medico-anthropology to social anthropology under the leadership of Malinowski. One of the professional differentiations between the schools/generations was that the younger social anthropologists largely ignored race. Race, as a biological subject matter for anthropology, was rapidly disappearing. But before moving to these new concerns, let us look at the American counterparts of the "British traditionalists."

[116] *The Races of England and Wales*, pp. 13, 18.

CHAPTER 2

American diversity

HAUNTED SENTINELS

The difference in the role of race relations in England and the United States directly influenced the concept of race in both countries. Not only was the discipline of anthropology defined differently in each country, but the two scientific communities had little contact with each other. The Americans looked mostly to Germany for intellectual guidance while the English disregarded totally any work done by Americans, especially Franz Boas. So while in retrospect the two communities may seem to have shared much – primarily little tolerance of Nazi racism – and finally to have rejected racism, their experience in the pre-war years was very different. Despite sharing a language, the professional discourse in each community was largely isolated.

In the post World War I period, the American scene was saturated with racism of different kinds. The various victims of racism had internalized much of the oppressive ideology and thus their critique of racism arose within. They shared much of the racist world view, including conceptual thinking and language. In hindsight, it is difficult to locate non-racist views, since race was viewed as a scientific fact both in its philosophical and popular versions. This was evident in the prevailing terminology in numerous debates which saw Darwinism replacing other religious metaphysics. From a historical perspective, anyone who followed social and cultural conventions on race could be branded a racist. This, however, would be a mistake, and would lump people of different racial convictions. The term racism has therefore to be used advisedly and to reflect the spectrum of opinions among scientists on racial questions. In order to reconstruct what American anthropologists said about race, it is necessary to establish who to include in this category. The field of anthropology in America has to be understood in relation to its internal power play as well as to the surrounding scientific community.

To begin with, an emphasis on race theories gives physical anthropology compared with other sub-disciplines in the anthropological community, greater weight than in other respects it warranted. Because anthropology was a small and fragmented discipline it is difficult to speak about schools; individualism ruled. Geographical and institutional affiliation were more important than the exact field of specialization, or professional training. New York City was the most important center, and in it Columbia University, the American Museum of Natural History and the Eugenics Society, were the three institutions accredited with professional recognition. These represented, with some simplification, the three national attitudes towards race. The most rigid hierarchical position was taken by the eugenicists, many of whom were closely associated with the racist Galton Society. The polarized egalitarian position is associated with the Anthropology Department at Columbia, and with Franz Boas who was the center of a school, and many who were his students at one time or another.

Between the Boasians and the Galtonians were a large number of scientists who never regarded themselves as belonging to a "group" as such, but who were especially influential in the years immediately after World War I. However, even members of the two extreme groups worked together in places like the American Museum of Natural History. Up to the 1920s the racist view was dominant; subsequently, changes in the Museum paralleled the national shift. Regardless of the precise nature of their views, New York scientists wrote more directly on race and were more involved in the politics of race than scientists who held similar views and positions to them across the country. The fact that professional interaction occurred between the Boasians and the members of the Galton Society suggests that, despite their confrontational substantive views, they were operating within a single discourse.

The Galton Society was the brainchild of the eugenicist-biologist-anthropologist Charles Benedict Davenport, and the notorious New York racist, Madison Grant. As Davenport explained to Henry Fairfield Osborn, a paleontologist and the President of the American Museum of Natural History, the Society was organized at the end of World War I, with the intention of having an anthropological society or somatological society as you call it here in New York City with a central governing body, self-elected and self-perpetuating, and very limited in members, and also confined to native Americans, who are anthropologically, socially and politically sound, no Bolsheviki need apply.

Officially the Society was described as a response to "the failure of the Anthropological Committee of the Research Council to accomplish anything substantial in securing anthropometric data among recruits."[1] Its members included prominent scientists such as the biologists Raymond Pearl and Edwin Conklin, the President of the Carnegie Institution John Campbell Merriam, the Columbia psychologist, E. L. Thorndike, and the anthropologists Clark Wissler and Earnest Hooton. Wissler was one of the handful of activists, while other anthropologists occasionally presented papers, but did not ordinarily participate in its activities. The Society, however, never achieved the status envisioned by its leaders. Bolsheviks and immigrants did not apply, and the level of participation of many of the "native Americans," WASPs whose names appeared on the letterhead of the society – was limited to the initial enrollment. Attendance at meetings was poor, and the Society – lamented the officers – acquired a bad name from the start, and its influence was accordingly "regrettably restricted."[2] Its one major achievement was to initiate a survey by the Rockefeller Foundation on the state of anthropology in Australia, but this was at best a partial success from the Society's point of view, since its execution was given to anthropologists with no connection to the Galton Society.[3] The Galton Society's membership was even more restricted than that of the Eugenics Society, and later attempts to suggest enrolling new members in either society failed, partly because of the founders' fear of the society being taken over by radicals. In debating a possible campaign to attract sociologists to the Eugenics Society, Davenport hesitated: "Do you not think," he wrote to Irving Fisher, "that we

---

[1] Davenport to Henry F. Osborn, March 9, 1918. Davenport to William K. Gregory, April 18, 1918. CBDP.
[2] William K. Gregory to Davenport, June 6, 1922. CBDP.
[3] The plan was conceived by Grant who counted among his "old friends" Raymond B. Fosdick, the President of the Rockefeller Foundation, and as Grant boasted to Davenport (March 30, 1923) "we discussed how Mr. Rockefeller's money could be wisely used for the benefit of the race on a very broad plan looking forward far into the future." CBDP. W. K. Gregory (secretary of the Galton Society, curator of Zoology, American Museum of Natural History), to M. Grant, Nov. 22, 1923. Minutes of the Rockefeller Foundation, 24031/2; 24075; 24241/2 (RFA 1.1/410D/3/23).

should be conservative and cautious in bringing in too many of the unconverted, less they divert the work of the society in a direction antagonistic to our aims?" The real danger was a development similar to the Rand school "which during the war became a hotbed of extreme radicalism."[4]

Madison Grant attained the status of a leading American racist theorist, the twentieth-century counterpart of the Europeans Count Gobineau and Houston Stuart Chamberlain. Every study which deals with the history of the idea of racism in America justly devoted much space to Grant's views. The interesting point about Grant is not so much the unmitigated vulgarity of his racist ideology, as that its proponent could command so much social respectability. Grant was a rich lawyer who spent so much time on his hobbies that he judged himself a naturalist and a historian. His status is readily recognized through the numerous semi-public positions he held. He was President of the New York Zoological Society and trustee of various other organizations. At the time when the growing prestige of scientific naturalism had misled many to accept racism as science, the English reviewer of Grant's book *The Passing of the Great Race* (1916) writing in *Man*, after World War I, found Grant's emphasis on race rather than on linguistics "refreshing," and added that it was "a clear statement of the case which should be of the utmost value to the lay public."[5] The book was received favorably, except by a small group of liberals, and became a success.

Grant's co-founder of the Galton Society, Charles Benedict Davenport, was the most prominent racist among American scientists. He had a proper scientific training, exhibited confidence and assurance, was a good organizer and enjoyed unique success in soliciting funds for studies. From the beginning of the twentieth century up until at least the mid-1920s Davenport thrived and his name became synonymous with eugenics. When eugenics was a popular creed and a movement, offering salvation from the joint menaces of modernization, industrialization and urbanization, Davenport was its prophet. His status fell with the decline of

---

[4] Davenport to Fisher, Feb. 11, 1924. CBDP.
[5] H. J. E. Peake in *Man*, 20 (Nov. 1920) 173. In 1921 a new edition was published, of which John Campbell Merriam, President of the Carnegie Institution, reviewed and approved a draft "most heartily." When the new edition was published, Merriam assured Grant of his interest, and added "[I am] incidentally having the pleasure of passing it on to several others to read as I keep it on my table at home along with various subjects which are always at the front for discussion." Merriam to Grant, Dec. 8, 1920; Oct. 10, 1921. JCMP.

eugenics, and when he died during World War II, even his most
faithful disciple wrote a defensive and apologetic obituary.[6]

Davenport came from an old Yankee family that divided its time
between Brooklyn and a summer house in Connecticut. He studied
zoology at Harvard, where he later taught before moving on to the
new University of Chicago. As a rising star in American biology, he
persuaded the newly founded Carnegie Institution to underwrite a
genetic institute for him at Cold Spring Harbor in 1904. The Station
for Experimental Evolution (after 1918, Department of Genetics)
became his home until his retirement three decades later. In
addition, he established the Eugenics Record Office and the Eugenics Research Association, which became his empire on the Long
Island shore. At the center of the American eugenics movement,
both the office and the association exerted enormous influence over
the content of human biology and science and their dissemination to
the American public up to the 1930s.[7]

Socially and politically, Davenport was closely associated with
the most notorious racists and kept especially close contact with
Madison Grant. They cooperated in the political campaigns against
immigration and in the eugenics movement. Grant financed directly
or helped raise the money for many of Davenport's ventures. They
mingled socially, with Grant introducing Davenport into Man-
hattan living-rooms where bigotry and racism was a popular
recreation. Although Davenport was not rich he felt comfortable in
this company, sharing its xenophobia. During World War I, he was
in charge of anthropology in the U.S. Army, and played a major role
in conducting the notorious Army mental tests. Among his lesser
known contributions as an American patriot was a scheme devised
for the selection of naval officers. The officers were to be chosen
based upon traits which were inherited in a Mendelian fashion and
included supposedly: (1) Love of the sea (an elementary instinct
"not yet fully studied"), (2) nomadism (sex-linked inheritance), (3)
hyperkinesis (dominant), (4) absence of fear, and (5) ability to

---

[6] Morris Steggerda, "Charles Benedict Davenport (1866–1944); The Man and His Contributions to Physical Anthropology," *AJPA*, n.s. 2, 2 (1944), 167–185

[7] For example Mark Haller, *Eugenics, Hereditarian Attitudes in American Thought* (1963; New
Brunswick: Rutgers University Press, 1984); Daniel Kevles, *In the Name of Eugenics. Genetics
and the Uses of Human Heredity* (New York: Knopf, 1985); Garland Allen, "The Misuse of
Biological Hierarchies: The American Eugenics Movement, 1900–1940," *History and
Philosophy of the Life Sciences*, 5 (1984), 105–128; and "The Eugenics Record Office, Cold
Spring Harbor, 1910–1940," *Osiris*, 2nd ser. 2 (1985); Charles Rosenberg, *No Other Gods: On
Science and American Social Thought* (Baltimore: Johns Hopkins University Press, 1976.)

command men.[8] The same kind of reasoning – farfetched scientific justification by self-assured WASPs – determined the Immigration Laws and consequently the demography of the American people. But the Army was not receptive to any of this scientific interference. While ready to accommodate limited mental testing, it would have nothing to do with the idea of changing the traditional criteria for selecting officers.

In the early 1920s, Davenport, Grant and others in the Eugenics and Galton Societies cooperated in their war against immigration – which from their perspective turned out to be a very successful campaign. Nevertheless, pessimism ruled, and their terminology betrayed the mood: facing the "great attack being prepared by the enemies of immigration restriction," those "unworthy citizens who would get rich quickly at the expense of America," Davenport could sound the alarm, but still feel confident.[9] Generally the racists were not satisfied with their success in barring further immigration and this dissatisfaction was aggravated a decade later, when racism had lost some of its popularity. Davenport lamented to Madison Grant that it was no longer fun: "I am sometimes appalled by the difficulty of opposing the view that all fertilized eggs of Homo sapiens are alike."[10]

Davenport, a conservative and a nativist, denied in the best American tradition the possibility that his world-view constituted ideology; he claimed merely to describe the truth in objective and pragmatic terms. In his address at the opening session of the International Congress of Eugenics, Davenport advocated more research rather than mere propaganda, because "People do not have heated discussions on the multiplication table; they will not dispute quantitative findings in any science."[11] With the growth of confidence in Mendelianism he declared "the imbecile is an imbecile for the same reason that a blue-eyed person is blue-

[8] Davenport, "On Utilizing the Facts of Juvenile Promise and Family History in Awarding Naval Commissions to Untried Men," *Proceedings of the National Academy of Sciences*, 3 (1917), 404–409.
[9] Davenport to Charles Gould, Nov. 22, 1922. Not all in the racist camp were close friends. Davenport, for example was not friendly to Lothrop Stoddard, who was introduced to him by Grant. Davenport's initial reaction was positive (Davenport to Madison Grant, May 3, 1920). Following the reading of Stoddard's book *The Rising Tide of Color*, Davenport wrote: "I read it through with the greatest of interest," but the two only corresponded occasionally thereafter. See also Grant correspondence with Davenport. CBDP.
[10] Davenport to Madison Grant, Nov. 6, 1933. CBDP.
[11] Davenport, "Research In Eugenics," *Science*, 54 (Oct. 1921), 397.

eyed."[12] The imbecile was seen as the most obvious result of bad heredity, and no one at the time suspected that environmental factors were involved. This was the reason for the tremendous impact Lionel Penrose's studies had in the 1930s, when he proved that mongolism was conditioned environmentally.[13]

Davenport's view of women as inferior beings whose destiny it was to raise a healthy stock also betrayed his misconceptions of the mechanism of heredity. One of the more revealing passages concerning the sanctity of the family as a middle class institution and the question of sterilization appeared in *Heredity in Relation to Eugenics*:

> I can well imagine ... the marrying of a well-to-do, mentally strong man and a high grade feeble-minded woman with beauty and social graces which should not only be productive of perfect domestic happiness, but also of a large family of normal happy children. Half of the germ cells of such children would indeed be defective, but as long as the children married into normal strains the offspring, through an indefinite number of generations, would continue to be normal. Yet in many states of the Union such a marriage cannot be legalized; and, in others, the potential mother might be sterilized.

And he condemned the sterilization laws as unscientific "because they attempt no definition of the class."[14] His paternalism and discriminatory attitude manifested itself also in the management of the Eugenics Record Office. Women were employed as field workers on a temporary basis for only three years and not longer "in the hope that [they] may marry and thus the Eugenics Record Office can not be charged with working cacogenically [sic] in inducing the excellent field workers whom we have secured to neglect more important social duties."[15]

Some of Davenport's research on individual heredity highlights to the modern reader the extent of the scientific ignorance of the time. Notable in this regard is a chapter on the "Influence of The

[12] Davenport, "Euthenics and Eugenics," *The Popular Science Monthly*, 78, 2 (1911) 16. Davenport wrote scores of similar articles, studying "Heredity, Culpability, Praiseworthiness, Punishment and Reward," *Heredity*, 83, 3 (1913), where among other things he spoke about the union of an artist with a woman who was a non-artist: "the children may not belong to the artistic biotype; but under appropriate matings, the characteristics of the biotype may reappear in later generations."

[13] See below, pp. 260–266.

[14] Davenport, *Heredity in Relation to Eugenics* (1911; New York: Arno Press and the New York Times reprint edition, 1972), p. 257.

[15] Davenport to H. H. Goddard, July 29, 1912. CBDP.

Individual on the Race" which featured Elizabeth Tuttle, "a woman of great beauty" who was born in 1667. In addition to her virtues, however, Elizabeth had evil traits "in the blood," a fact "proved" by her husband divorcing her on grounds of adultery. Her distinction was that many among her descendants were prominent people. However, it was her negative characteristics which left their mark. As Davenport emphasized himself, he manipulated the data to underscore the heritability of defects as manifested among the descendants of Elizabeth's character. One such progeny was Aaron Burr, Vice-President of the United States, who provided Davenport with the hallmark of his analysis of the germ plasm. In Burr "flowered the good and evil of Elizabeth Tuttle's blood. Here the lack of control of the sex impulse in the germ plasm of this wonderful woman has reappeared with imagination and other talents."[16]

During the twenties, Davenport still thought of himself as belonging to the mainstream and belittled the opposition. Lecturing to the anthropological section of the American Association for the Advancement of Science, he observed that "While the anthropologist may deplore the fact that increasing ease of communication is causing a hybridization of the different races of mankind," he was consoled by the fact that it also made it easier to transport the anthropologist to study the primitive races.[17] Though generally a staunch hereditarian, by the mid-1920s Davenport admitted the possibility of environmental influences, and compared with some of his fellow eugenicists such as H. H. Goddard, he may even on these grounds, be considered a kind of moderate. Yet he remained hereditarian, and in his last article on mental defects he tried to emulate Dr. Down's discovery of mongolism by comparing feeble-mindedness with Negro features.[18] His attitude to blacks was consistent throughout: they were a menace to the American society. He thus wrote to Wingate Todd, a moderate physical anthropologist, a mainliner if ever there was one: "The presence of the African negro in our country may be very fateful for its future, as its increase

[16] C. B. Davenport, *Heredity in Relation to Eugenics*, pp. 225–227. Davenport's data were at best incidental.

[17] Davenport, "Measurement of Men," read before Section H, American Association for the Advancement of Science, Dec. 29, 1926. *AJPA*, 10, 1 (1926), 68. Davenport to T. Wingate Todd, Oct. 27, 1928. CBDP.

[18] Davenport and Grace Allen, "Family Studies on Mongoloid Dwarfs," address at the 49th Annual Session of the American Association for the Study of Feeble Minded, *Journal of Psycho–Asthenics*, 29 (1925); Davenport, "Dr. Storr's Facial Type of the Feebleminded," *Journal of Mental Deficiency*, 68, 4 (April 1944), 339.

tends to overcrowd more and more the country to the detriment of the white race." These were the views that shaped his study of racial mixture in Jamaica.[19]

Against this background, some of his statements sound surprisingly environmentalist. Referring to the nature–nurture debate, he wrote: "The truth does not exactly lie between the doctrines; it comprehends them both. What a child becomes is always the resultant of two sets of forces acting from the moment the fertilized egg begins development – one is the set of internal tendencies and the other is a set of external influences." Or "there is no heredity without environment and few environmental effects which are not dependent also upon heredity."[20] While Davenport's social and political prejudice was straightforward and does not raise any conflicting interpretations, agnostic statements of this kind display changing views of which he was probably not even aware. Davenport combined environmental factors and a theory of hereditarian influence to provide an account of versatile racial development, but this legitimized, even in racist circles, the investigation of the environment.

When Davenport asserted himself as a professional scientist as compared to Grant the amateur, he pretended to act with scientific objectivity. Yet he manipulated data and abused method on numerous occasions. In discussing the original skin color of Homo sapiens, Davenport assumed in a private letter

that there is no doubt that the ancestors of all of us had a black skin. The white skin is highly abnormal and, no doubt, a relatively recent acquisition. The evidence for this is that all of the primates have a dark skin. I suppose the political consequences of the statement of a truth are the last things in the mind of a scientific writer.[21]

A short while later, however, in an article on "The Skin Colors of the Races of Mankind"[22] Davenport refrained from speculating on whether the black or the white skin was a later evolutionary mutation, and which of the two was more advanced. Superficially, this article may appear innocent and non-racist, but since Daven-

---

[19] Davenport to T. Wingate Todd, Oct. 27, 1928. CBDP.
[20] Davenport, "Euthenics and Eugenics," p. 18; "Research in Eugenics," *Science*, n.s. 54 (1921), 396.
[21] Davenport to Madison Grant, July 1, 1924. CBDP.
[22] *Natural History*, 26, 1 (1926), 44–49.

port privately viewed the white skin as a later mutation and therefore inferior, the article was a cover-up.[23]

Naturalism was the prevailing view in American science. When applied to human biology, anthropology or any of the social sciences, all practitioners accepted a rigid racial typology. Except for a few scientists who objected to simplistic interdisciplinary analogies, most shared the belief that either a contemporary crude Mendelian genetics or biological reductionism (Lamarckianism being still popular) could explain all human characteristics. Not all scientists were enthusiastic about eugenics, but few objected to the anti-immigration propaganda advanced in the name of science. The most prominent among the objectors were Herbert Spencer Jennings and Franz Boas. It took a few more years for some of the biologists to come to reject eugenics publicly, and even longer for those anthropologists outside the Boasian circle.

Historical studies of eugenics overlook the fact that Davenport's views were not static. Admittedly, he tenaciously held to his opinions: nevertheless, these changed in important details. Although he appeared to be the staunchest hereditarian, his participation in the scientific discourse forced him to respond to the growing environmentalism. It is therefore indicative that as an overall shift, Davenport – who represented the spectrum of racial theories on the right – also changed components of his theory, from exclusively asserting the significance of hereditary influences, to account for and minimize environmental factors. This was not only because the movement against racism was based upon the non-racists who actively opposed biological determinism as methodologically flawed and racist, but because in order to keep pace, the hereditarian school responded by trying to answer the environmentalists' criticism. In doing so, the subject matter of their investigations changed, and instead of studying heredity to prove its importance, Davenport examined the environment to show its insignificance. But once his subject matter had changed, ideology could serve only as a limited tool in manipulating the results. While his interpretations still emphasized differences which seemed negligible from his data, he could henceforth be challenged with direct

---

[23] In his obituary, Steggerda wrote that Davenport "has been criticized for publishing his ideas too hastily. I doubt whether he ever felt this to be true, although some of his most devoted students and colleagues were among those who held this opinion." Steggerda, "Charles Benedict Davenport," p. 177.

evidence from his own material. This became especially evident in 1929 in his *Race Crossing in Jamaica*.[24]

Davenport was the embodiment of the universal intellectual and the absolute savant. He enjoyed wide popularity within scientific circles, and was a leading scientist who wrote and disseminated his views to the public. His social position was analogous with that of the English biologists, who during the 1930s refuted scientific racism. Ideology and politics separated racists from non-racists on substantial matters, but in their professional standing over time they enjoyed a similar type of legitimacy. While the substance of the discourse had shifted, its locus in the professional scientific community meant that it was the relative power of the participants that produced the outcome.

EUROPEAN SKULLS AND THE PRIMITIVE MIND

The growth of anti-racist thought in the social sciences is often associated with the name of Franz Boas. Boas's overwhelming influence on American anthropology of the first half of the century, through his own work and that of his disciples, has been acknowledged in memoirs and anecdotal biographies, mostly by admiring students.[25] His list of honors during a long professional career, the numerous distinguished students he taught, and his recent popularity in historical literature, all testify to his justified importance. Boas's expertise included ethnology, physical anthropology, linguistics and archaeology. It was his mastery of these sub-disciplines

---

[24] See below, chapter 3.
[25] The bibliography is extensive. Among the examples was the volume published upon Boas's death by the American Anthropological Association. A. L. Kroeber *et al.*, *Franz Boas, 1858–1942*, Memoir 61 (Menasha, Wisconsin: American Anthropological Association, 1942). It included, among other pieces, Ruth Benedict, "Franz Boas as an Ethnologist," and Alfred L. Kroeber, "Franz Boas, The Man." Melville J. Herskovits wrote a biography, *Franz Boas: The Science of Man in the Making* (New York: Scribner's, 1953), and Robert H. Lowie wrote the memoir for the National Academy ("Franz Boas," *Biographical Memories of the National Academy of Science*, 24 [1947]: 303–322.) Walter Goldschmidt edited a volume to commemorate Boas's Centenary, *The Anthropology of Franz Boas*, American Anthropological Association, Memoir 89, 62, 5, pt. 2, which included Margaret Mead's, "Apprenticeship Under Boas." These scholars, as well as other Boas students, wrote about Boas on numerous other occasions. Among the more professional historical analyses of Boas's work, George W. Stocking, *Race, Culture, and Evolution: Essays in the History of Anthropology* (with a new preface) (Chicago: University of Chicago Press, 1982, 1974) are the best studies on Boas, primarily up to 1911. For a critical analysis of Boas, see Marvin Harris, *The Rise of Anthropological Theory: A History of Theories of Culture* (New York: Thomas Y. Crowell, 1968).

which contributed towards delineating anthropology's present boundaries in the United States, its European counterparts excluding one or the other of these sub-specialties. Boas's egalitarian views on race, first proclaimed in 1894, characterized his work until the very last moment of his life, when in a discussion on how to combat racism at the age of 85, at a Columbia Faculty Club luncheon, "Boas, with a comment on the need to press its exposure ... and without further sound, fell over backwards in his chair, dead."[26]

Boas's views on race were determined by his professional position, intellectual commitments and personal psychology. In his writings on race, Boas integrated information that ranged from biology through the social sciences to linguistics. To imagine that such a complex combination of sources could merge into a coherent and comprehensive framework was perhaps simplistic and unrealistic. Scientific theories have often evolved on faulty assumptions, especially when they have involved interdisciplinary applications. Boas's thought was not free from such errors, and at times he accepted conventional racial stereotypes. Nevertheless, his views on race were seen during his life as an egalitarian critique of conventional racism.

Boas formulated his ideas about race at a time when there was no agreement between the disciplines involved, and no clear epistemological choice among the contradictory alternatives. Towards the end of Boas's career, Mendelianism and biometrics unified into population genetics, and psychology and sociology incorporated cultural relativism, partially as a result of Boas's input. These disciplines, however, treated the study of race very differently. Boas's ideas should be evaluated against this background of scientific uncertainty and confusion. His anti-racist legacy stems as much from his ideas as from his actions to mobilize opinion among his peers and the public in favor of egalitarianism. His impact on the idea of race in American science and culture manifested itself on several levels: "the expert," whose scientific work, theoretical and empirical, shaped the discipline; "the professional," as an active participant in the scientific community, attested by his membership on committees and on editorial boards, as well as the ideas he professed in various honorary positions as a representative of anthropology and his impact through his students' work; and "the

[26] Herskovits, *Franz Boas*, pp. 120–121.

intellectual," who participated directly in public and political discourse. These components of his work were compounded over time, Boas the universal intellectual, the citizen, augmented the active role of Boas the scholar, the absolute savant, only later in life. It was this dual significance which explains Boas's centrality to the decline of scientific racism, one that divorced the biological from the cultural study of humankind. Boas first articulated this position during his studies in Germany.

Boas immigrated to the United States from Germany at the age of twenty-nine in 1887, after completing his studies in Heidelberg, Bonn, Kiel and, for one year following his doctorate, in Berlin. His university studies were primarily in physics, with a minor field in geography. His shift from physics to anthropology coincided with his emigration from Germany. He attributed this shift both to his desire to work on "physiological and psychological mechanics." In addition, his move to the United States was supposedly the result of the widespread anti-semitism in Germany, and his enthusiasm for the myth of American freedom and individualism.[27] While an element of long-term planning is evident in Boas's life, his pragmatism has been somewhat neglected by his biographers. If, indeed, there was a theme of continuity in Boas's life, it was his recognition and acceptance of the limitations he faced at different stages, whether scientific, cultural or social, and his consequent accommodation to reality. What drove Boas to America was not so much anti-semitism as the search for an academic career. This does not negate the reality of anti-semitism in the Second Reich, nor does it deny the story that the scars on Boas's face were a result of duels he fought over anti-semitic remarks,[28] but rather affirms his vocational commitment.

Fundamentally skeptical, Boas did not believe that he could overcome the many difficulties involved in obtaining a university professorship in Germany, difficulties which were especially complicated for Jews. Many others from similar backgrounds did overcome both the rigid system and anti-semitism, while American campuses were in fact, not more receptive of Jews. Yet for Boas, the

---

[27] Boas to his parents, May 2, 1883. Quoted in Stocking, *Race, Culture, and Evolution*, p. 139. Stocking studied Boas's correspondence for the period, and his explanation replaced the traditional descriptions given among others by Ruth Benedict in "Obituary of Franz Boas," *Science*, 47 (1943), 60; and Herskovits, *Franz Boas*.

[28] A. L. Kroeber, "Franz Boas, The Man," in A. L. Kroeber *et al.*, *Franz Boas, 1858–1942*, p. 8.

American alternative seemed easier, especially since his uncle, Abraham Jacobi, who was the first professor of pediatrics in the United States, was ready to help. One could speculate that Boas's emigration was mainly a coincidence rather than an ideologically committed migration, an interpretation that mitigates Boas's alleged ambivalence towards Germany.

When he initially planned his move, Boas was hoping to get a position at Johns Hopkins, but it did not materialize. He nevertheless decided to try to establish himself in the United States in 1884 on his way back from a trip to the Arctic. It was this field trip which for many years people believed was responsible for converting him from geography to anthropology.[29] Since academic opportunities were not abundant, Boas went back to Berlin, where he accepted a position at the Ethnological Museum. A second visit to America on the occasion of a field trip to British Columbia resulted, on his return, in an offer from *Science* to become an assistant editor, which he accepted. This position served as a temporary arrangement until, following an encounter with G. Stanley Hall, he received his first university position in the United States, at Clark University. For the next few years his professional fortunes in America were uneven, but Germany offered nothing better. In fact, if public involvement is a criterion for Boas's attitudes, then he did not assume an American identity until well into the twentieth century, some years after being appointed at Columbia.

By then Boas was the expert, but not yet the intellectual, and did not involve himself in any public affairs. Much was made of his ambivalence toward the German culture and society as a reason for his emigration, but this view is largely anachronistic. Once in the United States he maintained his German sympathies, and was part of the New York Jewish German community. In contrast he was reluctant to assume an active American identity, and generally displayed anti-nationalist and cosmopolitan feelings which were most likely directed in the spirit of classical liberalism against hyper-Americanism. This also explains his anti-racist and egalitarian approach, which was motivated by fundamental skepticism and which charted his shift from physics to anthropology.

In his studies of perceptions of light and psychophysics, Boas contested the accepted view that the perception of light is the sole result of the intensity of light, and instead suggested a qualitative

29 Stocking, *Race, Culture, and Evolution*, pp. 135–160.

analysis taking into account the state of mind of the perceiver. This relativistic and subjective approach, which transcended the physicist's training, became part of Boas's intellectual baggage. Interaction between perceptions and reality was an underlying theme in much of his work, not least his studies on race. In his first encounter with "savages" on the cartographic trip to the Arctic, he was attracted by their similarity to civilized people, and displayed a philosophical egalitarian approach characteristic of his future treatment of the subject of race:

> I often ask myself what advantages our "good society" possesses over that of the "savages." The more I see of their customs, the more I realize that we have no right to look down on them. . . . As a thinking person, for me the most important result of this trip lies in the *strengthening* of my point of view that the idea of a "cultured" individual is merely relative and that a person's worth should be judged by his Herzensbildung.[30]

Here was no shift or break, only a strengthening of previous beliefs. Subjective perceptions determined the reality, as Boas would most likely have put it, and the liberal German Jew found among the Eskimos a confirmation of his beliefs in individuality, humanity and the supremacy of truth. The only true and total reality was the perspective of the individual. The German philosophical-historical tradition, especially Dilthey's influence, was asserting itself in Boas's studies on the peoples of America.

Once in New York, Boas became partially integrated in the city's Jewish-German-American milieu. He joined the American Museum of Natural History in 1896, became a curator in 1901, and left it after a fight in 1905. In the meantime he received an appointment at Columbia, and in 1899 was appointed to a professorship. He stayed there until his retirement. New York's intellectual life was a microcosm of the conflicting interests among the public at large, and the scientific community in particular. Boas's pragmatism and accommodation had to be sustained at a peak level for him to survive and to assert his principles. Although he had some support from Jewish philanthropists, he did not keep close contacts with the Jewish world. At the same time he had to maintain cordial professional relations with prominent Anglo-Saxons who, as a group, were blatantly xenophobic.

Boas's earlier and important contributions to the study of race

---

[30] Letter Diary, 12/23/1883. Quoted in Stocking, *Race, Culture, and Evolution*, p. 148 (emphasis added).

were published in 1911 in *The Mind of Primitive Man*. The thesis of the book was that race, culture and language are independent variables and should not be confused. Migration and historical changes have caused the three categories to overlap, but in principle they remain separated. Generally speaking, Boas argued that "the biological unit . . . is much larger than the linguistic unit."[31] Secondly, Boas showed that the claim for racial superiority of the whites in general, and the Anglo-Saxons in particular, had no scientific backing. Boas had addressed the question almost twenty years earlier in 1894, and at the turn of the century had used the title "The Mind of Primitive Man" for an article published in *Science*.[32] Concurrently with his theoretical writings, he was working on physical measurements of various "races" in a series of investigations in which he argued that the environment modified the physical features of migrated populations.

For Boas the egalitarian approach was a prerequisite for the study of anthropology. The researcher "must adapt his own mind, so far as feasible, to that of the people whom he is studying." It implied that no unbridgeable gulf existed between the mind of primitives and that of civilized persons. Each would adapt to the other. Lack of logic and lack of control were supposedly fundamental primitive characteristics.[33] While not denying the obvious differences between Western industrial society and a tribal society, Boas suggested an alternative analysis. Divorcing the mechanism of thought from its manifestations, he limited the differences to the latter, indicating that "the organization of mind is practically identical among all races of man; that mental activity follows the same laws everywhere, but that its manifestations depend upon the

---

[31] Franz Boas, *The Mind of Primitive Man* (New York: Macmillan, 1911). A course of lectures delivered before the Lowell Institute, Boston and the University of Mexico 1910–1911, revised and enlarged edition, 1938.

[32] Franz Boas, "Human Faculty as Determined by Race," *Proceedings of the American Association for the Advancement of Science*, 43 (1894), 301–327; "The Mind of Primitive Man," *Science*, 13, 321 (Feb. 1901), 281–287; The differences between the versions were meaningful and point to the evolution in Boas's thought. Especially important was the treatment of the question of domestication in the 1911 and 1938 versions. In the earlier version, Boas argued that the differences between primitives and civilized people were similar to those between wild and domestic animals, while in the 1938 version the argument disappeared. See Herskovits, *Franz Boas*, p. 31. Whether this meant Boas changed his view of the differences between people or between animals was not made explicit.

[33] The French sociological school of Durkheim, for instance, was elaborating the distinction between the irrational primitive and the socially rational industrial society, which was most explicit in Levi-Bruhl's work.

character of individual experience that is subjected to the action of these laws."[34]

The rediscovery of Mendelian laws of heredity in 1900 posed a major new challenge in the interpretation of evolution. And while genetics progressed relatively quickly in research on lower organisms and fruit flies, its application to human heredity was long in the making, especially on questions of temperament, intelligence and character which still puzzle scientists today. Many of the claims advanced in the name of genetics were totally unfounded, but its seemingly overall power of explanation was seductive. Nevertheless, Boas refused to submit to the exaggerations in the name of Mendelianism and addressed the question of heredity in the early years of the century cautiously. Hesitating between biometrics and Mendelianism he did not commit himself to either, but rather developed his own quantitative tools as suited to the specific problems under study.[35]

Boas's creativity has led at times to a wild-goose chase. Scientists often are tempted to speculate beyond their knowledge in their field of expertise on a topic with political implications, and the resulting confusion can be especially great. The expertise cannot be questioned by a layperson, and the sanction of science gives credence even to the most absurd claims. If since the post-World War II years a measure of skepticism has entered public discourse concerning the incontestability of scientific wisdom, its impeachable status before the war was hardly ever questioned. On one of the rare occasions when Boas was tempted to venture beyond his field, he reputedly gave a talk on "The History of the American Race" in which, after warning the lay audience that he was dealing with an uncharted territory, he speculated on the Europeans' growing resemblance to the Indians in America. Because the paper was "so lucid and simple" it was adopted by many as an actual reference to the history of the Indians, and as an indication of the racial future of America. Consequently, Boas had to deny a misconception which persisted

[34] Franz Boas, "The Mind of Primitive Man," p. 281.
[35] Franz Boas, "Heredity in Head Form," *American Anthropologist*, 5 (1903), 530–538. On Boas's use of coefficients, see W. W. Howells, "Boas as Statistician," in Goldschmidt (ed.), *The Anthropology of Franz Boas*, pp. 112–116. Stocking (*Race Culture and Evolution*, pp. 167–168) shows how Galton's methods must have been congenial to Boas, who had training in physics but not in biology or medicine, and argues that Boas developed independently the application of statistics to anthropology. Nevertheless, Boas rarely employed coefficient analysis and his statistical work was severely criticized by Pearson.

for many years that his studies supposedly supported the claim that Europeans in America tended to resemble the Indians.[36]

This was especially pertinent because Boas's most important research on human heredity was on "Changes in the Bodily Form of Descendants of Immigrants." It was originally conducted on behalf of the U.S. Congress Immigration Commission, which had been organized to study the deterioration of the American stock caused by the new immigrants. The Commission's work, the Dillingham Report, was published in forty volumes in 1911, and symbolized the high point of political propaganda for immigration restriction before the Immigration laws were enacted in the twenties. Boas's work was out of tune with the rest of the volumes in the series, yet with the help of J. Jenks of Cornell University, a member of the Commission, he managed to have his research plan approved and financed.[37] Boas examined the skull measurements of first-generation Americans of Italian and Jewish descent, and compared their cephalic index[38] to that of the populations in the country of origin. He concluded that the differences between first- and second-generation Americans born of different ethnicities was smaller than between the respective European populations.[39] This became a source for much confusion and criticism directed at Boas, not least because it savored of Lamarckianism. None the less, this study undermined the traditional approach to physical anthropology. As a result of Boas's critique, the discipline which already lacked coherent methodology lost even the semblance of an agreed subject matter. Not only did different measurements lead to conflicting typologies even before Boas studied immigrants' skulls, he now refuted the very notion of a physical stability which was at the base of any racial theory. These conclusions were amplified, often in a distorted form, in semi-popularist writings. Boas's claim of the plasticity of skull was not welcome from a professional point of view, but it raised a score of more profound fears, the most prevalent being the suggestion that Boas had discovered a new American type, which in its simplistic and popular version, meant that white Americans were beginning to

[36] Alexander Lesser, "Franz Boas," in Sydel Silverman (ed.), *Totems and Teachers: Perspectives in the History of Anthropology* (New York: Columbia University Press, 1981), pp. 1–31.

[37] Stocking, *The Shaping of American Anthropology 1883–1911: A Franz Boas Reader*, pp. 202–214.

[38] Measure of the breadth of the human head as a percentage of its length.

[39] Franz Boas, *Changes in the Bodily Form of Descendants of Immigrants*, Senate Document 208, 1911, 61st Congress, 2nd Session, Washington 1911. Also a short version in *American Anthropologist*, 14, 3 (1912), 556–557.

resemble the Indians. In the long run, Boas lost the battle; the skepticism towards his results remained, notwithstanding his publications of all the data in 1928. But he won the war: the unquestionable stability of the skull as a classificatory tool of races, vanished.[40]

Boas used his studies of the plasticity of skulls also in a direct political way. As the most prominent scientist active against immigration restriction his expert advice was solicited in legal matters. One such occasion presented itself with regard to the racial status of Armenians. During the twenties, Armenians were not allowed to own property in the State of Washington because they were thought to be Orientals, not Caucasians. The racial classification was based on their "rounded," "brachycephalic" heads, a proof of their Mongoloid racial characteristics. Boas was asked by Armenians to testify in court that they were Caucasians and therefore should be permitted to own property. Boas agreed, but instead of presenting a theoretical testimony, or one based on data from traditional sources, he used the opportunity to study the Armenians, adding them to his earlier investigations on immigrants. This time the research was supported by his clients.[41] As in his previous studies, he compared foreign to American-born Armenians and showed statistically that the two series varied meaningfully. Boas attributed the change in the shape of the skull to the different way babies were cared for. In Armenia, as in Eastern Europe, babies used to be put on their backs on a cradle board, unable to move. The weight of the head pressing against the board suppressed the development of the occiput and produced a high ratio of breadth to length. In the United States, with changing habits this racial characteristic disappeared. Notwithstanding later scientific reservations about the validity of the argument, the Armenians were allowed to own property. This was one of the occasions when Boas was able to further his scientific

[40] Boas, *Materials for the Study of Inheritance in Man* (New York: Columbia University Press, 1928). A modern analysis of the debate was carried out by Tanner, who examined Ronald Fisher's critique of Boas. Tanner, however, leaves open the question whether Fisher's suggestion of a high rate of illegitimacy among the first generation Italian-Americans was justified. Tanner accepts Fisher's "conceivable explanation" which was done with "supporting calculations." He does not point to the fact that the "explanation" and the "calculations" were unrelated. See below chapter 4. J. M. Tanner, "Boas' Contribution to Knowledge of Human Growth and Form," in Goldschmidt (ed.), *The Anthropology of Franz Boas*, pp. 76–111.

[41] Boas tried to get financial support from the Laura Spellman Rockefeller Memorial (Franz Boas to Dr. Beardly Ruml, Jan. 16, 1925; reply, Jan. 20) but failed because the money for such studies was held by R. Yerkes in the Committee on Human Migration of the National Research Council and by Merriam of the Social Science Research Council, both active in the eugenics movement. FBP.

research while simultaneously disseminating anti-racist information. In the thirties it turned into his full-time occupation.[42]

For many years Boas had to defend, with only limited success, his
rather moderate anthropometric results against critics who mis-
stated his conclusions. The significance of the immigrants' study,
together with its flavor of Lamarckianism and seeming incompatibility with Mendelian genetics, opened it to biological criticism. But
Boas was most vulnerable because he left the problematic unans-
wered, with only tentative suggestions: in his own words, "I, at
least, am more inclined to ask for further material from other
sources than to force a solution that must be speculative." Boas
refrained from assigning the changes of the skull to genetic modifications or claiming that these were permanent in nature: he left
these questions open. He assigned the changes to the ecotype (in
modern terminology phenotype,) which was determined by
environmental or ecological conditions.[43] The theory also left open
the possibility that a return to the old environment would see the
reappearance of the former physiological types. Boas took his clues
from various sources, including the city–country dichotomy, but he
rejected as an explanation selection through migration. "I have
shown that selection is extremely unlikely to bring the results
observed. That the essential causes may be the city conditions is
possible but not proven. I have not ventured to claim that I have
discovered these causes."[44] A similar hypothesis led a few years
later to studies by Boas and his students to prove that higher I.Q.
scores of blacks in the North were not a result of selective migration.

Straddling the factual and the hypothetical, Boas's interpretations were egalitarian in nature: he attributed civilization and
progress to historical events, the outcome of a good fortune rather
than a proof of superiority. Referring to the physical changes which
resulted from migration and their relation to mental faculties, Boas

[42] On another occasion, Boas tried to initiate a similar study in response to a similar request
by a lawyer representing the Armenians on account of attempts by the Attorney General of
the United States to test in the Supreme Court the right of Armenians to American citizenship. Boas's plan for research was rejected because the lawyers refused to take a chance of
what the results might show. Boas's correspondence with Vernon B. Malcolm, 1924. Also
Boas-R. Dixon correspondence. Ronald Dixon cooperated with Boas in preparing the
Armenian case. FBP.
[43] He was quick to point out that changes in ecotypes did not include pigmentation.
[44] Franz Boas, "Changes in the Bodily Form of Descendants of Immigrants," 556–557. Also
"New Evidence in Regard to the Instability of Human Types," *Proceedings of The National
Academy of Sciences*, 2 (December 1916), 713–718.

concluded that the latter were influenced far more by the environment: "It is true that this is a conclusion by inference; but if we have succeeded in proving changes in the form of the body, the burden of proof will rest with those who ... continue to claim the absolute permanence of other forms and functions of the body."[45] It was this kind of challenge which began to undermine the rigidity of racial typology.

His findings addressed an even more deeply rooted misconception concerning the relation of intelligence to skull size. While the topic had been presumably exhausted scientifically by the American School of Ethnology in the mid-nineteenth century, the argument was repeatedly regenerated. Physical anthropologists continued to measure skulls and, notwithstanding statistical criticism, viewed the difference in brain size among the races as meaningful. So entrenched was this view that Boas prefaced his egalitarian argument by admitting: "We find that on the average the size of the brain of the negroid races is less than the size of the brain of the other races; and the difference in favor of the mongoloid and white races is so great, that we are justified in assuming a certain correlation between their mental ability and the increased size of their brain."[46] A comparably bizarre claim to be advanced in the name of anti-racism was that women's brain is smaller than that of men of equal stature. But, he added, "the faculty of woman, while perhaps qualitatively different from that of man, cannot be deemed to be of inferior character. This is therefore a case in which smaller brain weight is accompanied throughout by equal faculty."[47]

It is too easy to condemn such statements as racist or to dismiss them as mere rhetoric. Boas was no racist, but he did reflect the values of his society. His explanation was not to deny the correlation of brain size with intelligence, rather to point out that "the bulk of the two groups of races have brains of the same capacities," although "individuals with heavy brains are proportionately more frequent among the mongoloid and white races than among the negroid races." Civilization, however, did not contribute to an increase in the size of the brain. This Boas concluded from a comparison of "civilized people of any race with uncivilized people of the same race." The result showed no "anatomical differences"

[45] Boas, *The Mind of Primitive Man*, pp. 17, 65.
[46] Boas, "The Mind of Primitive Man," p. 282.
[47] Boas, *The Mind of Primitive Man*, p. 27.

that would justify an assumption of "any fundamental differences in mental constitution."[48] This rationale persisted in anti-racist literature for years. It lumped the majority of the world's population together but concurrently satisfied class prejudice by distinguishing between the majority of the people and the elite. The mass of the whites and blacks were similar; only a minority among the whites, the carriers of civilization, were superior. Few among blacks were inferior. This approach left much to be desired from an egalitarian perspective: nevertheless it limited the question of differentiation to a small minority – to the exception rather than the rule. As a tool in race relations against discrimination it could have been very powerful. There were enough data to contradict such a preposterous correlation, and it is not to Boas's credit, nor to that of other anti-racists, that the idea of a superior minority was used. But that should not diminish the egalitarian achievement in historical perspective. Egalitarianism grew out of the context of racism and accordingly both the ideas and the scientists were captives of the standards of the era.

Boas concluded that from an anatomical perspective a basic equality of mental capacity exists among races. He was more agnostic on questions of temperament and impulses. Like his contemporaries, and many modern writers, Boas did not include the factor of time in his evolutionary analysis. Accepting evolution as a general proposition, Boas avoided speculations on the differentiation of races or on the development of various faculties: he limited himself to arguing that at present all humans share these capabilities.[49] Boas was not a biologist and did not study the origin of

[48] *The Mind of Primitive Man*, p. 283.
[49] Leslie White condemned Boas as an anti-evolutionist, calling his critique of Spencerian biological reductionism reactionary science ("Diffusion Versus Evolution:. An Anti-evolutionist Fallacy," *American Anthropologist*, 47, [1945], 339–536; "Evolutionist in Cultural Anthropology: A Rejoinder," *American Anthropologist*, 49 [1947], 400–411; *The Science of Culture* [New York: Grove Press, 1949], p. 110). The question has gained some prominence primarily because of the lack of distinction between cultural and biological evolution. Among the respondents was Robert Lowie, who presented the Boasian perspective and argued that Boas and other anthropologists were not against evolution, but rather opposed specific interpretations of evolution, such as Morgan's or Spencer's. "Professor White and 'Anti-evolutionist' Schools," *Southwestern Journal of Anthropology*, 2 (1946), 240–241; *Social Organization* (New York: Rinehart, 1948), p. 227. Also Stocking, *A Franz Boas Reader*, pp. 129–130. The confusion resulted from mistakenly equating opposition to natural selection with anti-Darwinism and anti-evolution. The mechanism was confused with the principle. Boas was never an antievolutionist, though he opposed some theories of evolution, and was never an enthusiastic Mendelian. The question of whether Boas was a Lamarckian is analyzed by Stocking, *Race, Culture, and Evolution*, p. 184, who shows that in

humankind: his acceptance or rejection of natural selection reflected conventions among peers rather than an informed scientific opinion. The important question is how such understanding influenced his work. Boas's approach to biology should also be viewed in light of his effort to maintain the interaction between natural history and the social sciences. British social anthropology in comparison rejected physical anthropology and natural history altogether.[50] It is revealing that at this stage Boas still had a progressive, hierarchical concept of culture, though individuals were already seen as equal: "the development of *culture* must not be confounded with the development of *mind*." Boas tried in future years to defend his position by providing more supporting data. The presumed lack of power for the logical interpretation of sensations among primitive man, but ... rather, in the character of the ideas with which the new perception associates itself." Individuals did not become more logical in civilization, but rather progressed because of the "traditional material which is handed down to each individual [and] has been thought out and worked out more thoroughly and more carefully."[51]

Part of Boas's argument for a fundamental equality among races also pointed to the limited logic of individuals in civilized societies. Both civilized and primitive man carry the explanation of a phenomenon "only so far as to amalgamate it with other previously known facts ... the results of the whole process depends entirely upon the character of the traditional material."[52] This skeptical approach to the primacy of one system over another, can be traced back to his shift from physics to ethnology. Confronted with the choice between the physical sciences and history, he assigned equal value to both.[53] Despite this equality, Boas had initially foreseen the integration of the various immigrant groups in biological terms, thereby implying the primacy of biology. Whether described as "Americanism" or the "melting pot" theory, the ethnic-racial plurality was going to converge to an American type. European groups would intermix faster among themselves than with the

the 1890s Boas did not reject the possibility of inheritance of characteristics modified by the environment, though in the twentieth century he refrained from supporting the idea.
50 Marian W. Smith, "Boas's 'Natural History' Approach to Field Method," in W. Goldschmidt (ed.), *The Anthropology of Franz Boas*.
51 Stocking, *Race, Culture, and Evolution*, pp. 197–233, 285–288.
52 Boas, *The Mind of Primitive Man*, p. 204.
53 Franz Boas, "The Study of Geography," *Science*, 9 (1887), 137–141. Reprinted in Boas, *Race, Language and Culture* (New York: MacMillan, 1938).

blacks, but eventually the solution to the race problem lay in biological fusion.[54]

Boas has been portrayed as particularly concerned with public affairs all his life, from his student days, when he was too proud not to retaliate to an anti-semitic offense, to his old age glorified by his anti-racist campaign.[55] There is much retrospective reading in this view. Excluding the famous scars,[56] there is no evidence of any meaningful public or political activity during his German years. Once in the United States he refrained from almost all non-professional activity for twenty years, and even thereafter he ventured into the public arena only rarely, adopting a mild tone and a noncontroversial manner. This is not to deny his combative personality in scientific circles. His public involvement increased during and after World War I. From then on his public exposure was almost permanent. He was involved in one controversial subject after another, becoming one of the vocal leaders of the liberal intellectual community in New York. This shift into the role of public figure took place when Boas was sixty years old. Although in his earlier academic work Boas addressed political issues of vital concern to the United States, primarily on immigration and race questions, such action, as he knew better than anyone, was not synonymous to direct political involvement. The exception to his earlier abstention from public affairs was university politics. While almost immediately following his immigration Boas felt confident enough to fight over professional and academic policies, the ivory tower remained a secluded haven for him during the next thirty years.

Like most immigrants, his first political controversy involved ethnic politics. Opposed to the war, Boas suddenly faced a growing anti-German feeling in America in addition to the growing involvement of the United States with the Allies. He rose to defend the *Vaterland*, and the German-American perspective remained the driving force in his public commitments up to 1933. In 1919, his opposition to government policies, together with a defense of the integrity of academic research, led him to attack certain American

---

[54] Franz Boas, "Race Problems in America," address as Vice President of Section H, American Association of the Advancement of Science, Baltimore, 1908, incorporated in *The Mind of Primitive Man* (1911.) Stocking, *A Franz Boas Reader*, pp. 318–330.
[55] Stocking, "Anthropology as a Kulturkampf: Science and Politics in the Career of Franz Boas," in Goldschmidt (ed.), *The Uses of Anthropology*, pp. 33–50.
[56] See fn. 28 on p. 78 above.

anthropologists who spied during the war under the guise of field
study. This instigated a turmoil of condemnations that followed his
exposure of the affair in the *Nation*, and he was removed from the
American Anthropological Association.[57] His pro-German activities turned after the war into efforts to reinstate Germany into the
scientific community, from which she was excluded on account of
German war crimes. The French were adamant, and successful, in
their efforts to boycott German science. Boas, with a handful of
colleagues, attempted to assist German scientists, through grants
and research money, as well as endless efforts to have them
included in international congresses.[58] This was Boas's first experience in intensive international academic diplomacy, an activity
which he never relinquished for the next twenty years. During these
years he also began to attack American racism, primarily "the
Nordic Nonsense," as well as to cooperate with politicians against
immigration restriction.[59] From the volume of his correspondence,
Boas seems to have devoted more time and energy to the politics of
anthropology than he did to any other external interest. This
professional activity discloses some of the intricate relations in the
American scientific community, including processes of accommodation and exclusion among rivaling factions. Especially interesting in this context was the racist/non-racist axis, as it was manifested in professional factionalism, and the growing role of the
Boasians.

THE BOASIANS

The notion of a Boasian school is used to describe Boas's influence
on anthropology through his disciples. Paradoxically the term is
often a target rather than a podium. Critics attack the school, while
many admiring students preface a description of Boas's impact
with a denial of the very existence of such a school, because of the

---

[57] Franz Boas, "Scientists as Spies," *Nation*, 109 (1919), 797. Boas believed other anthropologists had also done the same, and that this was the source for the condemnation. Boas to
G. Stanley Hall, Jan. 25, 1921. By not naming the anthropologists who spied, Boas
implicated many others. For a detailed study of the affair, see Stocking, *Race, Culture, and
Evolution*, pp. 270–307.

[58] Boas's correspondence during the early twenties testifies to these efforts. On the boycott,
see Brigitte Schroeder-Gudehus, "Challenge to Transitional Loyalties: International
Scientific Organization After First World War," *Science Studies*, 3 (1973), 93–118.

[59] Franz Boas, "This Nordic Nonsense," *Forum*, 41 (October 1925), 501–511. Boas worked
mainly with Emanuel Celler of the US Congress. FBP.

great diversity among its members.[60] More intriguing than the overall coherence of the Boasians' work, is the question of the extent to which Boas the teacher, the theorist, and the person, shaped the work of his students, especially in regard to the question of race. Critics have questioned how far Boas's theoretical definitions determined the development of American anthropology. This topic still awaits close study. However, what is needed for tracing anthropological views on race and their leaven on society is more a social and cultural reading of the Boasian school as the context against which to evaluate their theoretical contributions.

As with Boas himself, his students' role in rejecting rigid racial typologies was important both on account of their writings and their professional politics. They can conveniently be grouped by age: the older generation were by the early 1920s already at the height of their professional careers (including Alfred Kroeber, Robert Lowie, Alexander Goldenweiser, and Paul Radin); the younger ones were then in training with Boas (Melville Herskovits, Ruth Benedict, Margaret Mead and Otto Klineberg, primarily a psychologist but also a member of this group). The term Boasians suits them primarily because they saw themselves as such in one way or another, at least for part of the period. Yet the two groups differed in more than age. The older anthropologists carried out their own work, and by the 1920s their interpretations of race were molded by their own interests, though they shared with other Boasians a common world-view. The younger group formulated their research programs more directly as an attempt to substantiate the separation of race and culture by elucidating the relative impact of heredity and environment.

[60] Leslie A. White, *The Science of Culture* (New York: The Grove Press, 1949) and Marvin Harris, *The Rise of Anthropological Theory: A History of Theories of Culture* (New York: Thomas Y. Crowell, 1968) were the most critical of the Boasians' theoretical contributions. Stocking, *A Franz Boas Reader*, pp. 1–21, argues for implicit assumptions shared by Boas students, and distinguishes between three types of Boasians: "strict" (Spier, Lowie, Herskovits); "evolved" (Benedict, Mead); and "rebelling" (Kroeber, Radin and Sapir). Among Boas's students who deny the existence of such a school were Kroeber ("Franz Boas, The Man,") and Lowie (R. H. Lowie, "Evolution in Cultural Anthropology: A Reply to Leslie White," *American Anthropologist*, 47 (1946), 223–233). Herskovits, in his classical biography *Franz Boas* (p. 23), rejects the unity implied by the term school, but speaks of a common denominator with emphasis on the distinction between heredity and learned behavior. Margaret Mead, like Herskovits, minimizes Boas's role in suggesting dissertation topics. (To her, however, Boas did suggest a topic, and in fact described his expectations of the context and the results he hoped her work would achieve. M. Mead, "Apprenticeship Under Boas," in Goldschmidt [ed.], *The Anthropology of Franz Boas*, pp. 31–33. And Boas-Mead correspondence, FBP.)

The rivalry between the Boasians and other anthropologists was manifested in the institutional development of the discipline. As was mentioned above, the Galton Society was an institutional WASPish effort to tilt the balance in anthropology against the Boasians. A prosopography of the politics of the anthropology community between 1919 and 1923 shows this last effort by the old order, including some semi-amateurish anthropologists, to fend off the influence of Boas and his disciples also within the traditional institutional setting.[61] The anti-Boas campaign succeeded in 1919 when he was censored, but this was reversed within four years as anthropology committed itself to Boas's point of view for at least a generation. In the larger perspective of American science, Boas's institutional power was growing at a much slower and uneven pace. The offensive against Boas in 1919 was due to political, personal, as well as scholarly motives. The predominantly German and Jewish ethnic background and the liberal-left ideology that characterized the Boasian school had only inflamed the xenophobia of the old-guard antagonists, who were primarily Anglo-Saxon conservatives. Beyond that lingered the question of cultural anthropology. Was the business of anthropology a racial classification of humankind, or was it cultural relativism? The sides were drawn around the heredity–environment debate.

The controversy was dynamic. Initially cultural anthropology strove to accommodate itself to the biological perspective. Then the environmentalists began to assemble data to oppose biological determinism, and cultural theory made its first strides in asserting its own identity. Boas himself always explicitly emphasized his agnosticism regarding the biological basis of personality and temperament. A number of anthropologists in both groups, especially Alfred Kroeber and Clark Wissler, attempted to reach accommodation on questions of the biological basis of psychology. Later on, while the old racial classification based on anthropometry was losing ground because of internal incoherence based on conflicting and erroneous data, the major assault of biological thinking against cultural anthropology came from new theories based on (simplistic) Mendelism and biometrics. This meant that while within anthropology the cultural school achieved the upper hand, by the mid-twenties it still had to confront scientists from other disciplines,

---

[61] Stocking, *Race, Culture, and Evolution*, pp. 270–307, offers the best account of anthropology during these years.

primarily eugenists and bio-anthropologists, who sustained their commitments to racial interpretations of culture.

Following the reaction of those who believed in rigid racial typologies in the immediate post-World War I years, Boas and his supporters consulted the dominant school in anthropology. Among Boas's first generation students, Alfred Kroeber and Robert Lowie were the more prominent, and both spent most of their careers at Berkeley. Neither had written any major treatise on the question of race: both, however, had criticized racism. Alfred Kroeber had already completed his linguistic training by the time he became one of Boas's very first students at Columbia. Born in New York, Kroeber lived in a liberal German enclave that had relatively little contact with the Anglo-Saxons. The affluent Jewish-German symbiosis that was flourishing in Germany had its counterpart in the New World, and this served as Kroeber's background. He encountered anti-semitism during his adolescence in a Yankee boarding school when he was mistaken for a Jew. Following his studies in New York, he moved to California, where he earned his distinction as a scientist primarily through the study of Californian Indians. It is perhaps not surprising, therefore, that Kroeber rejected racism a priori and supplied scientific justifications later.

Kroeber's early writings accentuated the divorce of the biological from the cultural, calling organic and social evolution "fundamentally different, unconnected, and even in a sense opposite."[62] He opposed eugenics and rehearsed the anti-racist credo in a lucid manner. In his most influential article, "The Superorganic," he separated the social context (actually meaning "cultural" without using the term) from the biological by placing human culture in a different category: that of the superorganic.[63] His arrows were directed against social Darwinism, racism and psycho-biological reductionism, and provided a conceptual tool for social scientists to

---

[62] Alfred L. Kroeber, "Inheritance by Magic," *American Anthropologist*, 18, 1 (1916), 32. Kroeber claimed to speak "for at least a majority of [his] colleagues" who reject any biological "interpretations of human institutions or national attainments." Like Boas, he did not deny the possibility of biological impact on the personality; he only pleaded ignorance in the name of science and added that "there is every probability that such inborn differences exist between many of the races." Biologists and psychologists were to work on heredity, anthropologists should study the environment. "Heredity, Environment and Civilization," *American Museum Journal*, 18 (1918), 351–359.

[63] Alfred L. Kroeber, "The Superorganic," *American Anthropologist*, 19 (1917), 163–213. Reprinted in Kroeber, *The Nature of Culture* (Chicago: Chicago University Press, 1952), pp. 22–51.

reinterpret and reject such determinism. Kroeber followed this with an analysis of the misuse of the Army Mental tests, pointing out that the data did not support the argument for black inferiority since the Northern blacks scored better than Southern whites.[64] Precisely this point was to carry much weight when a few years later it was popularized by a younger Boasian, Otto Klineberg. Kroeber enjoyed a powerful professional standing; well respected as a scientist, he was considered the most influential American anthropologist after Boas. Kroeber though, was not politically inclined. In response to his first wife's death from which he recovered slowly and painfully, he invested most of his extra professional energy, up to 1926, in psychoanalysis. In addition, the geographical distance between California and the East enabled him to refrain from intensive participation in professional politics, which his academic standing would have allowed. His work over the years on cultural evolution, on the context of historical theory and on its relation to biology leaves open the question as to what degree his views changed in time. Even if his infusion of naturalism into cultural studies in the post World War II era pointed by then to a more biological world view, this later formulation was done in a different context from the fight over scientific racism of the early twenties. During the earlier period, when the political stakes were high, Kroeber contributed to the anti-racist campaign. With the clear rejection of racism by the early 1950s, a potential space was reopened for studies of the biological basis of culture.[65]

Robert Lowie, Kroeber's colleague at Berkeley, was the more devoted disciple of Boas. On various occasions during his career he was engaged in professional polemics to defend Boas's views. While still in New York, he contributed to the evolving anti-racist school. But like Kroeber, once he moved to the West Coast, he kept his racial egalitarianism mostly out of the political arena. Similar to other Boasians, Lowie's background was Jewish-German: he came from Vienna, which from a New York perspective was close enough. His upbringing was not unlike Kroeber's either. Following edu-

[64] Alfred L. Kroeber, *Anthropology* (New York: Harcourt, 1923), p. 77.
[65] Alfred L. Kroeber, "Historical Reconstruction of Culture and Organic Evolution," *American Anthropologist*, 33 (1931), 149–156. Reprinted in Kroeber, *The Nature of Culture*. Theodora Kroeber, *Alfred Kroeber: A Personal Configuration* (Berkeley: University of California Press, 1970). Julian H. Steward, *Alfred Kroeber* (New York: Columbia University Press, 1973). Eric R. Wolf, "Alfred L. Kroeber," in Sydel Silverman (ed.), *Totems and Teachers: Perspectives in the History of Anthropology* (New York: Columbia University Press, 1981), pp. 35–64.

cation in New York public schools, he came to Columbia only at the graduate stage, where in a very unsystematic way, intertwined with work at the American Museum, he became an ethnographer. Much of his work was done in the field, and in various memoirs he regretted his own lack of theoretical preparation for some of his general books, primarily his commercially most successful work, *Primitive Society*. For fifteen years before 1921 Lowie worked at the Museum under Clark Wissler: none the less he remained a Boasian, interacting with anthropologists such as Alexander Goldenweiser, Paul Radin, Leslie Spier, and Elsie Clews Parsons. It was this cultural context that was so important in the formulation of his egalitarian views.[66]

In New York the Boasians and the racists competed for influence, while sharing similar institutional space. At the same time as the rest in the anthropology community were shifting professional alliances in an ad-hoc manner, the Boasians were gaining strength, until in the mid-twenties they became the dominant force, controlling the politics of the discipline by sheer numbers. By then, the younger generation of Boasians was coming of age. But before examining their impact, there is a need to chart the developments during the earlier period in physical anthropology, which was the professional locus for studies of race.

AMERICAN PHYSICAL ANTHROPOLOGY

A brief survey of American anthropology at the end of World War I shows that little mattered outside the East Coast. Although there were departments of anthropology in other parts of the country such as Chicago and San Francisco, and though the anatomist Wingate Todd at Case Western Reserve worked on physical anthropology, the undisputed center was in the East. Distance prevented anthropologists outside of Boston, New York and Washington from participating in professional activity. Committee membership particularly illustrates this phenomenon. In the capital, an active local anthropological society together with the Smithsonian Institution

---

[66] Lowie, *Robert H. Lowie, Ethnologist. A Personal Record* (Berkeley: California University Press, 1959). Robert F. Murphy, *Robert H. Lowie* (New York: Columbia University Press, 1972). Cora Du Bois, *Lowie's Selected Papers in Anthropology* (Berkeley: University of California Press, 1960). For a straightforward criticism of racism by Lowie, especially on Madison Grant and H. F. Osborn, see his "Psychology, Anthropology and Race," *American Anthropologist*, 25 (1923), 291–303.

partially compensated for the lack of a major university center. Washington's prime was before World War I, but it remained active during the interwar years. Harvard's anthropology department together with its affiliated Peabody Museum was second only to New York in significance for the profession. During most of this period, Ronald Dixon, Alfred Tozzer, and Earnest Hooton were Harvard's leading anthropologists. While certainly very different from each other, they maintained the facade of a team. The distance from New York meant that the Harvard anthropologists could profess partial unity based upon geography, at the same time it was not too far for Harvard to be secluded from the centers of power.

As the intellectual center of the country, New York attracted several active anthropological institutions, with close contacts to major philanthropic sources. The Galton Society and Cold Spring Harbor were the centers for the eugenicists and racists, while the New School for Social Research provided a liberal outlet for the Columbia faculty. Both the American Museum of Natural History and Columbia University were the core of anthropological activity and employed anthropologists of liberal and conservative commitments. Despite the ideological diversity, there was contact, at times close, between the opposing camps. The interaction resulted partly from institutional constraints, and partly from association with a larger anthropological community that included many neutrals. Surrounded by, and being part of, the intellectual activity of the city, New York anthropologists were, generally speaking, much more involved in public debates and retreated far less into the ivory tower. Columbia's anthropology was synonymous with Boas, but he was the exception and many faculty members kept close contacts with eugenics circles. A comparable situation existed in the American Museum where the liberal and conservative groups worked together, though not in cooperation. Henry Fairfield Osborn, the President of the Museum was a close associate of Madison Grant and an adamant Anglo-Saxon supremacist. Nevertheless Boas worked in the Museum for several years, as did Robert Lowie, and later Harry Shapiro and Margaret Mead. The tension and rivalry made a non-partisan approach difficult, and therefore neutrality was not as much a determining force in New York, as it was in Washington and Cambridge.

A CONSERVATIVE OUTSIDER

Anthropology in Washington had two centers: the Smithsonian Institution and, up to the end of World War I, the more influential Bureau of Ethnology. To the rest of the country Washington presented a more or less unified group, personified during the interwar years by Ales Hrdlicka, curator of anthropology at the Smithsonian and the editor of the *American Journal of Physical Anthropology*, which he founded and managed in an uncompromising manner.[67] Hrdlicka was born in Bohemia and immigrated to America at the age of twelve. Following some years of economic hardship, he studied medicine and in 1895 began his anthropological career. After serving at the American Museum of Natural History between 1899 and 1903 under the direction of Frederick W. Putnam, he enjoyed a prosperous career at the Smithsonian Institution until his death. Not a major theoretician, Hrdlicka collected enormous amount of data. Due to his lack of biological and mathematical training, he avoided genetics and modern statistics, even to the point of denying their importance. Consequently he tried to shape physical anthropology solely along morphological lines.[68]

During World War I Hrdlicka participated in the efforts to collect anthropometric data by measuring recruits. One of those with whom he cooperated was Madison Grant, whose role was to raise the money for the survey since the government was reluctant to finance the enterprise. In return, Grant offered his "expertise" on matters such as how the blanks were to be filled by the soldiers. These contacts were useful also in raising money for the new *American Journal of Physical Anthropology*, which Hrdlicka was establishing simultaneously. Grant played a major role in the financing of the new journal. When the Galton Society was founded, it was suggested to Hrdlicka that the new Society would assume the financial responsibilities for the journal, while he would remain its editor. Hrdlicka declined the offer because he was afraid of a takeover, even before the journal was published. It is of more than passing interest to note that Hrdlicka was encouraged to accept the support of the Galton Society from a most unexpected source,

[67] For example, Hrdlicka wrote a significant proportion of the reviews in *AJPA*. This was not so much a sign of diligence or of lack of reviewers, as of his wish to keep the review copy for himself. It caused a dispute and extensive correspondence with Ashley Montagu. AHP.

[68] A. H. Schultz, "Ales Hrdlicka, 1869–1943," *National Academy of Sciences Biographical Memoirs*, 23 (1945), 313. Schultz's obituary is very critical, but not inaccurate.

namely Franz Boas. Boas who was on the editorial board of the *American Journal of Physical Anthropology*, suggested that Edwin Conklin of Princeton would represent the Galton Society but strongly objected to Grant and Davenport. He was very surprised to learn that Davenport had already been on the board.[69]

Hrdlicka's views on race were shaped by his unsophisticated approach to the debate of heredity versus environment. This was repeatedly illustrated in his studies, including his best known *Old Americans*.[70] Among his sources of information on the new biology was, not surprisingly, Davenport, who in response to Hrdlicka's request, avowed "a personal conception of the mechanism of heredity in man" identical with the mechanism that applied to plants and animals.[71] Hrdlicka defined "Old Americans" as whites who had four grandparents born in the United States. His motivation was partly to examine a conventional misconception of how Europeans in America start to resemble the Indians, and partly to investigate Boas's claim that immigrants tend in the second generation to have intermediate bodily forms between the norm in their country of origin and the average in America. In brief remarks that served as conclusions for the research, which took fourteen years to complete and over 400 pages to describe, Hrdlicka observed that this is "a group that already comes closely to deserving the characterization of an anthropological unit." The "Old Americans" were a variation of the English, Irish, and Scotch, but are "at least different from any of these as these are different from each other." This was perceived as enhancing the perception of an independent American identity. The American type was seen as an improved variation of its West European ancestor. The most contemporary conclusion in the study addressed the new immigrants. Though of different national origins, "the latecomers . . . have been undergoing a gradual physical improvement, leaning in stature and other respects in the direction of the type of the Old Americans."[72]

[69] Letters in Davenport and Boas files (series 1. Ca 1903–1925); Grant and Gregory (Box 14) AHP. Also in FBP; Boas asked Professor Henry H. Donaldson (the Wistar Institute of Anatomy and Physiology; April 9, 1919), for help in rallying the support of the Galton Society, which "is backed by a few rich women," to assist Hrdlicka finance the *AJPA*. Boas objected that "Madison Grant and Davenport should be given control of the journal" because "this, of course, would be entirely unfair and would disturb the usefulness of the whole undertaking."
[70] Hrdlicka, *Old Americans* (Baltimore: Williams and Wilkins, 1925).
[71] Hrdlicka–Davenport correspondence, May 3 and 5, 1915. AHP.
[72] *Old Americans*, pp. 408, 412.

Hrdlicka himself belonged to the immigrant group, and the conclusion was definitely self-serving.

Although such was precisely the scientific information needed to combat immigration restriction, Hrdlicka did not become active outside professional politics. He would involve himself politically during the post-Munich crisis of 1938 because it directly concerned his Bohemian background, an ethnic affiliation which he cherished. In the early twenties, however, he was a member of the Eugenics Society and kept neutral on the immigration question. He was not a restrictionist and, if at all possible, avoided participation in a public campaign. In a display of impartiality he refused to help either the immigrants or the restrictionists. It was one more instance in which the victim adopted the aggressor's point of view. He declined a suggestion that he should take the initiative to testify before the House Committee, arguing that he and the Chairman of the Committee, A. Johnson, did not get along. In addition, his government employment served as a good excuse.[73] By then, Hrdlicka felt confident enough explicitly to oppose Grant, who headed the Immigration Committee of the Eugenics Society, while trying to refrain from a confrontation. This hesitancy would repeat itself a decade later when he was asked to take part in the fight against Nazism. Hrdlicka displayed the ambivalence of an immigrant outsider, who tried to be accepted by the establishment, and in an effort to gain respectability adopted much of its bigotry, although for scientific as well as more personal reasons he was inclined to refute racism on scientific grounds rather than for ethnic reasons.

Hrdlicka upheld such a conventional line that there was little in his scientific views to arouse antagonism by any member of the profession. As the years passed, his views became more outdated, but never quarrelsome, unlike his personal relations.[74] His case illustrates the limit of a critique motivated primarily by ethnic status without the support of liberal or egalitarian politics. In addition, the flavor of Lamarckianism was always present in his work, founded on conventional misconceptions rather than on

[73] Hrdlicka: "Two years ago [Johnson] attended my lectures on 'The Origin and Composition of the European Nations' and showed that he held strong pre-formed opinions." Letter to Irving Fisher, Nov. 27, 1923. Also to Boas, May 6 and 29, 1918. AHP.

[74] There were numerous instances in his and other anthropologists' correspondence that testify to the constant way in which he antagonized his peers: from the fights with Boas in 1919, to his editorial handling of the *American Journal of Physical Anthropology*. The shift upon his departure was so welcomed that the *AJPA* began a new series.

science.[75] These two facets of his conservatism – scientific and political – were relatively autonomous. While illuminating Hrdlicka's personality, this configuration also presents the tension between conflicting political and ethnic commitments, underscoring the contingency in the development of anti-racist thought.

IDIOSYNCRASY AT HARVARD

The Harvard anthropological community occupied a middle ground on the question of race. Two of its three major anthropologists throughout the period, Ronald Dixon and Earnest Hooton, had published on racial classification, and both deserve mention for different reasons. Dixon was far less influential in the long run, though he was the more senior of the two, and his book *The Racial History of Man* was mostly notable as a mark of the sophistry racial studies attained, without substantively supporting or refuting a racist perspective.

Dixon described the study as an experiment, and emphasized that he was working with facts and not theory, in the extreme. Generally, physical anthropology described local variation in charting racial typology but implied universal validity. Dixon adopted, quite literally, the global approach and concentrated solely on the "raw facts of physical measurements." He presented his approach as aiming "to be wholly unprejudiced, to have no thesis to prove, to take nothing for granted, to be able to apply to the whole body of data on man's physical characteristics one single method of analysis, and to follow the evidence fearlessly to whatever conclusions it might logically lead."[76] The result resembled a farce on physical anthropology, but none among the anthropologists was amused.

Dixon began with the proposition that race is a group defined by physical characters, but since the complexity of classification is so great, and because each criterion used in different studies produced conflicting results and no general agreement existed on what traits were important and what secondary, his solution was to "set up arbitrary standards, and, using these as our measure, determine the character and relationships of people *in terms of our arbitrarily selected units.*"[77] Dixon chose three physical measurements, and

[75] "It is known that changed environment and consequent changed habits of life react ... upon the body permanently." *Old Americans*, p. 2.
[76] Ronald B. Dixon, *The Racial History of Man* (New York: Scribner's, 1923), p. v.
[77] Dixon, *Racial History*, p. 8 (emphasis original).

collected all the information he could to produce close to 600 pages of classification that grouped together the most unlikely populations. Whether Dixon's original intention was to refute physical anthropology through sarcasm is difficult to say.

Casting his vote in favor of biometrics as more applicable than Mendelism to anthropology, Dixon pretended that he did not see why his method was unacceptable: "I must confess I am puzzled to understand why the method is to be condemned in toto, when if applied to the data which others have treated in elaborate biometric fashion, it leads to strikingly identical results. Can a method which is intrinsically wrong, lead again and again to results which the biometricians regard as correct?"[78] Of the various criticisms Dixon received, Boas's view is interesting. Boas helped Dixon greatly with many details of the study, yet the two had totally disagreed on the substance. In a way, Dixon's work could be seen as the most devastating critique of racial typology, insofar as it suggested that any arbitrary assortment of measurements is as good as another. But Boas was more interested in the method, and did not accept arbitrariness as a sufficient methodological critique.[79]

Dixon's unsociable personality and his lack of students meant that what little influence he had on the discipline disappeared upon his death. Yet, during his life time, his prestigious position assured his views a hearing. He was more receptive to the anti-racist position, and cooperated with Boas in defending the Armenians against attempts to brand them Asians, a clearly exceptional view for a Boston Brahmin and a second generation Harvardian who was more likely to become a member of the Immigration Restriction League. A different type of idiosyncrasy was exhibited by Dixon's colleague, E. A. Hooton, who became the most influential physical anthropologist in the country during the interwar years.

Earnest Albert Hooton was a professor of physical anthropology at Harvard. He was born in 1887 in Wisconsin, where he went to college. Hooton earned his PhD. at Oxford in classics, and came to

[78] Ronald B. Dixon to F. Boas, Jan. 21, 1923. Also their correspondence during the previous two years. On his objection to Mendelism: "I was particularly interested to find that you do not regard the case as at all settled in the matter of Mendelian inheritance. It had seemed to me that there was so much doubt in the matter, and the laws, if any were so complicated, that it was futile at present to attempt to include them in any general study of racial origin." Dixon to Boas, Oct. 31, 1922. FBP.

[79] Boas-Dixon correspondence, 1923. FBP. Dixon's reputation as an anthropologist had suffered heavily as a result. He continued to teach at Harvard, and cooperated with Boas on various topics, until he died in 1937. His papers were destroyed.

Harvard in 1913, where he taught for the next forty years. A very conscientious worker with high professional standards, he built up an excellent laboratory and trained many students. However, his contribution to anthropological theory was minimal.[80] Hooton's style was sometimes as revealing as the content of his writing. What has been termed "facetious" and "lurid"[81] may actually have been morbid. It is difficult to read some of his works and not get the impression that if he did not regard some races as superior to others, it was only because he saw *all* races as inferior. His attitude was that of a misanthrope. While he may have been kind and pleasant as a person, his cynicism and bad taste often exceeded acceptable bounds for scholarly work.

His views on what constitutes race represented the conventions prevailing in physical anthropology up to World War II. Since he trained most physical anthropologists in the United States, his impact was correspondingly wide. His first and best book, *Up From The Ape* (1931), became a widely used textbook and even appeared in a second edition after World War II.[82] Despite its popularity, it was a scholarly work, filled with technical details, illustrations and pictures, but above all it displayed the utter turmoil which physical anthropology was undergoing.

"A great group of men can be classified as a 'race'," explained Hooton, "only if its members present, individually, identical combinations of a number of physical features which they owe to their common descent." Since the various measurements were not ranked in order of importance, the number of morphological races was likely to grow larger and more complex with the accumulation of data. Without an agreement about what constitutes similarity, attempts at taxonomy were useless. Hooton, therefore, resorted to classifying humans into "four great groups which are larger and more comprehensive than the term 'race' implies." These groups – Negroids, Mongoloids, Whites, Composites – he consequently divided into races. Hooton would probably have used the name species for the larger groups, but preferred to avoid the controversy such a definition would entail. Consequently his classification was

---

[80] Boas to Cattell, July 9, 1926; Boas to W. F. Ogburn, Nov. 7, 1928. FBP.
[81] Clyde K. Kluckhohn, "Earnest Albert Hooton." Reprint. *Year Book of the American Philosophical Society* (1955), 418–422.
[82] Earnest Albert Hooton, *Up from the Ape* (New York: Macmillan, 1931).

based on large groups defined as races, subdivided into small races, and so on.[83]

In evaluating racial differences, Hooton rejected direct correlation between race and culture, but supported the hypothesis "that the physical characteristics which determine race are associated, in the main, with specific intangible and non-measurable, but nevertheless real and important, temperamental and mental variations." Referring to psychological tests, Hooton claimed "that the data derived from such psychological tests put the burden of the proof upon those who refuse to admit the existence of such racial differences." It was a similar argument to the one Boas had advanced, requiring the opponents to prove their point. Hooton's use of this technique testified to the shift in scientific opinion. By the early 1930s racial typology was no longer an undisputed view; in fact environmental relativism became so widespread that casting doubt on its validity seemed meaningful.[84] For Hooton like others, acceptance of racial differences in mental ability was a matter of cultural preference. He did not think that the scientific case for strong racial typology was stronger than a relativistic position, but he felt more comfortable with the former position. It was principally the same line of thought that made him support Lamarckianism: "simply because we do not know of any mechanism whereby acquired modifications may affect the germ plasm and thus be fixed in heredity, it does not follow that the process is nonexistent." For Hooton the alternative explanation of evolution by natural selection was a very troublesome prospect. If "individual strivings are of no avail for future generations, every unfortunate infant has to start over again with nothing but the obsolete outfit of his inheritance. If evolution has happened this way it is a depressing business." This pessimism explains his growing sarcasm.[85]

---

[83] Hooton, *Up from the Ape*, p. 502. Also "the differences between the several races are quite as marked as usually serve to distinguish species in other animals" (p. 395). The distinction is meaningful. While races imply biological similarity, species imply a disjunction. This raised the question of interfertility, but Hooton negated the possibility that racial mixture would lead to sterility (p. 587).

[84] Hooton, *Up from the Ape*, pp. 593–594. As in the rest of his writing the data were not necessarily coherent. On the same page he wrote: "Until we know exactly how to distinguish a race and exactly what intelligence tests test, we shall have to hold in suspension the problem of racial mental differences."

[85] Hooton, *Up from the Ape*, p. 601. Intellectually the alternatives he presented were rather simplistic. "If the evolution is not mainly a chance process it must be an intelligent or purposeful process. It seems to me quite immaterial whether we believe that the postulated

Hooton's writing reflected the shift in the balance of power from the racists to the egalitarians during the twenties. Methodologically, Hooton considered himself closest to the biometricians, despite his awareness that they did not "isolate racial types in the populations" they studied, and dealt "with them as if they were racially homogeneous." Apparently, Hooton aimed to fill this gap. He divided the scientific views of race into three schools: the biometricians, the environmentalists, and the racists. The Boasians (though not mentioned by name) were "disposed to deny that there are any cultural or psychological correlates of race." For them race is significant "principally because it effects differences in outward appearance which arouse the prejudice in the ignorant." Directly opposed to them were "the ethnomaniacs," who saw a close affinity between "cultural and psychological characteristics with physical types on wholly insufficient evidence." This group consisted largely of unprofessional anthropologists, but – perhaps not surprisingly, given his other writings – he concurred with their conclusions, even though none of these, as he admitted, has "been scientifically established."[86] It was Hooton's professional mission to fill this lacuna with the help of biometrics.

If Hooton's choice between alternative systems was arbitrary, though coherent, his interpretation of anthropometric data was often extremely puzzling and self-contradictory. Such was his position when he rejected Boas's studies of the changes in the shape of the skull on account of their insignificance. The two percent shift was considered inconsequential because Hooton claimed a "five unit change is necessary to shift a head from dolichocephaly to brachycephaly or the reverse, according to the conventional subdivisions of the index." Actually the cephalic index was divided into categories of dolichocephalic, with a breadth less than 75 percent of the length of the skull, mesocephalic, between 75 percent and 80 percent, and brachycephalic, above 80 percent. A population, or race, which was borderline would shift from one category to the other with less than one percentile change in average. A two-point difference was forty percent of the range from the one extreme category to the other. In any study, forty percent change cannot be regarded as inconsequential, but this is how Hooton preferred to present Boas's egalitarian

source of the intelligence or purposeful causation is a divine being or a set of natural 'Laws.' What difference does it make whether God is Nature or Nature is God?"
[86] Hooton, *Up from the Ape*, pp. 396–397.

studies.[87] Similarly, he simplified genetics in his speculation that "The replacement of long-heads by round-heads which is a widespread modern phenomenon" was "probably due to the Mendelian dominance of great head breadths over lesser head breadths." The significance of the skull shape was to enable a recognition of race relationships.[88] Hooton's rejection of Boas's statistics and his replacement of these with conjectures about Mendelian heredity of a unit character of skull shape is illustrative of the methodological anarchy in the discipline. Professional legitimacy provided the credence to almost any speculative theoretical position. But even as Hooton was writing, this type of arbitrariness was being refuted by biologists.

From 1926 onwards, Hooton's primary research concentrated on the biological basis for criminality. It led to a dead end, similar to Dixon's racial classifications and to English craniometry as represented by Morant.[89] The story of Hooton's collection of data on "the relation of race and nationality to crime in the United States" is a fascinating illustration of how the mechanism of a scientific community, respectability, and mutual back-scratching sustained a study for over a decade, with significant financial support from various sources. When it was finally published the study was criticized but also, more importantly, ignored. It belonged to the genre of criminal anthropology, a branch that had flourished late in the nineteenth century but diminished in importance before World War I. Historically, the significance of this work for the study of race is twofold: first as an illustration of how physical anthropology operated – Harvard after all had the best department in the United States during the interwar years – and as an explanation of its failure, and secondly, as background to Hooton's brief political cooperation with Boas in denouncing racism.[90]

Hooton studied 17,000 criminals and non-criminals in ten states. Each person was measured or evaluated for approximately 125 characteristics. In his original research proposal, submitted to the Social Science Research Council in request for a grant, Hooton made sure to distance himself from Lombroso, not in principle but

---

[87] Hooton, *Up from the Ape*, p. 410. Similar questions could be raised on his explanations of other characters such as the nasal index, p. 427.
[88] Hooton, *Up from the Ape*, p. 414.   [89] See below, chapter 3.
[90] A list of Hooton's supporters is too long to recount, and it included Boas's qualified endorsement for the continued collection of data. EAHP, Box 2abc. Grant proposal, no date. (April 1927).

rather in technique. Hooton argued that anthropometry had been improved since Lombroso, whom he portrayed as having sound ideas but poor training. Hooton judged his criminals to be inferior anatomically and mentally to the rest of the population just as Lombroso did, but in order to improve on his predecessor's simplistic types, Hooton divided his data by race and nationality. The classification was rigid, and though he did not assign particular crimes uniquely to any one group, he definitely found patterns. Without directly paralleling Lombroso's theory of atavism, Hooton none the less described the criminals as contributing to the "degenerative trends in human evolution." In a similarly deterministic fashion, he predicted "that it will be a comparatively easy and short matter to determine the correlations of human body types with disease." Even better, he thought, was the chance to establish from an individual's physique the mental disease "which he is liable to develop." Hooton avoided stating explicitly that it was possible to infer from the individual's anthropology "what particular form of criminality or other antisocial behavior his organism may produce," but it was possible "to catalogue and to describe anatomical indications of organic inferiority and to predict that the more numerous and accentuated these are in any individual the more surely he is to be of low mentality and worthless character."[91]

The mass of data made the publication almost inconceivable. It took Hooton a few years to resign himself to the idea that he would find no publisher for the work as one unit, and consented to have it divided into two books: one for general readership, the other – to include the data, to be published in installments, financed by the expected profits from the popular volume. As it turned out, the book found very few readers. The popular version, *Crime and the Man*, sold 1751 copies in ten years. Of the more scholarly version, *American Criminal*, only one volume was published and it sold 350 copies.[92] The meager attention received came mostly from reviewers who were generally not supportive. An English reviewer was particularly annoyed at Hooton's suggestions for directing and controlling "the progress of human evolution by breeding better types and by the

[91] Hooton, *Crime and the Man* (Cambridge: Harvard University Press, 1939), pp. 393, 395; 389–390. Hooton referred to "the great Italian criminologist" (p. 13). For a recent critique, see Gould "The Ape in Some of Us: Criminal Anthropology," in *The Mismeasure of Man* (New York: W. W. Norton, 1982), pp. 122–145.

[92] W. W. Smith, Harvard University Press, to Hooton, Nov. 5, 1948. EAHP, Box 5. Also Hooton correspondence with other publishers.

ruthless elimination of inferior types, if only we are willing to found and to practice a science of human genetics." The review justly compared these suggestions to Nazi legislation, in particular the "Law for the prevention of progeny afflicted by hereditary diseases," and the Marriage Law of 1938.[93]

Hooton was not very surprised at the book's reception and in fact was well aware that his work was out of vogue: "the mere proposal to investigate seriously the racial anatomical characters which are the outward signs of inheritance, in their relations to psychological or sociological phenomena, is regarded as a sin against the Holy Ghost of Science." Hooton's sense of being a pariah persisted despite his continuous central position in the discipline. He began the study at a time when criminal anthropology was going out of fashion but when biological determinism was still very popular. The response to the book at the outbreak of World War II in a totally changed political and intellectual climate testified to the shift in scientific opinion. If criminal anthropology vanished with the decline of racism in the forties, it has certainly done better since its resurrection as part of sociobiology.[94]

Hooton's language was as offensive as his conclusions and his illustrations were anything but "facetious." In addition to the graphs which in his own description were meant to "embellish or deface ... nasty little human figures," there were what Hooton called mosaics – not actually portraits – of "some professionally drawn and admirably executed heads." These were done with the intention of being "handsome rather than ugly. I wanted the criminals to be as good-looking as is compatible with the prescribed combination of features." Alas, the most outstanding feature of these mosaics was that the men portrayed were not well groomed. This did not quite show the hereditary feature claimed by Hooton, but it did make them look sinister.[95]

Hooton's greatest impact was through his students. Those trained in anthropology became the leaders of physical anthropology in the United States. Perhaps even more important were the numerous undergraduates who attended his courses on human evolution, many of whom later went on to join medical professions.

[93] *Man*, 40, 111 (June 1940), 90–92. The quote is from Hooton, *Crime and the Man*, p. 397.
[94] Richard J. Herrnstein and James Q. Wilson, *Crime and Human Nature* (New York: Simon and Schuster, 1985), is a testimony that Hooton's ideas have been rejuvenated at Harvard.
[95] *Crime and the Man*, preface, and the various illustrations; for example, pp. 57, 59.

Although Hooton believed in racial typology, was socially conservative and mingled with racists – which would have ordinarily put him
unequivocally in the racist camp – his position on race was more
complex, as is suggested by his role in the political campaign against
racism, and his cooperation with Boas during the thirties.[96]

THE POLITICS OF COEXISTENCE

The congenial relations between racists and anti-racists, and the
cooperation between supporters of rigid racial typology and cultural
relativists blurred the classification of scientists into precise categories. One could profess rigid racial views yet be part of – and
cooperate with – the most egalitarian element within the scientific
community; occasionally, indeed, even promote an anti-racist idea.
Hooton belonged in this category, but an even more striking case
was that of Clark Wissler, the most prominent anthropologist
actively involved in the Galton Society, the New York racist group,
who nevertheless kept good working relations with the Boasians.
His case is particularly interesting because his theoretical studies of
culture, primarily the development of the concept of cultural area,
placed him among the few racists of that time who actually
contributed to scientific thinking.[97] His central position in both the
anthropology community and the scientific establishment reveals
the professional mechanism and tension which slowed the pace of
anti-racism within anthropology but kept it closer to the center stage
of the scientific activity in the United States.

Wissler was of Old American ancestry, his family came from
England and Swabia. He was born in Indiana, where he spent
practically all his time before coming to Columbia at the age of
twenty-nine. He studied psychology and anthropology with J. M.
Cattell, Boas and Livingston Farrand. While some have seen Boas
as a major influence on his career, Wissler had little time to be
influenced by Boas before "the affair" at the American Museum,
which culminated in Boas's resignation and Wissler's succession to
the vacant post. Whether from intellectual curiosity or the opportunity for field work and a position at the Museum, Wissler – whose

---

[96] See below, part III.
[97] Stanley A. Freed and Ruth S. Freed bemoan the lost memory of Wissler in the history of
anthropology, retrace his contributions and argue for his current relevance as an earlier
forerunner of sociobiology in "Clark Wissler and the Development of Anthropology in the
United States," *American Anthropologist*, 85 (1983), 800–825.

principle training was in psychology – opted for anthropology. Once established at the Museum as a curator (1905), Wissler and Boas had to coexist peacefully. The Museum was a great center for teaching anthropology, and possessed abundant means; Boas and Columbia supplied the academic prestige and the intellectual leadership.[98] This cooperation, however, should not lead to the conclusion that Wissler was a Boasian. His cultural background was different, and he strongly preferred the company of members of the Galton Society – of upper-class Yankees.

Wissler's discussion of race in terms of universal patterns of culture is most explicitly put in *Man and Culture*. The book has been recently called "one of the most important anthropological books of the early decades of the 20th century."[99] In it, Wissler developed his concept of cultural area in holistic terms, combining biological and cultural phenomena. For Wissler, cultural evolution meant that each culture had to go through a rigid structural universal pattern – from a primitive state through a slow predetermined accumulation of culture before reaching civilization. Although he did not ascribe to a gap between primitive and civilized societies, he emphasized the stages of cultures as levels of "enrichment of these complexes" and in a deterministic fashion denied the possibility of overcoming the universal pattern. Moderately pessimistic, Wissler found within the pattern "spaces for tremendous expansion." In his case, it opened the way for an analysis of the superiority of the Nordics.[100]

Correlating biological, geographical and cultural processes, Wissler described Asia and Europe as the sources of man's evolution. The inhabitants of this area he termed the "main body" of humanity, while the rest of the world was relegated to a marginal position. Based on these definitions, Wissler erected a comprehensive classification. The primitives, the dark skinned, were the marginal peoples with marginal cultures who occupied the geographical margins of the world. This self-fulfilling correlation Wissler termed "striking." He then spoke of the marginal people as the most specialized in their bodily characters, and of the peoples who belonged to the "main body" as having the most general characteristics. At this stage Wissler introduced the concept of youth for a nation-race, which he ascribed to the ability of a race to

[98] Freed and Freed, "Clark Wissler," is a convenient starting point.
[99] Freed and Freed, "Clark Wissler," p. 819.
[100] Wissler, *Man and Culture* (New York: Crowell, 1923), pp. 78, 79.

keep the general character "indefinitely," by not specializing, and to
manifest a "vigorous type." In order to overcome the apparent
contradiction between specialization as a character associated with
civilization and progress while maintaining the vigorousness of the
primitive, he interpreted the condition of the civilized to be of a
unique type: "its breadth and diversity is too great for a specialized
unity of action." Let it be.

Wissler presented the Nordics as the youngest type among the
"main body," because they were the "wild untamed barbarians of
Europe" as manifested through "conquest and pillage." War and
militarism was turned into the rule of chivalry, and following the
"domestication of the Nordic masses," the uniqueness of Western
civilization developed. Although Wissler's analysis underscored the
point that no single race, not even the Nordics, could lay claim to
more than an incidental contribution to culture, he nevertheless
found the type most suited for keeping the culture flourishing is the
less specialized, the wildest, namely the Nordics.

So the Nordics stand out as the new generation in the family of the world,
the hope of the immediate future; it is theirs to carry forward the lamp of
civilization . . . Faced with such a responsibility, it would be criminal not to
give the best thought of the time to the conservation of whatever virtues this
stock possesses.[101]

Wissler was a member of the inner circle of the Galton Society, a
position which in itself would have been a sufficient indicator of his
racist stand. This was further amplified by his theory of a universal
pattern of culture in which he displayed an explicitly ethnocentric
position. His support of Nordic superiority was politically motivated and was published as part of the restrictionists' propaganda
during the Congressional debate over immigration.

Having worked in the vicinity of Boas left only nominal marks on
Wissler's views on race. He admitted the difficulties in using the
term "race," but once he replaced it by "type," he felt free to preach
racism. His only critical comment on Madison Grant and Lothrop
Stoddard was that all cultural groups have claimed superiority, but
he did not distance himself from their views. The Boasians surely
had a great distaste for Wissler, but his position at the Museum and
good contacts in the national scientific community made cooper-

[101] Wissler, *Man and Culture*, pp. 354–359. Hrdlicka read Wissler's book with
"astonishment." His comment on these quotes was "What is this?" A. Hrdlicka to
F. Boas, April 2, 1923. AHP.

ation with him indispensable. This was most evident in the work of committees and in the allocation of grants.

During the early twenties, race psychology was a popular topic in the social sciences. Yet, despite the overwhelming dominance of hereditarian explanations, the environmental argument was beginning to receive attention. In part, this was a withdrawal in the face of exaggeration in the name of nature and a response to criticism from Boasians and sociologists. The degree of skepticism, however, was a matter of taste: scientific studies of cultural conditioning were in their infancy, sporadic studies could suggest any number of alternatives to biological determinism, but were yet insufficient to substantiate a cultural interpretation. The specificity was left rather to personal choice. Castigating these racist positions as pseudoscience is therefore anachronistic. Consequently, efforts were made to devise methods for resolving disagreements within the scientific community by setting up committees, research programs, and soliciting financial support. The details of the retreat of scientists from racism was determined in part by the composition of these greatly varied committees. More often than not their members shared basic beliefs and excluded those scientists with whom they had little chance of reaching an agreement. This mechanism did not resolve disagreements, but it presented to outsiders what was considered the leading opinion within the disciplines. These committees represented a firm control over the discipline as the supporters of rigid racial classification had at the end of World War I. Later in the twenties, following a power shift, the discipline became more balanced between the camps, and the committee provided the mechanism of a clearing house, primarily to divide grants among the competing schools when the big Foundations, or national scientific organizations could not resolve conflicting scientific opinions and internal political rivalry.

The first important organizational effort to study racial questions after World War I was the formation of the Committee on Scientific Problems of Human Migrations.[102] It was organized under the auspices of the Division of Anthropology and Psychology in the

---

[102] Earlier attempts included Kroeber (and others) in Berkeley who tried through a Committee of International Relations to study race psychology. They suggested practical applications and scientific questions, but were directed by the Carnegie to solicit funds from Yerkes and Wissler on the Committee on Scientific Problems of Human Migrations which because of conflicting ideologies never materialized. Kroeber–Merriam correspondence, Feb. 1921. JCMP.

National Research Council as part of the 1922 propaganda to restrict immigration. Its personnel reflected the partisan perspective. The chairman was Robert Yerkes, the psychologist who had conducted the Army Mental Testing during the war and had later moved from Harvard to Yale to establish the Institute of Human Relations. Another member was Clark Wissler, who by 1924 was spending a day a week at Yale and the rest of his time at the American Museum. Both were members of the Galton Society, and very influential in dividing the Committee's budget, which received help from the most prestigious scientific organizations. In addition to the sponsorship of the National Research Council, its budget came from the Laura Spelman Rockefeller Memorial, the Carnegie Institution and the Russel Sage Foundation. The list of attendance at its conferences reads like the selective Who's Who of American Science. The Committee on Scientific Problems of Human Migrations was active until 1929, and its annual appropriations were in the range of $50,000, more than any other comparable committee. Its policy was to locate researchers in various laboratories and to initiate investigations on questions related to migration. Initially all studies were meant to enhance the scientific basis of the hereditarian argument. Those who were investigating environmental factors were a priori excluded. Generally, Boasians "need[ed] not apply," though even that rule had exceptions.[103] The committee's studies would have been even more uniform had not some of the scientists switched horses midway. Most notable among these was Carl Brigham, who in 1930 publicly retracted his earlier claims of a scientific basis for racial interpretations of I.Q. results. The Committee on Scientific Problems of Human Migrations contributed little to the understanding of the dialectical relation of nature–nurture. But its impact was crucial in blocking major funding sources from scientists who were not associated with its work, and

[103] M. Herskovits, a student of Boas, received aid, after Wissler was pressured by peers, and the policies of the committee were a source of antagonism in the anthropology community. Tozzer to Boas, May 4, 1924; Boas (to Wissler, June 7, 1926) described his criticism in the Executive Committee meeting of the National Research Council Division of Psychology and Anthropology on the work of Committee on Migration: "When planning for any large investigation, the plan should be submitted to a wider circle for approval and suggestions and that the cooperation of the scientific societies devoted to this subject is indispensable." Since Wissler did not attend the meeting, Boas made sure Wissler received his version of the criticism. On the Social Sciences Research Council see Dixon to Boas, Sept. 29, 1926. FBP.

delayed for a few years the oncoming dominance of the cultural school.[104]

At the same time other committees were formed which slowly proved themselves as new sources of finance. Both the National Research Council and the Social Sciences Research Council elected committees for the study of the American blacks, in which the rivals had to accommodate each other. The Committee of the National Research Council on the Negro, through its membership and work, became a landmark in the shift against an exclusive hereditarian explanation. A. Kidder, who was the chairman of the National Research Council Division of Anthropology and Psychology, initiated a small committee whose members represented the spectrum of opinion on the race issue: Boas, Davenport, Hooton, Hrdlicka, T. W. Todd, and H. N. Woodworth. Because the major figures in the discipline were included, none could have afforded to boycott the committee or voice disapproval of its membership. Kidder's choice showed that the political balance in 1926 allowed the presence of Boas and Davenport on one committee, but neither was influential enough to veto his rival's participation. Boas and Davenport kept in cordial contact over the years but rarely did they ever cooperate.[105]

The Committee tried to devise a system by which different studies could be compared. To reach an abstract agreement was not very difficult. Terminology that included catchwords such as cooperation and coordinate methods of measurements were easily agreed upon. The premise of what amounted to an interdisciplinary approach was accepted by all members of the committee, with even the individual proposals of Davenport and Boas being surprisingly similar. Subjects such as collection of comparative material in Africa, special reference to mixed populations, stress on genetic influences with full consideration given to environmental conditions, were all part of the emerging consensus. The Committee even called cooperation with the Social Sciences Research Council "indispensable" since "the biological characteristics of

---

[104] Yerkes-Merriam Correspondence and annual reports during the 1920s. JCMP. Yerkes-Davenport, CBDP.

[105] Boas's bequest of his anthropometric data to Cold Spring Harbor was rather an act of desperation because there was no other place that would accept it. Boas reversed his decision once Columbia was ready to receive the gift. Davenport to Boas, May 28, 1924. FBP.

man do not depend solely upon descent but also upon social environment."[106] The highlight of this cooperation became the Conference on Racial Differences sponsored jointly by the National Research Council and the Social Sciences Research Council in 1928, but this – as it turned out – reflected more on race relations than on the science of race. The conference was held in Washington, where Jim Crow meant that blacks could not participate, since they could not stay at the hotel nor eat at the restaurant. Boas's last minute offer to move the conference to New York and have the participants meet at the Faculty Club of Columbia did not receive an answer, except that "the situation in Washington is what it is."[107] Under the auspices of the Committee on the Negro, no meaningful or unexpected cooperation developed, but in the late 1920s it supported some of the more important work which helped delineate the debate on race. Principal names here include Melville Herskovits and Otto Klineberg who worked under Boas and studied environmental influence, and Davenport and Morris Steggerda, who studied race mixture in Jamaica. The relative strengths and weaknesses of these studies played a role in charting the shift in favor of the environmental school.

Boas had become involved with anthropological studies of blacks following his departure from the American Museum in 1906. That year he gave the commencement address at Atlanta University, at the invitation of W. E. B. Du Bois, and tried raising funds for an "African Museum." The effort was aborted, but he continued to work sporadically on issues pertaining to American blacks as part of his interest in the question of race and civil rights. He even tried to offer a course on blacks, but the success and encouragement were such that he did not repeat the experience.[108] None the less he kept in close contact with various blacks, and made special efforts to enlist black students in the survey of black anthropometry such as the

[106] A. V. Kidder to Franz Boas (Oct. 19, 1926). Study of the American Negro (Dec. 2, 1927). Committee on the American Negro – Proposals for the Organization of Investigations on the American Negro. The proposed budget of the committee was less than a third of the Committee on Scientific Problems of Human Migrations (less than US$40,000 for three years as compared with US$50–60,000 during some years in the Committee on Scientific Problems of Human Migrations). FBP.

[107] Knight Dunlap to Franz Boas, Jan. 17, 1928. Boas's reply, Jan. 18. The Conference was held at the end of February.

[108] Boas to Goldenweiser, Nov. 18, 1921. FBP. Stocking, "Anthropology as Kulturkampf," p. 38.

work conducted by Herskovits which Boas initiated as part of his racial studies.[109]

Melville Herskovits was born in Illinois to Jewish immigrants from Germany and Hungary. Following a spell in Texas and Cincinnati, he graduated from Chicago in history and moved to New York and the New School of Social Research. There, like Ruth Benedict, he came under the tutelage of Alexander Goldenweiser and Elsie Clews Parsons. He next moved uptown, becoming a graduate student in anthropology at Columbia which was part of the City's bohemian scene in the early twenties. While graduate work was much shorter at the time, usually two to three years, Boas's students continued to hang around seminars for some time after completing their studies. The anthropology department was squeezed financially by the University as a retaliation for Boas's pacifist role during World War I and his "unpatriotic" position on various occasions. The only financial break during the early twenties came from the Board of Biological Science of the National Research Council in small grants that allowed for minimal graduate research. In Herskovits's case, it helped with his post-doctoral work from 1923 to 1926 on "Variability under Racial Crossing." During this period he also taught for a time at Howard University, where he met, and for the first time cooperated with, black intellectuals.[110]

Herskovit's anthropological work on heredity in race crossing began with measuring blacks in New York in 1923. Over the next few years his research widened and he drew his samples not only from New York but also Howard University, Tennessee, Alabama and West Virginia. Herskovits emphasized variability within the sample rather than mere statistical averages. This approach led later to his major conclusion that the blacks in America form a new Afro-American physical type. He opposed the perceived view that racial crossing increases the phenotype variability in a group, in this case among blacks, by claiming to the contrary that among blacks in the United States homogeneity increased and became the rule. In addition to the physical measurements, Herskovits studied gene-

---

[109] See Boas correspondence with Carter G. Woodson of the *Journal of Negro History*, who labored hard to find the right candidate to cooperate with Herskovits, for example, May 7, 1923. FBP.

[110] George E. Simpson, *Melville J. Herskovits* (New York: Columbia University Press, 1973). Alan Merriam, "Herskovits – Obituary," *American Anthropologist*, 66 (1964), 83–109. Herskovits did receive grants from Columbia in 1926, when three years after he finished his dissertation the opposition against Boas had somewhat abated. FBP.

alogies, as supplied by the blacks he studied. This was an open-ended method in that the answers were subjective, but probably more accurate than the alternative system practiced by Davenport and Steggerda who classified the people they studied into one of three categories according to appearance. Herskovits's major methodological problems were the reliability of data based on the genealogies and the representativeness of his sample.[111]

According to the sample, Herskovits concluded that interbreeding among blacks of mixed ancestry increased in the last generations and that far less mixing between whites and blacks occurred. He ascribed the growing segregation to social pressures which were getting progressively worse "among Negroes as it is among the White population." His conclusions applied to the black population of the United States as a whole, but the problem remained of whether this could be substantiated on the basis of his samples, a methodological shortcoming which Herskovits found difficult to overcome. Contrary to his style, he therefore added an emotional plea in the name of conventional wisdom, arguing: "That racial crossing between Negroes and Whites in this country is diminishing is evident, I believe, to anyone who has had intimate contact with the American Negro, and I know of no other hypothesis which will fit [the] observations."[112] This type of substantiation might have been more appropriate had it been advanced in support of prejudice, but apparently the methodological rift between the camps was minimal. A further difficulty, of which Herskovits was well aware, arose with the sociological character of his description of "Negro," given that the subject of the study was the biology of a mixed group. His anthropometric measurements showed that the blacks constituted an intermediate group between West Africans and Europeans, and despite the variability among the six series he used, there were no "apparent differences arising from the fact that

[111] Melville J. Herskovits, *The Anthropometry of The American Negro* (New York: Columbia University Press, 1930), pp. 1–18. Myrdal called Herskovits's study "by far the best available" but did not accept Herskovits's claims of the representativeness of his sample, adding: "The investigators of white samples have not even made efforts to get representativeness." Gunnar Myrdal, *An 'American Dilemma.' The Negro Problem and Modern Democracy*, 2 vols. (New York: Harper & Brothers, 1944), I, p. 137.

[112] Herskovits, *The Anthropometry of The American Negro*, pp. 41, 42, made great efforts to prove that. Boas was skeptic all the way, writing to Herskovits (following an earlier publication of *The American Negro, A Study in Racial Crossing* (New York: Knopf, 1928) an abridged version of the 1930 book, "I do not believe, as I told you several times, that the proof that you have sampled the whole Negro population is convincing." Boas to Herskovits, Jan. 31, 1928.

the rural West Virginia Negroes, whose ancestors for several generations had been living in the same few counties" and the New York blacks who were mostly migrants. The only significant physical deviation was among the Harlem professionals, whose lighter skin color was a result of sociological selection.[113]

The conclusion of the study – that the American black constitutes a unified type with greater homogeneity than the "unmixed ... peoples who have contributed to its ancestry" – was in Herskovits's words "sufficiently unexpected." This was not unlike Boas's conclusion regarding the changes of bodily form among immigrants. While the similarity between the two is not commented upon in the literature, and apparently neither Boas nor Herskovits referred to it, the impact of both studies was comparable: both provided a powerful critique of established views, rather than contributed to a formulation of a profoundly new position. The striking implication of Herskovits's work concerned the very existence of a pure race. Anthropologists and lay people alike accepted the notion that the physical variability of a population is an index of its racial purity: the more homogeneous a group, the purer it was supposed to be. But in this case Herskovits had dealt with a hybrid population by definition, the genealogies of the blacks showing that only 22 percent had no known white ancestry, and yet the group displayed homogeneity comparable to, or greater than, the standard among "pure" European populations. The greatest heterogeneity was found in a predominantly white population with some black ancestry, and not as expected by Herskovits at the point of a greatest mixture – half black, half white. At first his biological explanation was not very sophisticated, but he finally assigned his findings to "a very complex sort of multiple Mendelianism."[114] Herskovits did not conclude that the homogeneous group constituted a new race, as it is clear from his argument that the lowest variability was most evident at the point of mixture. Yet his conclusions, especially the observation of a growing segregation and diminishing racial admixture combined with the stability of type, led precisely to such popular perceptions.

Herskovits continued to work on black anthropology, studying

---

[113] Herskovits, *American Negro*, p. 240.

[114] Herskovits, *American Negro*, pp. 251, 275, 278. It was Boas the Lamarckian, who suggested to Herskovits that his earlier non-Mendelian interpretations will be objected to by geneticists because of the distinction between genotype and phenotype. Boas to Herskovits, Jan. 31, 1928. FBP.

African history, and he turned in time into the leader of Afro-American studies. Immediately after completing his dissertation, he began to collect anthropometric data in Harlem. He became involved in the public debate on the question of race and nationality, rejecting in the best Boasian tradition the confusion between physical and cultural attributes[115] and more importantly became a pro-black partisan. Once he had moved from physical to cultural measurements, he confronted the tradition of African inferiority, and concurrently with the New Negro movement of the 1920s, glorified African culture, and traced its survival among black Americans. On the basis of his professional expertise from field studies which extended to Africa and the West Indies, Herskovits enlisted explicitly in the service of black revival, ascribing the positive aspects of black life to African heritage and the negative ones to the American social impact. His belief was that the blacks' confidence in their own past would strengthen their present position in the United States. Ethnic pride was seen at the time as a double-edged sword, since highlighting strong connections with Africa could also mean inability to assimilate – and a rejection of the melting pot idea, still an unacceptable attitude. An unfavorable interpretation of the same data could have attributed to African heritage the negative aspects of black society, rather than as Herskovits did, its music and culture.[116] The importance of Herskovits's work resided in its conclusions more than in the data, comparable in its unwarranted assertions to the way mainline research on racial questions had underscored bigoted claims. Herskovits's anthropometric studies helped disprove misconceptions of the inferiority of blacks. Among physical anthropologists who studied blacks, Herskovits had done comparatively better work, and he used these earned credentials to comment on public affairs. He integrated the anthropological study of blacks with a commitment to promote good race relations while publishing on West Africa, West Indies, and Brazil – all part of the ethnohistorical aspects of the New World blacks. Herskovits also displayed interest in the interaction of psychology and anthropology, but his studies of

---

[115] A full bibliography can be found in Alan Merriam, "Herskovits – Obituary." Herskovits published on these questions in *Opportunity*, *The Nation* and elsewhere.

[116] Herskovits, *The Myth of the Negro Past* (New York: Harper & Brothers, 1941), p. 32. For critical response, see Myrdal, *An "American Dilemma"*, p. 1394. Herskovits's book was written as part of the Carnegie study conducted by Myrdal.

blacks' psychology were limited.[117] This field became the expertise of another of Boas's students, Otto Klineberg.

The most devastating and direct critique of the racist Army I.Q. tests conducted during World War I – which supposedly quantified the inferiority of blacks – was the reinterpretation which showed northern blacks to have scored better than southern whites. Since the tests were heralded by racists and immigration restrictionists to present their views as though these were supported by science, the critique was very pointed. Initially this was shown early in the twenties, and was later on amplified by Kleinberg who carried out his work in the name of racial equality, became one of the central figures in the UNESCO statements on race after World War II, and was instrumental in the Brown versus Board of Education case in the Supreme Court in 1954 which outlawed segregation in American education.

A different line of anti-racist studies came from the growing social and cultural anthropology as it was explicated in England and the United States under different names, but with similar effect which resurrected Rousseau's noble savage, and presented the primitives as a source of envy to Western society. The most prominent in this group were Bronislaw Malinowski and A. R. Radcliffe-Brown on the British side, and Margaret Mead and Ruth Benedict in the United States.

DIONYSIA IN THE PACIFIC

The disarray in which physical anthropology found itself during the 1920s and the 1930s was a result in part of its internal methodological problems, but even more so of the general decline of scientific naturalism. The professionalization of sociology and anthropology meant that institutionally they were drifting further apart and, at least in the United States, had little contact during the interwar years. In Britain and the United States anthropological theories shaped the reorientation of the social sciences away from biological reductionism. Social anthropologists, broadly defined, were explaining society under a host of theories: structuralism and

---

[117] Herskovits and M. M. Willey, "A Note on the Psychology of Servitude," *Journal of Social Forces*, 1 (1923), 228–234. Herskovits and M. M. Willey, "Psychology and Culture," *Psychological Bulletin*, 24 (1927), 253–283; Herskovits, "Freudian Mechanism in Primitive Negro Psychology," in Evans-Pritchard *et al.* (eds.), *Essays presented to C. G. Seligman* (London: Kegan Paul, 1934).

functionalism, cultural and social anthropology, historicism and diffusionism, and many of these were additionally flavored by psychological interpretations. The discontinuity of the various theories, increased by partisanship, ordinarily forestalls the treatment of the different schools together, yet these had compounded the impact on the decline of racial theories through the challenge presented to scientific naturalism.

The diversity of ethnology and social anthropology was a source of much disciplinary dispute, and personal questions often overshadowed theoretical disagreements. Bronislaw Malinowski and Alfred R. Radcliffe-Brown, together with their disciples in social anthropology, were engaged during the interwar years in an intense rivalry. This pales, however, compared with their disdainful attitude towards the Boasians. None the less, all factions held to a scientific world view which emphasized social interaction and the overriding importance of environment as compared with heredity. All, apart from Radcliffe-Brown, saw in the individual the source of social manifestations, accepting in various degrees psychological explanations. Most did not study the question of race, thereby rebelling against the traditional subject matter of anthropology. Those who did examine the racial question as part of a larger study pointed to its irrelevance in the understanding of culture. The influence of this shared anti-racist world view was somewhat mitigated by their style of refuting and denying any merit to the competing schools, which were also in their different ways, egalitarian. This was especially strong in Britain, had caused much turmoil in the discipline and may have postponed the decline of racial typologists who maintained an appearance of legitimacy, being one approach among a cluster of schools.

British social anthropologists based their method of structural functionalism on the concept of social solidarity as it was developed by Emile Durkheim.[118] In his studies of totemism and the division of labor, he pointed to the relevance of anthropology to the study of contemporary society. Hoping to reduce the complexity of modern capitalism to its essentials, Durkheim turned to Australian aborigines in search for clues. At the time, the evolutionary school was at its height. While rejecting some of its excesses, Durkheim accepted the basic premise of evolution as a tool to analyze social change. An

[118] Emile Durkheim, *The Rules of Sociological Method* (1895), trans. W. D. Halls, ed. Steven Lukes (New York: Free Press, 1982).

armchair anthropologist who subscribed to many of the contemporary chagrins of biological determinism (such as the correspondence between skull size and intelligence), he none the less did not study race as a social phenomenon because the sociological diversity within each race suggested to him that the explanation of social variables would not be biological but social. A non-sociological investigation of racial typology was, in Durkheim's eyes, a means of evading the real issues, which for him evolved around social cohesion. For similar methodological reasons he rejected psychological explanations.[119] Durkheim's choice to focus on society and to exclude both the racial and the psychological causal explanations *a priori*, shows how hard it is to categorize theories along a progressive-reactionary continuum. In hindsight his rejection of racial explanations seems if anything not to have gone far enough, while his dismissal of psychology is a major drawback of his theory. If the intellectual discourse is about opening new horizons and eliminating outmoded ones, then Durkheim's replacement of racial studies by sociology and cultural anthropology provided the professional setting for the new sciences. His synthesis, though evolutionary, was no longer unilinear and shifted emphasis to a more open-ended social development,[120] which later was elucidated in the work of Malinowski and Radcliffe-Brown.

RADCLIFFE-BROWN

Radcliffe-Brown was Durkheim's most faithful disciple among British anthropologists. He was born in Birmingham, where Prince Peter Kropotkin, the Russian anarchist-philosopher, was his neighbor. Reputedly, he adopted from Kropotkin the view that before trying to reform society one should understand it, which he felt was especially true with regard to the social complex known as Victorian England. "Anarchy Brown," as he was known at Cambridge, preferred, however, to try and understand modern society from the bottom up, that is, to study the primitive and simple communities, a theoretical approach he learnt from Durkheim.[121] Whether this

---

[119] Durkheim, *The Rules of Sociological Method* (1895).

[120] "Mechanic" and "organic" solidarity echoes the primitive–civilization polarity, yet leave enough space for varied interpretations. Emile Durkheim, *The Division of Labor in Society*, trans. W. D. Halls (New York: The Free Press, 1984).

[121] A. R. Radcliffe-Brown, *Method in Social Anthropology*, ed. M. N. Srinivas (Chicago: University of Chicago Press, 1958), p. xviii.

story accurately portrays Radcliffe-Brown's conversion to anthropology is secondary to the fact that this was his way to present the legacy to "friends and colleagues." In principle he was committed to study the intricacy of Western society, but he almost never practiced this commitment. Radcliffe-Brown left for the Pacific in 1908, remaining abroad for almost thirty years until he returned to England in 1936 to occupy the Chair in anthropology at Oxford. In the interval he was a professor on three other continents – at the universities of Cape Town, Sydney and Chicago – and became a central force in world anthropology, with close contacts to the Rockefeller Foundation. His impact was primarily on theoretical thinking and, on the issue of race, indirect, but the growing prestige of structural anthropology owed much to his forceful personality.

The editor of a recent collection of Radcliffe-Brown's papers prefaced the volume by commenting that Radcliffe-Brown's ideas are out of fashion in British social anthropology, adding "for a man so ready to dismiss his predecessors, there is perhaps a certain justice in this."[122] Radcliffe-Brown's work was characterized by his combative nature and antagonistic attitude towards peers. His field studies were seen as models of research, but his vigor was directed more to theoretical formulations. In defining a system which he called "scientific comparative sociology" he was influenced by the tradition of the evolutionary school deriving from both Herbert Spencer and Durkheim. He described society as an organism and dismissed as unimportant the role of the individual or the use of psychological explanations in deciphering the total social organization. His obduracy in refusing to admit the individual as a factor that influenced society was matched only by his opposition to anything resembling conjectural history. And while he adopted positivism and Spencer's organic metaphors he totally rejected the attempts to reconstruct the origin of humankind. Primitive societies did not lend themselves to any historical study, only speculations, and therefore the historical school as well as any attempt at reconstruction, was rejected as futile.

In his Presidential Address to Section E of the South African Association for the Advancement of Science in 1923, Radcliffe-Brown formally described his methodological approach as the separation of ethnology from social anthropology. Ethnology, pri-

[122] Adam Kuper (ed.), *The Social Anthropology of Radcliffe-Brown* (London: Routledge & Kegan Paul, 1977), p. 1.

marily American, was viewed as historical, while social anthropology was seen as inductive, scientific. In a characteristically condescending tone he described the relation between them as "one of one-sided dependence. Social anthropology can do without ethnology, but it would seem that ethnology cannot do without assumptions that belong specifically to social anthropology."[123] For Radcliffe-Brown, ethnology was part of the attempt to reconstruct racial history, the main interest of physical anthropology: it proved futile despite the extensive collection of data. In a rare understatement he described the results of ethnology as not "by any means proportionate to the time and energy expended." However, while he denied speculative history in principle, Radcliffe-Brown rejected race psychology only as much as he considered it to be theoretically premature, very much like Durkheim a generation earlier. He did not negate its importance as a possible fruitful study of racial differences in the future, but argued that it could not be as yet approached "as a scientific problem."[124]

His rigorous approach to science was largely divorced from social involvement, and while he might have been a reformer by nature, his views of applied anthropology were very much part of the social milieu of the colonial service. Despite his outright rejection of historical conjecture, he none the less accepted ethnology as applied anthropology, and was a powerful component of the British consensus, regardless of sub-disciplinary creed or school.

The study of the beliefs and customs of the native peoples, with the aim not of merely reconstructing their history but of discovering their meaning, their function, that is the place they occupy in the mental, moral and social life, can afford great help to the missionary or the public servant who is engaged in dealing with the practical problems of the adjustments of the native civilization to the new conditions that have resulted from our occupation of the country.[125]

Radcliffe-Brown resolved his hesitations between pure and applied science by advising scientists to investigate the problem and the administrators to implement the acquired knowledge. At a time

[123] Radcliffe-Brown, "The Methods of Ethnology and in Social Anthropology," *South African Journal of Science*, 20 (1923), 124–147; reprinted in Radcliffe-Brown, *Method in Social Anthropology*, p. 27.

[124] Radcliffe-Brown, "The Present Position of Anthropological Studies," A Presidential address to Section H of the British Association for the Advancement of Science, 1931. In Radcliffe-Brown, *Method in Social Anthropology*, pp. 43–45.

[125] Radcliffe-Brown, *Method in Social Anthropology*, p. 32.

when the International Institute of African Languages and Cultures in London was being endowed, these amounted to policy formulations. This suggestion, however, displayed the discrepancy between Radcliffe-Brown's view that a total social structure should be studied with scientific rigor and objectivity, and a view that the existing meager knowledge should be applied in a fragmentary fashion to colonial administration.

Radcliffe-Brown himself refrained from disputes outside the professional arena. Within his discipline he was involved in many arguments, primarily with Malinowski, and during the thirties in the United States when he taught in Chicago and exerted tremendous influence. None the less, he never used his influence and prestige in the fight against racism. For him, applied anthropology meant giving distant advice to colonial administrators.

MALINOWSKI

While Radcliffe-Brown was not appointed to a chair in England until 1936, Malinowski, who was an outsider to British society, was part and parcel of British anthropology throughout the interwar years. In fact his seminar at the London School of Economics constituted to a large degree social anthropology in Britain. He influenced the discipline as a teacher, a field researcher and, a theoretician – not unlike Boas in America. In contrast to Boas, his role as an intellectual was limited. Malinowski and Radcliffe-Brown played comparable roles in the anthropological communities in the rejection of biological interpretations, although their antagonism to each other caused them to accentuate their differences. Malinowski approached human behavior as a social phenomenon in a more theoretical manner than was usual for his time. While Radcliffe-Brown was interested in consolidating the theory of social order, Malinowski investigated how social order answered the natural needs of human beings. In a manner of the American school, he subordinated social structure to culture.

Another resemblance between Malinowski and Boas was their initial training in physics in their respective country of origin: Poland and Germany. In 1908 Malinowski had to give up this study because of illness. After a short stay in Germany he moved to England for postgraduate studies in the London School of Economics under Charles Seligman. In 1914, he travelled to Austra lia and for some years studied the Trobriand Islanders. This became known as one of the most famous field trips in the history of anthropology. He returned to London in 1922 and taught continuously at the London School of Economics until 1938. Never hesitant to trumpet his own fame and superiority, Malinowski placed himself at the center of the small anthropological community in Britain. This went well with students and disciples, but less so with colleagues. In his advocacy of social anthropology he quickly came to criticize W. H. R. Rivers and Charles Seligman, his predecessors and mentors during his early years in anthropology. Intellectually and professionally, he was the most prominent anthropologist in Britain, yet being a foreigner and one who antagonized his peers did not increase his popularity or centrality in English intellectual life.[126] He rarely intervened in public issues in Britain, and when not teaching he preferred to have long sojourns in Switzerland, a testimony to his cultural affinities.

Malinowski's contributions to and influence on anthropology stemmed foremost from the Trobriand Islands.[127] Malinowski's egalitarian influence, regardless of his personal feelings towards the natives, was displayed in his attempt to discover logic in the savage mind and to humanize the primitives in Western eyes by presenting a complex picture of their culture. In addition to a rigorous methodological approach, his theoretical work was significant especially for providing a model for fieldwork. His ethnology was revolutionary in style as well as in content: no longer was the anthropologist a detached superior Westerner who studied the prehistoric past in the contemporary laboratory of primitive life. He was rather the empiricist observer who wrote about living human beings, full of empathy for the dynamic of their society. While in hindsight his theoretical impact has been minimized by numerous

[126] Seligman felt Malinowski hurt him personally. Recounting his past help to Malinowski in a private letter he wrote: "I was your earliest and ... most constant backer," and testifying to his continued admiration for Malinowski's scientific work, he added: "I do not admire what I may call your semi-popular propaganda work, and I consider much of it definitely bad for anthropology. Your frequent railing against your colleagues cannot but produce a bad impression on the semi-instructed public, for you are a person whose opinion counts for a good deal." Seligman to Malinowski, Aug. 5, 1931. BMP-LSE. Also R. Firth, "Malinowski as Scientists and as Man," in Raymond Firth, (ed.), *Man and Culture: An Evaluation of the Work of Bronislaw Malinowski* (London: Routledge & Kegan Paul, 1957).

[127] Malinowski's publications which resulted from this trip included *Argonauts of the Western Pacific* (1922); *The Sexual Life of Savages in North Western Melanesia* (1929); and *Coral Gardens and their Magic* (1935).

critics, his historical significance stems from his ethnographic work, and the impact it had on contemporaries.[128]

Malinowski based his theory on his field work, as can be readily seen from some of his general books such as *Crime and Custom in Savage Society*, *Sex and Repression in Savage Society* and two posthumous publications, *A Scientific Theory of Culture* (1944), *The Dynamics of Cultural Change* (1945). These were written in direct opposition to some of the vogues in psychology of the period, specifically denying the notion of an illogical primitive mind. Malinowski also challenged Freud and psychoanalysis and denied the claim of the universality of the Oedipus complex. There is no absolute primordial configuration, he thought, rather "a functional formation dependent upon the structure and upon the culture of the society."[129] His premise was that all cultures were to be judged equally according to their relative value system. The basis for culture was, in Malinowski's opinion, a human nature grounded in permanent needs, and he therefore judged Functionalism as the transformation of organic, individual needs, into cultural imperatives.[130] Today these are commonplace both in anthropology and intellectual discourse in general, but during the twenties only a minority were receptive to the idea of treating all cultures and societies as fundamentally equal.

Malinowski's description of basic human institutions as functions of social organization was a direct attack on biological reductionism. He insisted on attributing to social organization topics which traditionally were explained as biological manifestations, these

[128] "Functionalism in its Malinowskian form has become repugnant," wrote Leach in a commemorative volume of Malinowski, and added: "Nor can I believe that this is merely a passing phase; the abstract theoretical writings of Malinowski are not merely dated, they are dead." This was said in a description of Malinowski's "anthropological greatness" and "imaginative genius." This paradox stemmed from Malinowski's "bias against abstract theory." E. R. Leach, "The Epistemological Background to Malinowski's Empiricism," in Firth (ed.), *Man and Culture*, pp. 119–120.

[129] Malinowski, *Sex and Repression in Savage Society* (New York: Harcourt, 1927), p. 143. Ernest Jones had criticized Malinowski for explaining everything by social institutions. Malinowski retaliated by focusing on the mechanic representation of psychoanalysis: "Where is then the repressed Oedipus complex to be found? Is there a sub-conscious below the actual unconscious, and what does the concept of repressed repression mean?" (p. 144).

[130] Malinowski's concept of culture ("compromises, inherited artifacts, goods, technical processes, ideas, habits and values," including social organization) was very close to Tylor's definition (1871). Similarly, Malinowski's and Radcliffe Brown's definitions of "institution" were not disparate enough to explain their disagreements. Audrey Richards "Culture in Malinowski's Work," pp. 16–17; Parsons, "Theory of Social Systems," p. 62, both in Firth (ed.), *Man and Culture*. Also Jerzy Szacki, *History of Sociological Thought* (Westport: Greenwood Press, 1979), p. 484.

included the family, religion, magic, language, aggressiveness, as well as education, law and economics. His treatment of the role of sex was an important part of this indirect attack on the biological imperatives. The academically unconventional manner in which his explicit language described sexuality underscored his belief that social constraints determined sexual behavior, including elementary biological functions such as mating, leaving nothing outside the social domain. Society and culture were seen as essential to human survival. Malinowski described the *Sexual Life of Savages* as a model to inspire envy in the British reader. Neither middle-class hypocrisy nor the image of the promiscuous savage had a place here. Malinowski claimed that "natives treat sex in the long run not only as a source of pleasure, but indeed as a thing serious and even sacred." What appeared "crude and uncontrolled" at first, under scrutiny resembled Western ideals. In the "richness and multiplicity of love lies its philosophic mystery, its charm for the poet and its interest for the anthropologist."[131] The chapter, "The Erotic Element in Games," described how the full moon brought an increase in play and pleasure-seeking – both of which were in short supply in Britain.

BENEDICT AND MEAD

If Functionalism did not take hold in the United States as it did in England, younger American anthropologists nevertheless worked along similar lines, though they preferred to call it "cultural anthropology." Perhaps the two most prominent among this group were Ruth Benedict and Margaret Mead, both disciples of Boas. Benedict and Mead were of "Old American" lineage, well placed in society with good prospects for a moderately successful life in traditional female roles. In their choice of anthropology, both sought to rebel against social conventions, each in her own style and temperament. Their social, professional and personal struggle for independence was waged largely within the anthropology department at Columbia, where the two developed an intimate relationship. Despite their differing personalities, styles, and careers, they represented to the educated American the practice of cultural

[131] Bronislaw Malinowski, *The Sexual Life of Savages in North Western Melanesia* (London: Routledge, 1929), pp. ix–x.

relativism, which made their work central to American culture far beyond professional circles.[132]

Ruth Benedict's interest in anthropology began at the age of thirty-one. In 1919, as an escape from the role of a domesticated wife in a childless marriage she entered The New School of Social Research. At the end of World War I, the New School provided a stimulating atmosphere, a hope of a better world, and an intellectual center. At the same time it was not too taxing, and did not force Benedict to abruptly desert the role of housewife. It took an additional two years for her to commit herself to the academic world.[133] Margaret Mead was an undergraduate at Barnard when she met Benedict, who was by then the instructor of anthropology at the college. Fifteen years her senior, Benedict was still only two years into her own graduate work. The two become close, Benedict providing the professional advice for a few years and Mead recipro-cating by introducing the shy and reserved Benedict to the city's radical intellectual setting. Mead who first came to Boas's graduate seminars as a protégée of Benedict, remained one, at least until leaving the department. Ruth Bunzel, who also belonged to this group of Boasians, listed these as the choices for their generation: fleeing to Paris, selling the *Daily Worker* on street corners, or going into anthropology. While this might not have quite exhausted the possibilities, the air of romanticism was very much part of their ethos.[134] Of Boas's students in the twenties, Benedict and Mead were the ones who were closely connected with some of the first-generation students, such as Alexander Goldenweiser, Paul

[132] Biographical data on Mead and Benedict is readily available. Recent biographies have been published: Judith S. Modell, *Ruth Benedict: Patterns of a Life* (Philadelphia, University of Pennsylvania Press, 1983) and Jane Howard, *Margaret Mead a Life* (New York: Simon and Schuster, 1984). Both are detailed on personal life and complement each other. Mead published an autobiography (*Blackberry Winter: My Earlier Years*, (New York: Morrow, 1972) on these years, as well as some of Benedict's papers in two different assortments with introductions (Mead, *An Anthropologist at Work. Writings of Ruth Benedict* (Boston: Houghton Mifflin, 1959); *Ruth Benedict* (New York: Columbia University Press, 1974). A different perspective on Mead is given by Mary Catherine Bateson, *With A Daughter's Eye* (New York: Washington Square Press, 1984). The work of Benedict and Mead is analyzed in any history of anthropology, including Harris who is very critical of their approach. M. Harris, *The Rise of Anthropological Theory* (New York: Crowell, 1968). The passion in Freeman's controversy of 1983 proves that this historical discussion is anything but dated.

[133] Modell, *Benedict*, pp. 110–111.

[134] Howard, *Mead*, p. 69. In this context, the choice of anthropology was mildly conservative. Mead described her friends in college as radicals "in terms of our sentiments rather than our adherence to any radical ideology." This explains why conservatives could be part of the group, but more importantly reflects on radicalism as a political movement where substance was secondary to appearance. Mead, *Blackberry Winter*, pp. 105, 107.

Radin, and Edward Sapir, cynically named "The American super-intelligensia."[135]

Benedict, even if more advanced in her training, was slower than Mead to internalize this new value system and transform it into her professional work. She began with traditional anthropological material of American Indians, preferred the library to the field as a setting for her dissertation research, and kept much of her life private. Mead was a public person all her life. That she did not end up in politics was circumstantial, though in later years she claimed not to have chosen politics because political success was both "too short and too exigent."[136] Be that as it may, Mead sought to be involved in contemporary affairs right from the start. For Benedict it took close to two decades, and she was very reserved about it. Mead was enthusiastic right from the beginning, and is reputed to have remarked early on that she would never be the best, but would be the most famous anthropologist. Consequently her academic work addressed the most hotly discussed intellectual topics of the day. In her M.A. research in psychology she conducted intelligence tests on Italian-American children and compared the results to the amount of English spoken in the children's home by their parents.[137] Mead learned the essence of what Boas had to teach; cultural relativism and the use of a scientific investigation to study a social problem and apply its method in a critical social analysis. The rest depended upon her creativity, and she travelled all the way to the South Seas to earn her reputation.

A study of racial differences among immigrants was a possible dissertation topic for Mead, but she was much more concerned with gender and sex. These were of prime concern in public discussion, among conservatives and radicals alike: eugenics and birth control, feminism and libertarianism were all popular issues. In her early twenties, these absorbed a substantial part of Mead's personal commitment. She married three times within a few years, and intimate matters were very much discussed among her friends. Her first husband recalled that "everything everyone did was just common gossip in that group. Our apartment was the center for much that went on in those remarkably social times."[138] By the time

---

[135] Lowie's phrase, who was offended by the group (he did not include Mead). Quoted in Modell, *Benedict*, p. 166.
[136] Mead, *Blackberry Winter*, p. 110.
[137] *American Journal of Sociology*, 31 (1926), 667. Howard, *Mead*, p. 64.
[138] Howard, *Mead*, p. 108.

she went to Polynesia to study Samoan adolescence, she had left
behind a husband who loved her but in whom she lost interest, a
disappointed lover, Edward Sapir, who had hoped to domesticate
her rather than have her as a colleague, and a resigned, longing
Benedict.

Mead's *Coming of Age in Samoa* received as many superlatives as
any anthropology book ever has. More than half a century after its
publication it was reexamined in the controversy that was part of a
sociobiology debate which attracted unprecedented public attention. In the twenties the book had all the ingredients for an instant
success, and it was celebrated by Malinowski, Havelock Ellis and
H. L. Mencken among others. It was science and it was readable; in
a clear and detailed language it described an exotic society, primitive but liberated. American intellectual and sexual anxieties were
set against the sexual liberation of adolescents roaming picturesque
South Sea beaches. The psychological dichotomy was complete.
Mead described primitives who did not ask for mercy, aliens who
were not immigrants begging for justice. Instead these enviable
strangers presented a society on which the American *id* could be
projected. And it was a successful cultural statement in the nature-
nurture debate.

The anthropological work was supplemented at the suggestion of
the publisher by two chapters analyzing the implications of the
study for American society. This appealed to Mead's sense of the
need for social involvement. It also improved the book sales. Few
readers, however, were concerned that the book lacked data.[139] For
the public, this was perhaps its greatest virtue, the vivid descriptions
making it all the more realistic. For the anthropologists, many of
whom were by then Boasians, the book substantiated their prejudices in favor of cultural relativism, and was additionally welcomed because it bestowed such popularity on the small discipline
not accustomed to public exposure. During the next decade, Mead
was in and out of field trips, working in the American Museum
primarily on her own writings, enhancing her reputation by public
lectures, marrying and getting divorced, and publishing books
mostly on the primitives of the South Sea. But she kept out of the
political American scene, and this changed only during the World
War II years and later.

[139] Criticism by Kroeber in a letter (October 11, 1928) and by Mary Austin in the *Birth
Control Review*, June 1929. Quoted in Howard, *Mead*, p. 128.

In the meantime Benedict was, at her slower pace, learning about the American Indians, teaching at Columbia, editing the *Journal of American Folk-Lore*, and preparing her own most famous contribution to anthropology, *Patterns of Culture*. Together with Mead's, these volumes were to further Boas's historical particularism of cultural dominant interpretations. Benedict's analysis of Nietzsche's Apollonian and Dionysian types as *Gestalt* configurations of two different cultures became a source of inspiration for much of the anthropology which followed. Beyond the discipline, the popularity of the book made "patterns" and "culture" conventional household words. It also addressed explicitly the relevance of the study to the political question of racism in 1934.

The first chapter of the book was "The Science of Custom,"[140] an anti-racist plea, based on illustrations taken from contemporary anthropology, but written in a moral, educational style. Its message was that culture mattered, not blood. The intensive contact in modern societies among different nationalities is the source of racial hatred; "we have come to the point where we entertain race prejudice against our blood brothers the Irish." The conclusion was that it was not against blood that discrimination was practiced. There is nothing in the biological structure of man that makes it difficult for any people to adopt different cultures, and there is no commitment in detail by the "biological constitution to any particular variety of behaviour.... Culture is not a biologically transmitted complex." Benedict spoke of the single origin of humankind and emphasized that even universal beliefs are "not equivalent to regarding them as biologically determined, for they may have been very early inventions of the human race, 'cradle' traits which have become fundamental in all human thinking."[141] She argued that because close geographical and biological groups displayed opposing cultural configurations the nature of society was far more complicated even if the optimal biological claims were acceptable explanations. In a rudimentary way she also injected the time factor, hardly ever referred to in racial debates: "The most radical changes in psychological behaviour have taken place in groups whose biological constitution has not appreciably altered."[142] Her conclusion – that even if there were a biological base to human

---

[140] An earlier version, in *Century*, 117 (1929), 641–649.
[141] Benedict, *Patterns of Culture*, pp. 10–19.
[142] *Patterns of Culture*, pp. 234–235.

behavior it would be largely irrelevant – was not revolutionary, and within a few years it became the dogma. Today, however, it is again a source for major conflict among scientists.

Like other successful authors, Benedict was not spared criticism.[143] The attacks on Mead and Benedict, even if years apart, stressed a similar point: that both had presented selective and limited data. Critics are no doubt correct in that alternative and additional information on the case studies in the two books is missing. In this, critics and future studies supplemented a supposedly one-sided description by presenting a more complicated view. But both Mead and Benedict expressed sufficient reservation in their own texts, indicating that their conclusions ought to be considered as "ideal types." The more accurate ethnographical part of the study was presented by both in the description of the deviants within the society. What the critics objected to mostly was the public legacy of the books, the simplified conclusions generated by lay and professional reviewers alike. The simplified message was partly a result of the wide appeal of the books: in its dissemination, it was diluted, and qualified statements were ignored. Instead, the focus was on psychological configurations and types which were accessible ideas. In place of biological simplification, the cultural type was introduced, but it too remained on the declarative level. Both authors have been blamed for having "succumbed to the temptation to exaggerate the decisiveness with which both individual and cultural personality types can be identified and contrasted."[144] This must be understood against the background not of modern fragmented social sciences, but rather in view of the biological, sociological and psychological holistic explanations in the context of which they were written. When the older schools were either describing the rift between the primitives and the civilized as unbridgeable, or alternatively placing them on a ladder where

---

[143] Raymond Firth was representative when he wrote: "One of the best anthropological books that have appeared for some time." But he added: "Application of the discipline of scientific method to ... [certain] statements scattered throughout the book reveals a somewhat small observational basis for them and the introduction of a great many assumptions about behaviour for which no justification is offered." A review in *Man*, 36 (1936), 31–32. For a description of the critical reception of *Patterns of Culture*, see Victor Barnouw, *Culture and Personality* (Homewood, IL: Dorsey Press, 1963). Also M. Harris, *Anthropological Theory*, ch. 15.

[144] Harris, *Anthropological Theory*, p. 409.

primitives rank along with civilized children and neurotic adults, Mead's and Benedict's solutions were far more sophisticated.[145]

This evidently raises the difficult question of similarity and differences between Western and non-Western societies. Without exploring the complexity of the problem, it is sufficient to show that Mead and Benedict were not consistent on the issue. *Coming of Age in Samoa* was based on differentiating between the cultures. Had the description of the Samoan adolescence sexuality come from the pen of a hereditarian racist, enough in American culture would have sustained the argument of a Samoan's inferiority and a traditionally over-sexed primitive. This no doubt would have fitted part of the American scene as well as, or better than, the exotic interpretations supplied by Mead. Despite the sexual liberation of some Americans, the majority adhered to the older Victorian morality. Sexual liberation was accepted by only a very limited group. Mead did not repeat the dichotomy in her other studies of the South Sea Islands, illustrating instead the similarity between primitives and the civilized. Benedict, for the sake of clarity, divided the Indians into two types, Dionysian and Apollonian. Although this blurred the real differentiation within the Indian diversity, the polarized division was no longer primitives versus the Western world; but was replaced by a dichotomy, according to types, and applicable to all humans. This was the main reason for describing the configurations, and the reason for its success. The content of the studies was important, but from the perspective of the debate over race and the environment-heredity controversy, these were even more significant in that they were the outcome of scientific work based upon the best credentials. Differences could be meaningful or not, normal or deviant, ascribed to biological or cultural factors, but it was up to the author to interpret the finding, as long as the data could support it. In this Benedict and Mead presented an alternative to race studies. Their writings became popular at the time when Americans were distancing themselves from scientific naturalism and ready to

---

[145] In England, Charles Seligman published *Psychology and Modern Problems* (1935) and spoke about definite evidence that psychological differences exist between Australians and European Caucasians, and compared Benedict's Dionysian and Apollonian types to Extrovert and Introvert. This was also the subject of a symposium of the British Psychological Society (Medical Section) and the Royal Anthropological Institute in 1936. See *Man*, 36 (1936), 113–114.

embrace a new understanding of the primitives. Cultural relativism had freed anthropology from the shackles of biology, which concurrently was divested by its own experts of any claims to pertinent knowledge which could explain cultural attributes.

PART II

Biology

CHAPTER 3

In search of a biology of race

Anthropologists were more eager to classify races than to define them. Ever since Darwin, the perception of biology as a science that uncovered the mystery of life and deciphered the enigma of evolution had captured the imagination of non-biologists. It was believed that biology held the key to solving social problems. Most of the anthropologists who classified races assumed that biologists had defined the essence of human races, a belief many biologists encouraged. After 1900, enthusiasm for racial classification combined with the hereditarian fervor kindled by the rediscovery of Mendel's Laws brought the popularity of race studies to new heights.

As shown above, anthropologists, and especially physical anthropologists, had no means of evaluating competing methodologies, and their commitment to the study of race was based on a blind faith that their important subject enjoyed fundamental scientific support, even if the details were not all clear. Elucidation was left finally in the hands of biologists who, with the growth of experimental genetics, were becoming more skeptical of their ability to deliver a methodology for racial classification. This inability of biology to supply satisfactory answers to social questions allowed social scientists to carve for themselves a growing space. Cultural and social anthropology largely replaced both physical anthropology and the old ethnology which was based on biological explanation as the frontier of the discipline. Yet anthropologists remained committed to accepting the judgment of biology, were one provided. So while the professional expertise of the anthropologists was sought in classifying races, and even in deciphering the meaning and implication of race, it was left to the biologists' expertise to define the applicability of biology to the study of human races.

Biology, in the meantime, was in a methodological chaos of its own. Continuous – discontinuous, mutation, contamination, ortho-genesis, Neo-Lamarckism, Mendelism, biometrics. These were some of the alternatives proposed by the unparalleled theoretical turmoil in biology during the first two decades of the century.[1] Which of them was supposed to be Darwinian? The public and even scientists in other disciplines were aware of the turmoil only in varying degrees, and knew even less about its exact substance and the relative positions of the various schools. Natural selection had supposedly been established as the mechanism of evolution, though opinions varied as to the exact meaning,[2] and Lamarckianism still had its supporters. George Bernard Shaw (*Back to Methuselah*, 1921) was its leading popularizer-philosopher and the Austrian biologist-charlatan Paul Kammerer, presented experimental results on toads in the twenties which supposedly showed an inherited morpho-logical change resulting from a change in environment. Most biologists rejected these experimental results – which, apparently were a fraud – but the whole episode did not add confidence or stability to the discipline in the short run. Many scientists continued to believe in the existence of use inheritance, including a number of biologists headed by the Englishman E. W. MacBride who throughout the twenties maintained a high profile in the public discussion on biological questions. Genetics grew rapidly after 1900. In Britain William Bateson, the Cambridge zoologist, became the prophet of the new discovery, which within a few years he named genetics. But Mendelianism, as the school was known in the early years in Britain, was not accepted without a scientific struggle. In the controversy between the biometricians and the Mendelians, the biometricians, headed by Ralph Weldon and Karl Pearson, contes-ted Mendelianism as metaphysical because the genes, the supposed units of heredity, could not be observed.[3] Biometrics was the

[1] The literature on the history of biology is growing fast and it would be presumptuous to attempt a detailed bibliography. A good synthetic work is Peter Bowler, *Evolution, The History of an Idea* (Berkeley: California University Press, 1984). A more detailed work, though accessible to the lay reader, is Ernst Mayr, *The Growth of Biological Thought: Diversity, Evolution and Inheritance* (Cambridge: Harvard University Press, 1982).

[2] P. Bowler, *The Non-Darwinian Revolution* (Baltimore: Johns Hopkins University Press, 1988).

[3] This is a well documented scientific dispute. See William B. Provine, *The Origins of Population Genetics* (Chicago: Chicago University Press, 1971), chs. 2–3. P. Froggart and N.C. Nevin, "The 'Law of Ancestral Heredity' and the Mendelian Ancestrian Controversy in England, 1889–1906," *Journal of Medical Genetics*, 8 (1971), 1–36; and "The 'Law of Ancestral Heredity': Its Influence on the Early Development of Human Genetics," *History Of Science*, 10 (1971), 1–27. L.A. Farrall "Controversy and Conflict in Science: A Case

application of statistical methods to biological questions. An early example of it was Galton's "law of ancestral inheritance," on the basis of which Pearson had shown that a selection of a specialized segment in the population would have a permanent inherited effect.[4] If, in hindsight, the biometrician challenge seems to have been a mole hill rather than a mountain, this was certainly not the case during the first decade of the century. In 1902 the academic credentials of the biometricians were superior to those of the Mendelians. Weldon had been a Professor of Zoology at University College during the 1890s and became Professor of Comparative Anatomy at Oxford; Pearson was Professor of Statistics at University College, while Bateson had a relatively junior position as a Fellow at St John's College. The rediscovery of Mendel's work came when both biometricians were at the height of their careers and when Bateson was already engaged in a dispute with them over the question of variations.

The biometricians – the Darwinians – were committed to explain evolution in terms of continuous variations, while Mendelians believed that they were dealing with discontinuous characters. Since Bateson was the first in England to adopt Mendelism, his version of it was discontinuous heredity, almost forced the biometricians to reject the idea. For Bateson, peas were either green or yellow, tall or small, while the biometricians preferred the bell-shaped curve as a model for describing continuous small variations. Darwinism and Mendelism were thus understood as conflicting alternatives not as complementary concepts. Mendel's laws were supposed at first to explain heredity, not evolution; the transmission of characters, not their change. In retrospect it is easier to understand their mistakes. First, the distinction between phenotype and genotype did not exist. Genetics also meant a one-to-one relation, each gene being responsible for one character which in turn was determined by only that gene. The belief was "what you see is what you have." If characters alternate, that would mean lack of continuity. But would evidence of continuity mean soft (Lamarckian) inheritance or was there an intermediate stage? The concept of

Study – The English Biometric School and Mendel's Laws," *Social Studies of Science*, 5 (1975), 269–301. Donald A. MacKenzie, *Statistics in Britain, 1865–1930. The Social Construction of Scientific Knowledge* (Edinburgh: Edinburgh University Press, 1981), ch. 6.

[4] For example, inbreeding among tall people would produce a taller population in the next generation. Galton himself believed, however, that they would regress to the average, and that only mutations can explain evolution.

genes was introduced, but then these were good only as long as one believed in them. At the time they were often treated merely as theoretical entities. While the biometricians' rejection of genetics as metaphysical was generally disputed within a decade, their position that variation and heredity were not contradictory but mutually reinforcing functions, turned out to be an important factor in the later synthesis.

Despite the methodological disagreements, members of both schools subscribed to the widely held racist beliefs which were grounded in the speculative nature of much of the early genetics. The best antidote to the conjectural nature of these theories was experimental work. Within a short period it was recognized that mutations, the mechanism of genetic change, were neither large nor directed. Biologists began to look for a synthesis of Mendelianism and selection upon recognizing the complexity of heredity even in the simple organism. This experimental knowledge did not lend itself to the explication of social and cultural characteristics either at the individual or at the racial level. To the degree that internal developments in biology shaped the refutation of scientific racism, it was this growing sophistication of experimental work which closed off many earlier viable options. Genetics forced scientists to tread carefully and to acknowledge the falsity of many previous claims, but it still left sufficient space for bigoted racial conjectures. Population genetics and the new evolutionary synthesis could lend credibility to either a racist or an egalitarian interpretation. It turned out to be predominantly anti-racist, but that was for political reasons.

In 1920, biologists accepted and advocated simplistic biological reductionism as an explanation of human differences, and where contradictory interpretations existed, they were a result of emphasis. Over the next two decades, many biologists sought greater sophistication in explaining the relations of environment and heredity in the making of an organism. A few became, as a result, more egalitarian, placing greater stress on environmental aspects and acknowledging that scientists were ignorant with regard to the possible cultural implications of biology. At the other end of the spectrum were those who sought to rank the classification of human groups as species, attributing differences to earlier prehistorical or even zoological periods, and claiming these to be so deeply entrenched that they could not be bridged by any social changes.

Despite unresolved scientific questions, the egalitarians were to prevail, both for epistemological reasons but even more so due to the political contexts of the debate.

The early studies of human heredity both in England and the United States were closely associated with eugenics. But by 1930 British human biologists began to carve themselves a new space beyond eugenics and gained an edge over their American counterparts. Subsequently, this proved to be crucial to the shift in the meaning of race. This relative flourishing of human biology in Britain was partially a historical coincidence – the convergence of a few truly outstanding personalities among the British biologists. Most of them entertained liberal or left-wing sympathies and translated these during the thirties into an anti-racist commitment. But perhaps more important was the relative lack of interest among the British public in the question of race: hence racism did not encapsulate the field of human genetics. This left a somewhat more open space for scientific research, relatively free of political bigotry. The American situation, by contrast, was dominated by the rabid racism of the xenophobic 1920s. This militated against any intensive study of human biology which, as a result, barely existed in the United States.

Biologists who wrote as universal savants and popularizers were often partisans. With the overall growing political polarization during the 1930s, the subtleties of the debate on race left even the educated public confused. Yet, despite the presence of rival interpretations, the knowledge of genetics and the prestige of biologists grew. Concurrently, there was a generational shift in the discipline of biology. The savants of the older generation, were replaced by younger – mostly socially progressive – biologists who became leaders of public opinion during the thirties. This trend had many exceptions. Biology was not then – any more than it is now, as the debate on sociobiology shows – a unified science with an agreed subject matter, research program, or way of interpreting data. None the less, by divorcing "scientific" from "political" discourse, biologists conveyed to the public the sense that there was a paradigmatic science, ignoring the political agenda at the very heart of human genetics.

The following description begins with a kaleidoscopic view of race among the first post-1900 generation: The focus then shifts to the biometric school and the work of Karl Pearson, a founder of the statistical approach to biology and, up to the mid-1930s, an active participant in its application to the question of race. It then describes the work of two geneticists who maintained their racist positions throughout life, almost regardless of the changes taking place around them. These were the American leader of the eugenics movement, Charles Davenport, and the British conservative Ruggles Gates. Neither enjoys a lasting intellectual legacy, but at the time both exercised great professional power. The story then moves to the liberal wing and examines the view of one American, H. S. Jennings, and one English leading biologist, J. S. Huxley, illuminating the close affinity and shared vocabulary between them and the conservatives. This becomes more apparent when compared with the conservative Raymond Pearl, who was Jennings's colleague at Johns Hopkins. The received historical view that Pearl was an anti-eugenicist is investigated and reevaluated. Another politically conservative and even more prominent geneticist was Ronald Fisher, who serves as the best proof that internal advances in science did not, in and by itself, force a rejection of racism. Fisher's position illustrates how a traditional view of eugenics was compatible with population genetics.

After examining these several movements which did *not* lead to the decline of racism, the discussion moves to the group of biologists who provided the leadership in the refutation of racism. Their work is described firstly in terms of how it facilitated the non-racist application of biology. This is followed by account of their explicit denunciation of racism, and their cooperation with anthropologists.

The broad-based account offered here tries to emphasize the substantial overlapping of ideas among those who were perceived as uncompromising rivals. The obvious differences between racists and non-racists should not be minimized. None the less, the debate over the application of biological knowledge to the classification of human groups, and the distinction between nature and nurture was essentially conjectural, and both parties presented hypotheses divorced from scientific data. Specific knowledge of racial differentiation mostly disproved earlier claims, but provided no pertinent solutions. Applying new experimental or theoretical knowledge to the question of race was therefore shaped largely by external non-scientific factors. There was no telling that the legacy of the British biologists of the thirties would be anti-racist, nor that their

American counterparts would hedge their bets. This was a result of an interplay of social, political and scientific beliefs.

A number of prominent geneticists who had written on race and eugenics during the early 1900s remained during the next two or three decades the leaders of the discipline holding prestigious academic positions despite the growing rejection of their work. It is only with great limitations that one can point to "representative" scientists within this older, small group. Nevertheless, there was a shared attitude among geneticists on the question of race, exemplified by William E. Castle and Edward M. East, professors of genetics at Harvard during most of the period under discussion, and Reginald C. Punnett who held a similar position at Cambridge. Despite the general fundamental consensus British and American geneticists differed substantially in their interpretations of how the data on flora and fauna should be correlated to the taxonomy and nature of human beings, namely racial classifications.

The most obvious difference between the two scientific communities was that up to the mid-twenties, American biologists were more involved in commenting on racial questions publicly, a role which the British mostly avoided. When the British wrote on race, they refrained from duplicating the commitment and exaggerated claims advanced by Americans to explicate race in the name of biology. The imprudence of some of these earlier American comments was in part the reason for the relative absence of younger American geneticists from public involvement during most of the thirties who refrained from confronting the elders of the discipline, and concentrated in alternative areas. In contrast the earlier British reticence was partly a result of the harsher professorial rivalry in Britain, which diminished the social stature of these scientists as universal savants. This, however, exposed biologists less to public criticism, a situation which facilitated the later public prominence of the younger British group before World War II.

William Castle began his career before the rediscovery of Mendel's Laws on heredity, adopted the new science, and became one of its leaders. East, who was younger, joined the ranks a few years later. Both displayed idiosyncrasies and misconceptions while contributing to the developing field of genetics, but if ever there were representative geneticists during those early years, they were Castle and East. Their views illuminate the way geneticists perceived how the embryonic science interacted with social and political questions, and more specifically exhibit the sort of speculation which shaped this vastly unknown field. In the name of progress and liberalism, against religious fundamentalism and anti-evolutionism, and in face of rapid social change, these scientists reasserted social values by virtue of their scientific credentials. Did their scientific knowledge determine their substantive position on the question of race? Was it pertinent to their role as intellectuals in the cultural discourse? Conventional wisdom answered yes to both questions: the scientists believed it to be the case and the public consented. But that perception is dispelled by their writings.

Both Castle and East were born into Old American families in the Midwest, where they began their careers before moving to the East. With great talent and hard work they achieved the highest positions in American academic life, teaching at a top university and belonging to important national scientific institutions. In the second and third decades of the century, when they offered commentaries on the present and future of Homo sapiens and American society, they were at the height of their careers. Both belonged to the establishment, were members and advisers of various academic societies and boards, taught many of the rising stars of the younger generation, and quoted each other's work. Their views on race represented the mainstream, while others who held similar hierarchical positions – for instance, Herbert Jennings or Raymond Pearl – were characterized by a more individualist approach which deserves a special analysis. A historical reconstruction which relates scientific research to social views faces the risk of reversed determinism. Notwithstanding, we must be aware of the fact that although these scientists translated their research results into social opinions it did not mean that the latter were actually related to their science. Science might very well have been just an instrument to distill social prejudice.

Castle was a zoologist whose research centered ·on small mammals. His main interest was in discontinuous variations, which he analyzed through experimentation on various Mendelian traits in guinea pigs and rats. Up to 1919 he rejected the basic Mendelian premise that genes, the units of heredity, pass "pure" and unmodified to the next generation. He preferred to explain intermediate characters with a "blending" theory which countered the alternative multiple factor hypothesis. He recanted his – by then anachronistic – views in a public statement in his seminar at Harvard, opening his remarks by saying that when he told his wife he was going to "correct" his views her response was that "he had spent a good deal of time recently in unsaying what he had said in previous years." Castle admitted this, but for him it represented the essence of progress.[5] Shortly afterwards Castle began to criticize eugenics publicly. Since he was one of the first geneticists to do so, his change of heart dealt a major blow to the presumed consensus among biologists on the matter. His criticism was amplified in the late twenties, and following his attack on Davenport's study of race mixture in Jamaica, the dispute between them became public.[6]

Castle wrote mostly for scientific journals and refrained from semi-popularization. His *Genetics and Eugenics*, the most successful textbook on the subject,[7] best conveys his views on eugenics by 1920. Even in the earlier edition, Castle directed incipient criticism at Davenport and the eugenics school, although he remained a member of the Eugenics Society. The book's message is confused; not only did Castle present both the hereditary and the environmental positions while adding his own critique, he also made hypothetical and contradictory statements. Ostensibly, he claimed to present a scientific epistemology with eugenics as an addendum – barely one seventh of the book. He left himself an escape route by implying a pluralistic position: "there is room for difference of opinion concerning such matters, which are not primarily biological, but sociological."[8] One may assume this awareness would have inhibited his enchantment with conjectures, but such was not the case. When he cited, for instance, Eugen Fischer on race-crossing between the Boer and the Hottentot in South-West Africa (which was on the whole favorable with "no evil consequences," a

[5] Years later Castle referred to his "stubbornness" on the issue. L.C. Dunn, "William E. Castle," *Biographical Memories of the National Academy of Sciences*, 38 (1965), 43–44. Castle used the term "contamination" to explain why meiosis in heterozygotes caused white color to appear in black coated guinea pigs. This was the last theory of "soft" inheritance. Mayr, *The Growth of Biological Thought*, p. 785.

[6] Davenport-Castle correspondence in CBDP. Also Ludmerer, *Genetics and the American Society* (Baltimore: Johns Hopkins University Press, 1972), pp. 79–80.

[7] The book had four editions and numerous printings, 1916–1929. Quotations are from the 1920 second edition, the 1921 printing. Castle, *Genetics and Eugenics* (Cambridge: Harvard University Press). Also Kevles, *In the Name of Eugenics* (New York: Knopf, 1985), p. 69.

[8] Castle, *Genetics and Eugenics*, p. 267.

mixture which, indeed "produces a vigorous sound race") he maintained despite the empirical study that "from the viewpoint of the superior race there is nothing to be gained by crossing with an inferior race." Although the superiority of a race could not be ascertained purely by biology, Castle opposed race-crossing, justifying it by analogy to horses. The good, pure race horses are never crossed "unless a new type of animal is desired," indicating there was no need for racial crossing since no one was planning a new human type.[9] In a sense, Castle can almost be said to have displayed prejudice by default since he merely repeated conventional beliefs. In later years, his analysis highlighted the flaws in the eugenics argument. He overcame his hesitations to confront Davenport, his former teacher, and many of the conventions of his class and peers. As a member of the original community of eugenicists, the significance and limitations of Castle's criticism are illustrated when he is compared with his close associate at the Bussey Institute for Applied Biology at Harvard, Edward East.

By 1910, a few years after completing his dissertation and the year he was appointed to his Harvard professorship, East had made his most significant contribution to genetics as an almost co-discoverer of multiple factors in heredity. The Swede Nilsson-Ehle had made the finding a year earlier, but East's discovery was none the less independent and important, and it meant that there was no further need for the "blending" hypothesis. This was part of his life work on hybrid corn, which had significant economic consequences. However, from the perspective of race concepts, his views on different kinds of hybrids had far more dramatic implications. He published much on social questions, especially on biological consequences of birth control and Neo-Malthusian concerns over population explosion.[10] It seems that the best approach to East's positions on the racial question is by way of the two chapters from his book *Heredity and Human Affairs*, which directly addressed the race question.[11] East prefaced his chapter on "Some Specific Race Problems" with a statement in favor of rationalism, and against the emotionalism characteristic of the racial generalization which is "so

---

[9] Castle, *Genetics and Eugenics*, pp. 269, 265.

[10] For example, "Population," *Scientific Monthly*, 10 (1920), 603–624; "Civilization at the Crossways," *Birth Control Review*, 7 (1923), 328–332; *Mankind at the Crossroad* (New York: Scribner, 1923), with many other popular articles in these as well as in *Scribner's Magazine* on similar themes.

[11] East, *Heredity and Human Affairs* (New York: Charles Scribner's Sons, 1927).

inarticulate as to appear almost instinctive. Upon analysis, many of these prejudices become absurd." He went on to describe some of the irrationality in Jim Crow and other racial prejudice, but was quick to add that he did not mean to object to the practices: "I merely want to see our customs take on some degree of rationalism; I should like to have a just treatment for all if that is possible." Alas, if only racial prejudice could be substantiated rationally, it would have been a notable stage in the improvement of the race. His "unprejudiced maxims" included enrollment in university according to merit, as well as severe restrictions on immigration, "but on scientific grounds," taking into consideration "racial amalgamation with eugenic standards ... in mind."[12] East knew that these kinds of mores could not be expected to please any side in the political debate, but that was exactly his proof of why his prejudices were apparently rational and based on scientific objectivity. He rejected as "sheer nonsense" the claims that attributed defects "of a mongrel stock to hybridization." But despite these reservations, he retained a belief in racial hierarchy and asserted that "some stocks are undesirable grafts upon other stocks." As opposed to Castle, who was happy to point out the existence of successful amalgamation among various races, East interpreted the results of miscegenation as poor, even in the best of cases such as the same Boer-Hottentot mixture. While the offsprings were "admirably fitted for primitive agriculture," as well as "strong, healthy reasonably industrious, and highly efficient at reproduction," he felt confident that none would argue "they are superior even to the dull and stolid Dutch peasant who gave them one side of their ancestry." East, a geneticist and a rationalist, resorted in the final analysis to intuition: "there is a residuum of race prejudice having a sound biological basis."[13]

East could not offer biological support for his prejudices. He spoke about the geneticist's reluctance "to recommend union between extreme racial types on theoretical grounds – a position not determined by preconceptions of racial superiorities or inferiorities," adding that as groups the colored and the American Indian "have little of genetic value to contribute to the higher white or yellow subraces." This he tried to substantiate with a series of demographic speculations aimed at proving that the black population did not produce eminent men. Any eminence there was in that race was a result of the heredity from whites through the

12 *Heredity*, pp. 180, 182.   13 *Heredity*, pp. 186, 184.

mulattos. Such was his response to *The New Negro: An Interpretation*, which presented the cultural achievements of blacks in the United States, and was a hallmark in the Harlem Renaissance. By and large, East did not contest its intent ("despite some nonsense it contained about the value of primitive negro art"); rather he disputed that the achievements were those of blacks. Of the personalities described, "No single one is indubitably a negro in the genetic sense. As one who has a wide experience in making genetic judgments, I am forced to conclude that the developed germ-plasm causing the making of this book is nine-tenths white at least." Presumably the rest was "nonsense primitive art."[14] East's wording is instructive. His claim of "making genetic judgments" highlights the false use of scientific credentials. His "genetic" evaluation was at best conducted in a manner of a beauty contest, because all he did was to look at the "polychromic portraits of the contributors." His next step was to quantify the conjecture: "nine-tenths white"![15]

Such an analysis presented a plausible social solution for East. In his view, the white germ-plasm was so overwhelmingly dominant that it could endow even the Negro with eminence. But that obviously was not good enough, because: "In the genetic sense the black germ-plasm will remain because the inheritance of genes is alternative." East tried to offer some concrete social remedies. He rejected the idea that blacks "would be deported or sterilized" and settled for an unspecified eugenic solution.[16] East's views were in no way unusual among biologists. The social economic background, the Anglo-Saxon xenophobia, and the horizons which were opened as a result of the first years of genetic work, all tempted the scientists to offer imaginary interpretations. By the mid-twenties there was a

[14] *Heredity*, p. 196. A. Locke (ed.), *The New Negro: An Interpretation* (New York: A and C Boni, 1925).
[15] At another point he guessed that, though races overlapped, the differences amounted up to one quarter: "If the measurements of each race, for any character, are divided into about 20 equal sized classes, the average difference between races may range from a vanishingly small figure to a figure as high as five of these classes." Though the statement was abstract enough to be disregarded, its language suggests East's mode of thought. For him each 5 per cent of the population could be classified in a different racial grouping, and in order to enhance the scientific facade he quantified his speculative examples. East, *Heredity*, p. 173.
[16] East, *Heredity*, p. 199–200. In an effort to show the importance of heredity over environment, East discussed Boas's data about immigrants in New York. He interpreted the change in the skull measurements as the result of greater variability. He stated that even under controlled conditions in a laboratory there is some crossing, adding in his offensive vein of humor "and the New York women of the East Side are not grown in pint milk-bottles" (pp. 202–203). Fisher advanced a similar suggestion.

growing consensus which relied on biology to explain human nature and culture. Yet it was only then that developments in genetics, together with critical feed-back from the social sciences, began to influence individual biologists to reform their conceptions and attitudes to race.

A professional position comparable to those of Castle and East was held by Reginald C. Punnett in England. Punnett belonged to the old school and was of a "comfortably bourgeois, conservative and churchgoing" background. He joined Bateson in 1902 in Mendelian experimentation, and for the next few years the two turned Cambridge into the most important center of genetics. In 1910, when Bateson left Cambridge, Punnett became Professor of Genetics and retained the position until 1940. Despite their phenomenal early success, Bateson and Punnett were left behind by 1912, because they did not accept Morgan's hypothesis that linkage between genes (which they discovered and named "gametic coupling") was a result of the presence of different genes on one chromosome. From then on, Punnett made numerous small contributions, but was never again at the frontier of science.[17] But compared with his American counterparts, Punnett was very careful about applying genetic principles to social questions in England, as was evident from his limited treatment of eugenics in *Mendelism*. He believed in biological determinism, but was not quite sure what that meant. Accepting education as beneficial to the educated, he did not consider it to have any permanent impact on society because "it will not alter one jot the irrevocable nature of their offspring. Permanent progress is a question of breeding rather than of pedagogics." But when he tried to describe the application of scientific knowledge to concrete social questions, he was careful to limit his claims to only several traits such as eye color or disease.[18]

More interesting perhaps than what *Mendelism* holds, is what it lacks: primarily the extensive conjectural treatise on the implication of Mendelism for Homo sapiens. This guarded approach was the source of Punnett's most important, if indirect, contribution, to the eugenic debate in Britain where the mentally defective aroused more interest than the distanced question of racial miscegenation. In 1917, at the height of enthusiasm for the immediate possibilities

---

[17] F.A.E. Crew, "Reginald Crundall Punnett," *Dictionary of Scientific Biography*; L.C. Dunn, *A Short History of Genetics*, pp. 71–2.
[18] Punnett, *Mendelism* (1905; New York: Wilshire Book, 1909), pp. 65, 88.

of improving the human race (or least part of it), Punnett asked
G.H. Hardy to calculate how long it would take to eliminate the
condition of "feeblemindedness' which was a major factor in the
eugenics campaign to legalize sterilization in England. Punnett
refined an earlier estimate by East, but both based their calculations
on Goddard's assumption that there were three in every thousand
(Americans) who were feebleminded as a result of genetic defect,
and that the "real menace" of the feebleminded lay in the huge
number of heterozygotic carriers who did not display the trait.[19]
Hardy concluded that under optimal conditions – whereby none of
the feebleminded is ever allowed to reproduce – it would take 8,000
years to reduce their number from 3 in 1,000 to 1 in 100,000. The
millennium seemed quite a way off.[20]

This had a tremendous impact in raising doubts as to the effects of
sterilization and the scientific claims by eugenicists in general.
Years later, it remained a point of contention. When Fisher tried to
recalculate Hardy's results under different assumptions, Hogben
rebuked him and Penrose showed that whatever results the statistics
produced, they would be of very limited significance, since the trait
was not a unit character and, in addition, one had to reckon with the
importance of the environment.[21] Punnett was not a eugenicist and
never became seriously involved in politics. His intent to enhance
eugenic efforts stemmed from his moderate conservative views and
he did not object to isolating or sterilizing the feebleminded.
Although, like his peers among the older generation of geneticists,
Punnett believed in the heritability of social ills, his reasoning led to

[19] Diane Paul, "The 'Real Menace' of the Feebleminded: Scientists and Sterilization,
1917–1930," Ms.
[20] R.C. Punnett "Eliminating Feeblemindedness," *Journal of Heredity*, 8 (1917), 464–465,
quoted in Stepan, *Race*, p. 150.
[21] Diane Paul has recently shown that "Fisher's views were more reasonable than Punnett's." Paul argues that what matters from the eugenics point of view was the initial rapid
selection, and not the attempt to "rid the world of the last few feebleminded individuals."
Instead, adhering to Punnett's assumptions about feebleminded, the rapid decline is
evident if the frequency is expressed in the number of defectives per 10,000. Their number
would decline from 100 to 82.6 in the first generation; from 82.6 to 69.4 in the second
generation and to 59.2 in the third generation. Selection – sterilization and segregation –
could therefore reduce the number of defectives by 17 percent in the first generation, and
by 40 percent within three generations. Fisher also questioned Punnett's two assumptions
that (1) feeblemindedness is transmitted as a Mendelian recessive, (2) mating is random.
The feebleminded are more likely to marry each other, he claimed, and therefore the effect
of selection would probably be closer to 36 percent in the first generation. Fisher's
theoretical assumptions were more realistic than Punnett's, but a recalculation of his work
by Richard Lewontin shows that the first generation selection would, under the most
favorable conditions, be only 7 percent. Paul, "Scientists and Sterilization."

different conclusions and his analysis was used by opponents of eugenics to show its ineffectiveness. This middle of the road attitude became a predecessor to the liberal critique in the thirties.

Eugenics was invented by Galton and bequeathed to Pearson, who as a statistician was interested in human biology, especially from the eugenic perspective. However, his continued opposition to Mendelism distanced him from the biological community. Pearson did not pretend to separate science from ethics or philosophy. On a tour of Germany in 1879 he became a socialist, replacing his lost Christian faith, and later mingled socially with the Fabians. He summed up his ethics by saying: "Morality is what is social," that is anything that was socially justified, is morally sound.[22] In his attempts to distinguish science from belief, Pearson chose positivism. His *Grammar of Science* denied metaphysics, rejected the search for the essence of things as opposed to their appearance, and limited scientific knowledge to what can be perceived by the senses.[23] Part of his overall scientific epistemology, Pearson's initial rejection of genetics was due to his insistence on continuous variations and to a misconception that the gene was a metaphysical entity.

His rationalism and belief in progress determined his adherence to Darwinism, which resulted from his socialism perhaps more than from his interest in biology. If eugenics was a synthesis between social and scientific views, nobody exhibited it better than Pearson, though his was a very individualistic solution. Pearson broke with the Eugenics Education Society as a result of a conflict on social and

[22] Quoted in MacKenzie, *Statistics in Britain, 1865–1930. The Social Construction of Scientific Knowledge* (Edinburgh: Edinburgh University Press, 1981), p. 80, who sees (ch. 4) Pearson as a representative of the Fabians' expression of the emerging professional class who opted for socialism. Kevles, *In The Name of Eugenics* (New York: Knopf, 1985), p. 24, argues that "Pearson was concerned less with the shape of the society than with where the Karl Pearsons would fit into it." These deductions from Pearson's world view are reductions which fall short of explaining why many Victorians of a similar background and beliefs opted for different solutions. The various concepts of race are a case in point. MacKenzie adds that Pearson's "intellectual position was unique" in that he "reflected professional middle-class interests uncomplicated by particularistic commitments" (pp. 91, 92). Also B.J. Norton, "Biology and Philosophy: The Methodological Foundations of Biometry," *Journal of the History of Biology*, 8 (1975), 85–93; and "The Biometric Defense of Darwinism," *Journal of the History of Biology*, 6 (1973), 283–316.
[23] K. Pearson, *Grammar of Science* (London: Walter Scott, 1892). Also, Norton, "Karl Pearson and Statistics: The Social Origins of Scientific Innovation," *Social Studies of Science*, 8 (1978), 3–34.

scientific issues. He viewed the members of the Eugenics Society as primarily Mendelians, and opposed their moral conservatism on social questions, such as feminism or temperance. In an open conflict, Pearson accused the society of being unscientific and propagandistic.[24] Yet despite his progressivism and sophisticated statistics, his views on race manifested bias disguised by unfounded biological claims.

In 1920, Pearson delivered the Presidential address to the anthropology section of the British Association, in which he challenged conventional racialist interpretations. The editorial in *Nature* commented that it was "a severe indictment of the traditional subject matter and methods of anthropology." In particular, it attacked anthropometry, arguing that the object of study should really be psychometry "and what I have termed ... vigometry" rather than the bodily measurements. In a kind of self-criticism, Pearson asked rhetorically: "Have we trained men during a long life of study and research to represent our science in the arena, or do we largely trust to dilettanti – to retired civil servants, to untrained travellers or colonial medical men for our knowledge, and to the anatomist, the surgeon, or the archaeologist for our teaching?" Recognizing that "as anthropologists we are inclined to speak as if at the dawn of history there were a number of pure races, each with definite physical and mental characteristics," Pearson declared his skepticism regarding the existence of pure races, but added that if these had ever existed, then in Europe they carried even less of a meaning since the continent "has never recovered from the general hybridization of the folk wanderings."[25]

This was a strong statement against rigid race typology. Pearson emphasized the methodological, historical and personal reasons for denying both the existence of purer races in the past and the importance of studying bodily differences. Yet, Pearson himself had devoted much time and energy to the study of anthropology, and as a disciple of Galton believed in the improvement of the human race, as well as in racial differentiation. Pearson's long-term contribution

---

[24] MacKenzie, *Statistics in Britain*, pp. 86–87; Kevles, *Eugenics*, pp. 104–105. Eugenicists found Pearson's emphasis on environmental causes for tuberculosis and his rejection of the claim that alcoholism has negative heredity impact particularly offensive.

[25] The theoretical aspect was part of his anti-Mendelian campaign, and he called for utilization of anthropology in the service of the state. Pearson, "The Science of Man: Its Needs and Prospects," Reprint. *The Smithsonian Report* (1921), 423–441. Editorial on Pearson's lecture, *Nature*, 106 (1920), 233.

to science was in modern statistics, specifically correlation coefficients: comparing the correlation between two sets of variables
through measuring how a change in one set determines another.[26]
Pearson combined his statistics with biology and conducted studies
on numerous topics with social and political implications. Never
hesitant to display originality in thought or be called heretical as the
case may have been, Pearson declared his opposition to pure science
("for its own sake") by widening the meaning of "applied" to
include intellectual training. Within these boundaries he also
managed to capture the theory of relativity as "utilized" science.[27]
His political and social views are therefore of direct consequence for
the understanding of his science, though he would have opposed
such an interpretation. Proclaiming his scientific objectivity to be
"the cold light of statistical inquiry," he wrote: "We firmly believe
that we have no political, no religious and no social prejudices ... we
rejoice in numbers and figures for their own sake and ... collect our
data ... to find out the truth that is in them."[28]

Of Quaker middle-class origin, Karl (reputedly, it had been
changed from Carl, in honor of Marx) Pearson's family could be
seen as an ideal, or a caricature, of the Victorian family: hard-
working, puritan, patriarchal, with strict discipline for good
measure. Whatever the psychological baggage Pearson had carried
from his childhood,[29] it included a non-revolutionary socialism,
with a blend of German idealism, a liberal approach to the women's
questions (including liberal attitudes to sex) and much English
upper-class elitism. His contempt for the lower classes, which many
socialists shared, meant that unlike the Fabians with many of whom
he was friendly, he opposed enfranchising the uneducated. Pearson's legacy is impressive if uneven, yet his academic experience was
not at all congenial. He started his career as a mathematics
professor in an attempt to escape his father, who pressed him to
study criminal law. Addressing biological questions, he found that

---

[26] The results are between 1.0 and −1.0. The higher the score, the closer the correlation, and
all the scores below zero means that an increase in one variable reflects a decrease in the
second variable.

[27] Pearson, "The Science of Man," *The Smithsonian Report*, p. 424.

[28] Karl Pearson and Margaret Moul, "The Problem of Alien Immigration into Great Britain
Illustrated by an Examination of Russian and Polish Jewish Children," *Annals of Eugenics*, 1
(1925), 8.

[29] For a recent attempt to evaluate this impact, see Kevles, *Eugenics*, pp. 20–40. His
world-view was a personal synthesis which reflected various currents among reformers in
England at the turn of the century.

biologists at the turn of the century were opposed to the new combination of biology with statistics. While mathematical ignorance among biologists was an important factor, the aversion for Pearson also fed on his intense opposition to Mendelism.

By the end of World War I, Pearson was prominent in the English scientific community, yet his biological theories were mostly rejected. Estranged from the Eugenics Society, his efforts were directed towards building a school of his own, a project which was eventually to be confined to a single laboratory at University College, London. His impact on statistics was second to none, though this did not console him. His interest was in biology, but his theory of heredity was coming under harsher criticism as time passed. While over the years he trained many students, and lectured at University College London for a generation, few of his students were appointed to academic positions, and even with those who were, he often fought on account of their opposition to his anti-Mendelism.[30]

Race theories, as has been shown so far, were often molded strongly by personal beliefs disclosing internal contradiction. Pearson was no exception. If Pearson chose to address the question of race, especially its social implications on Britain, he had, like many of his fellow countrymen, practically to invent it. Granting his socialism, his sophisticated statistics, his denial of the supposed pure origin of races, and his awareness of the impact of large migration in history on biological mixture of contemporary population, one could have assumed Pearson to be an egalitarian. But apparently he entertained even stronger prejudices.

His major scientific investigation into the question of race was on "The Problem of Alien Immigration into Great Britain, Illustrated by an Examination of Russian and Polish Jewish Children."

---

[30] See for example, the relation between Pearson and Raymond Pearl. Pearl was trained by Pearson, and considered himself a disciple. When Pearson founded *Biometrika*, Pearl was invited to join the editorial board. By 1910, Pearson removed Pearl from the editorial board because Pearl accepted Mendelism and rejected the "law of ancestral inheritance." Pearl's only criticism, besides claiming that research (and time) would settle the debate of heredity, was that Pearson's policy was destructive to the journal. Yet he was very respectful and continued to treat Pearson as a mentor in statistics. Before the dust settled, however, Pearl became so upset that he responded to denunciations of his work as "superficial and careless": "I should regret exceedingly to think that I had ever published any work so extremely superficial and careless as some of the work from your biometric laboratory is from a biological standpoint." Pearson-Pearl correspondence, Feb. 15, March 12, 1910. A decade later the wounds had healed, at least partially: Dec. 15, 1932, Nov. 15, 1934. KPP-UCL, 782. Provine, *The Origins of Population Genetics*, ch. 2, p. 3.

Pearson inaugurated his new journal, the *Annals of Eugenics*, with the publication of this study. The article was stretched over three years, in five installments totalling 416 pages, and ended with the note "to be continued." Pearson published the study forty years after he first became a mathematics professor at University College London. The *Annals of Eugenics* was to be the most important periodical in the field. With its abundant scientific jargon and statistical formulas, it was directed at a limited and professional readership. His study of the alien immigration was to provide an important example of integrating scientific research with social planning. Pearson conducted his studies over many years, and his interest in the subject stemmed from earlier days when Jewish immigration into Britain was a political issue. Yet in 1925, there was no problem of alien immigration into Great Britain. The eugenicists who campaigned vigorously and successfully against immigration in the early 1920s were Pearson's peers on the other side of the Atlantic.

Twenty years earlier, in 1903, Pearson had delivered the Huxley Lecture, the most prestigious annual lecture at the Royal Anthropological Institute. Speaking "On the Inheritance of the Mental and Moral Characteristics in Man, and Its Comparison With the Inheritance of the Physical Characters," Pearson declared "I came to this inquiry without prejudice. I expected *a priori* to find the home environment largely affecting the resemblance in moral qualities of brothers and sisters," but the results, Pearson argued, compelled him to conclude that the environmental influence on physical characters was not meaningful.

Discovering that parental somatic influence and home environment complemented rather than contradicted each other, Pearson confused the influence of heredity and environment in a scholastic manner to conclude triumphantly: "Occam's razor will enable us at once to cut off such a theory. We are forced, I think literally forced, to the general conclusion that the physical and psychical characters in man are inherited within broad lines in the same manner, and with the same intensity."[31] Pearson assumed all characters to be inherited along a continuous curve. But he measured many of the data in discontinuous units – eye color as light, medium or dark, temperament in the polarized categories of quite-

---

[31] Pearson, "On the Inheritance of the Mental and Moral Characters," *JRAI*, 32 (1903), 201, 203–204.

noisy, shy-self-assertive, self-conscious-unself-conscious, popular-unpopular, and mental quality (ability and handwriting) in five sub-categories.[32]

Despite these limitations, Pearson synthesized his findings into a comprehensive philosophy of science. Anthropology must suggest how its laws "can be applied to render our human society both more stable and more efficient." Projecting the complementary action of nature and nurture in the nuclear family into society, he concluded: "education is of small service, unless it be applied to an intelligent race of men." Pearson was pessimistic: intelligence among the British was waning, reforms in education would be ineffectual, "the mentally better stock in the nation is not reproducing itself." The only remedy was "to alter the relative fertility of the good and the bad stocks."[33] To such a policy, unexpected or unplanned immigration would be detrimental. Therefore, claimed Pearson, he opposed Jewish immigration. This bias against immigration evident in Pearson's investigation of Jewish children was aimed at establishing grounds for "discrimination" against immigration in "an already crowded country like Great Britain." Pearson even outdid his American peers. Arguing that in "the present state of psychological and medical knowledge" it was possible to set high standards for immigration, Pearson raised the specter of a race of immigrants who would score well on tests but later prove unsuitable.[34] He claimed to study Jewish immigrants from Russia not because they were Jews "but because they formed a large and accessible body of immigrants." Though he praised the individual contributions of English Jews who were well integrated ("the differences are no greater than Catholic fellow-subjects"), he considered that such instances could not yield the satisfactory conclusions that only a statistical inquiry could. Probably only a few of the possible immigrants were brilliant: "no breeder of cattle, however, would purchase an entire herd because he anticipated finding one or two fine specimens included in it; still less would he do it, if his byres and pastures were already full."[35]

Pearson's study covered every aspect of Jewish heredity from

32 Pearson, "Inheritance," pp. 213–237.   33 "Inheritance," p. 207.
34 Admitting to the ignorance of science about the question of hybridization, Pearson was able to offer only an analogy concerning crosses between dogs of "the 'nordic' Pomeranian with the 'oriental' Pekinese," but even he presented this only "as a caution, not as an argument."
35 *Annals of Eugenics*, 1 (1925), 127.

historical speculations, over the intermarriage of Jews with the local population in Eastern Europe (racial homogeneity), through physique, to cleanliness of hair and body, and tidiness of clothes. These and other categories were correlated with intelligence – such as hours of sleep, ventilation of home, rent and so forth. The study concluded that Jewish girls were distinctly less intelligent than Gentile girls, whereas Jewish boys scored worse than Gentiles in good schools but better than those in poor schools.[36] Faced with statistics which could be variously interpreted, Pearson quickly concluded: "our alien Jewish boys do not form from the standpoint of intelligence a group markedly superior to the natives. But that is the sole condition under which we are prepared to admit that immigration should be allowed." Aggregate average placed the Jewish population rather low physically and mentally, besides which no one could say how adaptable their progeny would become. Despite the risk that Britain may "exclude a future Spinoza," any future immigration would violate "the law of patriotism."[37]

Pearson's idiosyncrasy underscored his racialist views. His comments about the blacks' inferiority and unsuitability to life even in Africa were undermined by his secularism; he enjoyed outraging his audience by declaring it likely that Adam was "negroid."[38] He continued to write until his death in 1936, but his fiefdom in University College London underwent a tripartite division among his son, Egon S. Pearson, Ronald A. Fisher and J. B. S. Haldane. The last two were to interpret the application of statistics to race in genetic terms, but with conflicting conclusions.

How are we to know that a given scientific theory is wrong or that

---

[36] The study was financed partially by English Jews. Pearson's litmus test of non-chauvinistic humanitarianism was of whether when it came to settle "a sparsely populated country" an individual "thinks only of his own race, or of the actual suitability of other races." Pearson after setting the rules, excelled in the test: "From this standpoint it is probable that the Japanese would be far more valuable than the men of Nordic race in many of the Pacific islands, and that the Hindoo and still more the Chinaman might, to the great advantage of world progress, replace the negro in many districts of Africa." *Annals of Eugenics*, 1 (1925), 6–7.

[37] Pearson's solution for the hardships of Eastern European Jewry was a Zionist one – strangely not that of the accommodationists among the Zionists, rather of the militants: "the Jewish immigrant must go as the Danes went to Yorkshire, with a spade in one hand and a weapon in the other. For it is not town-workers, but fruit and corn-growers that are needed, and the Arab race will not indefinitely allow soil to the man who cannot defend it." This came from a representative of the Empire who spoke of science as a vehicle of social improvement, keeping order, and assisting in governing the Empire. *Annals of Eugenics*, 1 (1925), 127.

[38] Kevles, *Eugenics*, p. 76.

it leads to a dead end? When the scientific community excommuni-
cates a scientist, a school, or a theory, the lay public accepts the
verdict. However, rivalry among specialists and schools leaves the
uninitiated puzzled. Before the mid-thirties, despite the overwhelming progress of genetics, Pearson vigorously held on to his biometrics
at University College London, training students who became colleagues, running a laboratory and publishing scientific journals. By
professional criteria, biometrics was still a viable alternative, but it
was more likely a scientific ghost, one that was put to rest upon
Pearson's retirement in 1933. The reorganization of the Department
of Applied Statistics was an overhaul accentuated by the antagonism displayed by Pearson's successor, Ronald Fisher, which was
reflected in a boycott against anyone connected to the old professor.
And none fared worse than Pearson's faithful disciple G.M. Morant.

Geoffrey Mackay Morant (1899–1964) could have been a very
competent scientist had he not climbed onto the wrong scientific
wagon. A scrupulous worker, he began as a student to cooperate
with Pearson. For twenty years he measured skulls. After Pearson's
retirement, Morant became a member of Ronald Fisher's department. But he continued to cooperate with Pearson, and was totally
boycotted by Fisher, until finally eased out during World War Two.
Morant's only support came from J. B. S. Haldane, but this for
humane rather than scientific reasons.[39] Craniometary which was at
the heart of European racial taxonomy a generation earlier, could
not by 1940 command any academic position in London. In
advocating that a readership appointment be given to Morant,
Haldane wrote that "his field is rather narrow," yet on the "metrical
side of human craniology" a "topic which is not wholly trivial," he
had "a serious claim to know more than anyone else in the world."[40]

Morant was among the most professional physical anthropolo-

[39] On Fisher and Haldane, see below.
[40] No doubt some Americans would have contested the statement, but in England Morant
did have more experience than others. Haldane to Fawcett, June 18, 1940, JBSHP-UCL,
Box 18. Morant chose to join Fisher because in his words "I had no reason to believe that I
was wanted in the statistics department." The Provost of University College London had
seemed discouraging about joining another department, and the only alternative was to
leave. Morant complained to Pearson about Fisher: "He has kept to the letter of his
bargain in leaving me alone to get on with my own work, but he has allowed me no
assistance of any kind – not even in bringing skulls up from downstairs – and has been
covertly hostile all the time." G.M. Morant to Karl Pearson, February 7, 1936, KPP-UCL.
Morant moved to the Institute of Aviation Medicine in the Air-Force, where he stayed till
retirement. John C. Gilson, "Geoffrey Mackay Morant (1899–1964)," *Dictionary of
National Biography*.

gists in England, and his activities for the standardization of the techniques of measurement were among the only internal attempts at a rejuvenation of the discipline conducted on an international scale during the thirties.[41] But the enterprise failed. The more data were gathered, the less reliable racial classification became – and the greater the confusion. One theoretical attempt to overcome the uncertainty was the elaboration of the "coefficient of racial likeness" by Pearson and Morant. This was a single numerical expression designed to measure resemblance between two racial groups by including all the known physical data, without assigning any order of importance to the various characteristics, and many calculations were done in efforts to find the coefficient among various groups. The most devastating critic was Ronald Fisher, who wrote that "while the purpose of the measurements is questionable, it is useless to criticise the details of the formula." As Fisher pointed out, the undifferentiated coefficient was "not a true measure of absolute divergence" and did not measure absolute racial affinity.[42]

Fisher's critique was published directly following articles by Morant on racial affinities in the *Journal of the Royal Anthropological Institute*. One of Morant's articles deserves a somewhat detailed reconstruction as an illustration of why physical anthropology was

[41] Morant together with M.L. Tildesley and L.H. Dudley Buxton, constituted the British committee. They had counterparts in Europe and America, and the story of the work of the committee if traced would provide a fascinating case study for the failure of a discipline through personal and international rivalry. The reports of the committee appeared periodically in *Man*, and archival material exists in the papers of Hooton, Hrdlicka, and Davenport among others. For example see "The International Committee for Standardization of the Technique of Physical Anthropology – A General Statement of Aims and Methods," *Man*, 34, 109 (June 1934), 83–86, which describes the formation of the committee: "In July, 1932, in the absence of any truly international organization in physical anthropology – the Congress of Anthropological and Ethnological Sciences not having been founded at that time – the President of the International Federation of Eugenics Organizations invited a small group of four anthropologists to form a standardization committee (with power of co-option), under I.F.E.O. auspices ... "

[42] The statistical criticism was that as a measure of racial difference "it combines various elements and the coefficient might be large, even if one feature is markedly different, whatever it may be." Fisher also pointed out that "If our value greatly exceeds the limit it only shows that our samples are larger than would be needed for the purpose. High values of the coefficient of racial likeness do not demonstrate that races showing them differ more in their cranial measurements than races showing lower, though significant values." R.A. Fisher " 'The Coefficient of Racial Likeness' and the Future of Craniometry," *JRAI*, 66 (1936), 57–63. Also in Fisher, *Collected Works*, V, pp. 484–490. Morant thought it incredible that Fisher would admit that he did not value paleontological evidence, and would concentrate solely on living populations. Morant to Pearson, July 21, 1935. KPP.

reaching a dead end.[43] The anthropometry of the people of the Swat and Hunza Valleys was of special interest as Morant described it because "they are said to possess characters which made them practically indistinguishable from some European races. Their presumed distinctness from all other races of Asia has led to some startling conjectures, such as the one that assigned them to the *Homo Alpinus* type." Morant was not a field researcher, and in this case he made it clear that he had relied on measurements by Sir Aurel Stein, himself no anthropologist. Morant was careful in recalculating data. Knowing all too well that inaccurate results were almost the rule rather than the exception, he consulted Stein on how to interpret the results. Morant worked on data Stein had collected on two different occasions, in 1926 and 1934. Naively he asked Stein: "Can each of the two groups be considered to represent a racially homogeneous population, as far as can be told from cultural and historical evidence, or should they be divided in any way?" Morant was aiming to classify the population according to racial (physical) criteria based on the Coefficient of Racial Likeness, and predividing the group into subcultural and historical units skewed the exercise.[44] Interpreting data to suit preconceived ideas of racial division was characteristic of racial studies. In this particular case the evidence shows that the adjustments of data to theory were crude.

Stein's results puzzled Morant until he discovered that "the scale had been read on the wrong side of the arm." Undaunted, Morant assumed that he could make accurate corrections even though the right way of holding the caliper[45] had been foreign to Sir Aurel Stein. Morant recalculated for the best part of the summer of 1934, verging on despair. Finally Stein sent him the original calipers in an effort to salvage the adjustments. Morant did his best with the faulty data within the theoretical limitations, which in any case did not represent reality accurately. The article was published in the official *Journal of the Royal Anthropological Institute.*[46] While few went to such an extent to adjust the data, everyone had to rely on material collected by others for comparative study. Such was the status of craniometry and physical anthropology before World War II, a once important branch in human biology that had lost touch with

[43] G.M. Morant, "A Contribution to the Physical Anthropology of the Records Collected by Sir Aurel Stein," *JRAI*, 65 (1936), 19–42.
[44] G.M. Morant to Stein, July 3, 1934, Ms. Stein 100, fol. 67, Bodleian Library.
[45] An instrument to measure various diameters of the head.
[46] Morant-Stein correspondence, Ms. Stein 100 fol. 67–92, Bodleian Library.

scientific progress. Only after the War was the discipline invigorated and brought up to date with biology.

Following his retirement Pearson, together with Morant, reexamined Boas's famous studies of the anthropometry of immigrants in New York a quarter of a century earlier. Boas's initial work had been preformed when racial typology was widely accepted, genetics and the mechanism of heredity were understood far less, and biometrics and craniometry were the only approach to racial classification. Pearson and Morant, however, were adamant in their attempts to salvage their discipline. Morant believed professionally in racial typology, but was not a racist. Concurrently with his racial studies, he participated in the Race and Culture Committee,[47] and when World War II began, he lamented that anthropologists did not do more to combat racism.

In the light of Pearson's views on Jewish immigration, it was ironic that Morant collaborated with Otto Samson, a Jewish refugee from Nazi Germany, in his attempts to rescue the notion of the stability of racial classification. Samson had been a curator in the ethnographical museum at Hamburg, specializing in Oriental ethnology. Obliged to resign, he emigrated in 1933. When he failed to get an anthropological post in Jerusalem he had to be retrained. Charles Seligman suggested physical anthropology, which was a new subject for him. Morant taught Samson "the literature providing measurements of Jews" because he said "it appeared likely that Samson would need to be acquainted with this material."[48] Even that spelled hope in the bleak prospect of a refugee. Fortuna must have been joking. The reexamination of Boas's data by Morant and Samson did not bridge the polarized position: either the change occurred because a new environment caused a shift in cranial measurements, or because Jews intermarried with Gentiles. This was precisely the same argument Pearson had advanced years earlier.[49]

---

[47] See pp. 285–296 below.   [48] Morant to Pearson, August 12, 1935.

[49] G.M. Morant and Otto Samson, "An Examination of Investigations by Dr. Maurice Fishberg and Professor Franz Boas Dealing with Measurements of Jews in New York," *Biometrika*, 28 (1936), 1–31. Pearson's assumptions of a high rate of Jewish – Gentile marriage over the generations, the only alternative suggested to Boas's environmental explanation, was unfounded. Pearson based his statistics on data of German Jewry at the height of their assimilation during the Second Reich and the Weimar Republic and claimed this to represent Jewish history as a whole. These at best measured what percentage of the Jews assimilated into German society, but not how many Gentiles were assimilated into the Jewish community. Similarly, the passing of Blacks into the white

Morant went on to retract traditional racial typology in *The Races of Central Europe*, which, as one reviewer called it, was a "carefully prepared statement." He concluded "that distinctions between races in Central Europe mean no more than very small differences between averages," and he finally accepted that cultural and linguistic differences when "accepted as a racial map" raise "the differences between populations ... to a fictitious maximum."[50] Morant had finally yielded to his data. He wrote against Nazi racism and lamented the earlier anthropologists' connivance with it.[51] This came too late to rectify almost anything except his own position. But it did indicate the direction anthropology would take after the War.

RACE CROSSING IN JAMAICA

Morant considered himself a biometrician and a physical anthropologist. Because of the legacy of the biometrics – Mendelism controversy at the beginning of the century he, like his biometrician peers, refrained even from getting acquainted with genetics. The result was that there was no field of human genetics in Britain for some time. Racial studies were not conducted by geneticists, and so the application of genetics to questions of race was largely left open to the younger, mathematically oriented biologists. These included Ronald Fisher, Lancelot Hogben, J. B. S. Haldane and Lionel Penrose, the last three of whom became major critics of racial typology. In the United States, unlike in Britain, eugenics had monopolized human biology. Claiming credentials in the name of genetics, it had given the topic a bad name. Yet, operating within the constrains of genetics, even the eugenicists of the late twenties had to contend with objections based on an environmentalist position. They tried to salvage the hereditarian position by conducting field studies to prove, first, that within a similar environment

society in the United States could not be measured. Despite the inaccurate measurements and the uniqueness in Jewish history of the German Jewry phenomenon, Pearson preferred these speculations over Boas's interpretation because these "would be widely destructive of modern anthropological conceptions." Pearson, "On Jewish – Gentile Relationships," pp. 32–33.

50 Le Gros Clark review of Morant, *The Races of Central Europe* (London: Allen and Unwin, 1939), in *Man*, 40 (1940), 191.

51 G.M. Morant, "Racial Theories and International Relations," *JRAI*, 69 (1939), 151–162. Morant, "An Attempt to Estimate the Variability of Various Populations," *Zeitschrift für Rassenkunde*, 1939.

racial heredity prevailed and, secondly, that whites were superior to blacks.

Davenport's last major study investigated race crossing in Jamaica, and was done with Morris Steggerda in the late twenties. The specific intention was to show that race crossing caused disharmonies, and thereby to refute environmentalism. A physical disharmony in this case was a statistical score that did not match the average and it did not imply any disability or disharmony in the ordinary usage of the term. While the study came under more criticism than Davenport's previous work, it was treated very much as sound science and not – as in retrospect it could be seen – as pseudo-science. The critics focused on Davenport's data, and it is important to examine parts of his argument in order to understand how he reached his conclusions. This study could be seen as representing a potential shift in Davenport's work: in this major research, he set out to compare heredity and environment. Although he minimized the importance of environmental factors, he did not ignore them. Davenport evaluated the work as a continuation of his previous position, and had the hereditarian school continued to dominate science, there would have been little reason to suspect his claim. However, the shift which, if unwillingly, he represented, is implicit in the subject matter of the investigation and the focus on environment.

The worst confusion in the study stemmed from the definition of race. In Davenport's obituary, Steggerda, his field worker and co-author on race crossing, was on the defensive: the scientific community had changed, and Davenport had become a pariah. Thus Steggerda wrote: "In all fairness, let him define race as he saw it." And he went on to give the definition from "The Effect of Race Intermingling" (1917): "A race is a more or less bred 'group' of individuals that differs from other groups by at least one character, or, strictly, a genetically connected group whose germ plasm is characterized by a difference, in one or more genes, from other groups."[52] This led Davenport to the absurd distinction of eye color as "elementary species," and such a definition remained the working hypothesis for the Jamaica study. Distinctions in eye color might be easy to observe in principle, but not in Jamaica. By definition, the decisive difference between blacks and browns ought to be skin color. Yet this was insufficient, and as even Davenport

[52] Steggerda, p. 174.

found out it was impossible "from observation of skin color alone
[... to] draw an accurate conclusion as to the genetic constitution of
a person." Therefore additional information was solicited for race
classification, such as the teacher's opinion, "for he is generally
acquainted with the parents of his school-children."[53] In practice
"along with the opinion of the teacher, a system was devised
whereby the author could make a hasty estimate and convey to the
recorder the estimate without the child being aware of the observation." The accuracy of the data can be surmised from a picturesque
description by Steggerda, who conducted a eugenic competition
similar to popular eugenic events in America: "The kind nurses in
the hospitals have given me all the babies I want [ed] ... If your
imagination is good you might imagine me in the middle of 50 nigger
babies and 75 nigger ladies, 3 Negro nurses and 3 assistants. What a
turmoil but I did it."[54]

If the definitions and classifications were muddled, the differences between the groups were mostly negligible, even on the
occasions when they were made to look important. Statistically,
the most significant physical disharmony alleged by Davenport
was the coefficient between arm length and leg length. In the
general discussion, Davenport argued against race mixture
because it produced what he claimed to be physical disharmony in
browns. The average was not sufficiently disharmonious, but "this
harmonious mean is made up of some very disharmonious individuals,"[55] a conclusion strengthened by examples of six disharmonious brown women. When one reexamines the data upon which
the conclusions were based, the discrepancies are evident. The
number of individuals upon which the averages were calculated is
not given. The total number studied ranged between fifty and
seventy-two in each race. An overall impression was given –
though not explicitly stated – that all individuals in each group
were measured for each trait. However, this was not so. In the
case of leg and arm length for instance, no average was given for
the white females "because of small numbers, only five having
been measured" (out of fifty). The number measured in the other
groups was not given, but the description of six brown women
with disharmony could be either substantial if it comprised a

[53] Davenport and Steggerda, *Race Crossing in Jamaica* (Washington DC: Carnegie Institution
of Washington, 1929), p. 374.
[54] Steggerda to Davenport, Oct. 8, 1926. Written from Kingston, Jamaica. CBDP.
[55] Davenport and Steggerda, *Race Crossing in Jamaica*, pp. 470–471.

meaningful part of the sample (and then one must wonder why five whites were too small a sample), or negligible if these were the only disharmonies discovered among seventy-two individuals in this category.

Among males, the results were practically identical for the three groups, while for the females the scores were given only for blacks and browns, with substantial differences.[56] Davenport concluded that the correlation of physical measurements "is always smaller in the females than the males, and apparently quite vanishes in White females."[57] "Vanishes" in this context should be read as "omitted," and supposedly, since lower correlation meant disharmony, Davenport's intention was not to imply that White females were disharmonious. Nevertheless, this was the most important physical disharmony Davenport found in hybrids. The conclusion did not result from an analysis of the data, but predated the study. In 1917, Davenport wrote that "miscegenation commonly spells disharmony – disharmony of physical, mental and temperamental qualities – and this means also disharmony with environment."[58] By disharmony, Davenport meant in principle, a statistical deviation, but in practice he used the term to mean incompatibility with nature.

Conventions of the scientific discourse at the time are highlighted not merely by Davenport's presentation of such discrepancies, but rather by the fact that these were accepted, and that the influence of the study was based on its summarized conclusions with little reexamination of its faulty data. Even Davenport himself presented intermediate results and interpretations which, had he remained consistent, would have turned the final conclusions upside down. For example, in comments on the psychological tests he argued that "the Brown's score is significantly better than that of the Blacks or Whites," and this was crucial in a "triangles test" which was the "most difficult."[59] But his acknowledgement of such statistical superiority did not translate into a modification of his conclusions of the overwhelming dominance of disharmonies based on a ratio of arm to leg.

[56] Males: Blacks 0.81; Whites 0.80; Browns 0.79. Females: Blacks 0.7; Browns 0.37.

[57] Davenport and Steggerda, *Race Crossing in Jamaica*, p. 297.

[58] Davenport, "The Effect of Race Intermingling," *Proceedings of the American Philosophical Society*, 65 (1917), 367. At the time Davenport postulated these striking conclusions, he differentiated between races to the degree that he viewed "a blue-eyed Scotsman" as belonging "to a different race from some of the dark Scotch. Strictly, as the term is employed by geneticists, they may be said to belong to a different elementary species" (p. 364).

[59] Davenport and Steggerda, *Race Crossing in Jamaica*, pp. 322, 327.

Physical measurements were a fertile ground for speculation. Davenport continued to presume that the blacks and the whites were "relatively pure-blooded," though "the Blacks [we]re consistently more variable than the Browns when judged from the standard deviations." But the most interesting conjectures were a result of his belief in the sanctity of a pure race. Davenport presented a hypothesis that "in the case of the Black women who carried a mulatto child *in utero*, her narrow pelvic outlet and the child's large head might offer an important disharmony." While no evidence supported this, as Davenport admitted, the motive for presenting an argument against racial mixture was strong enough for him to disregard his own finding of "the apparent ease at childbirth among the Negroes" and that "the difference in weights between Blacks and Browns is not statistically significant."[60]

Criticisms of *Race Crossing in Jamaica* were based on both anthropometric and biological grounds. In a well publicized review in *Science*, Castle argued that gene differences of the kind Davenport meant "do not involve disharmonies." Castle's attack on Davenport and his most prestigious supporter Herbert Spencer Jennings[61] was the culmination of opposition to eugenic determinism over a number of years. In England, Karl Pearson had raised many methodological objections from a biometric perspective. He pointed to inadequate sample size and disregard of family histories (were the Browns first or second generation?) but above all to the choice of Jamaica, which because of "its centuries of racial intermixture is the last place where a study of the relative physical and mental traits of White and Negro can be made."[62] While it is easy to concur with Pearson's technical criticism, his fundamental objection recalls the different developments in England and America in racial studies. Pearson suggested that Europeans of "reasonably homogeneous race" should be compared to West Africans. His interest lay primarily in the biometrics–Mendelism debate: he therefore wanted to find clear-cut differences between the groups, which would

---

[60] Davenport and Steggerda, *Race Crossing in Jamaica*, pp. 419, 421.

[61] William Castle, "Race Mixture and Physical Disharmonies," *Science*, 71 (1930), 604–605. Castle to Davenport, Nov. 18, 1930. CBDP. Davenport to Castle (Dec. 8, 1930. CBDP): "I should not have responded at all excepting that a writer in the *Journal of Heredity* referred to your criticism as having deprived "Race Crossing In Jamaica" of a certain part of its importance and I felt it might be desirable to insist that our knowledge was not so complete as your somewhat dogmatic way of putting it might indicate." Jennings approved the reply; for Jennings's support see below, pp. 204–208.

[62] Pearson, Review of *Race Crossing in Jamaica*, *Nature*, 126 (1930), 427.

indicate the mechanism of heredity. Davenport, however, was responding to the heredity–environment debate, and therefore chose groups that lived in environments as similar as possible. Notwithstanding Davenport's many faults and the inexcusable execution of the study, Pearson's principal objections were not pertinent to Davenport's environmental investigation.

Criticism of Davenport's work was becoming widespread even among his supporters. His collaborators included Frances G. Benedict, from the Nutrition Laboratory of the Carnegie Institution, who had trained Steggerda in his preparations for the field research. Benedict had been invited to contribute a chapter to the book already in 1927, well before the study was completed. He responded by saying that "it would be better to accumulate the material first and not 'draw the net' as it were, until it was pretty well in hand, for I feel as if the 'general picture' is the only one that will be of real value. Local conditions might lead to a wholly erroneous general deduction." He never wrote the desired piece.[63] Davenport hoped to receive Carl Brigham's support, who at the time was going through his own transformation. A decade earlier Brigham had written the standard text on race differences in intelligence tests. Brigham responded to Davenport:

The more I work in this field the more I am convinced that the psychologists have done a bad job in naming tests, and that the psychologists have sinned greatly in sliding easily from the name of the test to the function or trait measured ... Tests have encouraged an enormous series of hypothesized 'traits.' I feel that we should all stop naming tests and saying what they measure.[64]

In private, even Davenport was tentative in his conclusions. He admitted "that very little information existed" on "the biological results of crossing different nationalities and races," because "no suitable quantitative methods have been devised for measuring temperament, including self control, the essential elements of the ability to be able to conduct one's self in relation to the mores which is, after all, the matter in which Society is especially concerned."[65]

From a wider perspective his study of Jamaica was an admission of failure. In a larger context, Davenport was interested in race relations in the United States, and he should have studied blacks in

[63] Benedict to Davenport, Dec. 15, 1927. CBDP.
[64] Davenport to Brigham, Nov. 27, 1929. Brigham to Davenport, Dec. 8, 1929. CBDP.
[65] Davenport to Edwin Conklin, Dec. 29, 1930. CBDP.

the United States. But he never did, because he lacked the financial backing (and the methodology) to approach such a formidable subject. Hence he limited himself to Jamaica, but persisted in commenting on the race relations in America with a pretense of scientific knowledge. He postulated that "excess of neurotic conditions or ineffectiveness possibly [arose] from a disharmony of instincts introduced by the crossing." He hypothesized "that the large amount of psychosis that we have in this country may be a consequence of the co-mingling of various European and the African races," and suggested "as a specific problem a study of the crosses of the small increment of the negro population in the north and, in general an investigation of the comparative growth of negro, white, mulatto populations."[66] This taxing project, so attractive to many anthropologists, was always postponed in favor of more manageable locations such as Hawaii and Jamaica.

During the thirties, Davenport became a sort of pariah. Once retired from Cold Spring Harbor, his enterprise faltered. He had no followers, and the Carnegie Institution was waiting for his retirement in order to reorganize the laboratories. At the same time, the eugenics movement was being reformed under the active leadership of Frederick Osborn. Despite Davenport's "reformed" racism, he continued to personify American scientific racism up to World War II. In England he had a counterpart in Reginald Ruggles Gates, whose interest in the question of race spanned the six decades before his death in 1962. The racist views he advocated in the name of biology beginning in the early twenties, maintained their rigidity, despite a changing world.

A CANADIAN IN LONDON: RIGID REGINALD RUGGLES GATES

Gates was a botanist, a geneticist and an anthropologist, a conservative who on several occasions during his career was involved in major professional disputes, began his career at a time of theoretical conundrum, and never accepted the growing consensus in biology. Up to World War II he played a central role in British professional politics and presented, among geneticists, the most rigid position on race. Ruggles Gates was born in Nova Scotia to affluent parents who lived on a farm in partial seclusion, cherishing the family past and nature, tracing their English ancestry to the

[66] Davenport to Wingate Todd, Oct. 27, 1928. CBDP.

court of Henry VIII and their North American roots to Massachusetts of 1638. His conservatism and attachment to England were so strong that his greatest admiration was reserved for the memory of Brigadier General Timothy Ruggles, a maternal ancestor who had fought on the Loyalist side in the American Revolution. Gates could have chosen differently even within the family line. On his father's side he was related to Major General Horatio Gates, a prominent leader of the American Revolution. But he was a monarchist and a traditionalist, a loyal Canadian and a British subject, and an admirer of the British Empire. This conservatism determined almost all his attitudes. His attraction to England showed for the first time in 1910 when on visiting the motherland at the age of twenty eight "he immediately recognized [it] as his spiritual home." He then lived in England up to 1942, and again from 1957 to his death in 1962. Between 1919 and World War II, Gates taught at King's College, London, where he became a professor in 1921. During World War II, he left for the United States. Through his friendship with Earnest Hooton he became associated with Harvard University. Gates's professional honors included being made a Fellow of the Royal Society (1931), and Vice President of both the Linnean Society and the Royal Anthropological Institute (in 1937 he was even proposed as a president to the latter).[67] His association with the Eugenics Society was long, but he never belonged to the inner circle as his correspondence with the society's Secretary C.P. Blacker discloses. By the mid-1930s he was at the core of the British scientific establishment, commanding professional consideration whether one agreed with or opposed his views. Following World War II, Gates's support of racial typology was seen as so anachronistic and he became such an outcast, that even his obituary reflected it:

It was inevitable that, holding the scientific view he did, Gates should have become entangled in controversies on racial origins, racial differences, racial crossing and the like. But it must be made quite clear that his views were sincerely held and were the direct consequence of the scientific picture as he saw it.[68]

[67] Because Gates was in India at the time the idea did not materialize.
[68] J.A. Fraser Roberts, (former student of Gates), *Dictionary of National Biography*, together with data from R.R. Gates Papers, at King's College, London. RRGP. His notorious racism became known to wider audiences as a result of his stand on UNESCO statements on race in the early fifties, and even more so around the debate in *Mankind Quarterly*. Race formalists continued to associate themselves with Gates, and in 1967 the volume *Race and*

An examination of Gate's early racial theory in the twenties discloses surprisingly little to suggest of his future position among the most radical racists in British science and one who was to carry the banner of scientific racism for four decades. The substance of his writing in the twenties was indeed racist, but it was in no way out of line with his contemporaries. At the time, Gates and Seligman, for example, kept a cordial, friendly relationship. Seligman recommended Gates's work on Mendelism in Homo sapiens for publication in *Journal of the Royal Anthropological Institute* and relied on Gates's work for his lectures on "Races of Man."[69] Yet within a decade the friendship turned sour because of a conflict over racism. Gates's first important statement on race was published in 1923 in *Heredity and Eugenics*; although revised and enlarged, this work never fundamentally changed.[70]

At the outset, Gates ascribed the writing of the book to his moral and social commitments, since "I was impelled to write this book by my interest in Eugenics, which is in turn founded upon a knowledge of genetics."[71] Here was the specialist who volunteered to become a universal savant in the service of the general good, and who claimed a special status for his political and social views because of his professional expertise. This commitment and belief eventually turned into an almost messianic drive. When Gates entered the field of ethnology, he expected little opposition because he was trained in a different discipline. Since anthropologists could not agree "as to what constitutes a race," Gates proposed to fill the gap by the "biologists who have had acquaintance with many species of organisms and their variations" and would, by analogy, "be able to contribute something to the decision as to what characters should be regarded as racial." To this area of notorious disagreement Gates sought to add his controversial interpretations under the guise of

Modern Science edited by Robert E. Kuttner (New York: Social Science Press) was dedicated to Gates.
[69] Gates, "Mendelian Heredity and Racial Differences," *JRAI*, 55 (1925), 468–482; Gates acknowledged Seligman's help (p. 481). Also Seligman to Gates, Dec. 7 1925: "I was very interested to see in the note at the end of your paper that you think you have seen 'white' mentality as well as 'white' noses in hybrids with quite dark skins, and I am a little bit surprised too, for on the whole in studying family types I had come to regard temperament and intellect as tending to be inherited along with skin and hair colour." Also May 29, 1925. Occasionally, they cooperated on the study of race, both on the organizational level and planning a research program, as was the case in the search for "pure-blooded Ainu" in Japan. Seligman to Gates, May 26, 1930. RRGP.
[70] Gates, *Heredity and Eugenics* (London: Constable, 1923).
[71] Gates, *Heredity and Eugenics*, p. vii.

impartiality. "If these colour types could be viewed from a quite impersonal biological point of view it is probable that they would be recognized as differing in ways that are analogous to the differences between many animal species."[72]

Gates's insistence that various populations should be treated as species rather than as races placed his views on race in a unique category. He denied in principle that a single definition – such as interfertility – is sufficient to classify species, and in the following years applied different criteria to different organisms. Two decades later this led him to disagree with the biologists of the new synthesis. In 1923, when his opinions were being formed, Gates came very close to defining human races as species: "The fact that all the races of mankind are fertile with each other is no longer a sufficient reason for classifying them as one species. The present generation of naturalists is describing innumerable species of plants and animals as distinct species, although they are perfectly fertile with each other." And he thought that in *Homo sapiens* the differences "are quite as distinctive and varied as those between many described species of higher animals." This led to his inclination, and later insistence, on defining human populations in analogy to other species, though he recognized the uniqueness of "the number of differences between individuals . . . observed in man" larger than in any "other species of animal or plant."[73]

In most of his writings Gates displayed conventional bias, accepting simplistic biological determinism, such as Davenport's description of the "wandering instinct" and nomadism as biological entities. But on various points his position could be interpreted as skeptical regarding traditional racial typology, or the possibility of a eugenic improvement. Gates acknowledged that anthropologists were no longer speaking of a pure Caucasian race, but were instead considering modern European populations, and was skeptical about the practicality of eliminating racial defects.[74]

Since Gates did not believe in the biological reality of the species, and claimed it to be merely a taxonomical unit, his flexible definition shifted the evolutionary unit to the individual's level. When Gates translated this into concrete racial differentiation, he proceeded in an eclectic fashion. He adopted from Arthur Keith the

[72] Gates, "Mendelian Heredity and Racial Differences," *JRAI*, 55 (1925), 469.
[73] Gates, *Heredity and Environment*, pp. 224, 1.
[74] *Heredity and Environment*, pp. 162, 212, 159, 222.

emphasis on endocrine (and other glands) as an inherited racial character, to which he added mental differences (determined by the nervous system), and *illiteracy*.[75] Gates divorced racial traits as they were manifested in the individual from those evident in a group and, absurd as it may sound, argued that though racial characters might disappear at the group level, they were preserved at the individual level. This misconception of Mendelian segregation of racial traits was apparent in his contribution to the ever debated question on the ethnic composition of the British Isles: "Even after a thousand years of intermarriage, separate traits may still be traceable in the modern Englishman. The blend is only a blend when considered *en masse*. Alternative inheritance, and more or less complete segregation, still appear as regards single characters."[76] This separation of racial traits as entities divorced from any context enabled Gates to develop a unique theory of racism.

Gates accentuated a conventional belief that "it is folly to suppose that crosses between a progressive and a primitive race can lead to a desirable result from the point of view of the advanced race," "or even of the primitive race,"[77] into a rejection of intermarriage between any groups. While biologists were debating the merit of variation, Gates used a circular argument to turn his suppositions into theories and to claim that these were proven scientific facts which substantiated the superiority of civilized nations. Gates's point of departure was a wishful supposition: "Although the mental capacity of modern man has not increased during the historical period, yet it is *necessary to suppose* that the development of the human mind has consisted in something more than the mere accumulation of tradition" (emphasis added). Clearly, his wish, shared by so many, was to prove that civilization had gone through more than merely an acculturation process in its differentiation from savagery – that consequently the germ plasm had been affected. This he achieved in a literary master stroke by constructing a supposed hierarchy in which "the mental level of the

[75] *Heredity and Environment*, pp. 218, 221, 233.
[76] *Heredity and Environment*, pp. 232–233. "It may be added that some recent observations of my own on crosses between Europeans and negroes in Brazil make it clear that complete segregation between black skin colour and negro features can occur. One finds occasional cases of men with completely European physiognomy (including non-kinky hair) and mentality combined with dark skin, and also of negroid features combined with a white skin."
[77] *Heredity and Eugenics*, p. 225. In various forms the argument repeated itself on numerous occasions. See also p. 233.

average Paleolithic man can hardly have been higher than that of our modern feeble-minded. The Australian black-fellow appears to be an early Paleolithic survival."[78] One wonders what scientific method might have been used to evaluate the mental level of any Paleolithic man, let alone computing an average. Gates believed in the mental inferiority of the blacks in the United States, and his explanation reveals the logic in his conjectures.

Gates's method was to present a presumed, if insufficient, biological fact, to criticize its shortcoming, but none the less to use it as a point of departure for further speculation. A case in point was his proof of the blacks' inferiority: "The brain of the average negro weighs three or four ounces less than that of the average white man, but this in *itself* does not necessarily prove a lower intelligence, because it is well known that men of exceptional intelligence frequently have small brains" (emphasis added). The size of the brain could certainly not have been enough to prove inferiority in a period when the knowledge of the size of brains of prominent men was part of popular culture, and the earlier scientific nonsense on the subject had been widely discredited. Gates's argument represented the mainstream, and as a matter of course he cited psychological tests to enhance his argument. His supposition in 1923 was that the average mental ability of "pure negros" was probably much lower than the average negro which included many mulattoes. Gates linked skin color and mentality and rehearsed the popular claim that within racial mixtures the presence of white ancestry increased the average mental capacity of the blacks. This belief did not set him off from his contemporaries, but his adherence to it in the following decades pushed him outside the scientific consensus.[79]

In a divided scientific community, whenever the choice existed, Gates opted for the racist alternative. Addressing the question of differential fertility – namely, exposing the danger of a population explosion among the lower classes and the population decline of the upper classes – Gates opposed Carr-Saunders's claim "that there are only slight differences in intellectual capacities between the classes" as too moderate. His preferred alternative was McDougall's thesis, which "emphasize[d] the dangers associated with the differential birth-rate which has grown up during the last half-

---

[78] *Heredity and Eugenics*, p. 225.
[79] Gates, *Heredity and Environment*, p. 233. "Mental tests of coloured children in schools show that, on the average, lighter skin goes with higher intelligence."

century." Already in the twenties Gates considered Carr-Saunders as too egalitarian, while liberals were to reject these eugenic views in the thirties as too deterministic. Carr-Saunders revealed the ambivalence in English attitudes towards class and race. The lower classes in England presented an immediate social problem and left little room for risky academic speculation, while the peoples of the Empire were remote enough for a show of benevolence. At the same time as he hypothesized about biological differences between the classes, Carr-Saunders could speculate "that 'there seems to be no marked difference in innate intellectual power' between negroes and the modern Europeans."[80]

In 1931 Gates reiterated all these heredity speculations and conjectures in *Heredity in Man*. His writing in general tended to be eclectic, primarily relying on Keith and Davenport,[81] and denying any racial character as crucial for maintaining racial differentiation. Hence, he was ready to support fairly early the argument that the Cephalic Index "has probably been much over-rated by anthropologists as a racial character."[82] This was a strange type of relativism, which, in fact, Gates utilized to enhance his racism. No criterion was crucial; therefore, all were important. Any one criterion proven not to represent racial differences could therefore be cast aside and replaced by many others – not quite a rigorous scientific methodology and certainly one that could never be falsified. Gates was capable of declaring that "of course there is no sharp line between the most advanced and the most primitive races, but all intergrades occur."[83] But while this may sound as representing a continuum and therefore no rigid classification, for Gates it provided the essence of a racist system.

In his early writing on race-crossing, Gates outlined a possible research program integrating ethnology and genetics as part of physical anthropology. The interdisciplinary approach was perfect for "someone who is trained both as a geneticist and an anthropologist. Such an individual should be able to visit various parts of the world where interracial crosses have taken place, and where the

---

[80] A.M. Carr-Saunders, *The Population Problem* (Oxford: Oxford University Press, 1922). Gates, *Heredity and Eugenics*, p. 248. Gates chose to describe Carr-Saunders as "broad-minded and restrained," apparently not quite a compliment. Gates, *Heredity and Eugenics*, p. 241.

[81] Gates, *Heredity in Man* (New York: Macmillan, 1931), p. 314.

[82] *Heredity in Man*, pp. 324–325.

[83] *Heredity in Man*, p. 329.

original crosses are so recent that there are not more than three or four generations of descendants." Few would have answered the job description better than Gates himself, who travelled widely, first in North and South America, and later in many other regions.[84] Apparently, professional training was insufficient. Gates's conclusions were wrong because he based them on small samples in his eagerness to make a point – so much that he would infer the "Genetic Segregation In A Primary Cross" from a single family.[85] He studied four members of the family and found that satisfactory to generalize on miscegenation.[86]

This discrepancy between his flexible biological epistemology and his rigid social-racial interpretation illuminates the political and social components which determined his racial theories. At the other end of the ideological spectrum – but very similar in creating a scientific facade for a committed position in the debate on the politics of race – was the anti-racist alliance that developed since the late 1920s among liberals and left-wingers (see Chapter 5). Professional cooperation between scientists based upon ideology, was the foundation for the Marxist collegiate, just as it characterized their opponents on the political right and the relationships between Gates and Ronald Fisher. This ideological comradeship bridged at times over scientific disagreements. Hence Gates often quoted Fisher much, and Fisher supposedly had high regard for Gates's work. Though each had a quarrelsome personality, which was manifested in their relations with various other scientists, their mutual sympathy stemmed from their shared conservatism and carried over into scientific support. Both were quick on other occasions to criticize peers with whom they disagreed, but refrained from criticizing each other, thus forming an unofficial conservative united front.

But before moving on to analyze the polarized wings of the political spectrum, attention should be paid to two scientists who are remembered in the public memory as egalitarians: Julian

---

[84] "Mendelian Heredity and Racial Differences," *JRAI*, 55 (1925), 470. Also *Heredity and Eugenics*, p. 228.

[85] The title of a short typescript by Gates, n.d. probably 1940s. RRGP.

[86] Gates accepted Davenport's argument of disharmonies in miscegenation which for him meant an opposition to "marriages between North and South European races." These disharmonies included "the fitting of large teeth into small jaws, or serious malocclusion of the upper and lower jaw ... large men with small internal organs or inadequate circulatory systems, or other disharmonies which tax the adjustability of the organism and may lead to early death." Gates, *Heredity in Man*, p. 329.

Huxley and Herbert S. Jennings, both of whom provide a striking illustration of what was the liberal position on race among scientists in the early 1920s, and the degree to which scientists shifted their opinions in the late 1930s.

CHAPTER 4

The limit of traditional reform

The true extent of scientific racism can best be grasped through its appeal to what is not normally seen as its constituency, namely to the liberals among scientists. This group consisted of the scientists who due to their political beliefs were made aware of the sinister character and consequences of racism, and provided a potential intellectual leadership to combat racism. However, their acquiescence to contemporary conventional views illustrates the difficulties in disentangling the racist web. At the same time, it suggests why once they broke with the consensus their critique was so effective: as insiders their views enjoyed the respectability both of science (the expert) and culture (the intellectual). This type of involved scientist was much more prevalent in Britain than in the United States, but recently scholarship on eugenics has claimed American counterparts in Herbert Spencer Jennings and Raymond Pearl. Jennings, a liberal, and Pearl, a conservative, fell short in their critique of racism as compared with the British group. In tracing in some detail the development of racial thought among these biologists, it is possible to delineate national as well as individual differences. As will be shown, a distinct political discourse shaped the scientific perceptions of race, and may account for the lack of American biologists among the intellectual leadership in the anti-racist campaign before World War II. The British group included J. B. S. Haldane, Lancelot Hogben, Lionel Penrose and Julian Huxley, the last of whom changed his views on race most dramatically. It is through examining his views in the early 1920s that one can grasp the enormity of the transformation within fifteen years.

A RACIST LIBERAL: JULIAN HUXLEY'S EARLY YEARS

In 1924, upon returning to England from a tour of the United States, Julian Huxley wrote a series of articles for the *Spectator* in which he stated that "the negro mind is as different from the white mind as the negro from the white body."[1] Huxley was a young scientist who had captured the headlines with his discoveries of "the secret of perpetual youth and renewed vigour, the determination of sex, and the curing of certain human diseases."[2] Even if these claims sounded somewhat exaggerated, they gave him a good press. His impressions of America generated much interest, and were valued as scientific and newsworthy. The astonishing part, perhaps, was the substance of the articles, in which the liberal Julian Huxley, who was to become an emblem of global cooperation, revealed himself as a racist; he advocated the white Southerners' point of view against the blacks, and supported the attitude of the Congress of the United States against immigration.

Huxley's fame as a liberal and a humanist on the racial question rests foremost on his opposition to Nazism at a time when the majority of the scientific community reacted indecisively. One of the best studies of Huxley's intellectual milieu is provided by Gary Werskey's *The Visible College* on the scholars of the Left. Although not one of the Marxist collegians, "Huxley was prepared to accept the tutelage of his left-wing friends, when it came to three crucial issues: The U.S.S.R., eugenics and the social relations of science."[3] Later commentators have lumped Huxley with his radical associates, but he always insisted on drawing the line between his political outlook and that of the extreme left. In this interaction between science and society Julian Huxley played a central role from the early 1920s when he started publishing popular books and articles on science. Huxley combined, as few were able, the role of the expert and the intellectual. This raises the intriguing questions of how he integrated his science and social philosophy, and where he drew the line between good and bad science. For example, why did Huxley

[1] J. Huxley, "America Revisited. III. The Negro Problem," *The Spectator*, Nov. 29, 1924, 821. The articles became news because of Huxley's prominence. See cable of the Paris correspondent of the *New York Herald* of Dec. 4, 1924, and readers' letters to the editor in *The Spectator*.
[2] *Daily Mail*, Feb. 20, 1920, referring to Huxley's experiments with the thyroid gland in tadpoles.
[3] Gary Werskey, *The Visible College* (London: Allen Lane, 1978), pp. 240–243.

during the thirties support the eugenics class bias as scientifically sound but reject its racism?

The articles in the *Spectator* were written by an English liberal who supported Southern racism and sympathized with racist scientific theories. It exemplified the shared cultural values beyond political creed based on class affinity. Huxley was a prolific writer, and though race was not his main concern, he wrote on racial questions over a period of three decades. His interest in the subject sprang from his broad scientific activity as a biologist which he interpreted according to the specific cultural context. Huxley never hesitated to take sides, often in a polemical manner, a style which he believed represented his family tradition. The most important sequel to Julian Huxley's life was the biographical fact that he was the grandson of Thomas H. Huxley, Darwin's staunch supporter. Julian carried the legacy of his illustrious grandfather for three quarters of a century, working under the "probing" eyes of the portrait above the mantelpiece. T. H. Huxley personified all the family qualities, including depressions and ill temper. In fact, these "Huxley genes" (Huxley's phrase) seemed to have been recessive, and did not manifest themselves in Julian's father, Leonard Huxley, who was therefore not considered a typical member of the clan. On his mother's side, the members of the Arnold family of Rugby were just as liable to break social conventions. Being a Huxley meant being an extrovert, and Julian played the role at its best.[4]

Julian Huxley's reputation as an eminent biologist is well deserved. His most important scientific achievement, *Evolution, The Modern Synthesis*, published in 1942, came four years after he was elected to the Royal Society – a long overdue recognition, and four years before he achieved his pinnacle of public acclaim as the first Secretary General of UNESCO. These were different facades of his work which integrated public affairs and science – essential elements in forming his views on the question of race. Though Huxley did much experimental work, his claim to fame as a biologist rests mostly on the evolutionary synthesis, coupled with his renown as a champion of the scientist's responsibility to society. During World War II, Huxley participated in the "Brains Trust," one of the most popular radio programs of the BBC, and became a household name. This intellectual ability to synthesize and to disseminate

[4] J. Huxley, *Memories* (London: Allen and Unwin, 1970), I, preface, p. 15.

knowledge from diversified sources was also characteristic of Huxley's approach to the question of race.

Experts and scientists are reluctant to acknowledge contributions by intellectuals to the hard core of science. Popularization, yes, but not original contributions. Hence, writing for the general public, by implication, taints the "pure" scientist, which is what happened to Huxley's status. This was best exemplified by his painful experience of not being elected to the Royal Society, while many scientists his junior had been elected. It led to anxiety and frustration, the more so because his only association with the academia was an honorary professorship at King's College in London. In May 1927 Huxley had resigned his chair of zoology, after less than two years, in order to work with H. G. Wells and his son Gip Wells on *The Science of Life*. The scientific community was surprised by the resignation, but *Nature* supported Huxley: "A new situation is created with regard to the purveyors of knowledge and their relation to academic institutions." The spread of popular education, commented *Nature*, "cheap printing, broadcasting, instructional films, and the systematization of popular lectures" as well as the successful libraries of the "Home University" and "Sixpenny," and the University Extension Lectures, were all seen as part of a novel trend in the popularization of science, of which Wells was a symbol, and which Huxley was about to join. The report concluded that it would be "interesting to follow the success of this new and courageous venture of Prof. Huxley." Lancelot Hogben, the left-wing biologist and Huxley's friend, was more realistic about the establishment's reception. In July 1927 he conveyed to Huxley his hope that the writing of *The Science of Life* would not postpone his election as a Fellow of the Royal Society. It did by a decade.[5]

Huxley's sins amounted to more than merely writing popular expositions of science. In addition to his outspokenness, he was a convenient target for the last Lamarckians in their continuing battle against the Darwinists. Julian Huxley had encountered an animosity that was still aimed at his grandfather. Personal, institutional and scientific issues combined to prevent his election to the Royal Society. His position outside the university system became the stumbling block, as his peers and friends kept reminding him in

---

[5] *Nature*, 119 (May 14, 1927), 722. L. Hogben to Huxley, July 11, 1927, Huxley Papers, The Woodson Research Center, Fondren Library, Rice University, Houston, Texas. JSHP, box 9.

letters of consolation. These became a spring ritual during the thirties, when the new Fellows were announced, and Huxley's name was not among them. While he did not explicitly regret resigning the university chair, he did feel left out in the cold. Against this background his election to the position of secretary of the Zoological Society was a professional and financial boost.[6]

In March 1938, Huxley finally became a Fellow of the Royal Society. In the flood of letters from all quarters, the one by H. G. Fleure, the distinguished geographer and anthropologist, and an authority on the question of race, struck a representative note by stressing Huxley's "championship of science in our social life."[7] By then, the preoccupation with relations between science and society had become fashionable, with many journals, such as *Nature* and the *Smithsonian*, advocating social responsibility. It was in this field that Huxley left his mark, and recognition by the Royal Society came at a time when his social views were receiving growing support from the scientific community.

Huxley's early views on race did not anticipate his anti-racist position in the thirties. They embodied English social paternalism reacting to a distant esoteric problem which was believed to have no relevance to British society. His conclusions were based on ignorance and on exotic interest in a question which had a somewhat mythical quality to it. Writing on "The Negro Problem," Huxley rehearsed old stereotypes of "the minds of children:" "The typical negro servant, for instance, is wonderful with children, for the reason that she really enjoys doing the things that children do." This was followed by a long list of infantile traits, supposedly prevalent among blacks, most of all "imitating their so-called betters." To explain these, Huxley advanced two theories: one psychological and the other biological. At the time when the American Congress was justifying the restriction of immigration by the infamous IQ tests, Huxley was even more direct in his methods:

You have only to go to a nigger camp-meeting to see the African mind in operation – the shrieks, the dancing and yelling and sweating, the surrender to the most violent emotion, the ecstatic blending of the soul of the Congo with the practice of the Salvation Army. So far, no very satisfac-

---

[6] Joseph Needham congratulated Huxley (Aug. 8, 1934): "At least now you have got a position something approaching what you deserve." JSHP, box 11.
[7] Fleure to Huxley, March 1938. JSHP, box 13.

tory psychological measure has been found for racial differences: that will come, but meanwhile the differences are patent.[8]

Addressing the question of racial sex ratios, Huxley argued that the "American negroes show an unusually large deficit of males," "[T]here used to be a negro secret society which took upon itself the task of getting the occasional very white babies, who Mendelianly segregate from the marriage of pale mulattoes, palmed off as white." In order to strengthen his scientific case, Huxley quoted "biological authorities, such as Davenport" who believed that "what we should a priori expect is actually true – namely, that Mendelian recombination of the two sets of factors which co-operatively build up the well adapted negro and Caucasian type respectively, gives rise to all sorts of disharmonious organisms." Hence, it was inevitable that "whitening" aggravated the racial problem.

Then there is the undoubted fact that by putting some of the white man's mind into the mulatto you not only make him more capable and more ambitious (there are no well-authenticated cases of pure blacks rising to any eminence), but you increase his discontent and create an obvious injustice if you continue to treat him like any full blooded African. The American negro is making trouble because of the American white blood that is in him.

Social conscience tempted Huxley to offer a solution to this grave eugenic and racial question. He noticed "with relief" that, contrary to popular belief and because of their high mortality rate, "Afro-Americans" did not increase faster than the whites. He was nevertheless pessimistic because in the selection process the survival rate of the mulattoes was higher, which aggravated racial strife. He rejected various solutions discussed at the time, such as repatriation of blacks to Africa (impractical because no country would accept them,) sustaining a status quo (because of the deeply grounded prejudice, based on "a good deal of sound social and biological instinct") or total segregation, (because that would entail emigration of whites from future black states, and no one could be counted on to supervise the whites' migration.) Huxley "solved" the enigma by manipulating human geography. He advocated that the North should turn into a segregated society and the South into a multiracial society. He reasoned the plan's practicality because the migration of many blacks to the North had supposedly created a

[8] J. Huxley, "America Revisited. III. The Negro Problem," *The Spectator*, Nov. 29, 1924, 821.

demand for workers in the South. That demand could be met by Southern Europeans, who were used to the weather and "appear to have no particular prejudice against intermarriage with coloured races; and if they invade the South, it is at least on the cards that miscegenation on a large scale will occur, so that a great part of the population will be ... a new blended stock." Should this fantasy materialize, Huxley saw a need for the United States to be divided into the South, where no color line would exist, and the North, "where the negro could be kept out, or at least allowed no privileges."

While this illustrates the general extent of racial prejudice among liberals, Huxley's distinction between Northern and Southern Europe is instructive in light of his later relative egalitarianism in *We Europeans*. In his objection to racial mixture, Huxley emphasized "the well adapted negro and Caucasian type" whose mixture "gives rise to all sorts of disharmonious organisms." But the term Caucasian evidently referred only to the Nordic population of Europe. Speaking about the Southern European immigrants, in other words the Italians, or, in the anthropological terminology of the time, the Mediterranean race, he was no longer worried about the "disharmonious organism." Put differently, since miscegenation could supposedly succeed only between closely related types, Huxley's argument was that the Southern Europeans were racially closer to the blacks than to the Northern Europeans. However, like all racist theories, this was not consistent: commenting on the immigration laws, Huxley was very critical of the Americans' presumptuous claim of being Nordic: "Pure Nordics are, of course, very rare anywhere save in Scandinavia and some other parts of the Baltic Coast," and thinking about the racial history of the British Isles he added that the Nordic superiority "seems to be most productive" when "it is in harness with other bloods." Whilst agreeing that pure Nordics were "quite rare in the United States" and that the new immigrants were probably "inferior to the average American type," he justified the immigration restriction because the United States needed breathing space "to sit down and take stock of herself without changing too much during the operation."[9]

Huxley expected natural selection to sort out "the welter of genetic factors which here are thrown into interplay." Relative advantage will result in the survival of some and the change of the

[9] "America Revisited. V. 'The Quota'." *The Spectator*, Dec. 20, 1924, 980–982.

population type. Yet he was not alarmed and did not expect an apocalypse. "Personally," he wrote "I do not think that this effect will be of great magnitude ... maybe a slight average darkening of complexion." Did he imply that if the population was to become darker, the darker people had an evolutionary advantage over the lighter stocks? These quotations, in addition to their value for defining Huxley's position, are instructive for what they tell us about the dissemination of biology and the range of its applications to society in the early 1920s. If a respected scientist could use or misuse his science in such a way, one should not be surprised by the confusion in the mind of the public over the scientific verdict on the race question.

Huxley's initiation into thinking about racial theories took place when he taught at Rice University (Houston, Texas) between 1912 and 1916. He travelled much in the course of studying the Southern fauna, during which personal experiences molded his views on blacks. In an unpublished and unfinished manuscript from 1918 entitled "The Negro Minds" he wrote about some of those experiences and acknowledged their impact:

I had grown up in the transplanted Bostonian conviction, so common in Liberal circles in England, that the negro being a man is therefore a brother, being a brother is therefore an equal ... A little life in the Southern States soon taught me more about their minds, more about inborn differences of race.[10]

Many liberal intellectuals shared Huxley's racial aversions, despite the conventional misconception about English (and Bostonian) egalitarianism. Because it is relatively rare to find an explication on race by British scientists, Huxley's views, as well as illuminating his personal position, pointed to the footprints of many of his peers, whose attitude to the "lower" classes in Britain resembled the American elite's reaction to the blacks.

In principle Huxley's liberal humanism contradicted his support of Southern racism thereby afflicting a humiliating defeat to his ethical value system. Though he did not recognize it explicitly as such, when he retracted his racism a few years later he became very critical at those who did not. Already in 1924, feeling guilty, he expressed glee at the fact that the Yankees too were defeated by a similar contradiction: "The Middle Westerner and to a lesser extent the Yankee are for the first time experiencing the negro at balk and

[10] JSHP, box 58: 6.

at first hand; and there is a certain grim humour in seeing their high moral principles and lovely theoretic equalitarianism dissolving under the strain."[11]

Huxley's typology placed the "savages" closer to monkeys than the rest of human kind:

> I personally firmly believe that most men and women are appallingly far from realising the potentialities of their inheritance ... But baboons or Australian savages can have all these advantages, and will not blossom beyond their limits – limits set by their inheritance.[12]

Against this "clear" evolutionary perspective, Huxley posed the rhetorical question "Why then try to deny the equally obvious fact of inherited, germinal differences between human beings of a single nation?"[13] Huxley used racial analogies as an easy literary tool to introduce the reader to his main interest in eugenics, and to a similar but more doubtful argument that a comparable gap existed between classes in Britain. He separated eugenics from racial questions because eugenics was a political issue with immediate implications concerning the British class structure, while the race question had only international aspects, and could therefore be taken up with more or less commotion, as demanded by the changing circumstances.[14]

As compared to his occasional writings on race, Huxley devoted ample time and efforts to eugenics and the Eugenics Society. He held many official positions in the society, including that of President in 1962, and served on various committees. Perhaps his greatest influence came from his unofficial role as a member of the inner circle, involving consultations with Carlos Paton Blacker, the Secretary of the Eugenics Society during the thirties, who had been his student at Oxford after World War I, and others who could be termed the "progressives" in the society. The topics of population and birth control attracted liberal intellectuals because in addition to their scientific merit, they gave cultural legitimacy to a sexual revolution. Huxley's correspondence discloses the scientific facade

---

[11] "America Revisited. III. The Negro Problem."

[12] J. Huxley "Eugenics and Heredity," Letter to the Editor, *The New Statesman*, 1924, JSHP.

[13] J. Huxley, "Nature and Nurture," *The New Leader*, Feb., 29, 1924. JSHP.

[14] Stepan, *The Idea of Race in Science: Great Britain 1800–1960* (Hamden, Conn.: Archon Books, 1982, p. 146) points to Julian Huxley, J. B. S. Haldane and Lancelot Hogben as the three prominent biologists who "found themselves in the anti-eugenic camp by the 1930s" in varied degree. For a different interpretation see Diane Paul, "Eugenics and the Left," *Journal of the History of Ideas* (1984), 567–590. The inclusion of scientists on the left in the eugenics movement is one factor that explains the importance of the movement for the cultural history of the first four decades of the century.

given to petty superstitions concerning sex by his peers. In November 1926, the BBC tested whether the delicate subject of birth control could be discussed on the airwaves. Huxley was the chosen scapegoat and was left to face the storm that followed on his own, while the BBC publicly regretted its insensitivity in dealing with the topic.[15]

Perhaps the first written statement published by Huxley on eugenics was in a letter to the editor of the *Athenaeum* in 1920. It emphasized the extraordinary similarity between heredity in all organisms, "in all forms of life above the lowest," and argued that feeblemindedness is "due to factors in the genetical make-up which are inherited in a regular mendelian manner." Huxley's position exhibited shared ignorance among geneticists rather than a personal bigotry. This was reflected by his choice of scientific authorities, such as Davenport, who turned up numerous times in similar circumstances in Huxley's writings, and H. H. Goddard, whose volume *Feeble-mindedness: Its Causes and Consequences* was seen by Huxley as an "important book." Such naivete was common to other scientists and intellectuals during much of the twenties.[16]

Against such understanding of feeblemindedness it is not surprising that when the Mental Deficiency Committee found that there were more than 300,000 feebleminded in England in 1929, Huxley eagerly accepted the figure in support of eugenics, rather than as a testimony to the loose definition of the term. He had devoted much time as a biologist to the study of the distinction between nature and nurture, but was not as careful to point out the confusion over environmental and hereditary factors in the report. The committee defined feeblemindedness pathologically, but at the same time presented statistics which included the mentally poor who were so classified for environmental reasons.[17] His fear of the dysgenic effect was even greater: Huxley considered the 20 percent of the population

---

[15] For some of the sexual aspects of the eugenic activity, see Huxley papers. Questions dealt with ranged from popular education to "discoveries" by correspondents about masturbation. For example see JSHP, boxes 9 and 11. Also box 136, clippings of reports of his lectures in the press.

[16] J. Huxley, "Eugenics and Eugenists," *The Athenaeum*, Dec. 1920, 895; "The Influence of Heredity," *The Times*, April 2, 1930, letter to the Editor; "The Vital importance of Eugenics," *Harpers Monthly*, 163 (1931), 325; Norman Lockyer Lecture, Nov. 23, 1926, British Science Guild, (published in *Nature* [December 1926], 884–885.) For a recent study on Goddard's pseudoscience, see Gould, *The Mismeasure of Man* (New York: W. W. Norton, 1982), pp. 158–173.

[17] J. Huxley, "Eugenics and Heredity," letter to the Editor, *The New Statesman*, 1924, p. 282; "The Influence of Heredity," letter to the Editor, *The Times*, April 2, 1930. JSHP.

who were responsible for propagating a quarter of the next generation, to be "neither physically nor mentally as good as the other 80
percent." By 1930, many of Huxley's ideas on race and the inherited
capacity of human groups became more moderate. Yet his biological determination, especially his eugenic paternalism towards
the English lower classes, displayed hostility and enmity shared by
his contemporaries.

Public health and medicine aroused the Social Darwinist in
Huxley, who criticized their contribution to the rise in the survival
rate and the number of morons, because of the interference with
natural selection "especially at infancy."[18] He bemoaned in the *New
Statesman*: "The selection for survival has been enormously weak-
ened by modern medicine ... sanitation ... welfare ... pity," and
lamented that the trend "for the poorest and, on the whole, least
desirable elements of the population to have the largest families,"
had been accentuated in the previous six decades. Education was
only a fraction better than medicine, because its favorable impact
was only temporary, and hence sinister in concealing the effect of
inherently lower quality for a limited time and deceiving the public.
Both medicine and education were seen as detrimental to the
continuous evolution of the race through natural selection, the first
by keeping the morons alive, the second by camouflaging the facts
from the public eye.[19]

Huxley was among those who considered that racial degeneration
was best fought through sterilization. Unfortunately for the eugenicists, the majority of whom supported legislation to legalize voluntary sterilization, the opposition in England was hard to overcome.
Huxley envied the "successful" precedents in Switzerland and
various states in America, especially in California, where thousands
were sterilized, and was eager to lend his scientific credentials to
advocate sterilization. At times this was done too enthusiastically:
witness his claim of a possible reduction by 15 percent of the morons
within a generation, and cutting by half their number in four to five

[18] Huxley, "The Vital Importance of Eugenics – Letter to the Editor," *Harper's Monthly*, 163
(1931), 325, JSHP.
[19] See a footnote to Huxley's article inserted by the editor in Huxley, "Nature and Nurture,"
The New Leader, February 29, 1924. For an internal debate among eugenicists on the merit
of sterilization of the unfit see Huxley, Letters to the Editor, *Weekend Review*, Sept. 6, 1930,
in a polemical exchange with Haldane. Huxley admitted that "overzealous advocates of it
have here and there wished to employ it as a penal measure" but the "Committee for
legalising Eugenic Sterilisation is wholly opposed to it." "The case for sterilisation of
certain classes of abnormal or defective persons appears to me overwhelming."

generations.[20] Huxley's enthusiasm was restrained on various occasions by the watchful Secretary of the Eugenics Society, C. P. Blacker. As Blacker pointed out to Huxley, "For our purposes academic calculations based on ... erroneous premises have not much interest."[21]

In these eugenic views, Huxley the liberal supported conservative social policies, and thus it is not surprising, that he not only quoted Ronald Fisher's statistics, but also concurred with his suggestions for social reforms. The eugenic problem resulted from the fact that in any capitalist society

the two biologically independent variables of those tendencies making for success and those making for low fertility, of social necessity became coupled together. And since these tendencies are largely genetic, the result is a progressive and cumulative diminution within the population of the proportion of gene-units.

This gloomy picture pointed to the deterioration in the genes for success. Huxley enthusiastically supported Fisher's suggestions that a comprehensive system of family allowances be devised in which every family be compensated according to its expenses. The better off, mostly the professional middle-class who need more, would get more. "The injustice is seen to be apparent only. The scheme is simply to remedy the existing economic disadvantages of having children: it is an adjustment of wages or salaries to the conditions of family life." The flexible system was "design[ed] to equalize matters within each group." "It is a correction which has to be applied for biological reasons, and in applying it we must accept economic facts as we find them." For those to whom this sounded unacceptable, Huxley cordially advanced the alternative: a Bolshevik revolution.[22]

By the early 1930s Huxley had greatly modified his beliefs in a

[20] J. Huxley, "Eugenics and Heredity," letter to the Editor, *The New Statesman*, 1924, p. 282. JSHP. Blacker to Huxley, Aug. 29, 1930; Oct. 24, 1930, The Eugenics Society Archive (SA.EUG) C, 185.
[21] Some of the corrections were made before publication, as with Huxley's claim that *all* the sterilization operations in California were done with voluntary consent. Blacker's suggestion was to adhere to facts, and he tactfully changed the text to *most*. His more substantial criticism concerned Huxley's interpretation of the reduction in the incidence of mental defects. The claim was purely theoretical, based on several assumptions including the way in which feeblemindedness was inherited and the ability to stop all the feebleminded from reproducing, and therefore had no practical value. Blacker added: "I have not yet been able to find out what figure he [Fisher] is prepared to defend as being possible to achieve in practice." Blacker to Huxley, Aug. 29, 1930. JSHP.
[22] "The Vital Importance of Eugenics," pp. 326–327.

rigid racial hierarchy. The racial and the eugenic ladders were somewhat similar, both consisting of

> an astonishing variety and range of different kinds of men. From savage to Nordic business man, from hunting pygmy to Chinese sage, the race is prodigal in types: and even within the single race or nation we range from imbecile and moron to man of talent and genius ... from those who through inheritance lack moral or aesthetic feeling to those hypersensitive to virtue or to beauty.[23]

The importance of these statements resided in their supposedly non-ambivalent nature. The noncontroversial and undisputed illustrations were meant to clear the way before exposing the reader to the more dubious assertion that there were genetic differences between classes. Huxley's style may be judged as demagogy, but it is revealing in disclosing an emotional rather than intellectual racial prejudice, illogical rather than rational concepts. It asserted what is usually not mentioned – the obvious. Liberals, humanists and other egalitarians, who might have been expected to hold world views diametrically opposed to those of intransigent racists, apparently had more in common with them than they might in hindsight have wished. An illuminating example of this overlap was the American biologist Herbert Spencer Jennings.

HERBERT SPENCER JENNINGS AND PROGRESSIVE EUGENICS

Within the last few years, the historiography of eugenics has produced a sophisticated understanding of the movement. In place of a monolithic use of eugenics and social Darwinism as representing pseudoscientific reactionary politics,[24] the eugenics movement, especially of the period between the world wars, is now presented as versatile and multifaceted. At least two schools are delineated

---

[23] "The Vital Importance of Eugenics," p. 324.
[24] For the classical statement of Social Darwinism, see Richard Hofstadter, *Social Darwinism in American Thought, 1860–1915* (Philadelphia: University of Pennsylvania Press, 1944). Greta Jones, *Social Darwinism and English Thought: The Interaction Between Biological and Social Theory* (New Jersey: Humanities Press, 1980), argues for a comprehensive approach that includes everyone in the earlier part of this century as a Social Darwinist, while Robert C. Bannister, *Social Darwinism: Science and Myth in British – American Social Thought* (Philadelphia: 1979), claims that the whole thing has been made up by partisans and adversaries, and Donald C. Bellomy, "'Social Darwinism' Revisited," *Perspectives in American History*, n.s. 1 (1984), pp. 2–3, contends that Social Darwinism was a narrow phenomenon which appeared around the turn of the century, primarily in Europe, not in Britain or America, and that it was polemical from its inception.

within the movement: an older, mainline camp and a newer reform group. The dichotomy is best elucidated in Kevles's *In the Name of Eugenics* which is now the standard history of the movement in the United States and England. Garland Allen prefers the terms "old" and "new" eugenics, distinguishing between them "by the age, educational background, and ideologies of their practitioners. And in both the United States and Britain, the shift from old style to new style appears to have begun in the late twenties."[25] Current historians of social Darwinism and eugenics underscore the similarities among American and British scientists, and point to the parallel developments which took place in both countries. The debate on reform eugenics addresses then the public role of scientists as intellectuals as well as the substance of their critique as experts. Thus the following reinterpretation examines the substance of Jennings's eugenics and racial views and his public prominence. It accepts the recent scholarship which classifies Jennings as a reformer in the early twenties, but suggests that because his views subscribed to much of the eugenics world-view and remained static in the following decade, he came during the thirties to hold conservative positions while his public status remained that of an egalitarian. Thus the question is raised whether too heavy a

[25] Due to the different meaning ascribed to the terminology by Kevles and Allen, the precise nature of this transformation is in need of further clarification. Kevles formulated the concepts 1) "mainline," 2) "antimainline," 3) "reform," and 4) "new." The first two concepts are antithetical to each other, the third is closely related to the second, and the fourth refers to the period from the late 1960s onwards, and to work on DNA and genetic engineering. Allen also speaks of "new" eugenics, but for him this relates to Kevles's second and third concepts "antimainline" and "reform." Kevles's "antimainline" eugenics differs from "reform" in that it refers, respectively, to a critique of the old school, versus a formulation of a new program, moderate compared to the old school's. This distinction is important as a theoretical formulation: one can criticize the accepted version but not subscribe to any alternative eugenic plan. However, to the best of my understanding, all the scientists who in the twenties formulated a critique of eugenics (antimainliners) also subscribed to the main tenets of eugenics and supported some kind of a modified, if general, eugenics program. In this respect I treat concepts (2) and (3) during the period under discussion as referring to a similar trend, this notwithstanding Lancelot Hogben and Lionel Penrose who took a more radical stand in the 1930s, at the time when the distinction between reform and antimainline became more meaningful. Kevles, *Eugenics*, pp. 122–123, 172–175, 267–8, 295–6. Garland E. Allen, "Julian Huxley and the Eugenical View of Human Evolution," Ms. Also "The Eugenics Record Office, Cold Spring Harbor, 1910–1940. An Essay in Institutional History," *Osiris*, 2nd ser. 1 (1985), 225–264. A different interpretation is suggested by Barry Mehler who underscores the continuity of racism in eugenics. His use of the term "new eugenics" is in reference to "the resurgence of eugenics advocacy in the past three decades, i.e. since 1960." And even in this historical framework Mehler emphasizes similarities. Barry A. Mehler, "A History of the American Eugenics Society, 1921–1940," Ph.D. dissertation, University of Illinois, Urbana-Champaign, 1988, p. 21 n32.

historical burden has been placed upon Jennings's egalitarian views, and by implication whether the comparison between the transformation of eugenics in the United States and Britain should illuminate the distinctions rather than, as has been done so far, the similarities.

Herbert Spencer Jennings was born in 1868 in Tonica, Illinois. His father was a physician, and a founder of a local literary society, and his devotion to evolution and biology was a substitute for religion, evident by his sons' names: Herbert Spencer's brother was named after Darwin. Evolutionary thinking and intellectual concerns were embedded in Jennings's world view early on in life. The elder Jennings encouraged his sons to read widely in philosophy and biology, and despite unstable economic fortunes and an aborted migration to California, Herbert received a thorough education. His early career after graduating from high school took him to an undesirable teaching post in north western Iowa, which lasted three months. This was followed by three years of further studies intertwined with teaching positions, until he was finally introduced to college life as an assistant professor (before he ever attended college), when he was recruited by his former high school teacher, who in the meantime had become a professor of botany at Texas A&M. Jennings's academic career took him through Michigan to Harvard, where he studied in 1894–96 for his doctorate. There he came to know a number of biologists, two of whom he debated eugenics with, thirty years later: William Castle who was a graduate student like Jennings, and Charles Davenport, himself a young instructor, and possibly the dominant influence on Jennings during his Cambridge sojourn. Jennings not only studied with Davenport, but rented a room in his house. The course of studies turned out to be especially instructive. During the summer all three biologists [Castle, Jennings, and Davenport] worked together in Newport, Rhode Island, at the Agassiz Laboratory. Harvard provided Jennings's most enduring academic training, and Davenport's role was unique in this formative experience.[26] Yet, it seems that already by then Jennings questioned Davenport's metaphysical reductionism.[27]

[26] Based on T. M. Sonneborn, "Herbert Spencer Jennings, April 8, 1868–April 14, 1947," in *Biographical Memoirs of the National Academy of Sciences*, 47 (1975), 142–223. Here, 158–159.
[27] Biological reductionism is a useful term despite its widespread abuse in the literature. It refers to the process of explaining complex phenomena by referring to a simpler set of data. In this context, I take it to mean the belief that *contemporary* biological knowledge

Like many other American students at the time, Jennings travelled to Germany at the completion of his studies on a tour which was
as much a cultural as a scholarly experience. In his letters home he
presented his work on marine biology as a search for universal
truths through a specific research. Unicellular organisms provided
him with a rich source for analogies to human society, as he
commented on his dazzling experiences in Jena (1897)

I've been discovering some queer Paramecium tricks in the last few days.
I'm beginning to believe that one might as well stand off and watch a city
full of men, with a telescope, and make theories about the forces which
compel them to move to such a direction or stop moving at certain times.[28]

These analogies yielded two important aspects for Jennings's
work: his view of the environment as an integral part of the
development of the organism, and the search for "The Psychology of
a Protozoan."[29] Jennings considered the genetic code of unicellular
organisms to include their "gross structure," namely the environment which comprises other unicellular organisms and determined
their behaviour. He thus concluded: "Development is fundamentally adjustment to environment, in this case, to cellular
environment."[30]

In 1906 Jennings was invited to a professorship at Johns Hopkins
and at the same year published what became his most important
book, *The Behavior of Lower Organisms*. Jennings's view of the role of
environment in moulding the individual at all levels, including
unicellular organisms, was influential on, among others, John
Watson and early behaviorism. In the debate over reductionism,
Jennings clearly rejected the view that life amounted merely to
physical and chemical reactions. This unorthodoxy involved him in
the debate over vitalism, and later enabled him to disclose a greater
sensitivity to the interaction of environment and heredity; the
implication being that each level has additional properties that
cannot be reduced to its components, and therefore social characteristics could not be explained merely by biological properties.

By the end of World War I, Jennings – although only fifty years

sufficed to adequately explain cultural characteristics. It does not refer to the question of
whether such an explanation will be forthcoming, nor does it assign moral evaluation. It is,
however, a useful tool to distinguish between those scientists who viewed the available
knowledge as sufficient to buttress political decisions from those who took an agnostic
position.

[28] Sonneborn, *Jennings*, p. 163.   [29] Sonneborn, *Jennings*, p. 169.
[30] H. S. Jennings, *Genetics* (New York: W. W. Norton, 1935), p. 236.

old – began a period which his student and biographer T. M. Sonneborn termed "varied activities" as opposed to the earlier one of "intensive investigation."[31] At the time it was still customary to celebrate the 25th anniversary of a doctorate, and Jennings's festivity in 1921 was significant for two reasons: the first was his response on the occasion entitled "On the Advantage of Growing Old," which marked his anticipation of declining activity. The second was the identity of the main speaker at the dinner, Charles Davenport, testifying to a cordial, and perhaps friendly relationship with the most prominent eugenicist in the country.

This was especially suggestive, because already a year earlier, during the preparations for the Second International Congress of Eugenics which was organized in New York immediately after World War I, Jennings experienced his first antagonistic encounter with the eugenics establishment. He became entangled in the dispute over the national and international character of science when attempts by the French to exclude the Germans were echoed in the United States.[32] Jennings opposed nationalism in science, and especially the exclusion of Germans, since he still cherished his postgraduate days in Jena. He consequently resigned from the general committee of the Congress.[33] Evidently, this did not cause a rupture in his relations with the Eugenics Society. He participated in the Congress itself and remained on the advisory committee of the society.

In 1921 Jennings subscribed sufficiently to the central eugenic credo as to recommend with reservation studies by mainline eugenicists such as Davenport, Henry H. Goddard (of the Vineland School New Jersey) and Arthur Estabrook (of the Eugenics Record Office) on the inheritance of particular traits in man: "This work has necessarily to be done by inexact methods, as compared with work on other organisms, and the results taken by themselves, might not

---

[31] Sonneborn, *Jennings*, p. 183.
[32] D. J. Kevles "'Into Hostile Political Camps': The Reorganization of International Science in World War I," *Isis*, 62 (1971), 47–60. D. J. Kevles, *The Physicists* (New York: Vintage Books, 1971), ch. 10. Brigitte Schroeder-Gudehus, "Challenge to Transitional Loyalties: International Scientific Organization After First World War," *Science Studies*, 3 (1973), 93–118.
[33] April 14, 1920. Davenport to Jennings, April 17, 1920. Jennings to T. H. Morgan, April 14, 1920. Jennings Papers, American Philosophical Society, Philadelphia. HSJP.

carry conviction; but the way they fit into the general picture
coming to us from all sources does make a strong case."[34]

At this junction, Jennings's healthy skepticism illuminates how
minimal the disagreements were between himself and the mainliners. Agreeing with hereditarian statements, Jennings wrote:

> Taking humanity as we find it nowadays, the differences between indi-
> viduals, and particularly the great practically important differences, are
> much more frequently the result of original differences of germinal
> constitution; that is, are matters of heredity, – than they are matters of
> education or environment....
>
> It appears to me true that there is sufficient similarity in environment
> nowadays, so that marked differences of individuals are much more
> frequently the result of diverse inheritance than of diverse environment....
>
> It is perhaps a mere truism, yet nevertheless an important fact, that
> environment cannot make poets, scholars, statesmen, out of germ plasm
> that has not the property of responding to the environment in that way; and
> there is plenty of such germ plasm.[35]

Jennings did not accept every eugenic claim, but the line he drew
was at best nebulous. Treating the book by Popenoe and Johnson
Applied Eugenics with caution, and even calling it "a somewhat
partisan propagandist," he nonetheless concluded that their
"general contentions are supported by the progress of the investigation;" and the same applied for Davenport's old work.[36] By 1921
there was very little substance to distinguish Jennings from the most
adamant eugenicist. He was perhaps less flamboyant in his language, and was more inclined to egalitarianism by his nature, but he
accepted all the eugenic terminology as factual, thus closing any
potential space for debating the status of such assertions. One can
hardly argue on ethics against nature. By the time Jennings
commented in public on eugenics at the end of 1923, he was at (or
maybe just beyond), the peak of his career, and at the center of the
biological establishment with a sound eugenic track record.

Jenning's commentary on eugenics came at the height of the
immigration debate. Immigration from Europe was first restricted
during the war, when Congress overrode a presidential veto in 1917.

---

[34] This advice was given by Jennings, in the capacity of an expert, when he was consulted
by an insurance company. Jennings to P. Burnet, June 23, 1921. Davenport offered
Jennings in 1921 to cooperate in a book on statistics, which Jennings declined because
he claimed to be already writing a similar book. Jennings to Davenport, April 23, 1921.
HSJP.

[35] Jennings to P. Burnet, June 19, 1921. HSJP.

[36] Jennings to P. Burnet, June 23, 1921. HSJP.

The immigration legislation stipulated a literary requirement which had been a long sought measure by restrictionists, who believed this would keep out the undesirable. But the requirements were found unsatisfactory immediately upon passage. The prospective immigrants were apparently neither as degenerate nor as ignorant as they had been portrayed. But this newly recognized situation did not diminish the restrictionists' enthusiasm; on the contrary, they redirected their efforts to the alternative mode of restriction that had been considered by the Dillingham Commission of the pre-war years, namely, a system of national quotas. The fear of post-war immigration – it was claimed that once shipping conditions were reestablished, the annual number of immigrants could reach ten million – encouraged a flood of restrictionist bills, including many to bar immigration altogether. The 1921 Immigration Act set the first national quota at 3 percent of the 1910 census. The 1924 Immigration Act reduced the quota to 2 percent of the 1890 census. A 2 percent quota would have reduced total immigration by almost a third, but the shift to the 1890 census meant an additional comparable reduction,[37] with a heavy bias towards Western and Northern Europe. While the Act was directed against Eastern and Southern Europeans, its racial prejudice was even more evident in the extended exclusion of Asians: with little attention or opposition, it ended the "Gentlemen's Agreement" with Japan,[38] replacing it with a total bar.

The main eugenicist actor on the Congressional scene was Harry H. Laughlin, Davenport's adjutant at Cold Spring Harbor.[39] Nominated by the chairman Albert Johnson as the "Expert Eugenical Agent" of the House Committee on Immigration and Naturali-

[37] The 1921 Act allowed 357,801 immigrants annually, that is 3 percent of the 1910 census. 1 percent reduction, a Senate bill, would have allowed 240,459, while the House (Johnson) bill (2% of 1890 census) would have allowed 161,990. Congressional Record, 65:5942–3, quoted in E. P. Hutchinson, *Legislative History of American Immigration Policy, 1798–1965* (Philadelphia: University of Pennsylvania Press, 1981), p. 190

[38] The agreement went back to the late nineteenth century, when the two countries agreed to limit the number of immigrants, thereby absolving Congress of the need to pass restrictive legislation on a political divisive issue (much like the 1980s quotas on car imports from Japan.)

[39] Whether or not restriction was a foregone conclusion, it nonetheless still had to succeed in the political game. Garland Allen, "The Role of Experts in Scientific Controversy," in H. Tristram Engelhardt, and Arthur L. Caplan, *Scientific Controversies: Case Studies in the Resolution and Closure of Disputes in Science and Technology* (Cambridge: Cambridge University Press, 1987).

zation, Laughlin had a continuous influence on its members. He presented several reports, including "Biological Aspects of immigration," and "Analysis of America's Modern Melting Pot."[40]

The closest the opposition came to offering a fundamental scientific critique was Jennings's testimony before the Congressional Committee on Immigration directed against the data presented by the anti-immigration lobby, specifically refuting Laughlin's argument and evidence.[41] The committee's bias was clear and it avoided witnesses who did not support Nordic superiority. Jennings was only called to testify under pressure from Representative Emanuel Celler – a liberal Jewish Congressman who was a vocal pro-immigration force on the Committee – and was allotted a short time for comments.

Jennings's text was published as an article in the liberal journal *The Survey*. In the biological jungle of racism and xenophobia, with no other biologist speaking out to counter the racist propaganda advanced in the name of biology, Jennings's testimony to Congress showed civic commitment and made him the standard-bearer of biological egalitarianism.

One can almost sense on the part of contemporries and historians a quest for a hero, for an alternative to the conventional crowd of the eugenics movement, a quest which endowed Jennings with his unique position. Kenneth Ludmerer describes Jennings as being mistreated by the xenophobic committee, which adds a motif of sacrifice to the heroic testimony.[42] Yet the members of the committee treated Jennings fairly, and later he did not harbour resentment. This is clear from his letter to the Committee Chairman, Albert Johnson:

Permit me to say that I appreciate the extreme difficulty and complexity of the task in which you are engaged, and realize that the points made in my statement touch only one aspect out of many. Also that from my observa-

---

[40] *Hearing before the Committee on Immigration and Naturalization*, House of Representatives, 66th Congress, 2nd Session, 1921, and 67th Congress, 3rd Session, 1923, respectively. Frances J. Hassenchal, *Harry H. Laughlin, "Expert Eugenics Agent" for the U.S. House of Representatives Committee on Immigration and Naturalization, 1921 to 1931* (Ann Arbor: University Microfilm, 1971); Mark H. Haller, *Eugenics, Hereditarian Attitudes in American Thought* (1963, New Brunswick: Rutgers University Press, 1984), p. 155; Kevles, *Eugenics*, pp. 102–3.

[41] H. S. Jennings, "Undesirable Aliens," *The Survey*, Dec. 15, 1923, pp. 309–312, 364.

[42] Kenneth M. Ludmerer, *Genetics and the American Society, A Historical Appraisal* (Baltimore: Johns Hopkins University Press, 1972), p. 110.

tions last Friday, I admire the thoroughness, patience and fairmindedness with which you are handling your task.[43]

While this is principally a courteous note which accompanied Jennings's written report to the committee, it does suggest that he was treated at least politely during his testimony.

Ludmerer places Jennings at the center of a group of scientists who supposedly rejected a prejudiced interpretation of science. These objections, however, amounted at the time of the testimony merely to a few qualified supportive private letters from Jennings's peers. Nevertheless, Ludmerer is correct in drawing attention to these letters since this was all that American biologists did to oppose the immigration restriction.[44] T. H. Morgan and J. H. Müller, in contrast to Jennings, never participated in the immigration debate. For the next few months it seems that Jennings's critique of eugenics kept him busy. He protested publicly once more against Laughlin's studies on immigration in a letter to *Science*,[45] and followed it up by resigning from the Eugenics Society.[46] These sustained his public image as a critic of the eugenics movement.[47] Jennings certainly sympathized with the underdog and was generally progressive. Kevles judges this critique of eugenics to be a continuity of Jennings's populist sympathies during the 1890s.[48] Yet, at no stage was Jennings the leader of a biological school with any profound social interpretation or concern. And thus one has to look into the details of his views on eugenics in order to reconstruct the dichotomy between the "mainline" and "new" eugenics.

---

[43] Jennings to Albert Johnson, Jan. 8, 1924 – Jennings Papers, American Philosophical Society, handwritten. Also published in *Hearing Before The House Committee on Immigration and Naturalization*, 68th Congress, 1st Session (Washington: Government Printing Office, 1924), p. 512. I am grateful to Diane Paul for pointing out Jennings's letter, and for her helpful insights.

[44] Ludmerer refers to Jennings as "one of America's foremost expositors of applying only sound biology to human affairs." He refers (*Genetics*, p. 123.) to the letters from Raymond Pearl, Vernon Kellog, E. Carlton MacDowell and Samuel J. Holmes.

[45] Jennings, "Proportions of Defectives from the Northwest and from the Southeast of Europe," *Science*, 59 (March 14, 1924), 256–258.

[46] Jennings to Irving Fisher, Sept. 27, 1925. HSJP.

[47] For example, Frederick Osborn "Memorandum on the Eugenics Situation in the United States," 4 May 1933, American Eugenics Society Papers, quoted in Mehler, *American Eugenics Society*, p. 117.

[48] Kevles, *Eugenics*, p. 127.

$NINA$[49] – NO IRISH NEED APPLY

In the summer of 1923 Jennings was solicited by Bruno Lasker of *The Survey* to examine Laughlin's testimony. The liberal motivation for the request was explicitly spelled out. Lasker feared that Laughlin's data would be used in future "every time we plead for a liberal treatment of the immigration question," and wanted to prepare ammunition to combat such criticism. Acknowledging that non-biological counter-arguments were available, Lasker hoped to fill the lacuna where biological and sociological views "did not answer each other." Notwithstanding his liberalism, Lasker was very careful in probing Laughlin's credentials or conclusions, even those that referred to immigration as the "dumping of social inadequates": "We do not feel sure whether the evidence bears them out." He therefore requested "a review of Dr. Laughlin's statement by a biologist who will approach the subject in a scientific, unbiased manner." The emphasis was on Jennings's objectivity, assuming it to be sympathetic. And so for the sum of US$25 Jennings consented.[50] The outcome was an official biological, "objective," statement solicited by a liberal journal to counter a right wing conservative biology.

The article was written during the summer, rewritten in the fall, and published in December 1923, just a few days before Jennings testified to Congress on the biological aspects of immigration.[51] Earlier, in 1922, Walter Lippmann had criticized the biological interpretation of the Army I.Q. tests during the war. But Lippman was an intellectual with no scientific credentials, and he supported immigration restriction. It was up to Jennings to present a scientific counterpart to mainline eugenics and nativist xenophobia.

The spectrum of disagreement among biologists was quite narrow. If Jennings's position was supposedly the one polarized to Laughlin, one could see from Jennings's first response to Lasker how close they really were when viewed in hindsight. Jennings's reply

---

[49] A common insertion in the classified section at the time.
[50] Lasker to Jennings, June 12, 1923. HSJP.
[51] Jennings to "Undesirable Aliens," *The Survey*, Dec. 15, 1923, pp. 309–312, 364. "The Relative Number of European-Born Defectives from the Chief Sources of European Migration and the Effect of a Change in the Basis of Admission From the Census of 1910 to That of 1890," *Hearing before the Committee on Immigration and Naturalization, House of Representatives* (68th Congress, 1st Session, Jan. 1924), pp. 512–518. Jennings "Proportions of Defectives from the Northwest and From the Southeast of Europe," *Science*, 59 (1924), 256–257. Jennings-Lasker correspondence in HSJP.

was that Laughlin's "report seems to me to present a pretty strong case, although I have not studied it so critically as I shall desire to do before writing the paper." Jennings promised his response to be that "of an experimental biologist" and the premise was that professional integrity was to be the guiding light: "I shall not write an article designed to favor one side or the other, but merely to size up the evidence."[52] This initial answer is indicative of the prevailing world view on the application of biology to social characteristics. If Jennings as a biologist could not find anything wrong in Laughlin's report without a close reexamination, perhaps one should not be surprised in hindsight that few called Laughlin's bluff at the time. The success of immigration restriction was apparently due more to a national consensus than to any pressure group, whether they were scientists and intellectuals as the eugenicists were, or a political pressure group as were the labor leaders.[53] This consensus of biological reductionism and race formalism[54] embraced scientists and nonscientists alike, all for whom xenophobia based on nature was probable, if not quite yet proven.

Jennings reinterpreted, but did not question, the restrictionists' data, nor did he try to discredit the biological foundation of the concept of "undesirable characteristics." Laughlin argued that "the recent immigrants, as a whole, present a higher percentage of inborn socially inadequate qualities than do the older stocks." Jennings approved Laughlin's epistemology, he quoted his evidence and conclusion, but criticized the statistical interpretation, claiming that the data suggested the Irish were even more "degenerate" than the new immigrants: "all the lines of evidence presented thus converge upon Ireland as the chief source of defectives."[55]

Jennings argued that approving the proposed legislation would compensate the decline in the number of East and South European degenerates with a surge of Irish undesirable immigrants. The final result would be a similar overall proportion of "institutional defec-

---

[52] Jennings to Lasker, June 20, 1923. HSJP.

[53] From the numerous legislative initiatives on the question of immigration see Hutchinson, *Legislative History*, pp. 159–213. Frederic Osborn wrote that the eugenic movement's influence was exaggerated because of the prominent people who participated in the movement, but that labor was really responsible for the legislation. "Notes on Markle and Fox," 12/18/73, Osborn Papers, American Philosophical Society.

[54] Race formalism views racial groups (at the time, European nationalities and ethnic minorities were referred to as racial entities) as constituting a "real" biological unit, with significant recognizable social characteristics.

[55] *The Survey*, p. 364.

tives." The types of defect would, however, slightly change. Jennings's approach to oppose the proposed restriction was therefore to highlight "the more important facts," namely that the Irish were, if anything, more degenerate than other groups of immigrants.

Jennings prepared a written statement for the Congressional Committee. In oral testimony he added a short statement which underscored the distinction between his own and Laughlin's calculation. He did not, however, include a single word of caution or opposition regarding the basic premise of Laughlin's work, or about the conjectural unproven biological foundation for such presumed characteristics. His summary of the statistical reinterpretations was "that the largest proportion of defectives comes from Ireland; the smallest from Austria-Hungary," and he reached comparable conclusions concerning the insane. The characteristics he examined were: insanity, crime, feeble-mindedness, dependency, tuberculosis and epilepsy.[56] There is nothing in Jennings's report to suggest that the heritability of these might be questionable. While the debate was over immigration and not biology, it was conducted in this particular segment in biological terminology, and over the scientific status of the claim that the immigrants were inferior. Jennings's acceptance of the restrictionist language and epistemology let the restrictionists continue and determine the discourse. This was not an oversight. Jennings accepted this type of biological reasoning at least as legitimate and in line with the existent scientific knowledge as the environmental argument, and was even in sympathy with it personally. The debate over changing the basis of the quota from 1910 to 1890 was wholly internal: under which of the two quotas would the United States admit a smaller number of those who were likely to become institutionalized. Jennings did not contest these assumptions.

Laughlin responded to the various criticisms against his data in an additional appearance before Congress. He singled out Jennings's as the only one to merit a serious response. Jennings, said Laughlin

did not challenge the honesty of the survey nor the representative nature of the population studied. In the end Professor Jennings comes to the same main biological conclusion as that given in the "Melting Pot" paper, namely, that taking into consideration the racial distribution of the inmate populations of our present institutions for the socially inadequate, it would

---

[56] *Hearing Before the Committee on Immigration and Naturalization* (68th Congress, 1st session, Jan. 1924), *Serial 1-A*, pp. 510–11.

probably be necessary for our future immigration policy to consider the matter of family stocks in admitting immigrants.[57]

While it is necessary to consider the hidden political motivation of this statement, Laughlin was nonetheless essentially correct. Jennings did not depart from the eugenics view on immigration restriction, nor from the correlation of social inadequacy with racial origins. He seems to have believed that racial differences carried real social and cultural consequences which could be quantified.

It is unlikely that this was merely a political strategy: namely to agree to the premise of the eugenic argument in order to challenge the conclusions and to achieve a political compromise in Congress of maintaining the 1910 basis. The initial motivation for the article came from a socially conscious editor, aimed at a long term influence on public opinion and reformulating received views. Lasker, fearing a future political exploitation of the racist data, requested a serious scientific "review." Jennings devoted time and close attention to the article, and even revised it to clarify his critique. Neither Lasker nor Jennings dismissed Laughlin's data off hand. The significance of Jennings's critique was to lie primarily in its scientific value and its intellectual legitimation for an egalitarian position. The immediate political purpose was secondary, as immigration restriction was expected to pass. In place of presenting a radical critique, however, Jennings accepted Laughlin's work and terminology as a blueprint for his testimony to Congress on the crucial question of determining the future of American demography. This illustrates the scope of agreement among American biologists as much as internal demarcations. It is unlikely that Jennings merely avoided the more fundamental disagreements for pragmatic motives. His conclusions came closest to criticizing Laughlin's assumptions and suggested a movement away from racial categories and a more careful examination of prospective families of immigrants at the country of origin. In the midst of the worst display of American scientific racist consensus of public policy, Jennings offered a relatively enlightened compassion for the immigrants:

The immigrant classes are bound to show a greater proportion of defects due to environmental pressure than their native class ... Would an equal number of average Americans put through the process of immigration

---

[57] *Hearing Before the Committee on Immigration and Naturalization*, p. 1,316.

under the same conditions, show an equal number of breakdowns? No one knows. But the affirmative answer to these questions is not excluded by the data.[58]

Jennings speculated that Americans of the best stock, if immigrated in large numbers under extreme poverty might also show the psychic strain which would result in a certain amount of institutionalization. Jennings certainly humanized the immigrants with this conjecture: this could also happen to us.

Such a statement coming from a non-immigrant of Old American stock was rare, but it did not present an intellectual alternative to the eugenic dogma. But if Jennings did not question the fundamentals of eugenics at the time of the immigration debate, he elaborated on the details of his critique further in 1924.

At the time Congress deliberated the immigration question, the Eugenics Society had its own Immigration Committee submit a statement to the congressional investigation. Jennings presented his reservations to the committee in November 1923, just before he published his article in *The Survey*, arguing that Laughlin's data did not merit the change of restriction from the 1910 to the 1890 basis. The committee which supported Laughlin, did not incorporate Jennings's comments in its report. Although he denied being "sore" at it, he clearly was, and emphasized his anger through underscoring the committee's mistakes on this "matter of enormous importance."

As a result, Jennings severed his relations with the Eugenics Society. Offended, Jennings began to regret his involvement in the campaign, but before withdrawing from public discourse he made a final pitch against the eugenics propaganda. He justified his resignation from the Eugenics Society by subscribing to Bateson's assertion that "no man of science can afford to have anything to do with a eugenics society." Jennings thus presented his resignation as a principled act and a symbol for scholars disengaging themselves from public discourse:

I doubt whether [these societies] are places for men of pure research, the strength of whose work lies in as complete freedom as is possible from

[58] *The Survey*, p. 310.

prejudice and propaganda. Such men cannot afford to allow their names to be used in support of assertions which appear to them unsound.[59]

But even this cleavage with eugenics was not couched in anti-racist terms, and Jennings never retracted his racial views on the Irish. Yet, he did go on to publish a more fundamentally critical paper on "Heredity and Environment,"[60] in which he blasted the confusion of "the all-mighty inheritance" as a dead doctrine "though as yet, like the decapitated turtle, it is not sensible of it." He opposed the concept of unit character, emphasizing instead that "hundreds of genes are required to make a mind – even a feeble mind," and that the outcome is determined by the interaction of heredity and the environment. Shortly afterward, he published a small popular exposition *Prometheus or Biology and the Advancement of Man*,[61] which further articulated his opposition to the myth of heredity determines all.

By the end of 1924, Jennings had offered as much an alternative to mainline eugenics as had anyone. His new, reform version opposed the rabid xenophobia of the old school, but he nonetheless still subscribed to the belief that available knowledge sufficed to warrant his eugenic and racial beliefs, and justified appropriate political action. Here was the expert who ventured out of academic discourse and commented to the public, combining the role of the scholar with that of the intellectual. Thus his views carried weight both for the profession and for the educated public. Despite its limited scope, Jennings's critique had no equivalent at the time within the British scene. However, the precise extent of Jennings's position was shaped by personal political motivation. The sense of personal defeat in the Eugenics Society pushed him to articulate a much more elaborate opposition during 1924. But not having political inclinations to start with, he apparently decided not to repeat the experience, and to avoid future political involvement altogether.

By 1930, the situation had somewhat changed. Many scientists came to recognize the validity of Jennings's earlier views on the

---

[59] Jennings to Fisher, Sept. 27, 1924. HSJP. The quote from Bateson was taken out of context from the English scene, where it referred to the eugenics society which had been caught in the imbroglio between the biometricians and geneticists.

[60] *The Scientific Monthly*, 19 (Sept. 1924), 224–238.

[61] (New York: E. P. Dutton, 1925), Published in England 1933, and translated into Spanish and Chinese.

inherent interaction between heredity and environment, and even took his claims a step further, reflecting the declining status and influence of eugenics. In 1929 this was manifested in the chilled reception to Davenport's study (with the aid of an assistant, Morris Steggerda) on *Race Crossing in Jamaica*, discussed above. The work, although based on extensive field research, was thoroughly faulted, and elicited little enthusiasm. The conclusion that race crossing among peoples causes disharmonious combinations was generally rejected, especially by Lancelot Hogben in London, and William Castle of Harvard. Castle, who had been a graduate student there with Jennings thirty years earlier, was in the early 1920s a main-liner, but by the end of the decade had come around to a more sophisticated perception. In the meantime other biologists voiced criticism of eugenics, including Raymond Pearl, Jennings's colleagues at Johns Hopkins.[62]

Yet, Jennings provided a most unexpected source of support for Davenport. He accepted the study's conclusions despite the insignificant statistical differences,[63] and viewed the results as a proof "with respect to parts of the body that are measurable." He quoted approvingly Davenport on the disharmonious crosses who have "the long legs of the negro and the short arms of the white, which would put them at a disadvantage in picking up things from the ground."[64] In his supportive assessment Jennings resorted to conjectures on the basis of analogies of crosses between different species of fish: "It appears probable that similarly inharmonious combinations of a more serious character may likewise occur, giving rise to insufficiency of heart or kidneys, or to the crowding of teeth." This type of circular argument is very characteristic of racist arguments. The first stage is to establish that disharmony exists among different organisms. Then comes the reassuring statement that human races do not differ among themselves as other species (eg. fish), but, nevertheless, the variability needs to be accounted for, and the rest remains open to the idiosyncrasy of the writer's imagination, normally divorced from any biological evidence. In this particular case the probability of disharmonious internal organs was grounded

---

[62] See below.
[63] H. S. Jennings, *The Biological Basis of Human Nature* (New York: W. W. Norton, 1930), p. 282.
[64] H. S. Jennings, *The Biological Basis of Human Nature*, p. 282.

in crossing among different species of fish. Jennings was epistemologically aware of the prevalence of such writing, and warned against it in his catechism a few years later ("Biological Fallacies and Human Affairs") but could not resist the temptation himself.[65]

Jennings's egalitarian legacy did not interfere with his favourable reception of Davenport's eugenic message, its assumptions and conclusions. Racial mixture between stocks which "differ greatly in physique from others" caused "adulteration" to "the superior race." Jennings agreed with the analysis, and even on the question of racial superiority he concurred with Davenport's conclusion of conventional bigotry that "the blacks studied were superior in the matters that affect musical ability; the whites in matter of judgment, of adjustment to conditions."[66] He offered a sarcastic consolation to the American people: racial animosity had to be expected in a nation of different groups. History is written as a story of conflict, and "a nation composed of races in process of mixture will not be among those happy peoples whose annals are vacant."[67]

Given the substance of his critique, which included much of the immigration restrictionists' and eugenicists' lingo, and his acceptance of both Laughlin's framework and data, one could ask then how should Jennings's scientific position and political world-view be compared to the British biologists' critique of eugenics a decade later? and whether his prominence was achieved mainly on account of the alternatives? namely, was this also a testimony to the want of social involvement among American geneticists and to the character of disengagement among progressive and liberal scientists in the post World War I period?

Jennings's image was one of a reformer and an egalitarian. By the mid-twenties contemporaries understood his work to imply a rejection of racism. His support in 1930 for Davenport -- who epitomized the old traditional school -- which he refined in a concise form in *Genetics* (1935) did not interfere with public esteem for him as an anti-racist. In 1941 he participated/edited the publication of an anti-racist book, *Scientific Aspects of The Race Problem*,[68] which further strengthened his reputation. Jennings's early stand against

---

[65] Jennings, *Genetics*, ch. 10, pp. 206–220.   [66] Jennings, *Human Nature*, p. 286.
[67] Jennings, *Human Nature*, p. 288.
[68] H. S. Jennings *et al.*, *Scientific Aspects of The Race Problem* (London: Longmans, Green and Co., 1941), p. 73.

the anti-immigration camp sustained his image as a liberal anti-racist, though no doubt some of his writing did not.

Thus Jennings's work persistently displayed two antagonistic strains. The reconstruction by historians of Jennings's "reform" outlook accurately illuminates one of its aspects, one which also represented his important contemporary image. The question remains of how this might be integrated into an analysis of the substance of his writings. The above interpretation of his Congressional testimony underscores the affinity between his anti-xenophobia, liberalism and racism. In this context, his 1930 support of Davenport is consistent and consequential. Rather than an aberration of an "anti mainline" trend by sudden support for a hard core eugenicist, Jennings sustained his views on race as a determining factor in social interaction. Granting that the complexity of racial heredity could not be noticed in ordinary circumstances, he expected the worst of racial miscegenation. As is evident in his books from the twenties onwards, he was as aware as anybody of the logical fallacies in biological reductionism. This inability of his to choose between the alternatives calls for a more refined historical evaluation. In place of supporting "new" eugenics, Jennings ought to be seen as combining the old with the new, of subscribing to old tenets, while projecting egalitarian nuances. The 1941 anti-racist essay displayed the same tension: in it he referred to studies as different as those of Bauer, Fischer and Lenz (1931), Davenport or Hogben, as though all presented similar and comparable anti-racist scientific claims.[69] This further enhanced his legacy as a leading anti-racist, a legacy which relied mostly on the lack of any better prominent American biologist who could serve as a role model. How might this be explained?

In the early twenties, the opposition to eugenics voiced by Jennings was weakly echoed by a small group of scientists. They were reacting at least initially to the rabid racism of Madison Grant and his ilk, the views of whom many regarded as farcical. The old, mainline eugenicists offended scientific protocol in terms both of professional integrity and the proper use of scientific data. This was the focus of Jennings's critique of Laughlin. The racial substance of the claims was confronted only as a by product of the methodology debate. By the end of the decade, much of the fanfare of eugenics had disappeared, and the fading public image was that of a more

[69] Jennings et al., Scientific Aspects of The Race Problem, p. 73.

moderate and a less threatening movement, one which was more receptive to population thinking and less typological. Jennings had opposed all along Davenport's extreme reductionism, and called for a sophisticated view of the interaction between heredity and environment.

This does not mean, however, that he rejected at any stage the notion of a racial hierarchy. He chose to testify in Congress – in discussing the notion of biological inferiority and superiority – that among the Irish there were more "defectives" than in other European races. He reiterated this position in the 1930s in accepting Davenport's claim that different races excelled relatively in different fields, as well as the assertion about the disharmony of race crossing. But to the degree that there was a new American eugenics in 1924, Jennings represented it. If Kevles's concept of "reform eugenics" is taken as an ideal type in the Weberian sense, it may suggest that in the early 1920s Jennings was an anti-mainliner, but that within a decade the discourse changed and his static views came to disclose rigidity. This moved him into an alliance with the conservative and racist Davenport. What might have passed for a critique of eugenics in the early 1920s, itself became mainline eugenics a few years later. By then, a rift developed between the public image of Jennings as a reformer and his views on race. This discrepancy did not capture public attention because after 1925 Jennings abstained from public involvement, to the extent that he even declined Boas's request for an article against sterilization in Nazi Germany.[70]

In contrast, during the thirties, the British biologists who constituted reform eugenics were at their peak of public fame, writing and criticizing eugenics and racism. Jennings was somewhat older than his English peers, and his withdrawal from political activity was motivated not merely by physical weakness (he was rather frail) but by a conscious decision not to repeat his experience of the early 1920s. Jennings liked to think, and tell others, that the reason he did not participate in public debate was that he could not afford the time to accept socio-political responsibility, and was too busy with research. But as one biography[71] suggests, during the years under discussion, Jennings was not very energetic, either in his research or in other activities.

The inconsistency in Jennings's views is highlighted by his disillusion with the role of the scholar as a public commentator in

[70] Jennings to Boas, July 13, 1933, HSJP.   [71] T. M. Sonneborn, "Jennings," p. 183.

1923–24. He found the biologist's social role "of speaking oraculary on the problems of human life, on the constitution and conduct of human society . . ." to be an "intolerable burden." Yet his progressive and social conscience was eased due to the importance he assigned to "emergent evolution." Emergent evolution referred in this context to the unique way in which each organism had developed, and therefore biologists who did not study humans were not supposed to be more capable of evaluating human evolution than laymen. "The biologist who speaks authoritatively on such matters must be a specialist in the biology of the *Hominidae*," concluded Jennings. Accordingly, when a biologist compares "the behaviour of man with that of other organisms" he ought to do so "only critically, after detailed comparative study and demonstration of the respects in which they are identical and he will give full weight to any evidence that they are diverse."[72]

Jennings did not have the urge to be publicly involved, and while liberal and progressive, his social and intellectual responsibility was minimal.

Should a comparison between British and American eugenics examine not only the content of the scientists' opinions, but also the way they chose to disseminate their views? Clearly, my answer is yes. Eugenics aroused enthusiasm because of its social message, and its import was in its public impact. This was due largely to the involvement of scientists such as Davenport, who were scientific intellectuals as well as scholars. There was no similar political involvement on the liberal end of the spectrum in the United States. Suggesting that Jennings was not a reform eugenicist, in the sense that the members of the British "Visible College" were in the 1930s, is not to condemn Jennings for lack of greater political involvement, or for his belief in racial inequality. Rather, the purpose is to show that the perception of a similarity of eugenic thinking in the two countries – a similarity which no doubt existed – has to be refined.

During the thirties a number of biologists became politically more active.[73] Though Jennings did not participate in their activism, he was considered to be part of this group. For the history of eugenics, this is where his significance lies: in addition to what he wrote or

[72] "Diverse Doctrines of Evolution, Their Relation to the Practice of Science and Life," *Science*, 65, 1672 (January 14, 1927), 22.
[73] See below, Part III.

believed, his impact was in what he represented. Historical hindsight may indeed suggest that his reputation and legacy were more important than his actions. Not only was he reputedly the first biologist of consequence in the United States to contradict publicly the racist interpretations and to criticize eugenics in general: he also represented the limitations of a theoretical development among the older generation.

Political positions are relative, and Jennings represented a minimalist creed, yet there was no biologist in America who was consistent in his critique of traditional eugenics. This raises the question of why no American biologist participated in the rejection of scientific racism before World War II. Leslie Dunn came as close as anybody, but he never belonged to the forefront of human biology as did the British J. B. S. Haldane, Lancelot Hogben or Lionel Penrose, and his public significance was greater after the war.

A CONSERVATIVE CRITIQUE

Pearson, Davenport and Gates had all reached a dead end in their biological work. While they remained respectable scientists in a wider cultural setting, their work was rejected by a growing segment of their professional colleagues, especially within biology. This, however, was not the case with other conservatives in American and English science such as Raymond Pearl or Ronald Fisher. Pearl, like Edward East, belonged to the second generation of American biologists. He was a biometrician turned geneticist, who attempted to synthesize population control and eugenics.[74] This effort was rejected by Pearson from the biometrician perspective, and Pearl never participated in the development of population genetics during the thirties. Within its limits, Pearl's was among the most successful research on human biology in America before World War II. His views on eugenics and race are especially interesting because he aspired to correlate his biological research to social questions, to combine his role as an expert, the absolute savant, to that of the intellectual and leader of public opinion. Where Pearl limited his synthesis to eugenics and population control, Ronald Fisher was one of a triumvir – the other two included J. B. S. Haldane and Sewell Wright – responsible for the new population genetics and what came

[74] Allen, "Old Wine in New Bottles: From Eugenics to Population Control in the Work of Raymond Pearl," Ms.

to be known as the first stage of the modern synthesis. Fisher was second to none in mathematics and statistics, and his innovations in population genetics were as valuable as his conservative social views were adamant. Both Pearl and Fisher illustrate how solid scientific work could coexist with belief in the most rigid racial typologies. Furthermore, their efforts underscore the point that internal scientific progress, if divorced from political commitments, is limited in its ability to criticize racism.

RAYMOND PEARL

In the history of eugenics Raymond Pearl figures prominently among a group of scientists who by the early 1920s, already opposed racism.[75] This judgment accentuates one facet in Pearl's ambivalence towards eugenics, but ignores his racism, which admittedly was most evident in his private rather than public life. The historical significance of Pearl's critique of eugenics is that it underscores a division among conservatives concerning conventional racial bigotry. The shortening of this focus, however, is that it endows Pearl's and, by implication, the conservative approach with a greater potential for a racial critique than it really possessed. Pearl provides a very dramatic illustration of the ambivalence of this type of right-wing anti-racism, partly perhaps because he left a long and revealing paper trail, especially in his correspondence.

Raymond Pearl, a distinguished biologist at Johns Hopkins, was born in New Hampshire, educated at Dartmouth, Michigan, Leipzig, and University College in London, and served during the 1920s and 1930s as professor of biometry and vital statistics at the School of Hygiene and Public Health. Baltimore provided a very congenial social setting, the highlights of which were his close contacts with H. L. Mencken and the saturday night drinking parties where merry Baltimorians dwelled on the immorality of prohibition. Pearl was a scientific entrepreneur who had close contacts with the Carnegie and Rockefeller Foundations, which

---

[75] "Among those who publicly or privately attacked the claims of eugenicists after 1915 were T. H. Morgan, Herbert Spencer Jennings, Raymond Pearl, H. J. Muller and Sewell Wright. By 1925, even W. E. Castle began to question claims for eugenics." Garland Allen, "The Eugenics Record Office at Cold Spring Harbor, 1910–1940," *Osiris*, 2nd ser. 2 (1986), 225–264 (here, 250). "Pearl ... did not disapprove of eugenical aims, only the methods and overt racism that was emerging in eugenicists' presentations." Allen, "Old Wine," p. 24.

financed much of his research. He served on various executive boards of scientific bodies such as the National Research Council as well as on several committees. He was also editor of the *Quarterly Review of Biology* and *Human Biology*, and a member of the editorial boards of other journals. During World War I, Pearl was the chief of the Statistic Division in the United States Food Administration. Later he was the President of the International Union for the Scientific Investigation of Population and the list of his honors and memberships attests to his national and international professional prominence.[76] His frequent straightforwardness, especially in committee meetings, did not endear him to other participants,[77] and some of the more distressingly racist comments were happily missing from his writings.

In accounts of Pearl's public conversion against eugenics, he is commended mostly for his *American Mercury* article of November 1927, entitled "The Biology of Superiority," his first published criticism of eugenics. The popularity of this magazine added injury to insult: Pearl criticized eugenics for "emotional appeals to class and race prejudices, solemnly put forth as science, and unfortunately accepted as such by the general public."[78] What Pearl opposed, as his private correspondence shows, were the reactionary activists who, like Madison Grant and Harry Laughlin, "were likely in their zeal for the Nordic, to do a great deal of real harm."[79] The last chapter has shown that the American wing of this "new" reform eugenics was very fragile even when represented by its liberal and progressive leader, Herbert Spencer Jennings, Pearl's colleague at Johns Hopkins. The examination of Pearl's views on race and eugenics, reveals the limitation of the reform eugenics among the older generation even more. Although historians have described Pearl as a moderate among eugenicists even by the early

---

[76] Herbert S. Jennings, "Raymond Pearl," *National Academy of Sciences, Biographical Memoirs*, 22 (1943), 295–347.

[77] Much of the evidence is implicit in his correspondence. Referring to his relations with peers on central professional committees, he commented for example "I am well aware that I do not enjoy the confidence or esteem of at least certain of the responsible officers of the social science research council." Pearl to E. B. Wilson, Aug. 1, 1930. RPP. On another occasion Pearl wrote about a meeting of the Executive Committee of the National Research Council: "After sitting for half a day, I could restrain myself no longer and made a five-minute's speech on the elementary principles of logic and the importance of common sense in the affairs of the council ..." Pearl to Wheeler, Oct. 9, 1923. RPP.

[78] Pearl, "The Biology of Superiority," *American Mercury*, 12 (Nov. 1927), 257–266.

[79] Pearl to Jennings, Nov. 24, 1923, HSJP, quoted in Cravens, *The Triumph of Evolution* (Philadelphia: University of Pennsylvania Press, 1978), p. 177.

twenties,[80] his private record suggests that his earlier wholehearted support for eugenics did not fundamentally change.

Pearl had published numerous articles on eugenics, and he believed in future centers at universities together with government support for "Breeding Better Men."[81] By 1927, the "harm" he referred to in the *Mercury* article was to the status of science, not to the unjust discrimination against the "lower" classes and "inferior" races. The danger of eugenics stemmed from its propagandistic aspect, especially by the more vocal among the eugenicists, who diminished the public perception of science as an objective enterprise. Pearl opposed the exaggerated pretense in the name of eugenics for scientific credentials, but not its substantial claims. When he opposed the cooperation between eugenics and genetics[82] it was a professional stand, neither ideological nor social. For him, eugenics and birth control were both social movements, while genetics was an academic discipline. What Pearl came to oppose in the propaganda for immigration restriction was not its overt racism, but the scientific disguise. This type of criticism by a number of leading geneticists though very limited in its intentions, had a compounded impact which foreshadowed the decline of eugenics and the belief in racial typologies.

Pearl's critique of eugenics emphasized the scientists' dislike of "enterprises which savor ... of propaganda," and while published in a popular magazine, it was not a statement of cultural preference, but a report on research aimed at negating eugenic exaggeration. Here was Pearl the absolute savant, the expert participating in the intellectual debate while claiming independence from it on the grounds of scientific objectivity. For example, he investigated the familial prominence of the world's superior philosophers and poets, concluding that "the particular combinations of genes which made

---

[80] K. Ludmerer for example argues that Pearl lost interest in human genetics as a result of the propaganda campaign for eugenics in the early twenties and "its indifference to the truth." *Genetics and the American Society* (Baltimore: Johns Hopkins, 1972), pp. 27, 121–129, 139. D. Kevles points to Pearl's earlier criticism of Davenport's biological research (*In the Name of Eugenics*, p. 312). G. Allen cites numerous instances of his racism, but his overall picture of Pearl is of a leading scientist who charted the reshaping of eugenics into population control and became a sceptic with regard to eugenics by 1918 ("Old Wine"). Allen wrote numerous articles on the eugenics movement, specifically on the transition, "The Eugenics Record Office, Cold Spring Harbor, 1910–1940. An Essay in Institutional History," *Osiris*, 2nd ser. 2 (1985), 225–264.

[81] Raymond Pearl, "Breeding Better Men," *World's Work*, 125 (1908), 9, 824. Quoted in Ludmerer, *Genetics*, p. 139.

[82] Letter to William Bateson, May 27, 1920. Quoted in Allen, "Old Wine."

these greatest philosophers were derived from just an average lot of human beings" and that only five of the sixty-three philosophers he had examined had gifted or distinguished progeny. As a result, Pearl criticized the eugenicists on three accounts: first, their definition of superiority was styled after the group they belonged to; second, they based their claims on the fallacy that the essence of heredity is that "like produces like"; and third, with "a curious lack of even literary consistency" they claimed to base their theory on the principles of Mendelism set forth at the start of their books, but then advanced social and biological doctrines unrelated to those principles. Pearl was even more explicit in private. Writing to his friend, the Harvard biologist William Morton Wheeler (March 25, 1927) he promised to sharpen his critique in a lecture to the International Eugenics Congress in Berlin that summer, where he was the designated main speaker: "I am going to make the most of the opportunity to blow their camp wide open."[83] These seemingly unimpeachable reform credentials camouflaged Pearl's darker side, the crude Social Darwinist who ignored his own otherwise clear critique of eugenics.

Pearl's involvement in the political process spilled over into his scientific publications. The affinity between his conclusions as an expert and his political position could not have been coincidental. Two instances are instructive. In 1934 Pearl discussed "The Weight of the Negro Brain."[84] Starting with the "accepted view" that the "skull capacity and the brain weight of the Negro" are smaller than among whites, he went on to cite as evidence data collected by various studies, beginning with Morton and his work "Crania Americana" (1849), and enumerating studies with similar conclusions.[85] At a time when the first modern physical measurements of American blacks were being published by Melville Herskovits, Pearl analysed imperfect data from 1849 and concluded that blacks have smaller brains, and that the difference declines gradually as more white blood is mixed with the black. Notwithstanding his outdated and inaccurate data, Pearl's conjectures were directed towards minimizing the division yet maintaining a formal distinction.[86]

---

[83] RPP.   [84] *Science*, 80 (Nov. 9, 1934), 431–434.

[85] For a critical discussion of Morton, see S. J. Gould, *The Mismeasure of Man* (New York: W. W. Norton, 1982).

[86] Pearl and Herskovits had corresponded earlier about a formal "objective criteria of a racial group" and Pearl consented to Herskovits's objections, but added that he is "not quite so

A second study "The Influence of Alcohol on Duration of Life"[87] testified to Pearl's willingness to pursue investigations in support of his political and social views. Pearl was an outgoing person who liked alcohol, which was illegal and a subject of political polemics during prohibition. In a manner true to political partisanship, and not without a sense of humor, he dedicated *Alcohol and Longevity* to – as H. S. Jennings put it – the "group of choice spirits" in the Saturday Night Club.[88] Jennings commented on this interaction of scientific investigation and social habits: "This investigation led him to the conclusion that the moderate consumption of alcohol is not harmful, and on this conclusion he based his own practice."[89] While the role of moderation in prolonging life has been corroborated by recent investigators, the historian could perhaps not be blamed for evaluating the impact of Pearl's drinking habits on his conclusion as more meaningful than the eventual scientific validation. Indeed, one suspects that Jennings's statement itself was ironic. Pearl concluded that excessive drinking shortens life, but also that "it has not been possible up to this time to determine whether the consumption of alcoholic beverages *in moderation* has any effect upon life expectancy." Surely such a statement could be utilized in the anti-prohibition campaign. The "moderate" categories included various habits of drinking, but "*never enough to become intoxicated.*" The "heavy" drinkers and those "who are positively known *to have been in the habit of getting drunk.*" No intermediate category existed.[90] One may wonder how Pearl classified the habits of his companions at the Saturday Night parties on this scale.

In those gatherings Pearl had many moments when he candidly expressed his views, only a fraction of which are reflected in his correspondence. One description which addressed such topics as Americanism, medical education, and anti-semitism deserves a special mention, since it was written at the very time when Pearl had reputedly converted to a new view of eugenics.

After the war, discrimination against Jews in universities increased. The situation at Harvard received special attention

hopeless" on the subject. Pearl - Herskovits correspondence, Oct. 1929. RPP. Apparently, few years later, Pearl believed that his hope had materialized.

[87] *Proceedings of the National Academy of Sciences*, 10, 6 (1924), 231–237. Pearl published other accounts on the study in the *British Medical Journal*, (May 31, 1924), 948–950; *Eugenics Review*, 16 (1924), 9–30.

[88] Jennings, *Pearl*, pp. 309.   [89] Jennings, *Pearl*, pp. 304.

[90] Raymond Pearl, "The Influence of Alcohol on Duration of Life," pp. 236, 233. Also "The Racial Effect of Alcohol," *Eugenics Review* (1924), (emphasis added).

because the President of Harvard, A. Lawrence Lowell, publicly demanded that an official quota be set for the number of Jewish students at the university. He failed to receive the support of the university's Overseers, and officially Harvard abandoned the scheme. Yet the number of Jewish students in the next two decades was halved.[91] The affair caused embarrassment to some Harvard faculties, perhaps more on account of the public forum than its substance. Other schools kept their "quotas" discreet. Pearl, who was in favor of the practice if not of the publicity, gave a candid view of these happenings at Johns Hopkins in a letter to Lawrence J. Henderson.[92]

He remarked on the clumsiness with which Harvard had handled the question of admitting – or rather excluding – Jews, and offered his own experience at Johns Hopkins as guidance. Pearl prefaced his support for discrimination with a claim to being "completely free from racial prejudice."[93] The text of the letter belied Pearl's high moral statement, and could have been written by the most rabid racist or anti-Semite in Europe or America at the time. It ought to be stressed that the comments on the technique of discrimination came from a person who was the statistician of the Johns Hopkins Hospital (1919–1935) and worked at the Medical School. Pearl intertwined bigotry and "expertise" in a manner which deserves lengthy quotation:

I have noted with considerable glee from the newspapers that you are mixed up in the Jewish question. If you will permit an outsider to say so, it seems to me that you people at Harvard have so far handled the matter this spring in about the most unskillful way that could have been devised if you had put heads together and thought over how you could most completely mess up the situation. I think we do it much more neatly here. We make no noise about it, but, for a number of years past, very quietly and skillfully means have been taken and are being planned for the future to keep down our Jewish percentage. One of the most humorous methods is the one

[91] Seymour Martin Lipset and David Reisman, *Education and Politics at Harvard* (New York: McGraw-Hill, 1975), pp. 142–144.
[92] Professor of biological chemistry at Harvard, and close friend of Pearl.
[93] Historians appear to have agreed. In addition to the references above, other favorable statements include Cravens who classified Pearl, Jennings, Morgan and Castle as the group that published "thorough criticism of eugenics" (*Cravens*, p. 179); Ludmerer says that Pearl's "descriptions of immigrants lacked the belittling tone of that of Madison Grant" (*Genetics and the American Society*, pp. 27–28) and gives him a major role in the "repudiation of eugenics" (pp. 84, 113). Especially telling for the public's perception of Pearl is Ludmerer's judgment that Pearl was among the group that "express[ed] the common fear that selective restrictive legislation might pass" (p. 123).

which Whitridge Williams uses in the Medical School. To begin with, they restrict their numbers. In the second place, he makes it an absolute requirement that any candidate for admission, who lives within 200 miles of Baltimore, must present himself in person. If he lives more than 200 miles away, he must send in his photograph with application. Then Williams makes a careful study of the curvature of the nose and the facial characteristics, and gives these matters due weight in reaching a decision. I tell Williams that he should let me make a proper biometric study of the photographs and then on the basis of it, put a statement in the catalogue that anyone whose nose has a smaller radius of curvature than a certain value, need not bother to apply. Publicly, of course, Williams and everyone else denies that there is any discrimination against Jews. Practically, however, particularly in the Medical School, the proportion is held to a very satisfactory figure.[94]

The addressee, Henderson, supported Lowell's policy and defended the policy "all over the United States" in what Jacques Leob described as an effort "to stir up anti-Semitism with the purpose of excluding Jewish students from American universities."[95] Henderson was a powerful force at Harvard, and a close friend of Pearl. Earlier in the year, Pearl "institutionalized" their friendship in the formation of "the X-Club" the purpose of which was to include few eminent scientists, but mostly to exclude others. The motivation was to counter the growing versatility in the American Academy, and the club was to meet once a year during the Academy's meeting for social purposes, that is, chiefly to avoid the presence of other participants in the meeting. Initially, it included in addition to Pearl and L. Henderson, W. M. Wheeler and E. B. Wilson (all three of Harvard) and John McKeen Cattel. It was never meant to number more than ten.

Pearl's letter to Henderson was written at a time when WASPish anti-Semitism was at its peak. His cynicism in the letter was directed at the idea of publicizing the method (in reference to Lowell's public comments) not at the discrimination and he was very satisfied with the results. As a biometrician, Pearl joked about the possibility of inserting the nose curvature as a qualifying criterion for admission, an attempt at humor that not all the applicants to Johns Hopkins, especially to the Medical School, might

[94] Pearl to Henderson, June 27, 1922. RPP.
[95] Jacques Loeb to Leonor Michaelis, April 19, 1923, Leob papers, quoted in Kenneth R. Manning, *Black Apollo of Science, The Life of Ernest Everett Just* (New York: Oxford University Press 1983), p. 97.

have appreciated. Pearl, however, turned even more vicious in the following paragraph, where in a vehement Social Darwinist fashion, he spoke of a confrontation between the Jews and the Gentiles for mastery of the world. The two groups could not survive side by side: one would win and the other be defeated. In the name of 'biology' and the fight for 'survival' Pearl judged the struggle to be unavoidable.

You may wonder why one who is so completely free from racial prejudices as I think I am, should so seem to take for granted that there ought to be discrimination against the Jew in our universities. It is my reasoned conviction that there should be such discrimination, and it is on that ground that it is a necessary move in *the struggle for existence on the part of the rest of us*. This does not mean that I consider the Jew all round a better man than the non-Jew. But it seems to me that the events have shown that he has by and large a much higher survival value than the non-Jew in societies organized as ours at the moment happens to be. This high survival value arises as I analyse it primarily from the nearly complete absence in him of any inhibiting sense of morals or decency, as these [s]enses are interpreted and acted upon by non-Jews. In other words, the Jew will never let any considerations of morals or decency interfere with his personal advancement. The Gentiles sometimes will. In the second place, the Jewish mind has developed in the direction of versatility and superficiality. In the immediate struggle for existence, these traits will win out, I think, always over thoroughness and depth. If I wanted to write a treatise on the subject, I could give you many specific examples which would prove the contentions I have set forth above, but I do not propose to bore you in this way. The real question seems to me to come to this. *Whose world is this to be, ours, or the Jews?* If you will give equal opportunity, my bet is that it will be their world. Perhaps it ought to be, but it is distinctly unbiological to suppose that we are going to lie down and let that situation come about. In other words, if we are not prepared to look after our own survival, we are indeed in a bad way. (Emphasis added.)[96]

The biological terminology proves the abuse of scientific language and credentials by Pearl, especially when transferred to the political arena. Pearl employed the same terms simultaneously in biological studies and in bigoted social commentary. Earlier in the letter, Pearl discussed psychologically his own assimilation of an idea from Henderson, though in a book review he had claimed it to be his own, and went on to discuss its possible implication to the theory of evolution. Pearl used the concept of evolution in a theoretical, supposedly objective manner, but sentences later and almost in the

[96] Pearl to Henderson, June 27, 1922. RPP.

same line of thought he uses evolution to justify xenophobia. This suggests how artificial at times is the dichotomy between scientific and social ideas.

Pearl's anti-semitism had consequences which reached beyond his incidental commentary on Harvard's admission policies and the exclusion of Jews from Johns Hopkins. As a powerful politician in American science, he was involved in the nomination of scientists to the American Academy. In that role his letter to Professor Edwin Bidell Wilson of Harvard in 1925 is instructive:

> I gather from the Academy list of names that we are on the high road to becoming a home for incurable Hebrews. Are there no people in the country eligible to the Academy except Jews? ... It seems to me that if the mathematical section's names this year are the best the[y] can do, the Academy should pass a resolution to the effect that no further names will be accepted from the section in mathematics until such time as they have somebody to offer who is neither a Jew nor an ass.[97]

The X-club had a very specific target.

What are we to make of Pearl's bigotry? Judging by his published criticism of prejudice, he should certainly not be held a racist. Yet the letters prove that Pearl's opposition to prejudice was not what he claimed elsewhere. In the thirties, Franz Boas tried to solicit Pearl's help, without success, in combating Nazi propaganda on race. From Pearl's publications Boas might have had a good reason to expect cooperation, and though he was snubbed, he continued to try. In declining to cooperate, Pearl declared his "strong aversion to ... [any] pronouncement [which] is ... about political questions," and added that such pronouncements not only harm the scientists who take part but through them damage science itself.[98]

The reply, despite its almost routine formality suggests that the reason for Pearl's relative lack of involvement in public debate was motivated by the discrepancy between his public image and his genuine opinions. He probably preferred to retain both his public prominence and his private bigotry. One may wish such opportu-

[97] Pearl to E. B. Wilson, March 7, 1925. As so often with bigotry, this claim was factually wrong, and malicious. Wilson in his reply denied there were many Jews on the list (all German-and Russian-sounding names were presumed Jewish) and added some information about the "incurable Hebrew" in question. Lefchetz used to be an electrical engineer, but following his loss of two hands "turned his attention to mathematics" in which, as it turned out, he was very good because "he was trained on the continent and not in this country." Wilson to Pearl, March 11, 1925. RPP, APS.
[98] Pearl to Boas, Oct 3, 1935. FBP.

nism to be more widespread. Pearl certainly did not lack opinions on public issues. During the thirties, he was a member of the Association for the Defense of a Constitution (the enemy being F.D.R. and the New Deal), and on a different occasion declined a request to support the American Committee for Democracy and Intellectual Freedom, and instead cabled Boas a copy of his support for the Dies Committee against un-American activities.[99]

Pearl's anti-Semitism coexisted with his critique of eugenics. He opposed Madison Grant's racism, but the precise difference might have been more in their approach to science than to race. Pearl's etiquette forbade the public disclosure of his anti-Semitism, but there is no indication he ever reversed his racism. On the few occasions in which he participated in public debate, he felt injured, never more than when in 1929 his criticism of eugenics cost him a professorship at Harvard.[100] Furthermore, his claim in 1922 to be free of prejudice suggests a subjective perception which the historian might be justified in questioning. In an obituary on Pearl, Henderson commented: "throughout his life he felt himself a north of Boston man and cultivated and cherished the sentiments and some of the prejudices of his people."[101] Few could have known better.

Pearl's case illustrates how scientists intertwined "internal" and "external" motivations on questions of human sciences. Somewhere in the closest, traceable or not, scientific and cultural values influence each other. Yet one should not *a priori* assume that the correlation between the political and cultural position of scientific ideas is rational. Incoherence and contradictions are more likely – and Pearl is a case in point. A moderate conservative in the public eye turned out to be a bigot: a top ranked biologist interpreted evolution after the manner of a dilettante. The significance of Pearl's views to the understanding of the relations between eugenics and geneticists is primarily that the obvious ought not necessarily to be equated with the truth, and that gaps in knowledge cannot be bridged by assuming that the scientists were coherent in their views. Pearl chose to minimize his own role as an intellectual. As a biometrician his analysis of data contradicted some racist claims popular among eugenicists. This, however, conflicted with his

99 Telegram to Boas, Jan. 5, 1940. RPP.
100 E. B. Wilson and East led the opposition. Wilson to Pearl, Dec. 124, 1927; June 11, 1929. RPP. Already in 1927, Pearl was feeling the personal heat of breaking ranks with friends with whom he shared eugenics views. Allen, "Old Wine."
101 *American Philosophical Society Yearbook*, 1940.

conservative position and his congenial relationship with many of the hard core eugenicists. A conservative anti-racist critique, even when couched in terminology of population genetics, was very limited, it needed the political motivation which was to be found among those outside the system.

BRIDGING RACE FORMALISM AND POPULATION GENETICS

Raymond Pearl never played a leading role in the "New Synthesis," which bridged Darwinism and Mendelism during the thirties. While he accepted both Mendelism and Biometrics and had thought along lines of population control, it was left to Sewell Wright to represent American biologists among the first population geneticists. Sewell Wright, however, did not participate in the debate over race, as did his British counterpart Ronald Fisher. While most British geneticists during the thirties turned out to be politically liberal, and several of them participated in discrediting scientific racism, Fisher provides the prime instance of a scientist who participated in the "New Synthesis," yet insisted on a traditional racial typology. An expert, an intellectual and a rigid conservative: science was not preordained to refute scientific racism.

Ronald Aylmer Fisher was born in 1890 to a middle-class family as the youngest of seven surviving children. At first affluent, the father lost his fortune when Fisher was young. Academic excellence sent Fisher from Harrow to Cambridge on a scholarship. He studied mathematics and showed a strong interest in biology. He left Cambridge in 1913, a year after graduation, when financial constraints forced him to search for a paid position in an investment company, but he sustained his interests in the application of mathematics to biological questions. In 1918, while teaching in a public high school and only marginally connected with academic circles, he published his first significant paper on a consistency of biometric analysis with Mendelian heredity.[102] Following this publication, he received offers for employment both from the Galton Laboratories under Pearson and the Rothamsted Experimental Station, the most prestigious agricultural institute in England. He

---

[102] R. A. Fisher, "The Correlation Between Relations on the Supposition of Mendelian Inheritance," *Transactions of the Royal Society of Edinburgh*, 52 (1918), 339–433. Significantly, the publication was sponsored by the President of the Eugenic Educational Society, Leonard Darwin, after it had been declined by the Royal Society of London. Joan Fisher Box, *R. A. Fisher The Life of A Scientist* (New York: John Wiley and Sons, 1978), pp. 50–51.

chose the latter, and it was there that he recast the basis of statistics and developed his *Genetical Theory of Natural Selection* (1930) for which he is most famous.

While Fisher enjoyed the best England had to offer to its fortunate middle classes, he suffered from a bitter and scornful personality.[103] While his science is described in superlatives, his personality gave little cause for admiration. Fisher's interest in biology is traced at least by MacKenzie to his early involvement in eugenics,[104] and it is almost self-evident how his personal interests coincided with his conservative politics and social beliefs. Fisher's case is rare in that his first-rate scientific views were directly related to his class interests. With his quarrelsome character, Fisher enjoyed many of the personal and scientific controversies in which he was engaged. He responded to scientific disagreement on a personal level and on various occasions showed hostility to opponents, which at least once brought him into a squabble with the police. His commitment to traditional middle class English values manifested itself in a millennaristic belief in racial decadence. Social conditions caused an urgency that forced the scientist to assume responsibility and salvage the class debate from the fundamental scientific misconceptions. Scientists, Fisher argued, have "to distinguish between what is inevitable, and what is subject to control," and as citizens they had to see to it that possible control was actually exercised.[105]

The 1921 International Eugenics Congress represented a comprehensive consensus of biological racism in America and England never matched before or since. Few challenged the notion that the mental and moral qualities of humankind are inherited to the same extent as are the physical characters, and Ronald Fisher reminded

---

[103] The *Dictionary of Scientific Biography* describes him as "Slight, bearded, eloquent, reactionary and quirkish." N. T. Gridgeman, "Ronald Fisher," *DSB*, p. 8. MacKenzie (*Statistics in Britain* [Edinburgh: Edinburgh University Press, 1981], p. 184), describes him as "marked by an extreme egocentricity and violent temper."

[104] MacKenzie, *Statistics*, pp. 188, 191, shows how selection played an important role in correlating the two.

[105] R. Fisher, *The Social Selection of Human Fertility*, The Herbert Spencer Lecture (Oxford: Oxford Clarendon Press, 1932), in *Collected Papers of R. A. Fisher*, edited by J. H. Bennett (Adelaide, 1971; thereafter RAFCP), II, p. 66. In a review of *The Need For Eugenics Reform* by Leonard Darwin, Fisher emphasized urgency: "it is much to be feared that unless the great body of educated opinion informs itself rapidly, and *from impartial sources*, on this important movement, schemes may be framed in disregard of the racial consequences and an opportunity lost of performing, for the benefit of future generations, a service of the first magnitude," "Modern Eugenics," *Science Progress*, 21 (1926), 130–136, in *RAFCP*, II, p. 127–133 (emphasis added). No doubt there was no consensus on what Fisher saw as "impartial sources."

the audience that the situation was not always such: "[this] is now so firmly established that we have some difficulty in realizing the opposition which early investigators encountered in establishing this fact."[106] At the same time this consensus included the biologists who were defining the new frontiers of science, together with those whose lasting contribution was more to bigotry and professional rivalry than to biology. As Fisher's position proves, progressive science could go hand in hand with reactionary social ideas.

Fisher saw evolution as a center of "faith and hope" in contrast to its more conventional evaluation as "a soulless creed." In a synthesis of evolution and creation, Fisher argued that the latter "was not all finished a long while ago, but is still in progress, in the midst of its incredible duration."[107] Eugenics was therefore more than a political creed or a religion, but had bearing on both. As Fisher claimed, "it stands or falls by the great biological advances of the last two generations, and in a very special sense is a product of the evolutionary theory."[108] His treatment of science as a creed explains why rigorous statistics were manifested in a volatile personality. Joan Fisher Box, in a biography of her father, presented a similar view: "Fisher could never let pass what he believed to be wrong reasoning. He was known on other occasions to argue the case, even with someone who produced a correct answer, if the reasoning on which it was based was not sound. To leave unchallenged what was irrational was to open the door to all untruth."[109]

Fisher's career in eugenic thinking began in his undergraduate days at Cambridge. There, among peers and teachers, he had the opportunity to formulate his scientific and social views. With the fervor of a young man he discovered "the underlying principle . . . of civilized races." His discovery was that

In any society which is so organized that members of small families enjoy a social advantage over members of large ones, the qualities of all kinds, physical, mental, and moral which go to make up what may be called

---

[106] "The Evolution of Conscience in Civilised Communities (In special relation to Sexual Vices)" paper read at the International Eugenics Congress, 1921. Published in *Eugenics Review*, 14 (1922), 190–192, and *RAFCP*, I, p. 448. Fisher substantiated the consensus by citing the method of experimental psychology of Thorndike, the method of correlation between mental characters of Pearson, and the genealogical method of Galton as it was practiced by Davenport.

[107] Fisher, "The Renaissance of Darwinism," in *RAFCP*, IV, pp. 616–620.

[108] Fisher, "Modern Eugenics-Being A Review of *The Need For Eugenics Reform* by Leonard Darwin," *Science Progress*, 21 (1926), 130–136, in *RAFCP*, II, p. 122.

[109] Box, *R. A. Fisher*, p. 268.

"resultant sterility" tend, other things being equal, to rise steadily in the social scale; so that in such a society, the highest social strata, containing the finest representatives of ability, beauty and taste which the nation can provide, will have, apart from individual inducements, the smallest proportion of descendants; and this dysgenic effect of social selection will extend throughout every class in which any degree of resultant sterility provides a social advantage.[110]

Using this analysis, Fisher elaborated, but did not significantly change, his social views in the next five decades. He claimed to have elucidated the eugenic principles from scientific studies from which his influence and status stemmed. Yet his social views preceded any of his scientific contributions.

Fisher applied sophisticated mathematics and statistics to the study of biology. Yet, when it came to social questions, he accepted a simple dichotomy between the upper and lower classes, the civilized and the primitive, heredity and environment. This division Fisher sought to quantify, and though qualifying it as a "provisional examination of the existing data" he argued that it is "unlikely that more than 5 percent of the variance of the physical measurements of man is due to non-heritable causes." Regarding other moral and mental features for which the data were insufficient even in Fisher's eyes, he thought "it would be wisest to judge by comparison of the known facts with those of the physical measurements." Perhaps most revealing is that he advanced these claims concurrently with his early attempts to harmonize biometrics and genetics.[111]

The eugenicists' pessimism concerning the future of civilization did not suggest to them the possibility that their society was not the best of all possible worlds: rather they feared the consequences of any shift in social stratification. With little study of social mobility,

[110] Fisher adopted the idea from an article by J. A. Cobb, which appeared in the *Eugenics Review*, in January, 1913. Fisher called it "the greatest addition to our eugenics knowledge since the work of Galton." Fisher, "Some Hopes of A Eugenist," paper read before the Eugenics Education Society, Oct. 2, 1913, *Eugenics Review*, 6 (1914), 309–315, in *RAFCP*, I, p. 80.

[111] Fisher, "The Causes of Human Variability," *Eugenics Review*, 10 (1918), 213–220, in *RAFCP*, I, p. 176. When he tried to integrate heredity and environment it sounded more scholastic than scientific: "The supposed conflict between heredity and environment is quite superficial; the two are connected by double ties: first that the surest and probably the quickest way to improve the environment is to secure a sound stock; and secondly that for the eugenist, the best environment is that which effects the most rapid racial improvement. The ordinary social reformer sets out with a belief that no environment can be too good for humanity; it is without contradicting this, that the eugenist may add that man can never be too good for his environment." Fisher, "Some Hopes of A Eugenist," (1913) in *RAFCP*, I, p. 78.

Fisher could declare that "there is no doubt" that "the large proportion of 'new blood' which enters the professions in every generation," is "on the whole, inferior to the professional families of long standing."[112] Fisher judged social classes to represent more than the accumulation of capital, and objected to criticism that society is not stratified eugenically, and that wealth is a bad criterion of "eugenic worth." He argued that dysgenic evolution was a result of the fact that "the socially lower classes have a birth-rate, or, to speak more exactly, a survival rate, greatly in excess of those who are on the whole distinctly their eugenic superiors."[113] To this Haldane responded from a socialist perspective that, if one judged the phenomenon in Darwinian terminology, the higher survival rate proved the superiority of the lower classes, to which Fisher did not reply.[114]

Birth control seemed to provide a possible solution, and the different methods of contraception, including sterilization, engaged the British eugenicists. The greatest evolutionary danger to the eugenicists stemmed from greater control among the superior groups (namely, the middle class) of family size, and as Fisher observed they had all the financial motivations to limit the number of children. This meant that the future belonged to the inferior groups. The historical lesson was all too clear: the decline and fall of all previous empires.[115] Yet he certainly did not view the ruling English class as inferior to the elite of earlier empires.

When contraception is widely practiced, those who find such methods repugnant to their moral nature will on average have the largest number of children. Future generations will be more and more largely composed of those whose feelings towards the methods of contraception may be compared with those of the early Christians towards abortion. The greater the economic pressure to which they are exposed, the more severe will be

---

[112] Fisher, "Positive Eugenics," *Eugenics Review*, 9 (1917), 206–212. Also in *RAFCP*, I, p. 131.

[113] Fisher, "Some Hopes of A Eugenist," in *RAFCP*, I, p. 70.

[114] Fisher, "The Evolution of Conscience in Civilized Communities," quoted in *RAFCP*, I, p. 451.

[115] "In this peculiar tendency of civilized societies to concentrate in the lowest classes the task of producing the citizens of future generations, our modern civilization seems to be merely following the course traversed by the Graeco-Roman civilization." Fisher's conjecture was supplemented by confidence: "We know, it is true, practically nothing of the rate of reproduction of the lower orders of society under the Roman Empire, but there can be no doubt that the failure of reproduction among the aristocratic, and among the self-respecting families was extremely pronounced." Fisher, "Eugenics: Can It Solve the Problem of Decay of Civilizations?" *Eugenics Review*, 18 (1926), 128–136, in *RAFCP*, II, p. 113.

the selection, and the more fiercely and clearly will their new morality be branded upon their conscience.[116]

Fisher contributed to the future society eight children of his own. His program for social reform would have compensated families proportionally to their income for bringing up each additional child; namely, each family would receive from the state a sum equivalent to its cost of raising up a child. The rich who refrained from having further children because of the high cost of raising them would be induced by high governmental compensation. The poor, who were prolific parents anyhow, would be compensated according to their relatively small expenses per child. As Fisher put it: "A family allowance system provides no economic motive for having children, or for refraining from having them. It merely abolishes the economic bonus which at present we offer to both Smith and Brown for every child they refrain from having."[117]

Everything Fisher stated on selective breeding as a eugenic mechanism was said despite his recognition that biological knowledge was limited to the influence of single defective genes. Reflecting on East and Jones's studies of maize, Fisher asked: "Why are the recessive factors in maize harmful? Why do not unexpected advantages as well as unexpected defects appear in the inbred strains?" He believed that "inbreeding was no effect in itself but serves solely to bring recessives to light, [which] is in complete accord with the human attitude towards consanguinity," and argued that morals must prevail. Upon this, all applications of genetics to humans depended.[118] In an attempt to overcome the frustration – which was the result of the predicted long duration needed for selection – Fisher contradicted his recognition (in other respects) of the importance of the multiple genetic factors responsible for each trait by contending that "a large portion of the feeble

---

[116] Fisher, "The Evolution of Conscience in Civilised Communities," quoted in *RAFCP*, I, p. 451.

[117] Fisher, "Family Allowances – In the Contemporary Economic Situation," *Eugenics Review*, 24 (1932), 87–95, in *RAFCP*, II, p. 74.

[118] "Eugenists will be grateful for the criticisms ... of Davenport's advice that those who probably suffer from recessive defects should marry into sound stocks. The contamination of good stocks by bad is only a sacrifice of good stocks in order to cover up a defect, which will eventually show itself in spite of all efforts; the more readily if the heterozygous condition be encouraged to have children." Fisher, *Eugenics Review*, 12 (1920), 116–119, in *RAFCP*, I, pp. 203–204.

in mind owe their defect to a single Mendelian recessive,"[119] implying a feasible eugenic solution.

The use of professional jargon to enhance social prejudice often turns up in unlikely places, as shown by Fisher's use of the concept of selection. He compared the genetic distinction between the classes to the dichotomy between civilized and primitive societies, and attributed the latter polarization to the fact "that all long-civilised peoples have been purged of their more murderous elements by passing through this period of *severe selection* ..." This terminology came from the same person whose most important contribution to science was his 1930 book *The Genetical Theory of Natural Selection*. As with his consistent views on social reforms throughout life, Fisher's ethnological views had been shaped along nationalistic lines before World War I, and he continued to speak in the tone of a crude Social Darwinist. In the optimism of the pre-war years, Fisher predicted: "The widespread, fruitful and successful races of the future belong to the dominant nations of to-day," and he based that misconception on genetics. "Eugenics is not inherently associated with nationalism; but in the world of nations as we see it, nationalism may perform a valuable eugenic function. The modern nation is *a genetic, a territorial, and an economic organism*, and the modern tendency is to emphasise its essential unity."[120] Some eugenicists glorified a mythical past of a purified race. Others lauded the modern nation-race, while lamenting some of its constituents. Fisher's statement illustrates the confused periodization in eugenic and racialist thinking. If the contemporary races were superior, then evolution and selection were working well, and there was no rationale for eugenics. But if the prophecies of doom were correct, then how could a modern nation with all past migrations and the inferior lower classes which contaminated the gene pool, be the preferable unit of selection? Bigoted arguments are often incoherent, and in this case neither Fisher nor his readers distinguished between his scientific and his propagandistic writings.

Like other racial theorists, Fisher confused biological with his-

[119] Fisher qualified the statement by saying "there is considerable but by no means conclusive evidence" to support this position. Fisher, "Modern Eugenics-Being A Review of *The Need For Eugenics Reform* by Leonard Darwin," *Science Progress*, 21 (1926), 130–36, in *RAFCP*, II, p. 124. For his contradictory views, see his debate with Punnett and Jennings in the section on Punnett, pp. 149–150.

[120] Fisher, "Some Hopes of A Eugenist," *Eugenics Review*, 5 (1914), 309–315, in *RAFCP*, I, p. 79. (emphasis added).

torical time-scales. His arguments were formulated in biological durations interspersed with claims about selection along national lines within the short historical periods of national existence. At times, he was more careful to point out the "specious web of conjectural ethnology," especially if the conclusions hurt his British ego, as did *Inbreeding and Outbreeding* by East and Jones, in asserting that the Irish were "principally the product of the intermingling of two savage Mongolian tribes"![121] Fisher's work illustrates that science and social views were intertwined in the conservative credo in the same fashion as among radical liberals and leftwingers, and that both the old racialist argumentation, and its reform, depended as much on external cultural developments as on scientific ones.

[121] But for this aspect, Fisher reviewed the book very favorably. See *Eugenics Review*, 12 (1920), 116–119, in *RAFCP*, I, p. 204. Integrating data of blood groups which contradicted traditional Scandinavian influence made Fisher suggest that the Scottish and north English "may well be a proto-Scandinavian influence." Fisher and G. L. Taylor, "Scandinavian Influence in Scottish Ethnology," *Nature*, 145 (1940), 590, in *RAFCP*, IV, pp. 319–321.

CHAPTER 5

Mitigating racial differences

The refutation of scientific racism depended upon a group of scientists interpreting biological knowledge in an anti-racist manner. Science could lend itself as easily to either a racist or an anti-racist interpretation, whether by biologists or social scientists. If popular opinion holds that science has its own determinism and that it is applied in a coherent manner as a result of its substance and objectivity, historical records suggest otherwise. Conventional perceptions of the impartiality of science encourage an assumption that the growth of population genetics inherently lend support to a non-racist interpretation. Yet, as the analysis above of Ronald Fisher's work showed, the evolution of anti-racism in science was not inevitable.

Other geneticists, however, did criticize racist theories from a scientific perspective, and studied environmental influences on various organisms in order to minimize the space assigned by default to nature as compared with nurture. They opposed racism on ethical grounds, and – perhaps most important – disseminated the new scientific understanding to the public. In other words, these scientists used their scientific credentials to serve as intellectuals in the wider cultural debate over race. The scientific expertise on both sides of the debate was comparable, if not identical, and biology ceased to present a unified view of the nature of race. The public was exposed to the debate among the experts, and thus political space was created for competition among intellectual interest groups for the public mind.

The main actors among the biologists were British. They included scientists aware of social injustice, mostly of a leftist persuasion, but who, in contrast to their conservative peers, did not deny their social purport. The most prominent in the group included J. B. S. Haldane, Julian Huxley, Lionel Penrose, and Lancelot Hogben.

LANCELOT HOGBEN

While in some respects Hogben's legacy is relatively less known than that of Haldane or Huxley, his denunciation of scientific racism came earlier and was more poignant than that of his peers. Hogben first encountered university life in 1913 at Trinity College, Cambridge, where he came to know something of the English academic establishment. Of modest background, he was unimpressed by the experience, from the consumption of food at the College to the social pretensions in general, and developed "a lifelong dislike and mistrust of any cosy establishment."[1] This antagonism led Hogben to join the Fabians at Cambridge and, what was less well known, to become a member of the Society of Friends. His religious background (having a priest for a father) was perhaps less influential in this case than his rejection of war and imperialism. Following the outbreak of World War I, Hogben volunteered for an ambulance unit and helped to build civilian shelters for families made homeless by the war. But when conscription was introduced Hogben refused to participate or even return to his voluntary positions, and became a conscientious objector. This landed him in solitary confinement sewing mailbags. By the time the Quakers bailed him out, his health had broken down, and he was discharged by a medical panel. The whole episode lasted less than three months, but it displayed Hogben's readiness to back his beliefs with action.

The next decade took Hogben across three continents, the third stop being South Africa, where he landed in 1927. He had begun his academic career in London, where he worked at Imperial College under the direction of E. W. MacBride, but he picked up little of MacBride's Lamarckianism or politics. Following a two-year stay in Edinburgh and another in Canada, he arrived in Cape Town. This rapid change of location was hardly conducive to experimental studies, and he therefore concentrated on theoretical work. South Africa would have provided him with a wonderful opportunity for research, but social commitment interfered. Hogben shared with his demographer wife, Enid Charles, in addition to their four children, political beliefs and professional interests. In South Africa this attitude had its toll. Though not politically active, Hogben disregarded in his behaviour the growing strength of apartheid,

[1] George Philip Wells, "Lancelot Hogben," *Biographical Memoirs of Fellows of the Royal Society*, 24 (1978), 187.

accepted colored students in his class, and even addressed some students' gatherings. But perhaps most offensive to those supporting apartheid was their open house held on Saturday nights. At first, this drew only senior students and junior members of the faculty, but later it reputedly began to attract the city's intelligentsia, and the place turned into a hotbed of radicalism. These armchair radicals were not involved in politics, but their mere existence was a threat to the authoritarian power. Therefore, despite the flora and fauna of South Africa, two years after arrival Hogben had to look for a new position. As luck would have it, the British Association annual meeting was held at precisely the same time in South Africa, and Hogben made some additional crucial contacts, leaving the visitors with a favorable impression. As a result he was able to gain a post in London.

The London School of Economics had in the meantime been receiving a Rockefeller grant since 1925, a portion of which had not been utilized in five years for want of appropriate personnel. The grant was for a Chair of Social Biology, a compromise between the interests of the Rockefeller Foundation in biological studies and those of the London School of Economics in social research. The first contacts in 1923 were made between William Beveridge, in the name of the London School of Economics, and Beardsley Ruml, the Director of the Laura Spelman Rockefeller Memorial. These were followed by initial grants in 1924 of a quarter of a million dollars to the school. The Rockefeller Foundations were only too eager to finance the work of the school, especially on "the physical or natural bases of the Social Sciences, including Anthropology, Social Biology and Psychology," but was somewhat more reluctant to invest in cement or towards the school's endowment. Negotiations followed, and the Laura Spelman Rockefeller Memorial granted the school a further US $155,000 in 1925, followed by US $700,000 in January 1926. The sum was a combination of US $500,000 to promote the study of modern social conditions and of the natural basis of the social sciences and an additional US $200,000 which were given because, as Beveridge reported, "Mr. Ruml had more money to give away than I had at least felt at that stage certain of being able to spend advantageously on the 'Natural Basis'." Beside the additional money that went towards a Chair of International Law, the endowment was divided half to anthropology and social biology, a quarter to modern social conditions, and a quarter to international studies. Though the chairs in anthropology and international law were established, and several other positions were made full-time, "the establishment of a Chair of Social Biology was postponed till enquiries showed that suitable candidates were available." It took five years to find the appropriate candidate, which enabled Hogben to return to London.[2] The unusual appointment, the only professor of social biology in England and the prestige of a chair at London University, gave Hogben – who came close to becoming a refugee from South African apartheid – an advantageous position which he utilized to fight racism.

In his inaugural address at the School, Hogben delivered a "somewhat sarcastic attack upon eugenics" for stressing the similarities between "man and higher animals" at the expense of the differences. The change in "recent years," Hogben argued, was not properly grasped by eugenists, "who think that reproduction and inheritance in human beings proceed on the same lines as in albino mice, fruit flies and the garden pea."[3] During the following years Hogben became one of the most effective critics of eugenics. He emphasized every point that minimized the importance of genetics for an understanding of social behavior and stressed the role of the environment. This he did both in his research and in his publications, many of which aimed at the educated public. He devised mathematical methods and in cooperation with Enid Charles and others, initiated statistical studies on topics ranging from clinical problems (which eventually absorbed most of his attention) to elucidating the societal genetic waste due to lack of education as it was measured by intelligence tests. He also initiated a series of statistical studies of I.Q. differences which showed that the differentiation was not – as was conventionally assumed – predominantly due to genetics, and cut the heredity factor down to a maximum of 50 percent from the generally accepted figures of between 80 and 95 percent.[4]

Given his idiosyncratic personality, Hogben did not find peace even among the London School of Economics radical constituency,

---

[2] "Origin of Social Biology in the School of Economics," memo by WHB (William Beveridge) July 16, 1935. Beveridge Papers, London School of Economics.

[3] Blacker described Hogben to Huxley as looking "rather like what you see behind the counters in Selfridges." Huxley answered by saying that "[Hogben] is really on the verge of being a genius, but always damning himself by his nervousness and inferiority complex ..." Blacker to Huxley, Oct. 24, 1930, Huxley to Blacker, Nov. 4, 1930. SA/EUG/C 185.

[4] G. P. Wells, "L. T. Hogben," pp. 198–199.

to whom his self definition in the late thirties as a scientific humanist was not Marxist enough. Hogben commented about his own intellectual evolution:

If I had been asked to give a label to my creed, when I was starting in my profession as a scientific worker, I should have called it Socialism. That was twenty-five years ago. Today I prefer to call it scientific humanism. Scientific humanism is the creed I profess and the profession I try to practise.[5]

This synthesis was too individualistic and did not go well with part of his audience at the School, many of whom were members of the communist party. Suddenly, Hogben's position as a radical was endangered, a position aggravated by his election to the Royal Society in 1936, which "made his scientific status unimpeachable," and displayed the eagerness of even the most eccentric members among the British intellectuals to be coopted into the establishment.[6]

Hogben's anti-racist arguments gained a wide audience as his books grew in popularity. The press and the educated public that followed the debate over the merit of biological planning of society interpreted Hogben's writings as undermining the eugenic position, showing differences in environment as more important in heredity with respect to mentality and behavior. Carr-Saunders, who at the time was at the University of Liverpool, reported in 1932 to the Metropolis that his audience is "somehow of the opinion that [Hogben] .. has shown up eugenics." This, he thought, was a cause for alarm because "just as the public is waking up, the one man who holds an academic position in this field seems to have given the whole thing a *coup de grace*."[7] In fact, Hogben was not an anti-eugenist, and up to 1933 had even served on the Consultative Board of the Eugenics Society. But then, anti-racism had to become more explicit and the danger of Nazism had to be faced. Hogben resigned from the board and dissociated himself from the eugenics move-

[5] L. T. Hogben, *Dangerous Thoughts* (London: George Allen & Unwin, 1939), p. 13.
[6] "Professor Lancelot Hogben," Obituary, *The Times*, Aug. 23, 1975. Hogben thought his appointment should have come earlier, and he suspected that his "enemies were keeping him out." G. P. Wells, "L. T. Hogben," p. 200. In this Hogben was not alone, and in fact his election came earlier than that of his more senior friend, Julian Huxley.
[7] Carr-Saunders to Blacker, Feb. 17, 1932. SA/EUG/C 56. On June 6, 1932 Carr Saunders wrote that Hogben's and Ginsberg's anti-eugenics made the most pressing problem for the future of the eugenics movement to obtain academic support. Blacker did not see Hogben as such a danger, though Hogben was no favorite of his. Blacker to Carr Saunders, Feb. 23, 1932. SA/EUG/C 56.

ment, though like H. J. Müller, he continued to support the principle of a possible improvement of genetic stock.[8]

Hogben's clear views combining anthropological and genetic knowledge in an engaging style made his books very popular and consequently influential. Here was the embodiment of the expert as an intellectual, the absolute savant at his most influential position. Much of the biology in his arguments was not unknown to his peers, but rarely was it articulated in such a coherent form, with the legitimacy of a professorship attached. Despite his tendency to accentuate differences, Hogben tried at times to bridge theoretical conflicts and keep up an open dialogue with opponents, as when in the Mendelism–biometrics dispute he argued that the antithesis of heredity and environment in genetics was outdated. Hogben supported Fisher's criticism of the incompatibility of the biometrician's law of Ancestral Inheritance with the principle of genetic segregation, calling the law "trite" rather than "false," and summarizing it as "a mathematically sophisticated way of stating that like breeds like."[9]

Hogben spoke of the "great variety of skin colour" but emphasized a more general variability of characters, concluding that a "classification of mankind in geographical units defined by skin, colour, or head-form would lead to a very different system from that based on hair texture and nasal index." Though blood groups were the most advanced basis for classifying populations and provided the only "genetic analysis of human differences which are geographically localized," Hogben saw no reason to adopt them as an absolute criterion for racial classification, since blood type was "only a single anthropological character," and argued that it had certainly failed to revolutionize anthropology. He was, however, ready to utilize the studies of blood group in anti-racist argument, commenting that "in groups like the inhabitants of Europe the fluctuations of the group percentages do corroborate what is already conceded by everybody, that the inhabitants of Europe are thoroughly mixed."[10] From a genetic point of view the blood group classification was substantially superior to skull form, but none the

[8] Hogben was not a member of the inner circle, but that was more a result of (lack of) comradeship, than of ideology. For example, see Blacker to Huxley, Dec. 20, 1933. SA/EUG/C 185.

[9] Hogben, *Genetic Principles in Medicine and Social Science* (London: Williams and Norgate, 1931), pp. 201, 171. Also Hogben, *Nature and Nurture* (New York: Norton, 1933), p. 111.

[10] Hogben, *Genetic Principles*, pp. 124–126.

less he was willing to incorporate either methods in a critique of racial typology.

By 1931, Hogben challenged the likelihood that racial classification along genetic lines could be achieved in principle:

We have very little justification for assuming a close approximation to genetic purity when we define a group of human beings by a large and heterogeneous assemblage of physical traits. Conversely, the possibility of dividing mankind into discrete groups distinguished by some particular anatomical characteristic for which the peoples inhabiting a restricted geographical area are relatively pure in the genetic sense does not presuppose the probability that the same group will be differentiated from their neighbors by genetic differences affecting other anatomical or social characteristics.[11]

Hogben's commitment to fight racist interpretations was a result of his belief that biology was the mainstay of anti-egalitarianism. He viewed the golden past as one of equality, based on the "mythical beliefs concerning the brotherhood of man." This harmony was disrupted by the racist supremacists who injected the biological argument. Biology had consequently to reclaim its own, and he called for the biologist to adopt

A more reasonable position ... [which] would be an attitude of experimental scepticism. Experiment and experiment alone can decide the limits of development imposed by whatever genetic differences distinguish one racial group considered as a fictitious whole from another group considered as a fictitious whole.[12]

In his attack on the correlation between mental differences and physical characters, Hogben's ammunition consisted of the retractions and hesitations of earlier advocates such as Pearson and Brigham. Hogben analyzed Davenport and Steggerda's data[13] and showed that the variability of the brown-hybrid population in the majority of the psychological tests employed was not greater than that of either parent stock, and concluded that Mendelian principles had little to offer in interpreting differences in mental capacity. As in other cases, the main flow in Davenport's statistical data was over-prediction.[14] The criticism that racism had the tendency to present statistical results that were too good turned out to be very powerful. Davenport argued that mental capacity was segregated according to Mendelian principles, yet his data showed that

[11] *Genetic Principles*, p. 127.   [12] *Genetic Principles*, p. 133.   [13] See pp. 166–168.
[14] *Genetic Principles*, p. 143.

physical variability among the intermediate groups of "Browns" was greater than in any of the pure stocks of "Blacks" or "Whites." At the same time the variability in mental qualities among these groups was similar. Hogben argued that there was no reason to presuppose an analogy between the different categories, and the strength of his claim was that he reinterpreted the racist study.

Hogben criticized more than empirical discrepancies. He showed that the Black, Brown and White groups were not socially equal. The first two included 32 prisoners while the third did not. At the other end of the scale, 19 Blacks were students, while only one White belonged in that category. The differences between the samples were not explained in the study, one of the last field studies aimed at strengthening the racist position. Hogben commented: "Certainly the onus of proof lies on the shoulders of anyone who, on the basis of differences recorded in this investigation, would elaborate legislative policies and reinforce social barriers."[15]

In a way, all Hogben did was to illuminate the obvious. Yet in this area where confidence and conventions surpassed knowledge, Hogben's argument was part of the shift in the burden of proof from isolated egalitarians to the racists. Once scientists with sound credentials criticized the racist argument, the racists had to substantiate their position, an impossible task within the boundaries of science. Racist theories were guilty of conceptually confusing time scales and jumbling archaeological, biological and historical times. Against this tendency to over-simplify nature, Hogben reminded his peers that king crabs or certain lamp shells resisted evolution over vast geological periods. Accordingly, "there is no strong *prima facie* evidence to sustain the assumption that the course of social evolution must have been profoundly affected by genetic selection operating within historic period."[16] Despite such a critique, this kind of mistake had not been eradicated in the past half century.

"AFRICA VIEW" – HUXLEY'S CHANGING PERSPECTIVES

As has been shown above the liberal Julian Huxley displayed in the early twenties conventional racism. During the thirties, however, he had become a celebrated anti-racist. Huxley's switch provides a significant and interesting insight into a more general cultural transfiguration. An individual's cultural commitments are often

---

[15] *Genetic Principles*, p. 137–138.   [16] *Genetic Principles*, p. 168.

varied and incoherent but as long as no explicit internal confrontation occurs such ambiguity may remain. However, a resolution is
sought once the conflict becomes explicit. The process may be
subconscious, and an initial vexation may lead to a preliminary
shift which begins a process of justification accompanied by a
growing commitment to a new, more coherent, cultural view. This
process describes Huxley's changing position on race following his
experiences in Africa.

Huxley's emotional and rational attitudes to race were shaped by
his personal encounters, reflecting spontaneous fear and 'socially
acquired' aversion to strangers. However, the manifestation of these
emotions was rational and depended upon his choice of cultural
values. When his racism collided with his liberal values, he reversed
his racism. A second facet of his racism was grounded in scientific
discourse and presented Huxley's belief of the correct interpretation
of racial differences. The two spheres intertwined to form a personal
cultural synthesis which included science and ethics, spontaneous
fallacies together with long-held prejudices.

Among Huxley's most revealing accounts of his views on race is
the chapter on "Racial Chess" in *Africa View*. Here Huxley recounts
how he had first come to fear blacks:

I remember once, in central Texas, arriving by car in a little town whose
streets were crowded . . . almost wholly by negroes; there were hundreds of
black men to tens of white. I am bound to confess that this first experience
of mine of being in a small minority among human beings of another
physical type gave me an emotional jolt; and I began, without any process
of ratiocination, to understand why white men living in such circumstances generally took to carrying revolvers and developed a race complex.[17]

This race complex never left Huxley. By 1930, reflecting upon his
journey to Africa, Huxley implicitly admitted the duality of his own
attitude and hinted that he had been able to overcome his fears only
intellectually: "One could doubtless get over such feelings; but the
point is that they arose unbidden." It was a struggle between
intuitional and rational thinking that produced his confusion about
race, both in the American and African experiences. Huxley describes his thinking by distancing himself from it through generalization:

[17] J. Huxley, *Africa View* (New York: Harper & Brothers, 1931), p. 394.

Even the casual visitor like myself finds it difficult to escape the genius loci; the intellectual climate enfolds him, and because almost everyone he meets tacitly makes the same general assumptions, he very often falls into the current way of thinking. It is only when he gets away again and finds that other people live in other intellectual climates and have quite other ideas on the subject, that many of the local assumptions are seen to be really assumptions, and that he begins to try and think.[18]

Multicultural exposure provided the resolution. Getting away had taken Huxley close to two decades – from 1912, when he first arrived in Texas, until 1930. He endeavored to resolve his intellectual conflict when, faced with the political realities of England during the Depression, he reflected upon his own beliefs. Then his aversion to aliens was concealed by his more sophisticated views of what constitutes inequality among groups and by the recognition that within contemporary science adequate criteria for the study of races were lacking. At the same time the political scene was shifting, and the growing liberal opposition to racism had supplied Huxley with ample emotional support.

From Huxley's point of view, the difference between Africa and the American South was crucial. In the South, he was a foreigner whose ideas about race relations were mere speculations – social utopias favorable to his peers, like those for which his brother Aldous became so famous. (H. G. Wells, J. B. S. Haldane, Lancelot Hogben, and H. J. Müller were all popular utopians and close friends of Huxley.) The articles published in the *Spectator* betray the same state of mind. That Julian Huxley echoed Southern racism is unfortunate, but his views were the reflections of a tourist, and he lacked the ongoing intellectual debate to which he was later exposed in England.

In East Africa Huxley served as a delegate of the Colonial Office Advisory Committee on Native Education. With the burden of the Empire upon his shoulders, he assumed a seriousness characteristic of English liberals attempting to influence government policy. However, on the subject of race he now found himself emotionally in agreement with those he was expected to oppose, the Imperialists. His report had to accommodate both his notions of human equality and justice, and his racial prejudice. First and foremost a scientist, a beacon of secularism and rationality, Huxley had to make rec-

---

[18] *Africa View*, pp. 394, 391.

ommendations reflecting his rational conclusions, even if the chances for their approval were slim at best.

This accommodation was more likely the result of evasiveness than the outcome of a struggle. From Huxley's description, it seems he first chose to treat the subject scientifically and rationally. This aggravated the conflict between his political convictions and his racial prejudices, which he resolved by upholding political liberalism and attributing racial prejudice to a distant party, preferably dead or ignorant. Not surprisingly, his synthesis included many inconsistencies.

A century ago, the Dutch at the Cape, or the whites in the Southern States, quite sincerely believed that the black men were separated from white by a great gulf which could never be bridged; they were predestined slaves, the whites predestined masters. Such ideas, though they linger on in many quarters, are simply not tenable today. The progress, educational and practical, of the negro in the United States, or of the native African where he has had proper training and opportunity, gives it the lie. White and black overlap largely in regard to intelligence, energy, ability and character.[19]

In the first part of the statement Huxley ascribed essentially his own views of a few years earlier to the most racist groups in Western society, thereby distancing himself from them and presenting the proper enlightened modern conviction as his own. The transformation can be followed best in the text of *African View*.

His first step in shedding some of his racism was to realize that blacks were not all alike. In January 1930 Huxley published this great news in *The Times*. "The Africans, though the ignorant persist in classing them all as merely 'blacks,' 'natives,' or even 'niggers,' show more variety of physical type and way of life than is to be found in all Europe." The second step was to narrow the gap between the blacks and whites: "The most important point to realize is that not one of the East or South African tribes is pure Negro; all have a Hamitic admixture, and some are in blood and physical type as closely akin to men of Southern Europe or the Near East as to the negro of West Africa.'[20]

Where Huxley did not have contacts with blacks during his stay in the United States, in his African tour he met black Africans and did not just view them through the Colonial Office or the White

[19] J. Huxley, "Why Is The White Man In Africa?," *Fortnightly Review*, Jan., 1932, 65.
[20] Quoted in *Africa View*, pp. 6–7, 15.

settlers' perspectives. Having acquired new perceptions, he rebuked those who had not:

Most Europeans ignorant of that science [social anthropology] are as prone to dismiss the Africans as the merest savages, as those ignorant of racial anthropology are to class them all together as 'niggers.' As a matter of fact, all the peoples of Africa, save perhaps the Pygmies and Bushmen, have an elaborate social organization which contains many admirable features.[21]

Huxley attributed the inability of the European to empathize with the African perspective or even to understand it to the uniqueness of the African social organization and ideas which are alien to the European: "This attitude will overlook the one half of native life, and find the other half ridiculous or incomprehensible." Recognizing his prejudices, Huxley consequently changed his mind also about the American blacks.

Relevant here is the statement, often made, that the negroes in the United States have not made contributions to the national life proportionate to their number, and that those American negroes who have attained distinction almost invariably possess an admixture of white blood, though ranking as 'negro' to the inflexible race prejudice of America. The first part of this criticism must be largely discounted owing to this very fact of colour prejudice, which makes it far harder for the negro than for a white man to rise to wealth or eminence. There would appear to be more truth in the second assertion, though here again it is hard to know how much to ascribe the restlessness and 'divine discontent' generated by racial discrimination.[22]

Huxley could hardly have repudiated his own views of six years earlier more forcefully.

Under these circumstances he began to object to the concept of race. It conveyed more than was justified. "The term [race] is often used as if 'races' were definite biological entities, sharply marked off from each other. This is simply not true." Applying the terminology of population genetics, he continued: "Any given 'race' is characterized by containing within its boundaries a certain assortment of genes. One racial assortment will differ from another in the nature and proportionate abundance of the different kinds of genes of which it is made up, and every race will share some genes with many other races, probably with all." Through migration, slavery and commercialization, "every gradation [exists] between negro and full

[21] *Africa View*, pp. 15–16.   [22] *Africa View*, pp. 15–16, 399–400.

white." This egalitarian approach still carried with it the old belief that much of the mental progress of the blacks was due to their mixture with more advanced groups. Put in popular form, this read: "the Bantu, and still more the Hamitic peoples, have a considerable proportion of more or less 'white' and quite definitely Caucasian blood in their make-up."[23] It is this duality in language that gives the clue to Huxley's double standards: his use of "genes" in scientific discourse when the argument was empirical, rationalist and anti-racist; yielded to "blood" when racial prejudice gained the upper hand.

Huxley argued that backwardness in Africa is environmental. First "there is no particular reason to suppose that even the most intelligent peoples would have made all the important inventions had they been kept isolated from the rest of mankind." But "even if negro inventors had arisen, or outside inventions had penetrated into Africa, the country itself is against progress. The excessive luxuriance of nature, the heat of the climate, the prevalence of insidious and chronic disease, combine with the ease of gaining some reasonable livelihood with very little effort ..."[24]

An impression from these quotations might be that Huxley became a 'lumper,' and would go as far as to negate the very possibility of distinguishing races.[25] Nothing could be further from the truth. The egalitarian approach was achieved because, methodologically, Huxley preferred to limit his survey. Though there were tribes like the Bushmen and the Pygmies "who are generally acknowledged to be descendants of earlier and more primitive buddings of the human stock," Huxley was concerned with "the averages, and the average among the more widespread and successful tribes."

Moreover, Huxley maintained many prejudices when he came to conjectures. Criticizing Rousseau, the political prejudice of left-wing theorists, the "nonsense" about heredity prevalent among psychoanalysts, and the "whole behaviourist school," Huxley postulated that "there is not the least reason why races should not differ in the average of their inborn mental capacities as they do in their physical traits." In fact on biological grounds he expected such

[23] Africa View, pp. 395, 396, 400.   [24] Africa View, p. 399.
[25] For an enlightening exposition on 'lumpers' versus 'splitters' see Leonard Lieberman, "The Debate Over Race: A Study in the Sociology of Knowledge," Phylon, 20, 2 (1968), 127–141; Leonard Lieberman and Larry T. Raynolds, "The Debate Over Race Revisited: An Empirical Investigation," Phylon, 39, 4 (1978), 333–343.

differences to exist.[26] For this reconciliation between environment and innate capacity, Huxley chose Charles Davenport as his scientific authority. Six years earlier Huxley had concurred with the idea that intelligence tests projected hereditarian ability. By 1930, however, he was able to write that practically everyone admitted the crucial role of environment in the scores, because no test "has yet been devised which will discount really large differences of home environment and early training," and he rejected the assertion of the "negro inferiority in brains."

Despite the wide range of variation, and the overlapping, Huxley maintained part of Davenport's conclusions which he scaled down to support his own old prejudice: Davenport showed "that the negro average of pure intelligence was definitely but rather slightly below the white, and that the negro was rather more emotional and excelled in certain tests indicative of artistic appreciation."[27] There is much in this quotation for everyone: variation, overlapping, and superiority. Any one of these aspects can be emphasized to the detriment of others. But most instructive perhaps was the fact that Huxley quoted Davenport and was using him as a scientific authority for a statement that was to be his big anti-racist leap.

Fluent with ideas and in an elegant, journalistic style *Africa View* presented a dual position, which Huxley did not see as self-contradictory. By the time he directed his attention to education in 1930, Huxley had become fairly open-minded and indeterministic about its results. The general concern in Africa was the "falling off of intelligence among native boys at puberty," which Huxley attributed to the preoccupation with sex, in itself a very sensitive topic. He concluded that with the right background the interference should not be larger than with "the average white child, and [the black] can continue and mature with us." Following similar pros and cons, Huxley chose to suspend judgment; "We cannot appraise the Africans' capabilities in any accurate or scientific way until he has had several generations in which to demonstrate what they are."[28]

At this stage Huxley was non-racist in his descriptions and analyses, but continued to take a racist stand when it came to

[26] *Africa View*, pp. 404–405.
[27] *Africa View*, p. 400. For a different review of Davenport in England, and one which consequently influenced Huxley, see L. Hogben, "The Concept Of Race," in *Genetic Principles in Medicine and Social Science* (London: Williams & Norgate, 1931).
[28] *Africa View*, pp. 402, 404.

conjectures. He ended the article in *The Times* with a liberal criticism of Imperial policies, wondering whether their impact would destroy the variety in Africa, "insisting on large-scale production to suit the needs of Europe and Big Business, reducing the proud diversity of native tribes and races to a muddy mixture, their various cultures to a single inferior copy of our own?" None the less, this speculative exercise concerning potential evolution did not grant an equal footing to the Africans: "There is also a certain amount of evidence that the negro is an earlier product of human evolution than the Mongolian or the European, and as such might be expected to have advanced less, both in body and in mind." One might recall that earlier ancestry was a subject of much national rivalry in Europe and reputedly testified to a sort of superiority. For many, including Huxley at this stage, the fact that scientific discoveries shifted the balance of antiquity in favor of the Africans meant that the implications had to be reversed: earlier prehistory came to denote primitiveness. Thus traditional culture values could be sustained as long as the scientific findings were properly manipulated. In the same spirit, Huxley surmised that natural selection would also work against the blacks. In the tropical countries "there seems to be little driving force of selection to push the level of mental qualities upwards." Such scientific fiction was appropriately substantiated: "Popular belief and the few properly-conducted mental tests point in the same direction."[29]

This duality in Huxley's attitude led him to maintain a belief in European superiority, but to compromise and claim it was miniscule:

I am quite prepared to *believe* that if we ever devise a really satisfactory method measuring inborn mental attributes, we shall find the races of Africa slightly below the races of Europe in pure intelligence and probably certain other important qualities ... But – and the 'but' is a big one – I am perfectly certain that if this proves to be so, the differences between the racial averages will be small ... and that the great majority will overlap as regards their innate intellectual capacities.[30]

Such paternalistic views on race and class reflected the cultural (and scientific) values common among liberals and left-wingers in pre World War II Britain. These were the beliefs which defeated scientific racism as it was manifested a generation earlier. If these

[29] *Africa View*, p. 405.   [30] *Africa View*, pp. 405–406 (emphasis added).

views sound strange to modern ears, it is because these early nuances made an eventual greater shift possible.

If any scientist could be considered a liberal and a progressive, Huxley was one. His integration of scientific theories with a social and cultural world view, even during the earlier period of the twenties when his writings cannot be classified as anything but racist, testified to the general cultural confusion, the imbroglio of science and politics which resulted from the changing class structure. The confusion is reflected in the fact that while Huxley supported the biologically deterministic view of inequality among groups, he simultaneously advocated a fundamental human egalitarianism, without finding the two inconsistent. This duality was maintained even later once Huxley assigned a greater role to environmental factors and emphasized general equality while attributing to genetic endowment a crucial margin in creating an elite.

On October 13, 1922, *The Oxford Chronicle* ran the article "Science and Progress" with the headline: "Outspoken Professors at an Oxford Conference." The occasion was the Sociological Society's week-end conference at New College at which Huxley declared that at "a certain stage in human development the 'struggle for life' theory forfeited the sanction of biology, which pointed to cooperation as the only avenue to biological progress." The struggle had not ceased, he emphasized, it was merely restricted to ideas and traditions, and biology "pointed unhesitatingly" to some forms of federation as a means of progress. It might be difficult to discover "outspokenness" in such ideas, but this is the very point that need be stressed. Such ideas were considered unique, if not radical, in the cultural context of the early twenties, and Huxley was always tagged outspoken and liberal. Politically, Huxley stood somewhere to the right of the socialists, ready to embrace humanitarian causes in a liberal fashion, but without any specific political obligation. A freelance in politics and science, he supported the Soviet Union: a support turned into vocal denunciations by the 1930s upon the persecution of Soviet geneticists who opposed Lysenko.

By the mid-thirties Huxley had become a leader in the fight against racism. His commitment to, and central position in, the eugenics movement encouraged him to attempt a synthesis of eugenics and anti-racism. A unique opportunity presented itself when he delivered the Galton Lecture of 1936. Here was the occasion both to salvage the dwindling fortunes of eugenics and to accommodate it within the changing political circumstances. An expert, an intellectual and a politician, Huxley tried to bridge all three facets of his work.

Eager to challenge the conventional views of his listeners, Huxley chose to address the subject of race by talking about the blacks and not about Nazism. He argued from the most prestigious eugenicist podium that to grant the blacks equality was justified on moral grounds, because it could not be scientifically determined whether the blacks were equal or inferior to the whites. During the thirties Huxley was growing more convinced that science could not give the answers and that, regardless of anyone's personal aversion, the blacks should get their opportunity before any final judgment was passed. "To assert, as is often done, that the present barbarism of, say, the Bantu is proof of their genetic inferiority is a gross error of scientific method." This was, however, precisely Huxley's belief a few years earlier in *Africa View*, and to the rank-and-file eugenicist this was outright heresy. Huxley felt he had to defend his eugenic commitment and credentials, and establish a common ground with his listeners, which he did by resorting to his old superstition: "For instance, I regard it as wholly probable that the true negroes have a slightly lower average intelligence than the whites or yellows."[31] Huxley's personal prejudices were in line with the traditional eugenicists, and presumably this ought to have lubricated the acceptance of his scientific egalitarianism, even the extreme statement that no "eugenically significant point of racial differences has yet been scientifically established."

Among the audience were the socially and institutionally strong Lamarckians such as MacBride, who opposed Huxley on many fronts, including in the Eugenics Society itself, in the Zoological Society, and in extensive public correspondence in *Nature*. MacBride had also been a stumbling block to Huxley's election to the Royal Society, and confronted him on many committees. Huxley's views should thus be evaluated against the background of this dynamic discourse involving "internal" scientific issues as well as political struggle within the scientific community. Huxley spent time and energy on debates with biologists including Ruggles Gates and Captain Pitt Rivers, neither of whom was considered a charlatan. In this context, the declaration that in the lower classes "the

[31] Huxley, "Eugenics and Society," in *Man Stands Alone* (New York: Harpers & Brothers, 1940), pp. 50, 53.

Darwins and the Einsteins, like the Miltons, were mute and inglorious," was outright heresy when voiced by an apostate in the eugenic shrine. Huxley knew only too well who his listeners were and what was considered legitimate and respectable in their eyes. But perhaps the best illustration of the spectrum of opinion at the gathering is that the other speaker during the dinner, Colonel Sir Charles Close, viewed Nazi Germany "as a huge laboratory, where a vast eugenic experiment was going on which was of the greatest importance." And though he did not approve of many German policies, he endorsed the movement back to the land and the "theory of race uniformity on a classless basis."[32]

Huxley was a liberal, more so than the substance of his views might suggest in hindsight. His culture was liberal and his creed was a synthesis of "pure" intrinsic science, ideology and politics. His views are a testimony to liberalism, both in its open-mindedness and in its superficiality. His peers were the progressives, his theme was reform, his rivals were right-wingers, and he admired the nonconformism and liberalism in his family tradition. Huxley and liberal were synonyms. During the early thirties, the liberal shift against racism was gaining ground, and Huxley became one of its main proponents. The racial issue and eugenics were closely intertwined because both rested on the assumption of innate relations between the body and the psyche. As always, Huxley blended the change in his personal views and the shift in the public mind: "We are now beginning to have a better perspective about race and culture, migration and diffusion. Race need have little or nothing to do with culture: and diffusion of culture may take place without any mass migration."[33]

Huxley changed his views on race as much because of science as of the different cultural influences he encountered. This sequential intellectual shift, which could be traced to a period but should not be attributed to a single event, caused Huxley to gradually modify his scientific views on race. The truism that a scientific theory in one discipline is not applied immediately, or accurately, to another discipline deserves special emphasis when dealing with scientific theories of race. All too often there is an implicit assumption by historians that, since a new discovery or development has taken

[32] "Germany a Huge Laboratory," reported in *The Morning Post*, Feb. 18, 1936. JSHP.
[33] Huxley, "Diffusion of Culture," *Weekend Review* Sept. 30, 1933, 318–319 (review of Elliot Smith, *The Diffusion of Culture*).

place in a certain discipline it should be perceived as though it were disseminated instantly to other disciplines, and conceptualized and integrated in a way that our contemporary understanding would deem correct. The interaction between biology, anthropology, psychology and sociology, to mention the main disciplines in which theories of race were conceived, left much to be desired. Professional rivalry was a common obstacle, but even good intentions fell victim to ignorance, and interdisciplinary interpretations were often arbitrary. Huxley's choice of one theory over another in its application to the question of race was made by a biologist who ventured into psychology or anthropology as a layman. Yet he believed his interpretation of these allied disciplines to be professional and scientific, and the public accepted it. His pretensions to the gown of the expert when he was barely an intellectual led to a sorry outcome which was, however, no worse than when anthropologists and psychologists tried to interpret what they had understood to be the latest developments in genetics. Hogben mocked the contemporary state of interdisciplinary studies by saying: "geneticists believe that anthropologists have decided what race is. Ethnologists assume that their classifications embody principles which genetic science has proved to be correct." The third party, the politicians, "believe that their prejudices have the sanction of genetic laws and the findings of physical anthropology to sustain them."[34]

In the preface to his *Essays in Popular Science*, Huxley denied the need to apologize for writing popular essays in his field of speciality, but it stretches the imagination to see all the pieces in the book in the category of Huxley's scientific specialization.[35] The collection begins with a discussion on heredity and a refutation of the inheritance of acquired characters, but then ventures into popular philosophy. In this compartment, "An Hour's Psychology" illuminates Huxley's interdisciplinary approach. The piece is based on short notes on psychology, written after a lecture by Professor Janet at the Royal Society of Medicine. Huxley's main contention was that the human race constitutes more than a single species. Interfertility among offspring was not deemed sufficient in the human case:

when we come to diversity of racial constitution of mind, and still more to diversity of individual mental structure, we find that the variety of shapes assumed by mind in the human species – mental organism if you will – is as

[34] Hogben, *Genetic Principles in Medicine and Social Science*, p. 122.
[35] Huxley, *Essays in Popular Science* (New York: Knopf, 1927).

multifarious as the variety of physical shapes assumed by lower forms of life. Progress, divergence, specialization, adaptation, degeneration, play the same part as in physical evolution.

Huxley, primarily a zoologist, accepted a psychologist's definition of human species. This may suggest that once he acted as an intellectual he was prone to make the same mistakes lay persons do, even though he sustained the aura of the expert.

Demarcating social classes as different mental species "at different evolutionary levels," and perhaps even "along divergent evolutionary lines," translated into a conservative political ideology which accepted hierarchy in nature as a model for society, where "the higher being founded on the lower, the lower [are] definitely subordinate to the higher."[36] A decade later, in his Galton Lecture of 1936, Huxley again addressed the question of species, but this time he shifted sides, and contested Ruggles Gates's argument that major races, namely the color varieties, are true species: "This appears to me to be a grave error, arising from a failure to recognize the biological peculiarities of the human species, as a species."[37]

The change in Huxley's eugenic views was somewhat similar to the evolution of his opinion on race. Were it possible to draw a sharp distinction between the two, one would be tempted to say that it was a change in attitudes toward race that brought a greater sophistication to his eugenic and perhaps even biological thinking. This argument can be supported both chronologically and substantively. Huxley's new attitude to race seems to have taken shape in and around 1930: this is revealed by his description of Africa. His views on eugenics were then still very crude, but that has changed by 1936. In his Galton Lecture, the concept of eugenics had undergone a transubstantiation, not least for the sake of his campaign against Nazism. The political context in no way diminished the probable significance of the scientific change; it may have only increased the urgency for a synthesis of the two.

By 1936 the shift in Huxley's views was most evident in the way he readjusted the balance between environment and heredity and in his emphasis on contemporary ignorance of the science of eugenics. In his environmentalism he went so far as to declare that eugenics "falls within the province of Social Sciences not of the Natural Sciences" and that as such it was "a particular aspect of the study of

---

[36] Huxley, *Popular Science*, pp. 189–190.
[37] Huxley, "Eugenics and Society," in *Man Stands Alone*, p. 49.

man in society." He delineated the geneticist's understanding of what heredity is from popular misapprehensions. Genes and genetic outfit are inherited, but "any character whatsoever can only be a resultant between genes and environment."[38] This metamorphosis in the role he assigned to genetics in explaining culture and in the significance of eugenics, was reflected as well in the shift in Huxley's support from Carr-Saunders's position in 1926, to Lancelot Hogben's in 1936. Carr-Saunders, in his classic book on population, emphasized the genetic differences between classes, and in the twenties Huxley was all too eager to follow such a lead. His relations with Carr-Saunders remained very friendly even when they disagreed on scientific matters. Carr-Saunders himself had moderated his views, and contributed a chapter to Huxley's most influential collaborative anti-racist book, *We Europeans*. The two families were sufficiently close, for Mrs. Huxley to arrange for the Carr-Saunders to be the official guardians of the Huxley's children while the parents were on their tour of Africa. However by the thirties, Huxley came to support Hogben who exposed "the ambiguity of the concept of causation" inherent in the classical biometrical method which has "completely obscured the basic relativity of nature and nurture."[39] Studies have shown, wrote Huxley, "the strong probability . . . that most of the differences [among classes] are dependent on differences in nutrition," and this has "physical and mental effects far transcending what we originally thought possible."[40]

There are good reasons to believe that Hogben's influence on Huxley in this respect was crucial. Hogben was supported along his troubled academic career by Huxley, and the two were close friends, despite their differences of opinion. Like many family quarrels, Hogben's controversial views caused the greatest anxiety to those who valued them most, in this case the left-wingers and the eugenicists. In 1930, at a time when Huxley's opinions were changing, Hogben was there to spread the new gospel: evolution was not what Julian's illustrious grandfather had thought. It was therefore unsurprising that Carr-Saunders's more traditional eugenic views had to be updated.

---

[38] Huxley, "Eugenics and Society," in *Man Stands Alone*, pp. 38, 42.
[39] L. Hogben, *Nature and Nurture* (New York: W. W. Norton, 1933), p. 95.
[40] Huxley, "Eugenics and Society," *Man Stands Alone*, pp. 47–48.

J. B. S. HALDANE: A DEFIANT ARISTOCRAT

J. B. S. Haldane was a close associate of Hogben and Huxley, who came from both the British and the scientific aristocracy. His views on race were less original than those of his peers, and when he became an anti-racist after the rise of Nazism, his views reflected a more directly motivated political position. It endowed his position with the strength of a political commitment, but limited his horizon and sensitivity to racial questions which were less directly related to his politics. His views on blacks, for instance, reflected accepted bigotry. John Burdon Sanderson Haldane had all the ingredients of a hero. A mythic figure, surrounded by larger-than-life stories, attracting admiration and animosity, Haldane imposed his presence and views on his contemporaries. The superlatives attached to his eccentric personality repeat themselves in biographies and obituaries, in some cases verbatim, reflecting a personality cult. Haldane was of patrician Scottish descent, and at an early age showed unusual intellectual ability, which left its mark even on this not too shy family. Imbibed with science and philosophy by a father prominent in both, and with radicalism from an ardent feminist and imperialist mother, J. B. S. was set on the track to fame early in life. Numerous known episodes of J. B. S.'s life portray a person always too clever to be disregarded and too arrogant to be liked. The later view came especially from those who were hurt by his disregard for conventions. Those who overcame dislike of his arrogance were likely to become admirers. Though Haldane's fame does not rest on his athletic prowess, his physical appearance contributed to the making of the myth almost as much as his intellectual abilities. He was already tall and heavy during his Eton days, and following a rough start, his physique supposedly protected him against the excessive bullying of older students irked by the young insolent. Later in life his huge gruff voice took over from his muscles, and in his last years an Indian dress coupled with a large bold skull, embellished his dignity.

Haldane's intellectual claim to fame rests on true versatility. While his best known scientific contributions were to population genetics, his first academic position was in biochemistry, and during his career he worked on human genetics, animal behavior, as well as in cosmology, the physiology of diving and the origin of life. His success as a popularizer of science, as an intellectual and an expert, was shared by peers such as Hogben and Huxley, and was accomplished in face of professional antagonism. In the early twenties Haldane himself supported the view that a serious scientist should not waste his time writing for the public: when Huxley began writing popular articles, Haldane advised him to refrain from compromising his science. But it did not take long for Haldane to join in writing for the layman, and in doing it extremely well and on a variety of topics that ranged from utopianism to science fiction, and included philosophy and politics.[41]

Ordinarily, scientists who ventured into politics supported a cause with occasional essays, or statements, but did not become part of a political organization and were detached from daily involvement. Haldane in contrast became a political activist in the midthirties, joined the Communist party, and began to write a weekly column in the *Daily Worker* and to participate on numerous political committees. The rise of fascism and especially Nazism intensified his political commitment, perhaps even more than it motivated that of his peers. The reformist-philosophical socialism of Haldane's earlier career was transformed into a full-fledged activism. In addition to the traditional intellectual role of commenting on – and interpreting – events, Haldane participated in helping refugees from Germany, and advised the Spanish government during the civil war on technical matters, especially gas warfare. In World War II his research into the physiology of diving began when, at the request of the Amalgamated Engineering Union and the Electrical Trade Union, he investigated the disaster of the submarine Thetis, which had sunk off Liverpool before the outbreak of the war. A demonstrably political act turned into research conducted for the Royal Navy. Such research was characteristic of his eccentricity. While he carried out little experimental science, when he did he was likely to be both the experimenter and the subject of the experiment, sometimes risking his life. He participated in the first of these dangerous experiments under the watchful eyes of his father, who drew J. B. S.'s blood at the age of three for research purposes, and a

[41] Two informative biographies of Haldane are: N. W. Pirie, "John Burdon Sanderson Haldane," *Biographical Memoirs of Fellows of the Royal Society*, 12 (1966), and Ronald Clark, *J.B.S. The Life and Work of J. B. S. Haldane* (London: Quality Book Club, 1968). Another is by J. Maynard in the *Dictionary of National Biography*, 1961–1970. K. R. Dronamraju edited *Haldane and Modern Biology* (Baltimore: Johns Hopkins University Press, 1968), a collection of articles in memory of Haldane. One of these, "Beginnings," was written by J.B.S.'s sister, Naomi Mitchison. See also Werskey, *Visible College* (London: Allen Lane, 1968); Stepan, *The Idea of Race in Science* (Hamden, Conn.: Archon Books, 1982).

few years later the two went together on expeditions to investigate collapsed mines.[42] Later in life, self-experimentation turned into a habit and swelled the personality cult.[43]

Haldane enjoyed attracting attention by breaking social conventions. The most successful topic for raising petty social scandals was obviously sex, nothing else focused as much opposition and curiosity or was sure to be retold in all circles with superficial disgust. Perhaps Haldane's best known episode confronted him as a reader in biochemistry at Cambridge against the University's moral committee which was named the *sex viri* for the number of its participants. During the scandal Haldane nicknamed the committee the "sex weary," which promptly led to its reorganization (and the addition of a seventh member), but Haldane was temporarily expelled, all of which only contributed to the myth accumulating around him.

Haldane mocked such conventions also in his philosophical speculations about science. These he began in an undergraduate essay which was turned in 1924 into the small popular volume *Daedalus*, the success of which launched his career as a writer and a public figure.[44] *Daedalus* was written in the form of a fictional historical essay by a student at the end of the 21st century, and in it he addressed eugenics and ectogenesis (test-tube babies). In a speculative scientific spirit Haldane ventilated sexual issues, an explosive matter even in biological costume. At this earlier stage, in contrast to his later materialism, his understanding of the evolving new physics led him to forecast that scientists would accept Kantian idealism as a foundation of scientific thought. "The reign of Kantian idealism as the basal working hypothesis, first of physics, and then of everyday life, will in all probability last for some centuries."[45]

---

42 On one such occasion, J.B.S. was taught the effect of breathing methane. In a cave, in a pit, where methane, which is lighter than air, accumulated, J.B.S. was told to recite Anthony's speech from *Julius Caesar*. "I soon began to pant, and somewhere about the 'noble Brutus' my legs gave way and I collapsed on the floor, where, of course, the air was all right." Clark, *J.B.S.*, pp. 27–28.

43 Haldane "On Being One's Own Rabbit," in *Possible Worlds and Other Essays* (New York and London: Harper and Brothers, 1928), Also Pirie "Haldane," p. 234.

44 Clark, *J.B.S.*, pp. 70, 73. At about the same time, Haldane was portrayed as the subject of two novels, *Antic Hay* by Aldous Huxley and *The Flying Draper* by Ronald Fraser. Werskey, *Visible College*, p. 86, Clark, *J.B.S.*, p. 90.

45 J. S. Haldane's idealism still dominated his son's philosophy. J.B.S., not unlike Marx, had aged from idealism to materialism. Haldane, *Daedalus or Science and the Future* (New York: E. P. Dutton and Co., 1924). A Paper read to the Heretics' Club, Cambridge, Feb., 1923, p. 15.

Haldane was the first to recognize the limited value of scientific predictions and used to joke about his mistaken forecast before World War II that an atomic bomb could not be developed in his lifetime.

Over the years Haldane remained committed to popularizing science. In addition to his books aimed at a wide readership, he commented for years in a weekly column for the *Daily Worker* (over 300 articles) on the application of science to social and political questions. His commitment to popularizing science stemmed from a basic optimism that science "can do something far bigger for the human mind than the substitution of one set of beliefs for another" by disseminating "among humanity as a whole the point of view" that permitted the creation of modern civilization.[46] Haldane confused the growth of scientific knowledge that produced a mastery of the world with the belief that such knowledge would reach beyond technology to philosophy and answer some metaphysical questions. This wishful thinking was the source of his optimistic efforts to spread scientific knowledge not for its own sake but in order to achieve a better world. While his commitment to social improvement remained firm, his views of what constituted such progress changed dramatically during the interwar period.

A fascinating aspect of such eccentric biologists as Hogben, Huxley and Haldane was the similarity of their views – the common path along which these radical nonconformists developed their ideas, rejected the values of their larger group, rebelled against conventions and ended up largely conforming to a shared radical world view. Even the nuances had a pattern. Like his peers, Haldane manifested the prejudices of his class and supported various aspects of eugenics until the late twenties, when he became sceptical of its applications while remaining faithful to its ideals. Much like his friends – a shade more critical of eugenics than Julian Huxley, but less so than Lancelot Hogben – Haldane gradually steered his views away from his earlier prejudice.

Haldane's support for ectogenesis while still a student was based on a Malthusian argument. The alternative to an ectogenetic world was a collapsed civilization "within a measurable time owing to the greater fertility of the less desirable members of the population in almost all countries."[47] In retrospect we may say that Haldane and

---

[46] Haldane, *Science and Human Life* (New York: Harper and Brothers, 1933), p. 1.
[47] *Daedalus*, p. 66.

other eugenicists presented the alternatives accurately – and that their fear has materialized: other classes have proliferated, and the world as it was dominated by the English/Nordic upper-middle class has vanished. Yet the distinction between conservatives and progressives was that the latter understood the change – accepted it and accommodated themselves – while the former remained committed to an ideology of racial superiority and to doom-laden prophesy. By any measure, Haldane was a progressive. In the late twenties he still supported the idea of eugenics but was ready to voice criticism over some of its policies. He accepted conventional wisdom, for instance "that mental capacity is strongly hereditary" as non-controversial, and branded as evil the numerical fact that "the unskilled workers are breeding much faster than the skilled classes." Haldane congratulated the Eugenics Education Society for its "good work in persuading a certain number of intelligent people that it is their duty to have more children," but with this his support for eugenics stopped and his social criticism began to take shape. Haldane argued against not the Society but "many of their members" for opposing social measures "designed to ameliorate the lot of the children of the poor at the expense of the rich. It is a curious policy to combat evils due to economic inequality by perpetuating that inequality."[48]

From this vantage point, Haldane began his criticism of eugenic policies not by contradicting the biological validity of heredity, but rather by turning the eugenic argument upside down. In this his approach was clearly polemical. By 1928 Haldane argued that if eugenics was as important as certain people had claimed, then the social policy was bound to be "the complete abolition of hereditary property, and the free and compulsory attendance of all children at State schools." Equal opportunities would further the most talented, and "all legislation tending in these directions must be regarded as eugenic."[49] The tension, however, resulted from his real – not polemical – belief, in the impact of biological endowment on culture and intellectual achievements, and its social misinterpretation through prejudice. Men are unequal, but along a different classification from that conventionally used: "The progress of biology in the next century will lead to a recognition of the innate

[48] Haldane, *Possible Worlds – and Other Papers* (New York: Harper and Brothers, 1928), pp. 202–203.
[49] *Possible Worlds*, p. 204.

inequality of men [...] Universal education leads, not to equality, but to real inequality based on real differences of talent. Where there is equality of opportunity there is no excuse for failure."[50]

As the political polarization during the thirties increased, and Haldane's commitment to the egalitarian cause and to the Communist Party grew, so did his criticism of eugenic policies, which he increasingly viewed in terms of his opposition to capitalism. Yet even he shared with opponents more than in retrospect we might have expected. To the world-wide confusion over welfare programs, with major new national experiments taking place in the Soviet Union, the United States and Nazi Germany, with the capitalist world facing an imminent decline, Haldane contributed by sharing "considerable sympathy with Fisher's views" on welfare benefits, regretting only that these did not rely "on very complete evidence." Haldane thought Fisher's program of child allowances proportionate to the family's average expense on a child "a measure of social justice," even though it would have dramatically transferred payments from the tax payer to the middle classes. His main concern was "to arrange a system of family allowances for the professional groups such as lawyers and doctors who are a valuable class of men from the eugenic point of view" more than their economic rewards might show. In this biological and social tangle, Haldane also recognized the limitation of such views, and with literary grace stirred his readers' doubts: "My own views on the differential birth-rate are extremely tentative, but they are somewhat as follows: If the rich are infertile because they are rich, they might become less so if they were made less rich."[51]

Haldane provided two types of arguments for his opposition to eugenics – biological and social – but one senses that he felt much more at home with the ethical, social justification. Deserting his earlier idealism and belief that science could transcend metaphysics, Haldane was ready to grant that "irrational motives" such as compassion cannot be avoided.[52] Hence, his opposition to sterilization legislation. He used statistical analysis to show that

[50] Haldane, *Science and Human Life* (New York: Harper and Brothers, 1933), p. 18.
[51] Haldane, *Heredity and Politics* (New York: W. W. Norton and Co, 1938), pp. 132–134. By then Haldane had developed the same kind of scepticism on eutelegenesis – procreation of gifted children by artificial insemination – which his friend H. J. Muller had argued in *Out of the Night*: "Once again I am inclined to regard such a proposal as premature in view of our very slight knowledge of the genetical basis of those characters which are found in the 'great men' whom we regard as admirable." Haldane, *Heredity and Politics*, p. 133.
[52] *Heredity and Politics*, pp. 100–101.

"mental deficiency" was "a legal and not a biological conception," criticizing sterilization not for its ineffectiveness – he was ready to admit that as a result "some mentally defective children would not be born" – but rather because the price would be too high. As a result of sterilization, "a considerable proportion, perhaps ten times as many, normal children would not come into the world."[53] This was too costly in ethical terms, especially perhaps for J. B. S., who did not have a child of his own. The message of the scientist was that compassion had a greater role to play than science, morals were more important than abstract rationalism in formulating social policy. This ability of the expert to substantiate moral judgment with scientific claims strengthened the opposition to rigid racial typology, substituting for it plural – cultural, social and biological – approaches.[54]

By 1941 with the increased commitment due to the war, the intensity of propaganda generally simplified intellectual doubts. Evolution, in Haldane's eyes, casts its vote in favor of the working class: "The actual application of Darwinism to contemporary capitalist society is quite clear. The poor leave more offspring behind them in each generation than the rich. So they are fitter from a Darwinian point of view. And if, on the average, they differ genetically from the rich, their innate characteristics are spreading rapidly through the population."[55] In the post-war period, with growing animosity, Haldane the ardent communist directed his arrows at, among others, Julian and Aldous Huxley for stirring anxiety about the population explosion. Predicting the possibility of producing food faster than population could grow, Haldane saw the major obstacle as expense, not science. Governments would have to invest in agricultural research rather than in the military, otherwise doom would prevail. "I dare say the Huxleys will turn out to be perfectly right ... But if they are right it will not be because such a disaster was in any way unavoidable, but simply because our rulers

---

[53] *Heredity and Politics*, pp. 94–95.

[54] On the question of sterilization, Haldane contradicted the claim that there could be such a thing as voluntary sterilization of the mentally retarded, who were no match for the system that decided to sterilize them, and the "choice" was always made in their name. Haldane quoted this testimony of Dr. Turner: "I venture to say I should not be fitted to hold my present office of medical superintendent of an institute for the care of mentally defectives if I could not induce practically every one of my patients to be operated on or to refuse an operation just as I myself might wish." *Heredity and Politics*, p. 102; Haldane quoted from Penrose, *Mental Defect* (London: Sidgwick & Jackson), 1933, p. 170.

[55] Letter from Haldane to the editor, *Science and Society*, June 21, 1941, JBSHP, Box 12.

understood by security not the means of keeping our people from hunger but the means of killing foreigners."[56] Appearing in a communist paper at the height of the Cold War, the claim could not have carried much credibility, but it was one of his more accurate forecasts and as the 1980s show, food production could easily exceed demand.

Haldane's views on race evolved along with his views on eugenics. In time he became less of a determinist. As a member of the British upper-class he had little sensitivity to the abuses of racism. Like his peers, he could accept racial prejudice with ease, tending to use racist terminology with naivete. Nowhere was this more evident than in his use of the term "nigger" in his children's book *My Friend Mr. Leakey* (1937). Haldane wrote about Sasabonsum, a nasty demon who hangs on trees and "catches niggers round the neck with his toes ... Of course he doesn't hurt white men, because they don't believe in him. But niggers do and that's that." The book was in print for many years, and ran an American edition. Haldane's attention was directed to the offensive language (not to say the content) on different occasions, but he replied that "the term 'nigger' is merely a friendly nickname, and that the idea of superstition is more of a joke against those who believe in this 'stereotype' than against the negro."[57] Clearly the answer was nonsense. "Nigger" was recognized in Britain as an offensive term, public figures refrained from using it, and there was absolutely no excuse for such language. It can be interpreted as an indication of Haldane's racism. It can perhaps also reflect a strange insensitivity, out of character in a man who invested so much of his life working for classes and people less fortunate than the descendant of Scottish aristocracy.

Some of Haldane's other remarks are even more disturbing, but ought to be evaluated in historical context as part of the initial and gradual opposition to racism among British scientists around 1930. Compared with Hogben, Haldane's shift came relatively late, and one suspects that in his case anti-Nazi sentiments were more crucial than among his peers. In 1928 Haldane wrote: "It was only the emancipation of the negroes which *saved* the United States from

[56] *Daily Worker*, March 20, 1950, JBSHP. Box 10.
[57] Letter to Haldane from Jeanne Spriter James, Oct. 4, 1948. Reply, Haldane's secretary, Oct. 19, 1948. JBSHP. box 18. The quote is from "A Day in the Life of A Magician," *Leakey* (London: The Cresset Press), p. 88.

twice its present black population. This event gave them access to alcohol, venereal diseases, and consumption. Their rate of increase slowed down at once . . ."[58] His eccentricity was by no means always egalitarian. Five years later, Haldane claimed biological agnosticism, when he presented a similar argument as a dilemma rather than a conclusion. Biologists in Haldane's opinion could not resolve the American controversy over segregation and equal rights as it was grounded in the claim of inferiority. Biologists can present facts such as that the Negro's skull is more ape-like, while his hairless skin is less ape-like, than whites'. Haldane was more serious when he argued from the different birth and death rates for blacks in the North and in the South that blacks have a harder time surviving in the North because in "environment suitable to a white man, they die of consumption and other diseases, just as the white man dies on the west coast of Africa." Playing devil's advocate to all, Haldane presented an American catch: if the black is persecuted, lynched and excluded from jobs "you drive him back to the cotton fields where he lives healthily and breeds rapidly, thus creating a Negro problem for future generations." But if you help him integrate into society "you also infect him with your maladies, besides establishing in your midst a reservoir of disease germs."[59] This erroneous and simplistic view of adaptability of various populations to different climates, with its total disregard of the differences between disease endemic to a stable population and epidemics affecting migrations, was strange coming from a first-rate scientist. Yet such a statement was perhaps more likely to come from Haldane than conventional wisdom would lead one to expect. In his scientific studies he relied on data collected by other scientists, and it is not surprising that his interpretation of conflicting pieces of information led him to reach false conclusions on several occasions.[60]

The statement nevertheless is important because it discloses in its conventional racism a tendency towards egalitarianism. The detached agnosticism can only be understood if we see that his interest in American blacks was confined to an abstract level without consideration of the people themselves. Haldane concluded that the scientific "truth lies somewhere between" equality and

---

[58] *Possible Worlds – and Other Papers*, p. 204 (emphasis added).
[59] Haldane, *Science and Human Life* (New York: Harper & Brothers, 1933), pp. 3–4.
[60] Sewall Wright, "Contribution to Genetics," in K. R. Dronamraju (ed.), *Haldane and Modern Biology* (Baltimore: Johns Hopkins University Press, 1968), p. 2.

inequality among the races,[61] but shortly afterwards he became committed to the fight against fascism and in this context he articulated a rejection of biological racism.

Unlike Hogben, Haldane did not break much new ground in his anti-racism. His importance stemmed rather from his scientific and social credibility, of which his popular writing was the major vehicle. He was an expert, but his impact as an intellectual on the changes in the concept of race owed more to his being an activist with the credentials of a scientist. Many of his popularizing articles were written for the *Daily Worker*, which had a limited audience, but his views received wider publicity. One such article, "Heredity and Races," displayed Haldane's shift towards unequivocal anti-racism. It began by emphasizing the significant role played by the idea of superior races in Nazi propaganda. Having recognized an established evil, Haldane compared and criticized the same sort of arguments of "the British in India, and by many of the whites in South Africa and the southern states of the U.S.A." This political opposition led him to a scientific analysis of the term race which he defined "as a people who normally breed together, and who differ from all other peoples as regards inherited physical characters which are found in all members of the race," recognizing that "probably race mixture and race formation have been going on together as long as men [have] existed." Haldane no longer refrained from committing himself to the pluralistic cause: "mankind is probably very much the better for it. If there were no race differences the world would be a much duller place. If there were no race mixture there might be several different human species incapable of breeding together and the Nazi doctrine would be true." Haldane could have reached this conclusion as a result of his Darwinism, but he did not. Because his focus was primarily political, even in the late thirties he continued to condone a racist interpretation of the existence of differences among races. The Europeans were still seen as "on the whole superior to negroes in a cold climate," and the latter were "superior to the European in East Africa." Even a seemingly egalitarian statement with regard to intelligence implied that Haldane maintained his earlier prejudice: "it is certain that races overlap" in intelligence, "for clever negroes are cleverer than stupid Englishmen, and musical Englishmen are more musical than unmusical negroes." This nevertheless left the

[61] Haldane, *Science and Human Life*, p. 12.

impression that he concurred with popular prejudice which claimed the Englishman to be smarter and blacks more musical.[62]

In his most egalitarian phase Haldane persisted in his positivist views of race differences among populations even if these were evasively couched. The French and the Chinese "are undoubtedly different racially," but one "cannot draw a geographical line between races except where there are natural barriers of a very formidable kind," similar to the inability to "draw a line between mountains and valleys, though Snowdon is certainly not a valley."[63] The purpose of classification, however, was left vague.

Politically, Haldane was much more straightforward in his condemnation of the abuse of the term race. When Chamberlain referred to the Danzig question in racial terms, Haldane was up in arms: "No doubt the majority of the people of the Danzig are linguistically and presumably therefore culturally Germans. But racially this is not the case." If anything he preferred blood groups as a criteria for differences of racial origin in Europe. Elucidating to the uninitiated the patterns of blood type in Europe, he concluded: "I do not suggest that such facts as these ought to be taken into consideration in deciding the destinies of a folk. But if blood and race are to be considered in this connection, the facts concerning them may as well be stated correctly."[64] While this might seem redundant, it was too polemical and politically inadvisable, even by "excellent anti-Chamberlainites." Kingsley Runter of *The New Statesman* and *Nation* responded to Haldane: "We all use the word 'race' in the sense that he used it, and if we are wrong in doing so, you, as a scientist, are right in pointing it out. But if Chamberlain was doing Nazi propaganda in saying that the Danzigers were of German race, then so is every paper in England at the present time since they all use the word 'race' in the same way!"[65] Confronting the misuse of racial terminology in the political arena in Britain in

[62] A handwritten copy of the article, JBSHP, box 7. See also Haldane, *Heredity and Politics*, especially "The Race Problem Continued." Making an analogy with the genetics of rabbits, Haldane pointed to the independent segregation of genes, i.e., long hair and whiteness, and concluded: "This is of some importance because it means that the physical characters of races are due to a number of different genes which can be separated, and it follows that a racial mixture once made is to a very large extent irreversible, and cannot be undone on the basis of selection for some particular characters." While that conclusion was in no way revolutionary, it still needed emphasis (*Heredity and Politics*, pp. 170–171).
[63] Haldane letter to cousin Alec, April 28, 1942. JBSHP, box 37.
[64] "Query Heading." JBSHP, box 17.
[65] July 13, 1939. JBSHP, box 12.

1939 was – from a scientific vantage point – still polemical, and it is against such a background that one should evaluate the political anti-racist activities of scientists.

A different aspect of Haldane's anti-racism is illuminated by the various conjectures he was ready to entertain as a scientist. Haldane shared much scientific work with Ronald Fisher, yet their judgment on race theories was diametrically opposed. As shown earlier, Fisher rejected Boas's environmental approach, even if the only reason he could rally was an opposing speculation regarding the high illegitimacy rate among Italians in America. Despite the general criticism in Britain of Boas's studies of the environmental influence on the skull, Haldane defended the work as feasible and objected to its unsubstantiated dismissal. On the other hand, he was sufficiently respectful to call Davenport's study of Jamaica "important," as a pretext for a criticism of it.[66] Though Haldane was skeptical of the potential contributions which could be derived from craniometry, he was ready to give Morant – the only biometrician left at University College after Pearson's retirement – the benefit of the doubt and collaborated with him. A short while later Morant turned anti-racist. This was probably made easier by Haldane's attitude, especially in light of Fisher's quarrelsomeness towards him.

MEDICINE AND EUGENICS: EXPANDING THE ENVIRONMENT

The anti-racist critique was part of the expanding space created for nurture at the expense of nature. The two were beginning to be viewed as complementing each other, rather than disparate entities. The most dramatic study in this approach was conducted by Penrose who expanded the environmental influences back to the womb. It became apparent that heredity and environment could only be viewed as part of a synthesis. This received a striking institutional explication in the transformation of the eugenics movement in both the United States and Britain.

Cultural currents move in interwoven circles. An idea first establishes itself within a certain circle, and only after it becomes a convention among peers, is it ready to overflow and influence an adjacent circle, being transmitted among discourses in a relatively indetermine way. The scientist, as both expert and intellectual

---

[66] Haldane, "Anthropology and Human Biology," *Congrès International des Sciences Anthropologiques et Ethnologiques* (London: Royal Anthropological Institute, 1934), pp. 56, 59.

operates in circles at different levels simultaneously. This accounts for the wide impact of Haldane, Huxley, Hogben and for that matter Fisher. The meaning these scientists attached to the concept of race and the dissemination of their views to wider audience are reasonably accessible to historical research. More difficult and sketchy must be the understanding of the process by which these scientists mutually shaped each other's views. Partial answer exists in the correspondence and the direct references within the group. Hogben, Haldane, and Huxley represented a group of intellectuals who in addition to their scientific contributions were public figures in their own right, assuming the political responsibility to disseminate their ideology. Their mutual impact integrated friendship, intellectual concord and personal peculiarities. Outsiders knew them through their prominence and eccentricity; though their scientific credentials varied, all were among the most outstanding scientists of the time. To the internal scientific critique of race, Huxley and Haldane had contributed less than Hogben, but nevertheless *We Europeans*,[67] was very likely the best known among the anti-racist books of the thirties. Hogben was the most consistent anti-racist in the group, being the first to have articulated a critique founded on genetics. His exposé was picked up and expanded upon by the other two. Another member of this anti-racist group who was less known to the public before World War II, but had a profound impact on the transformation of the scientific understanding of the relation between heredity and environment, was Lionel Penrose. In the pre-war years he was much more the expert, but after the war he became more involved and assumed the role of an intellectual as well.

Lionel Sharples Penrose's reputation was very different from that of other anti-racists, though like them he integrated his moral commitment with his scientific work. Of Quaker descent and a pacifist, Penrose was no doubt a political outsider, and had opposed racism for political and moral reasons, but in the discourse of heredity and environment his initial contributions were 'internally' scientific, and unlike his peers, Penrose kept his politics mostly private.[68] His unique contributions were in his field studies; among the non-racist biologists he was the only one whose reputation rested

---

[67] See pp. 296–310 below.

[68] During the thirties, Penrose was associated with the Psychologists' Peace Society that was stimulated by luminaries such as Einstein and Freud. Harry Harris, "Lionel Sharples Penrose," *Biographical Memoirs of Fellows of the Royal Society*, 19 (1973), 549. His stay in Canada for the duration of World War II was not coincidental.

on his own empirical studies of human biology. This empiricism should in no way be seen as undermining his theoretical contributions. In their own way these studies lasted longer than other anti-racist writings, and proved a source for cooperation with Hogben and Haldane, who based part of their critique of extreme hereditarianism on Penrose's studies. Taking together the published work of the three, their citations of each other and letters, their mutual influence and the growing complexity in their view of the environment which defined the nonracist agenda, one can see a coherent anti-racist scientific discourse being developed and presented to the public.[69] Though in some respects Penrose was distanced from the group, his work on mental pathology provided the empirical convergence point for proving positively the influence of environment, rather than merely criticizing racist studies.[70]

Penrose's work before World War II rested primarily on the "Colchester Survey;" a study of mental deficiency. Following early training in psychology, Penrose completed medical studies and integrated the two in investigating mental defects, on which he was to focus for the rest of his career. From 1930 to 1939, Penrose was a research medical officer at the Royal Eastern Counties Institution, where he conducted his path breaking study. Among his first books was *The Influence of Heredity on Disease*,[71] in which he clearly summarized the declining weight attributed to heredity in analyzing mental defect.

Penrose was interested in mental defect primarily from a medical perspective. Heredity was synonymous with a fixed, permanent character, while environment conveyed a temporary situation, one that was potentially subject to alteration. Penrose rejected the accepted view in Mendelian studies of humans which had generally concluded that heredity was by far the more influential factor, because for him the practice of medicine, namely the improvement

---

[69] Mostly the correspondence in Penrose (LPP) and Haldane (JBSHP) papers at University College, London (UCL).

[70] From this perspective it is easy to see how Huxley, who remained a relatively traditional eugenicist, was left somewhat behind the more radical critique. Penrose accused Huxley that while he remained agnostic with regard to the potentiality for equality of "primitive races and half castes" he advocated discriminatory policies against "members of our own lowest social strata." Review by Penrose of J. S. Huxley, *Man Stands Alone*, in LPP, typed copy, pp. 1–2.

[71] (London: Lewis & Co, 1934). An earlier book, *Mental Defect* (London: Sidgwick & Jackson, 1933), gave a detailed account of the study and was published in a series of text books of social biology edited by Hogben.

of environment for therapeutic purposes, was diametrically opposed to the hereditarian claim. Otherwise medicine would have transformed into a practice "closely allied to that of the animal breeder." When later studies supported his position he argued that "if we can, by artificial means, neutralize the injurious hereditary effects, the importance of heredity, from the medical point of view, is very much diminished."[72] At the same time Penrose suggested that the reason mental disorders were assigned more frequently than physical diseases to heredity was the almost total ignorance on the topic.

The study of the correlation between Down's Syndrome – mongolism – and maternal age is his best-known investigation. It attracted wide attention primarily because of its relevance to all groups of the population. This study redefined the meaning of heredity by extending the influence of the environment much earlier to the embryo stage. This had a powerful effect since mongolism was judged to be the most crystallized example of genetical rather than nutritional or otherwise environmentally acquired defect. Penrose's humanitarian approach was evident from his choice of subject matter, questions, and methods. In addition to mathematical formulas which necessitate close reading, Penrose illustrated the environmental importance even in the case of mongoloids by presenting pictures of twins, one of whom was normal. This was in contrast to the frequently monstrous pictures of the feebleminded which appear in books such as that of Henry Goddard.[73] Penrose's pictures, however, portrayed the mongoloids in the company of normal foster parents, or against the background of greenery, rather than in desperate poverty.

The difficulty in the study of mental defect lay in the need to investigate complete family histories. In this case Penrose's investigation included 1,280 patients who had close to 7,000 siblings, in addition to other relatives who were included in the study. It is clear that the difference between Penrose and the American eugenicist Davenport lay not so much in method as in execution. "Family histories" is a generous term. Harry Laughlin and Penrose both studied the same subject matter, yet the dichotomy could not have been greater. Penrose's work was the first rigorous study of its kind, which was carried out with attention to every possible detail

---

[72] Penrose, *The Influence of Heredity on Disease*, pp. 6, 36.
[73] Henry H. Goddard, *Feeble-mindedness: Its Causes and Consequences* (New York: Macmillan, 1914; Arno Press, 1973), see Gould, *The Mismeasure of Man* (New York: W. W. Norton, 1982), pp. 169, 173.

through double checking the data, and finally evaluation of its reliability, which consequently relegated 35 percent of the records to "incomplete" and "very incomplete."[74]

Through a shift in perspective, Penrose was able to present a totally different interpretation, which contributed to the anti-hereditarian critique. One such example was his analysis of crime and mental illness: it showed that the two definitions were used interchangeably depending on the available institutional facilities. In the debate over superiority, the prevalence of crime and mental illness among various nationalities or ethnic groups in the United States played an important role. The relatively high position of the economically affluent (the Nordic) among the mentally diseased was puzzling to some, and provided others with the tool to negate their supposed superiority. Crime and mental disorder were very often regarded in popular culture as one and the same, especially among the poor, but Penrose was the first to point out that the overlapping of the two criteria was a result of class prejudice – a distaste in middle class aesthetics for the unfortunate poor rather than a clinical definition.

A different conceptual analysis emphasized by Penrose was his perception of mental ability as a continuum with no clear divisions at any level. Rather than treat discrete mental units as reality, as conventional practice would have dictated, Penrose reexamined his patients and concluded that "mental deficiency is not a clinical or biological entity, but only a legal concept useful for social and administrative purposes."[75] Since any society consists of a gradation between wizards and "simpletons," it was a social, not a biological, problem how the second group should be treated. The scientific questions and the medical treatment depended above all upon reclassification of the individuals into a biological rather than administrative groups. The scientific evidence contradicted the social norms. Idiots, the lowest on the scale, were likely to result from genetic defect and therefore more apt to have normal siblings than the simpletons, who were higher in their mental ability and presumably more "normal." One could not draw a line to define the undesirable. Penrose's marginal group belonged there as a result of a host of factors, and the demarcating line could be defined at any number of points, according to various criteria, equally senseless,

[74] Harris, "Penrose," pp. 525–526, 535.
[75] Mental Defect, quoted in Harris "Penrose," p. 524.

which would inevitably cause much individual injustice. Idiots, Penrose showed, resulted mostly from mutations and environmental factors, which meant that any policy aimed at limiting the propagation of such families who had unfortunate member(s) was not only morally unjust but, even worse, ineffective.

An important initial part of Penrose's work was to show that the various definitions of mental illness were full of discrepancies. Earlier social studies in England, such as Roundtree's, spoke of about 10 percent of the population in the category of economically deficient, yet these did not attribute the deprivation to heredity. In the twentieth century, however, studies of mental deficiencies and of the "social problem group" grew in number, and the earlier charitable approach was turned into sinister examination. Goddard's outlook of exposing the feebleminded as a threat to society behind the cover of normal appearance dominated professional views during the 1910s and 1920s. A study in Britain during the first decade of the century, which led to the Mental Deficiency Act of 1913, had addressed the problem in a restricted fashion. By 1929, the British Report of the Joint Committee of the Board of Education and the Board of Control examined the issue of mental defectiveness in a wider perspective and assigned to this category everyone who "by reason of incomplete mental development is incapable of independent social adaptation." This segment of the population, judged incapable socially included many from prostitutes to unemployed. To the eugenic alarmist this was valuable ammunition, but what it did was to redefine the lower tenth in the population as hereditary defectives.[76] In order to dramatize this misconception, Penrose reversed the argument: "the genetic backbone of the population is, in fact, the despised mentally inferior tenth."[77] The boundaries of scientific discourse is defined by polarized speculations which are presented by respected authorities. Penrose's hypotheses, even if too assertive, were less fantastic than Laughlin's and Goddard's, and redirected the scientific discourse towards an environmental, social interpretation.

Penrose's principles in investigating mental illness were directly related to the concept of race: humanizing the supposedly inferior;

[76] Penrose, *The Biology of Mental Defect* (London: Sidgwick and Jackson, revised edn 1954), pp. 1–12.
[77] Quoted in a review of Penrose's book *Outline of Human Genetics* (London: Heinemann, 1959), by Kenneth Mather in *Heredity*, 14, 1&2 (1960), 215–216.

abolishing artificial dichotomies and old taxonomies which had no biological basis but social and cultural bigotry; and negating the distinction between environment and heredity. All this became the basis of the non-racist credo. One possible reason for Penrose's choice of mental defect as subject matter was that in addition to being an "uncharted territory," and unpopular field of study, it allowed Penrose to keep away from involvement with public issues.[78] Penrose did not really popularize the significance of his studies, this was done by Haldane and Hogben who presented Penrose's findings to a much larger audience.[79] Beyond the issue of personal idiosyncrasies, the major intrinsic difficulty in popularizing the new studies in human biology stemmed from its inaccessibility for both the public and many scientists alike who could not follow the mathematics of the new approach.[80] In the uphill battle, there was one indication that environmental interpretations were gaining ground: though the different schools varied greatly, all kept reducing the percentages attributed to heredity.

In later years, Penrose discarded the term race altogether. In 1945 he replaced Ronald Fisher, who moved to Cambridge, at the Galton Laboratories at University College London. He became a public figure and assumed the responsibility of carrying the banner of anti-biological reductionism, operating from the shrine of the eugenics movement. As the holder of a chair endowed by Galton, his opposition to hereditarian determinism was more than mere symbolism, it was a revolution. Penrose participated in UNESCO's publications against racism and pursued what became the new level of post World War II commitment among scientists to combat scientific racism.

LESLIE CLEARANCE DUNN

In the post war years the English biologists found new partners among their American peers. Earlier, no major American biologist belonged in this category, and though Leslie Clearance Dunn of Columbia University was a loyal anti-racist for many years and was

[78] *Bio. Mem.*, p. 524.
[79] From the citations, cooperation in publishing and writing, and the small correspondence that survived, it is evident that the impact was mutual and fundamental. Letters include: Hogben-Penrose, July 28, 1931; March 3, 1932; April 17, 1932; Haldane-Penrose, Sept. 1934. LSPP.
[80] Penrose, *The Influence of Heredity on Disease*, p. 11.

involved in professional politics – including the reform of Cold Spring Harbor in its transition from the Davenport era to modern genetics – he refrained from combating racism in public until after the war. During the thirties human biology progressed in England, but there was no comparable serious work in America, where it became an anathema. Dunn was something of an exception because he had addressed the questions of human biology, and even more specifically the problem of race, as early as the twenties. His help was then solicited to analyze anthropological material along genetic lines, but he too refrained from pursuing further research on human genetics and did not publish again on race until after World War II.

Leslie Dunn was born in Upstate New York and, following undergraduate studies at Dartmouth, became William Castle's assistant at Harvard in 1915, where he worked mostly on the genetics of mice and rats. After returning from combat service in World War I he moved in 1920 to the Agricultural Experiment Station at Storrs, Connecticut, to work on poultry genetics. Coincidentally, Alfred Tozzer, who had finished his collection of anthropometrical measurements in Hawaii as part of a study on race mixture, asked Dunn to analyse the results, which were published separately in a few short articles during the twenties, and finally together in 1928.[81] The subject of race mixture was treated at the time in its most simplistic manner, and Dunn's analysis was all the more outstanding because it was based on primary anthropometrical material rather than on some speculations about secondary studies.

Dunn's conclusions showed all the scepticism that would characterize future genetics application to racial questions. His emphasis lay on rejecting the myth of race crossing degeneration or vigor, stressing impressions rather than affirmative conclusions. He advocated normalcy as the order of the day, underscoring the fact that "hybrids" of Hawaiians and the Chinese "were normal persons, frequently combining the more valuable personal characteristics of both parent type."[82] As to the Mendelian significance of the study – the reason he was asked to analyse the data – Dunn found it to be nil,

[81] *An Anthropometric Study of Hawaiians of Pure and Mixed Blood* (Cambridge: Harvard University, Peabody Museum). Other articles included "The Eugenics Congress 1923," in *Race in State and Society*, and "A Biological View of Race Mixture," *Proceedings of the American Sociological Society*, 1926. Dunn's biographical sketch in Th. Dobzhansky, "Leslie Clearance Dunn," *Biographical Memoirs of the National Academy of Science*, 49 (1978), 79–104.
[82] Dunn, *Anthropometric Study*, p. 148.

since no information was available that could furnish such interpretations: "Factorial analyses supported by clear segregation ratios can be expected to appear only in data involving large numbers of F2 or backcross progeny, obtained from complete family records in which the description of each trait in each ascendant is known."[83] No study could claim such data, nor was such a collection feasible; indeed what Dunn declared in a subtle way was that no valid Mendelian analysis was possible – a conclusion diametrically opposed to Davenport's on Jamaica.

When Dunn moved to Columbia University in 1928 he became an important supporter of the retreat from scientific naturalism because he spoke with scientific authority based on his prestige as an expert in genetics. While his cooperation was important in the reform of Cold Spring Harbor and in Boas's anti-racist campaign of the thirties, he did not contribute directly to the public debate on race until the end of World War II. He then assumed the role of expert, but not quite intellectual, and published two popular books condemning racism. While Penrose did original research in human biology, Dunn did not. In fact Penrose was critical of Dunn's knowledge of human biology. None the less, they shared a commitment to use their professional credentials to combat what in their view was the abuse of science in propagating racist views.[84] That no American human biologist provided new scientific investigations or a penetrating critique to rival the English was a testimony on the state of the discipline in America. Yet in both countries the strongest institutional basis for scientific racism during the twenties, namely the eugenics movement, had in the meantime changed.

EUGENICS REFORMED

The growing literature on eugenics in the United States and Britain describes a movement which reached a peak of popularity in the

---

[83] *Anthropometric Study*, p. 174.
[84] L. C. Dunn and Th. Dobzhansky, *Heredity, Race, and Society* (New York: New American Library, 1946; fourth edn 1972), over half a million copies sold. (Penrose lauded the book's over-all attitude, but criticized it for faults in describing human genetics: "the writers entirely fail to convince because they show over and over again that they have not the first-hand knowledge of the material." LPP 45/1, review of the 1952 revised edition. That Dunn was the American expert on the subject reflected on the state of the discipline in America more than it did on the author.) His other book was *Race and Biology* (UNESCO, 1951), written when Dunn was chosen to represent the biological sciences in UNESCO's declaration against racism.

early twenties and then underwent reform, emerging with a more sophisticated scientific approach and a moderate racism, thus providing in the long run an institutional base for genetic engineering and population control.[85] During its reform stage, the movement supposedly emphasized its apolitical nature and shunned controversies in an effort to gain new scientific respect. This new historical perception has shifted the balance away from earlier descriptions of the movement's death. Kevles ascribes the common denominator of the reform to the wish to update eugenics according to advanced genetics.[86] But such scientific commitment constituted the subjective perspective of every mainliner including Davenport, who was considered at the time a major geneticist. At a slower pace the older, mainline, scientists were also forced to recognize scientific advances. Thus, even Davenport was conducting studies to assess the impact of environmental factors. In a limited way, the older generation too would have refined the earlier crude methodology, but presumably would have maintained the underlying bigotry.

Kevles's term "mainliner" is more useful in understanding the role of the non-scientists in the movement, many of whom remained adamantly racist as ever. During the twenties and thirties the generational shift resulted in the relative decline in influence of the older hands such as Madison Grant in America and Leonard Darwin in England. This shift has been ascribed to the process of professionalization and the mounting opposition to Nazism, both of which played a major role. Yet, the specificity of the shift during the crucial years of the late twenties and early thirties – when the specter of Nazism was still mostly ignored, but when the political confrontation over discrediting racism was tipping in favor of a more egalitarian approach – has not been adequately studied. While filling this lacuna is beyond the scope of the present study, it is

[85] For an uncompromising critique of eugenics and population control as a movement that sustained its racism, see Allen Chase, *The Legacy of Malthus* (New York: Knopf, 1980). The best studies on "reform" and "new" eugenics are Kevles, *In the Name of Eugenics* (New York: Knopf, 1985) and Garland Allen, see p. 190. A recent work on eugenics by Richard A. Soloway (*Demography and Degeneration. Eugenics and the Declining Birthrate in Twentieth-Century Britain* (Chapel Hill: The University of North Carolina Press, 1990) suggests the degree to which Kevles's work has become an "orthodoxy".

[86] Kevles, *In The Name of Eugenics*, pp. 88, 172–173, attributes the reform in eugenics to a shift from mainliners to non-mainliners who attempted to adapt themselves to the changing circumstances. In this, Kevles seems to imply that the younger group was predominantly non-racist, including Ronald Fisher (p. 170). This clearly deserves some qualification in view of the analysis presented above.

possible to point to the locus of the difficulty, and to suggest that politics – national and institutional – occupied the protagonists' attention and played a leading role in the process of change.

From this perspective the question remains of whether the scientists among the reform eugenicists should be considered insiders or outsiders? By definition, once a reform takes place – as opposed to an abrupt takeover by a rival organization or an internal *coup d'etat* – the shift has to be made by insiders, who by the time of the reform became mainliners. To the degree that the reform took place as a result of internal pressures, one could presumably classify the reformers as mainliners. Going beyond the typology, however, the most significant changes for eugenics resulted not from internal reforms, but rather from external forces which led to its decline. Eugenics became a small peripheral movement, and though it retained the support of a few prominent scientists, its overall influence was negligible. Leading eugenicists sustained their interest in issues of population control, and eventually provided additional impetus for genetic engineering and population control, which, however, took place in a radically different context. The most significant feature in the history of eugenics during the interwar years was its falling influence in public discourse, a decline which paralleled the fate of scientific racism.

In Britain more than in the United States, the reform of the movement was the result of a change in intellectual milieu as well as an institutional shift. The earlier rift between the geneticists (Bateson, Punnet) and the biometricians (Pearson) and the frequent animosity of some of these scientists to the Eugenics Society (which was led by Leonard Darwin) ended with the gradual retirement of the main actors. By the early twenties, younger scientists such as Gates, Fisher and Huxley were becoming prominent in the work of the Eugenics Society. The new secretary, C. P. Blacker, was slow to carry out reforms and, like his predecessor, often found himself in a minority. But his hesitations resulted mostly from political considerations rather than from innate conservatism. Huxley's new role in the movement, together with his marked shift on the question of race in 1930, is the best testimony to the internal reform of eugenics and the affinity of this change with the rejection of racism.[87]

---

[87] Leonard Darwin was close to Fisher (see J. H. Bennett [ed.], *Natural Selection, Heredity and Eugenics* [New York: Oxford University Press, 1983].) Blacker was Huxley's student, and

The rejection of simplistic claims that social characteristics are determined by a single gene, signaled for the first time the difference between liberals and conservatives on the issues of eugenics and race during the late twenties. Fisher together with several of his friends who were active in the Eugenics Society failed to shape the society in their own image. Although the growing number of scientists on the committees increased their influence, they did not present a monolithic message. The ensuing conflict involved lay persons and scientists on both sides, and eventually led to a reaction against Fisher's circle, known as the "Rothamsted lobby." The rivalry was most evident in institutional politics, such as on the nominations to the General Policies Committee. Fisher pressed hard for immediate cooption of his supporters but failed. Joan Box describes the struggle from Fisher's perspective, the view of the losing camp. She sees the rivalry in terms of scientists versus lay members, especially against the secretary C. P. Blacker, "a sociologist." But since key members who opposed Fisher were scientists too, and as he received support from lay conservatives, the split seems to have been political rather than one of scientists versus the public. In 1934, to prevent the initial antagonism to Nazism from spilling over to eugenics, a special committee with emergency powers was formed and took control of the society. This committee represented a growing interest in environmentalism,[88] and an increased sensitivity to racism.

American eugenics declined as the phobias that fed the movement were partially quelled. The post-World War I isolation, the disappearance of immigration from the national agenda, and the economic prosperity of the twenties, all seemed to have alleviated the political urgency of the movement. An even more significant shift was the incipient defeat of racism by new social forces.

sustained a life long respect to him. Consequently, Huxley became more influential in the movement as a member of the very informal inner circle. Fisher, however, was kept at a distance. It is difficult to envisage a criterion by which Fisher would be more of a "mainliner" than Huxley.

[88] Joan Fisher Box (*R. A. Fisher: The Life of A Scientist* [New York: John Wiley and Sons, 1978], pp. 195–196,) describes the last efforts of the "hereditarians" in the society when they lost the fight to Blacker and his group: "The council was rendered impotent, and men like Fisher, Ford, Fraser Roberts and Thornton resigned from the society rather than lend their support to a movement whose policies they could no longer hope either to approve or amend. The scientific movement was routed and, with it, Fisher's hopes that the Eugenics Society would again serve genuinely eugenic ends. The report of the Committee on Family Allowances, a dead letter in a Eugenics Society without scientific ballast, was one of the last tasks Fisher performed with the Eugenics Society he had served for more than 20 years."

which were to shape the growing American cultural diversity.
However, at the micro-level the institutional reform of eugenics was
mainly the work of one person, Frederick Osborn. In 1928 Osborn
retired from a successful business career and joined the eugenics
movement with the substantial gift of US $10,000, which instantly
put him at the center of the movement.[89] Though Osborn himself
was a newcomer, his background made him anything but an
outsider. His two uncles were closely associated with eugenics.
Henry Fairfield Osborn, the President of the American Museum of
Nataural History, was a founding member and one of the insiders of
the movement. A second uncle, Cleveland H. Dodge contributed
large sums to the Society (and to the American Museum), and other
members of the family did the same. Frederick Osborn's contribution was therefore significant but not unexpected. He remained
an executive member of the Carnegie Corporation of New York, but
largely gave up business and immersed himself in eugenics. The
conventional history, based mainly on Osborn's own account, is
that for the next few years he sat at the American Museum and read
widely on social and biological sciences, emerging a transformed
person.[90]

This explanation, however, skips the period of the late 1920s. The
subtle internal politics in the eugenics movement during the years
between 1929 and 1933 ought to be the focus of any reconstruction of
the shift.[91] The enigma remains of what were Osborn's views on
eugenics when he decided to devote to it his career. The transformation took place before the Great Depression; racism if anything had quietened down, the economy was prospering, and
Osborn apparently had shown no particular intellectual interest in
any of the subjects involved since taking an undergraduate course at
Princeton in 1908 on biology and geology. For twenty years he was
in business, and there is little doubt that by 1928 he had just a

---

[89] The gift was to the Eugenics Research Association, whose director Davenport had written
to thank Osborn: "The soil has been prepared and yours is the seed which will develop into
something that we all have been looking forward to, namely the adequate support of
researches on normal (as opposed to pathelogical) man." Davenport to Osborn, Jan. 4,
1929.

[90] Ludmerer interviewed Osborn, who himself published the same version. (*Genetics and the
American Society* [1972] p. 174). Kevles, accepts Ludmerer's interpretation (*In the Name of
Eugenics*, p. 170).

[91] Unfortunately the available documents are limited. Osborn's own papers for these years
are very sketchy. Additional material is available in Davenport's papers, and in the papers
of Merriam (the President of the Carnegie Institution of Washington).

general interest in what in retrospect can be seen as population studies, though at the time he was thinking more in terms of processes of "contemporary evolution."' It is conceivable that Osborn came to the Eugenics Society with the notion of leading a general reform, since by any standards the society was in decline. This does not indicate, however, whether the reform envisioned was organizational or ideological. There is evidence to suggest that upon joining the eugenics movement, Osborn was as badly confused as most people at the time. Although a reductionist interpretation of his background would suggest that he held a racist upper class WASPish perspective, he quickly came to sympathize with ideas that symbolized reform eugenics.

One of his first encounters in eugenics was with the work of the "Committee on Scientific Aspects of Human Migration," which was then terminated but had impressed Osborn with its "courage and wisdom ... in attacking the basic problems."[92] The Committee, a bastion of tradition racial typologists, initiated and financed many of the racist studies of the twenties while stalling alternative research.[93] The Eugenics Research Association, with Osborn's support, planned to follow up on the Committee's work with a program under Davenport's direction. While both committees represented the racist wing in the scientific community, Osborn's participation in it redirected his attention to population questions, which he reinterpreted in the manner rather of a social scientist than of a biologist.

At this early stage of his initiation in the late 1920s, Osborn was devising a research program for eugenics, but found that human evolution was more complicated than he had assumed. His initial enthusiasm to reach practical conclusions had to be restrained by, of all people, Davenport who claimed that more basic research needed to be done before contemporary human evolution could be addressed: "It does not suffice merely to express a conviction that there is inheritance of physical and mental and emotional traits. It seems to be necessary to understand how they are inherited." Davenport recognized that only about six scientists in the world were engaged in the study of human genetics, and it seems that Osborn was getting the message that this line of research was not practical for eugenics.[94] Consequently he retreated to easier tasks of

[92] Osborn to Merriam, March 22, 1929. Copy to Davenport, CBDP.
[93] See pp. 111 on Kroeber.
[94] Davenport to Osborn, Feb. 10, 1930. CBDP.

literature surveys, demonstrating his open-minded approach in engaging a student of Boas in one of these surveys to prepare "the chapter on the distribution of races in the United States."[95] By 1930, when the Eugenics Society was a long way from being reformed, Davenport had already encountered some tough, if subtle, opposition at home.

If ever there was a break in eugenic policies, this was probably one. It manifested itself in a book Osborn sponsored and provided the preface for on the controversial subject of *Heredity and Environment*. The aim was to present the status of psychological measurements and the developmental origins of mental characteristics as they would apply to population studies. This traditional eugenic subject matter was prefaced by Osborn with a warning that such "studies can be easily perverted by uncritical use of psychological materials."[96] The scientific sources and advisers relied upon were not partisan in the old manner and the survey represented a cross section, its conclusions approaching a modern interpretation of asking not whether environment or heredity is more important, but rather shifting the question from limitations to potentiality embedded in each factor. Biological determinism remained, but it was enveloped with so many environmental clarifications and opened to such a dynamic approach that very little was left of the old type of reductionism. The only specific group differences which still seemed to be of consequence were those between socio-economic classes. American eugenicists were closing ranks with their English peers.[97] But in fact the trend had begun earlier. The Carnegie Institution, which was underwriting Davenport's work, was less than satisfied with the nature of eugenic activities. Criticism being raised in many quarters, it was decided to set up an Advisory Board to resolve the situation.[98] The Board included some traditional eugenicists, such as Wissler and Thorndike. But this time L. C. Dunn, who had just replaced Morgan at Columbia, was asked to participate. Carl Brigham, who was changing his views on the value

[95] Osborn to Davenport, May 28, 1930. CBDP.
[96] Gladys C. Schwesinger, *Heredity and Environment*, ed. Frederick Osborn (New York: Macmillan, 1933), p. vii.
[97] Schwesinger, *Heredity and Environment*, pp. 459–465. The study did not discuss racial groupings as such, had no "race" category in its index, and directed the readers to other works that included Klineberg but not Davenport (p. 245).
[98] In November 1928 Davenport presented a research proposal in a long meeting with Merriam, the President of the Carnegie, and as a result Merriam suggested setting up the Board. Davenport to Osborn, Nov. 9, 1928. CBDP.

of I.Q. testing, was also present. The real program of the Board was to find a way to reform eugenics. But it seems that Davenport was too strongly entrenched, and the attempt was quickly put to rest until his retirement a few years later. From then on the movement's reform progressed at a snail's pace. The old generation was eased out or retired. Osborn wrote a book on population, and later in the thirties cooperated with Boas in conducting an anti-racist investigation. In the meantime he nurtured good contacts with people who were alienated by the old eugenics such as Harry Shapiro, a physical anthropologist who was engaged at the American Museum of Natural History in the twenties, despite Grant's anti-Semitic opposition, and later even joined eugenics.[99] Yet during those years the possibility of reform seemed very remote, and racists remained vocal in the Society. Following the rise of Nazism, even such an adherent and activist as William K. Gregory, a prominent paleontologist at the American Museum and Henry F. Osborn's adjutant for many years who could not by any stretch of the imagination be considered anything but an Anglo-Saxon supremacist, felt by 1935 that he had to register a protest over the extreme form of the eugenicists' sympathy with Hitler, and resigned from the Society.[100] Race enthusiasm no longer enjoyed respectability.

Reform eugenics was partly the result of a generation gap. The younger eugenicists, headed by C. B. Blacker and F. Osborn were not outsiders, but they reflected the shift in opinion among scientists who by definition were the high priests of eugenics. The pendulum shift against the simplistic misconceptions of the old eugenics was enhanced by the Nazi aberrations which forced many more to recognize racism as abhorrent. The reform was limited by the class component in the ideology of the movement which clung to the inherited superiority of the upper classes. While the tone had changed and the racial language had become more moderate,

[99] Dunn was invited to take part in the committee, under the chairmanship of A. V. Kidder. See Merriam to Dunn, Feb. 16, 1929. Also for more information on the Committee's work. LCDP. On Shapiro's nomination to the American Museum, see Boas correspondence with Warburg, FBP.

[100] Gregory to Hooton, May 21, 1935. EAHP, box 4FG. In explaining his resignation to Hooton, Gregory also wrote: "Admitting that 'superior' and 'inferior' are purely subjective, I would still hold that the New England tradition and the people that carry it have a right to struggle for their protection and perpetuation. So too Germans perhaps had a right to struggle lawfully against the Jews, but [with] Deportation, Expropriation, Prison Camps, slanderous foul propaganda, false anthropology, they have honored the people they persecute."

eugenicists were reluctant to give up their social prejudice. Osborn, for instance, consistently refused to address the racial question, but retained a qualified belief in the higher biological capabilities of the rich.[101] This component was obviously stronger in Britain where social differentiation did not contradict a deep national myth of equality, and which the Nazi doctrine did not change directly.

[101] Frederick Osborn, *Preface to Eugenics* (1940; ref. edn New York: Harper & Brothers, 1951). He thought that in the case of racial differences "the problem of cultural assimilation overshadows any eugenic aspect" (p. 78). He also evaluated the class impact as small compared with individual differences, apart from the case of "widely contrasted groups" (p. 95).

PART III

Politics

CHAPTER 6

Confronting racism: scientists as politicians

1933 – EARLY HESITATIONS

Following Hitler's accession to power on January 30, 1933, the fight against racism became a primary concern for a small but growing number of scientists. The 1920s saw scientists moderating their earlier racial enthusiasm and moving in an egalitarian direction, becoming skeptical of racial typologies and beginning to contest the capability of contemporary scientific knowledge to resolve the heredity versus environment debate. The urgency of dealing with racist doctrines became more compelling with the rise of Nazism, and anthropologists found themselves at the center of public demand to rebuke "Aryan science." Most scientists, excluding right-wing radicals, dismissed Nazi scientific racism as mere nonsense right from 1933, as is evident from their correspondence. Their public commitment, however, differed according to their social and intellectual affinities, and prior to the late 1930s only a minority explicitly opposed racism. Consequently, the period can be subdivided into three phases.

The first, which occurred during 1933-34, included several initiatives motivated by the plight of refugees and the question of anti-Nazism, but in general the issue of race was faced only indirectly. The second phase amounted to a stalemate up to 1938; while efforts to counter racism through institutionalized scientific channels were frustrated, anti-racist publications by individuals became popular. It was during the third period, however, from 1938 on, that the scientific community declared itself against racism. Since the 1950s, public memory has been that the rejection of

Nazism led to the refutation of scientific racism,[1] but as discussed in the introduction was not a foregone conclusion. It took great efforts and political manoeuvering by committed scientists to facilitate this rejection of racism.[2] Most scientists were hesitant to join the political frontier in the intellectual battle to discredit racism. The first to do so were those who were already prepared; left-wingers, liberals and Jews. Despite an initial response of disbelief, a small contingent mobilized itself and became a focal point of rallying against Nazism. Their numbers increased slowly and their commitment grew. Before 1938 attempts to publish joint scientific anti-racist statements to represent the discipline's position, foundered and it was left to individual efforts to fill the gap through books and articles. While an institutional committee in England failed to reach a consensus to condemn racism, collective efforts never even reached the point of trying to formulate an official position in America. From December 1938 onwards, following the aggravation of the political situation and the growing impatience with Nazism in the West, earlier campaigns materialized in a number of anti-racist declarations. These included statements by the American Anthropological Association, the executive council of the Society for the Psychological Study of Social Issues, and a group of distinguished geneticists at the International Congress of Genetics in Edinburgh, which became known as the Geneticists' Manifesto.[3] All of them

[1] This account is agreed upon by those, including Stocking, who subscribe to the present egalitarian consensus as scientifically correct (G. Stocking, "Lamarckianism," in *Race, Culture, and Evolution* (1968; Chicago: University of Chicago Press, 1982, pp. 234–238), and by those including John Baker who bemoan equality. For Baker since 1928 no ideas against equality of races could be voiced. Sorokin's *Contemporary Sociological Theories* "marked the close of the period in which both sides in the ethnic controversy were free to put forward their views, and authors who wished to do so could give objective accounts of the evidence pointing in each direction. From the beginning of the thirties onwards scarcely anyone outside Germany and its allies dared to suggest that any race might be in any sense superior to any other, lest it should appear that the author was supporting or excusing a Nazi cause. Those who believed in the equality of all races were free to write what they liked, without fear of contradiction ... Sorokin's chapter is well worth reading today, as a reminder of what was still possible before the curtain came down." John R. Baker, *Race* (Oxford: Oxford University Press, 1974), p. 61. See also Stepan, *The Idea of Race in Science: Great Britain 1800–1960* (Hamden, Conn.: Archon Books, 1982).

[2] Peter J. Kuznick (*Beyond the Laboratory: Scientists as Political Activists on 1930s America* (Chicago: Chicago University Press, 1987), describes the campaign against Fascism and pays attention to the fight against racism. See especially chs. 7–8.

[3] Ruth Benedict, *Race: Science and Culture* (1940; New York: The Viking Press, 1943), pp. 195–199. "Geneticists' Manifesto at the International Congress of Genetics in Edinburgh," *Journal of Heredity*, 30 (1939), 371–374. Diane Paul, "Eugenics and the Left," *Journal of the History of Ideas*, 45 (1984), 567–590. William B. Provine, "Geneticists and Race," *American Zoologist*, 26 (1986), 857–887.

asserted the principle of opposing Nazi racial theories, but did not go far towards defining race in egalitarian cultural terms. This was postponed until UNESCO initiated its first statement on race in 1950.

The single most active American scientist to combat racism in science was Franz Boas who remained the central figure of American anthropology up to his death in 1942. During the thirties his main contribution became more political, primarily in assisting refugees from Germany and fighting against scientific and political racism. In 1933, at the age of seventy five, Boas was still teaching full time at Columbia, where he supervised more (and better) PhD.s in anthropology than found at any other school in the country. Reputedly, his hopes of early retirement did not materialize due to the Depression and Columbia's refusal to hire replacements, especially Boasians. A veteran of many public campaigns, with contacts mostly in Europe and few in England, Boas suddenly found himself in the midst of a new turmoil, combating prejudice and conducting an intensive research program in an endeavour that continued literally till the last day of his life, ten years later.[4]

For more than a decade before 1933, Boas was active on behalf of German-American cooperation, especially in science. Although he visited Germany in 1932, and kept up his activities in the Germanistic Society of America, he did not comment on the internal politics of the country prior to March 1933. He seemed reluctant to adopt a position of blank opposition to the regime of a country with which he retained a profound cultural identification. During March and April 1933, requests for help from Germany started to accumulate in Boas's files, but despite his efforts to help, he felt "hopeless." The crisis came to dominate Boas's work. The first initiative for international cooperation was coordinated from London, where a committee to help the German refugee scientists was formed under the chairmanship of Gilbert Murray, and included Sir William Beveridge, Sir Gowland Hopkins (President of the Royal Society) and George Trevelyan. Boas organized the American side,[5] neglecting his scientific activity as well as many of his previous social interests, including his involvement with minorities questions in the United States. By May 1933, Boas found himself engaged both in helping individuals find haven in the United States and in organizing

[4] Herskovits, *Franz Boas: The Science of Man in the Making* (New York: Scribner's 1953.)
[5] Boas to R. Pound, May 23, 1933. FBP.

opposition to anti-Semitism and racism. This was part of the wider response to the refugees' plight, and it is in this context that peer pressure upon biologists and anthropologists to renounce the scientific credentials of racism became critical.

Boas joined the American Committee Against Fascist Oppression in Germany when it was organized in March. His first public act was to address an open letter to President Hindenburg on March 27, which became the manifesto of Boas's later work. In his political activities Boas continued to apply rigid standards of accuracy, and refused to support propaganda which he believed did not measure up to these standards. When the Committee published a "Black Book of German Fascist Atrocities," Boas withdrew from the Committee because he believed these did not represent a systematic policy, only "unfavorable ruffianism in days of revolution."[6] By late April he had tried to get the Council of the National Academy of Sciences to pass a resolution against "the tendency to control scientific work from non-scientific viewpoints that are [sic] spreading particularly among the nations of Europe." Such an unspecified target was to be used often in resolutions over the next few years because it could be seen as "directed [not] against Germany alone, but equally against Italy or Russia or any other state that is guilty of the same offense." When this effort failed, Boas sought to have a similar resolution passed by the American College of Physicians and Surgeons.[7] As more detailed reports of the "utter despair of all classes of Jews in Germany" began to reach him, and as he became aware of "a well organized attempt in New York, and probably in other parts of the country, to propagate anti-Semitism," his Jewish commitment overshadowed any prior loyalties to Germany. In June, he took the lead in organizing the Lessing League to combat "the anti-Semitic agitation which is being carried on in this country by the Silver Shirts Party."[8] Boas, who had devoted so much of his life to liberal causes and campaigned incessantly to influence public opinion, was realistic and skeptical about the impact of such efforts through writing because, he commented sadly, "only people who agree will read it."[9] Here, nonetheless, his contributions turned out to have a lasting importance. Boas undertook a systematic effort to

[6] Boas to M. Trent, April 23; to M. Butler, May 3. FBP.
[7] Boas to C. Abbott, April 17; Boas to M. Butler, May 3; Boas to H. Cushing, April 25. FBP.
[8] B. Liebowitz to E. Boas, May 4; Boas to L. Posner, May 26. FBP.
[9] Boas to Kaempfert, *New York Times* Science Editor, April 10, 1933. Boas to W. M. Wheeler, Harvard, May 23, 1933. FBP.

"counteract the vicious, pseudo-scientific activity of so-called scientists who try to prove the close relation between racial descent and mental character." He launched a research program aimed at providing data to "attack the racial craze" by "undermin[ing] its alleged scientific basis" and creating opportunities to combat racist fallacies in an educational campaign.

Boas recognized that he would be considered a partisan in conducting an investigation on racial questions, specifically if it involved the Jewish question, and therefore organized a committee which consisted largely of non-Jews. Financial support, however, was mostly Jewish since non-Jews had declined solicitations. The enterprise was carried out under the auspices of the Council of Research of the Social Sciences at Columbia University, which included the sociologist Robert MacIver, the psychologist A. T. Poffenberger and the geneticist Leslie Dunn, all nationally prominent. The committee was largely a facade for the work of Boas and his students.[10] For some time the council had been supporting the research of Otto Klineberg, who demonstrated the predominant role of environment in determining the mental characteristics of American blacks. Boas's goal was to show that "individual heredity and racial heredity are entirely different things and that while we may find that certain characteristic traits are inherited in a family, the race is altogether too complex to infer that racial characteristics as such are inherited."[11] The essential aim of the Council was to achieve wide publicity, hoping to shorten the time lag of publication by issuing pamphlets. The council also planned to publish books of which Boas's *Anthropology and Modern Life* [1928] was the model. Boas paid great attention to media coverage, and invested much effort in writing letters to editors and issuing press releases. His article "Aryans and Non-Aryans" was submitted to the *Atlantic Monthly*, *Harper's*, *Scribner's* and *Esquire*, before being finally published in June 1934 in *Mercury*, eight months after the initial

---

[10] Boas called for a meeting at the City Club in November 1933, to organize the campaign, aiming to raise $10,000 annually to study "Racial and Social Differences in Mental Ability," and refute alleged racial characteristics. The American Museum of Natural History declined the invitation, Frederick Osborn would not help financially, and Boas had to rely only on Jewish financial support. Since June 1934, Dunn was away, and gave Boas an official *carte blanche* in running the committee. Boas to M. Warburg, Dec. 29, 1933; to F. Warburg, Nov. 24, 1933. Other non-Jews who were suggested included, in psychiatry William A. White (Washington), Macfie Campbell (Boston). See E. M. Friedman to Boas, Nov. 13. FBP.

[11] Boas to F. Warburg, Oct. 9, 1933. FBP.

attempt.[12] Boas even explored the possibility of producing an educational movie to combat anti-Semitic propaganda, to be based on his studies of gestures of Jewish and Italian immigrants.[13] He also tried to mobilize scientists to speak out publicly against scientific assumptions underlying racism and insisted that even popular publications, devised only as propaganda tools, should be accurate in content. On similar grounds he opposed Ignaz Zollschan over the years, as being too much of a Jewish nationalist.[14]

Perhaps the most telling of Boas's commitments to civil rights was his struggle to give fair protection to Nazis in the U.S.[15] Boas refrained from party politics, but was very active on public issues. This included membership in many organizations, among them the American Committee Against Fascist Oppression in Germany, the National Committee for the Defence of Political Prisoners, and a committee for civil rights of Indians. In addition, he served as the national chairman of the American Committee of Democracy and Intellectual Freedom and of the Committee on Race Relations of the Society of Friends. He also corresponded with many political organizations, recruiting participants and speakers on their behalf. At Columbia he was involved with the branch of The League of Struggle for Negro Rights (1933) as well as with defence of academic freedom. Occasionally, Boas became an advocate for the rights of minorities, such as the Korean students, who rarely captured public attention.[16]

[12] Boas to Sadgwick, Nov. 8, 1933; Marion Sanders to Boas, Dec. 20, 1933.
[13] Boas to Harry Warner, June 30, 1938.
[14] Boas to the members of the Council, April 21, 1933. On the Council's plans, Boas, circular, n.d. (1935?). Boas asked Hooton to find an opportunity to publish an anti-racist statement and arranged the contacts with media agencies to assure coverage. Boas to Berneys, Jan. 27, 1936; For a session at the National Academy of Science Boas solicited interviews by journalists for himself, Hrdlicka, Todd and Hooton, April 13, 1936. The "gestures" study was targeted to the Sunday Magazine of the *New York Times*. On Zollschan, see below pp. 318–325.
[15] He demanded that "proper public judicial procedure" should also be applied in the case of those "guilty of the numerous outrages." Boas withdrew from the National Committee for the Defence of Political Prisoners because they declared their intention of not defending a Nazi group, and he supported the appointment of Furtwaengler as Director of the New York Philharmonic Orchestra, because opposition to it was based solely on political motives. Boas to Hirsch, Jan. 15, 1935; to the Editor, *New York Times*, March 2, 1936.
[16] Boas to S. Dickstein, Jan 16, 1940. It is interesting to note that he was totally unaware of racial discrimination against the Japanese on the West Coast. Boas's "Japanese sources" ascribed anti-Japanese sentiments and actions to be politically motivated, not racially (Boas to M. Hillyer, April 29, 1942). Boas's support of the black minority was long and extensive. In this context it should be mentioned that he supported political efforts to combat anti-black legislation, affirmative action in education " in principle and in practice

His political experience during the thirties made him into a sophisticated political observer.[17] Despite repeated disappointments, and echoing Tocqueville's fear of democracy, Boas maintained a belief in the impact of words, and in the ability of the individual to shape society:

I do not believe that the simple term 'Democracy,' which we connect with intellectual freedom, applies to every kind of democracy, because ... an intolerant or bigoted democracy may be as bad as any form of absolutism ... My own personal experience has been that on account of my consistent stand for intellectual freedom I have been ostracized by the American democracy in 1919, by Russian scientists in 1932, and by Germany at the present time.[18]

Aside from general political anti-fascist activity, there was very little organized response to Nazism among scientists and almost none from official scientific institutions. Scientists reserved their comments, and except for excluding a small number of investigations financed at Columbia, no organized initiative was taken to undermine the scientific claims of Nazi racism. While racism was on the wane in American science, little immediate response to the Nazi threat emerged among scientists.

BRITAIN – RACE AND CULTURE COMMITTEE

In contrast to the United States, where the Boasian critique of racial typology had been central to the formation of anthropology during the first three decades of the century, in Britain the question of race did not become prominent until after 1933, before that date the primary debate had been over class relations.[19] Functional and social anthropology became the dominant form of the discipline

– by giving blacks the opportunity to participate in anthropological and psychological studies of their own people. His participation in a symposium of Fascism and Lynch-terror emphasized his twofold opposition to racism ("Leipzig and Scottsboro – A Tale of Two Cities." Dec 6, 1933, FBP) as did his activities in combating racial legislation on the state level. For The League of Struggle for Negro Rights see FBP, Nov. 25, 1933. He was particularly influential in the State of Washington where the anti-racial-miscegnation bill was finally defeated in 1939. Boas testified, and urged others to do the same. Boas and M. Jacobs correspondence, especially March 21, 1939. FBP.

[17] Previously Boas had been politically naïve, as his correspondence with the Soviet Union and Germany suggests, but in this he was not alone. Until his breach with Germany, his correspondence does not include any comments on the political situation in Germany, where he summered in 1932. His remarks concerning the Soviet Union display ignorance.

[18] Boas to Schneiderman, May 15, 1939. FBP.

[19] Kevles, *Eugenics*; Stepan, *Race*; Paul, "Eugenics and the Left."

more by secession from nineteenth century evolutionary tradition than by confrontation. Rather than being marginalized by institutional anthropology in the 1920s, as were the American hereditarians, British racialists remained respected figures in the profession and dominated the Royal Anthropological Institute into the thirties. Consequently egalitarianism was almost non-existent among the British.[20] It was only when British liberals were forced to reconcile their overall world-view with their racial prejudices and had to wrestle with their long accepted social intellectual conventions that they began to advocate anti-racism. A few of those who had displayed ugly racism at an earlier date, such as Julian Huxley or J. B. S. Haldane, began to shift in an anti-racist direction around 1930 and within few years became the symbols of anti-racism. Others, however, committed themselves to the nonracist position only later. In 1931 Arthur Keith updated his 1916 theory of racial antagonism as part of human nature. John Linton Myres called it "provocative" in a review for *Man* but did not confront it critically.[21] Keith's position sparked a minor controversy, but it was not until three years later, and under different circumstances, that the anthropology community embarked on its first institutionalized attempt to face racism.

By the spring of 1934, British scientists had encountered the question of a response to Nazism – privately or in scientific circles – either in regard to the immigration of persecuted fellow scientists or as a political question. Left-wingers and liberals voiced a growing demand for an active response, part of which was reflected in the political tension and internal pressure, which led the Royal Anthropological Institute with the support of the Institute of Sociology, to establish on April 24, 1934, a committee to study the "racial factor in cultural development." Among the British anthropologists, the driving force to form the Race and Culture Committee seems to have been Charles Seligman. A major stimulus from outside the

[20] G. Stocking (ed.), *Functionalism Historicized. Essays on British Social Anthropology*, History of Anthropology II (Madison: University of Wisconsin Press, 1984).

[21] Sir Arthur Keith, *Ethnos, or the Problem of Race* (London: K. Paul, 1931). Keith's public stature was enhanced by his official role in the Royal College of Surgeons in London and his position as Rector of the University of Aberdeen. He first formulated his nationalistic theory in 1916, under the impact of World War I, and the updated version received publicity in two distinguished lectures: his Huxley memorial lecture, and the Rectorial address in Aberdeen. Myres, *Man*, 32 (1932), 246. Keith's position promised that the theory would continue to arouse public opinion throughout the 1930s (see correspondence in *Man*, March-June 1940), and even in the post-war period.

Confronting racism 287

anthropological establishment had come from Ignaz Zollschan, a Czechoslovakian Jewish physician then in Britain as part of his European tour in a personal campaign to combat Nazi anti-Semitism.

The Race and Culture Committee was established under constraints which made its task impossible. When, in the spring of 1936, the committee published what it called an interim report,[22] even the editorial in the moderate *Nature* had some harsh comments: it had taken the committee two years to deliberate on the question of "a simple definition of race to serve as a guide to the general public in the discussions of the problems of to-day," and then it did not deliver. "Not only are alternative definitions offered, but also several members append observations which at times almost amount to minority reports." *Nature* found the two definitions "inexceptionable," and added: "these definitions are far from being generalizations from concrete realities and empirical, [these] are no more than logical concepts, postulated for the purpose of classification and investigation." Examining the existing distribution of physical characters among the population groups of the world, *Nature* remarked that "race is pure abstraction." Taken at face value, this view would have placed *Nature* among later date extreme anti-racialists. But this was not so much a result of *Nature*'s egalitarianism as a display of its frustration with the committee's work; impatience which resulted from the recognition that "racial distinctions have emerged from the sphere of intellectual inquiry and have been made the practical basis of discrimination." Consequently it was the task of scholars to agree upon and publish a resolution which would return the debate to its appropriate domain.[23] The visibility of the racial question turned anthropology into a popular topic and this, coupled with a belief in objectivity and rationality, united the anthropologists under the auspices of the Royal Anthropological Institute to solicit contributions for studies on the racial history and population of Britain, justified by the claim that Britain lagged behind many other countries in such studies. The list of twenty signatories appended to the request included Gates, Huxley, Keith and Seligman.[24] *Nature*'s editorial displayed the misconce-

[22] Royal Anthropological Institute and the Institute of Sociology, *Race and Culture* (London: Le Play House, 1936).
[23] *Nature*, 137 (April 18, 1936), 635–637.
[24] *Times*, March 13, 1935, also published in *Man*, 35 (April 1935).

ption that a scientific debate can return the spectre of racism to its previously "respected" dimensions. Anthropologists and biologists were presumed objective in their scientific analysis of the question of race, and there was not even a hint that the reverse might be the case, namely that prejudice was the source of scientific justification and that scientists were trapped by the same blindness as the public at large. *Nature*'s "objectivity" was illustrated in several editorials such as "The Aryan Doctrine," which attacked German dogmatism, and in the same spirit reproached the Americans (by implication, Boas and his disciples) who resorted to the easier alternative of egalitarianism, following the "voice of the facile theorist . . . while the scientific investigator of race, who refrains from dogmatism pending fuller inquiry, is still crying in the wilderness."[25]

This middle-of-the-road attitude was also manifested in a letter to *The Times* from Alfred Haddon, Sir Gowland Hopkins, the President of the Royal Society, and J. B. S. Haldane, in which they admonished Sir John Simon, a Cabinet Minister, for exhibiting his Aryan extraction.[26] The editorial emphasized the widespread ignorance among the public concerning the race issue, and partially blamed the divided anthropologists for being unable to communicate a clear message to the public. After explaining the Nordic and Aryan theories, the editorial concluded: "Such dogmatic assumptions, unfortunately have their attraction for the political doctrinaire and the agitator; and it is perhaps to be regretted therefore, that the International Congress of Anthropological and Ethnological Sciences did not see its way to promote investigation into such racial problems on broad lines. The machinery may seem overweighty; but at least the truth would have been made available in authoritative form to all."[27] The hopes of the summer of 1934 evidently did not materialize: by 1936 the Race and Culture Committee showed that a clear authoritative statement in the name of the profession was unattainable.

Professional politics rendered the Race and Culture Committee's efforts futile. The most prominent racist among British anthropologists was Arthur Keith, and the staunch racists on the committee were G. H. L. F. Pitt-Rivers, and Reginald Ruggles Gates, all of

[25] "The Delusion of Race," *Nature*, 137 (April 18, 1936), 635–637. "Genetics and Race," *Nature*, 137 (Dec. 12, 1936), 998–999.
[26] Quoted in, *Nature*, 134 (August 7, 1934).
[27] "The Aryan Doctrine," *Nature*, 134 (August 18, 1934), 229–231.

whom belonged to the mainstream of the profession. Despite the relatively few records pertaining to the Race and Culture Committee, the cooperation between Pitt-Rivers and Gates in presenting a racist front is clear. The anti-racists on the committee, however, were certainly better represented. The classification of British scientists as anti-racists in the mid-thirties, when a formalist approach to race was still widespread and the Boasian critique hardly present, may cast doubts on the whole exercise. Yet if the definition employed is narrow enough and politically oriented, it is possible even at this stage to distinguish racists from anti-racists. Anti-racists included scientists who opposed political racism, classified themselves as such and objected to the use of scientific theories to justify racial discrimination. The members of the Race and Culture Committee who published such views before World War II included the chairman G. Elliot Smith, the anatomist Le Gros Clark, the geographer Herbert J. Fleure, the cultural anthropologist Raymond Firth, the biometrician Geoffrey Morant and the biologist J. B. S. Haldane.

This narrow definition of anti-racism has to be understood in its historical context, one that excluded Jews from the Committee because they were deemed too subjective to participate in such a scientific elucidation. Simplistic objectivism was the norm to such a degree that even liberals and the victims themselves, in this case the Jews, accepted ostracism; and so because of Gates's opposition, the sociologist Morris Ginsberg was not included.[28] The same attitude of appeasement guided the British opposition to a Czech initiative to organize an international race congress. John Linton Myres, the British diplomat of anthropology, consented to such congress if it could be kept "strictly scientific." But in his view, this was unlikely since "it appears at present to be sponsored by Czechoslovakia, Austria and France," countries which, as victims, were expected to retaliate. A further prerequisite was the inclusion of the Germans who, Myres thought were unlikely "to come to a Prague-Vienna-Paris enterprise."[29] Surely Myres did not expect that the inclusion of an official German delegation was to turn a race congress into a dispassionate scholarly enterprise. At least by implication, he

---

[28] Seligman to Gates, April 22, 1935. RRGP.
[29] Myres to Farquharson, confidential (March 1934?) 121 fol. 106; Myres to Fleure, March 10, 1934, 121 fol. 112. JLMP.

claimed that as a result of the political situation the topic evaded scientific analysis.

Although the culture of British science was very formal, disagreements among scientists often reached the public domain. Individually, several scientists entertained themselves by engaging in lively disputes, which included much correspondence with the editors of the *Times* and *Nature*. Yet the British scientific establishment was almost sacred, or at least tried to present itself as such. Its best strategy for preserving unity was to *avoid* issues that could not be settled peacefully. Scientific legitimacy stemmed from very few tradition-bound institutions and societies. Oxford, Cambridge, and London were the only centers that mattered; other universities only counted when they conformed. Opposition was never meaningful if mounted from the provinces. The key to success was incorporation and accommodation. As long as no viable institutional alternative existed, everyone had to fall in line, even the "Visible College."[30] The Race and Culture Committee should therefore be viewed as an effort in accommodation.

If the fear of Nazism motivated left-wingers to establish the Committee, right-wingers were encouraged by the Nazi success to increase their activities. Gates's xenophobia, for example, was manifested in his anti-miscegenation campaign, which he began in 1933. Although his aim was to show that "there is no method of knowing how many [colored people] are born" in Britain, he defined it as "an increasingly difficult" problem. Undaunted by this lacuna in knowledge, he based his argument on studies that included 500 children – "no doubt a very small fraction of the whole number." Gates was worried "that the only force against [racial] crossing is that of social ostracism which can be evaded in various ways," especially in port towns where colored people had their own streets.[31] Like other racists Gates denied that his views had any connection with Nazi doctrines, and Seligman even solicited, perhaps perfunctorily, his cooperation in the campaign against German racism. Ostensibly there was no institutional cleavage between racists and anti-racists in British science, but in the case of

---

[30] Gary Werskey, *The Visible College* (London: Allen Lane, 1978), uses the term with regard to the left, though Werskey does not make this particular analysis. For Huxley's case, see above, chapter 5.

[31] Gates's views were too "outspoken" for the *Nineteenth Century*, which declined the contribution. Fleming to Gates, Oct. 13, 1933; Gates to Blacker, Oct. 16, 1933. RRGP.

the Race and Culture Committee this overzealousness in pursuing a
consensus where none existed became self defeating.[32]

Gates's comments for the Race and Culture Committee presented
adequately his disagreement with other members. Gates believed
that "in the taxonomy of animals and plants the conception of
groups within groups had long held sway and it is difficult to see how
it could be otherwise with man if evolution has taken place."[33] From
this basic analogy the rest followed. Because Gates looked for
"groups within groups," and applied the same terminology to
mankind as to the rest of nature, he chose to speak about species and
races "or smaller population groups." He considered fertility an
"obsolete" criterion for a species and therefore "if an Australian
aborigine and an Eskimo were bred together there is no reason to
doubt that they would show full fertility, but this is not a sufficient
reason for placing them in one species. If the same criteria of species
were applied to mankind as to other mammals, it appears that the
White, Black and Yellow types of man at least would be regarded as
belonging to separate species." Gates thought that anthropological
data which showed no considerable geographical area to be
inhabited exclusively by any one race did not "nullify the value of
these types as anthropological conceptions," and concluded: "It
appears clear that within historical times the reverse process of
racial migration and intermixture has been taking place at an even
accelerating rate ... This process has led not merely to an undoing
of the evolution which has taken place under condition of geographical isolation. Evolution has not ceased, but intermixture has
largely taken the place of isolation as an evolutionary factor."[34]

The other racist on the Committee was Captain George H. L. F.
Pitt-Rivers, the grandson of the founder of the Pitt-Rivers Museum
at Oxford. After a career in the army and the colonial service,
H. L. F. Pitt-Rivers became active in anthropological circles in the
1920s, as well as a close friend of Bronislaw Malinowski. Author of
the influential volume on *The Clash of Culture and the Conflict of the
Races*, Pitt-Rivers was a member of the Eugenics Society and

[32] Seligman introduced Zollschan, an anti-racist activist, to Gates in the spring of 1934.
Seligman to Gates, March 15, 1934, RRGP. Did Seligman actually believe that Gates
would cooperate in such an effort? One would doubt that, but perhaps Seligman's
intention in soliciting Gates was to deter him from public opposition.
[33] Gates, "The Conception of Race," August 6, 1934, in the Bodleian, Ms. 121 f. 162–3.
JLMP. Published in the report as his addendum.
[34] Gates, "The Conception of Race."

Secretary-General and Honorary Treasurer of the International
Union for Scientific Investigation of Population Problems from 1928
to 1937. His support for Nazi Germany went a long way beyond
mere vocal Aryanism. He taught in Germany during the 1930s, and
following the outbreak of the war was held a political prisoner in
England during 1940–1942. The scientific contribution he treasured
most was the science of "ethnogenics," a method for the study of the
"interaction of race, population and culture." Among his rec-
reations he listed "refuting politicians," and it is evident why
Pitt-Rivers spared no efforts to have his racial views aired in the
Committee's report.[35]

Pitt-Rivers's concern was that "the looseness with which the term
race is used" obscures "the process of race-extinction." He accepted
that migration confused the linkage of race with a geographical
region, and therefore replaced traditional race formalism with rigid
ethnic identity and "race-types" which were dissociated from their
customary "geographical habitats." In this context, the important
distinction was culture. Pitt-Rivers described the "Nordic,"
"Alpine" and "Mediterranean" as standardization of the characteristics of existing race-types although, as he added, these were
arbitrary. The meaningful distinction lay in a "race-cultural
complex" of "People" – namely, Celtic, Aryan, English. This
critique of traditional racial divisions from a racist perspective
shows that the answer to cultural relativism and biological complexity was not necessarily egalitarian. Pitt-Rivers credited Arthur
Keith as the writer who had refuted the idea of the fixity of
race-types not from an egalitarian, but from a nationalist and
racialist, perspective. An evolutionary view of race implies continuous development; where Gates emphasized the biological aspect
alone, Pitt-Rivers combined it with the cultural.

Even when the Committee managed to agree on an abstract
principle, political compromise remained a constant impediment.[36]

---

[35] *Who Was Who*, 1961–1970; "A. H. L. F. Pitt-Rivers," *Dictionary of Scientific Biography*. The
centrality of the *Journal of the International Union for Scientific Investigation of Population Problems*
is attested by the contributors to its first issue. These included among others J. Huxley,
Carr-Saunders, and Crew.

[36] Such was the case when Seligman tried to persuade Gates to endorse a call from the
International Institute for Intellectual Cooperation for "a general investigation of the
anthropological and ethnological basis of Western civilization." Seligman, assured of the
support of Malinowski, Elliot Smith, Myres and Firth, added that on the Continent
"considerable progress seems to have been made ... in the organization of research
groups" on similar matters. Seligman to Gates, March 17, 1935. RRGP.

Of the report's twenty-three pages, only the three pages of the preamble were agreed upon by all of the members, but even these reflected disagreement. Although Boas's article in the *Encyclopedia of Social Sciences* on "Race" was given as a bibliographical source, Pitt-Rivers suggested a critical addendum to the effect that Boas's approach was "not compatible with the most recent approach of human ecologists or of ethnologists." The compromise was a supplementary reference to a recent book on human ecology.[37] The Committee debated Boas's work, and Elliot Smith requested from Boas for the Race and Culture Committee thirty copies of his essay "Aryans and Non-Aryans": "As chairman I want all the members to read your pamphlet before we draft our final report." It was in Elliot Smith's opinion "extremely valuable at the moment when I am deeply involved in the task of trying to combat the racial non-sense that now plays so large a part in current journals and discussions."[38]

The committee in effect offered two definitions of race: nominalist and realist, emphasizing the limitation of scientific knowledge of the physical aspects of human groups, and suggesting only that "innate psychological characters may later be found to differentiate them." The nominalist definition called for caution in the use of statistical averages based on "descriptive and measurable characters" (i.e., phenotype) which might in fact "obscure . . . several diverse strains" (i.e., genotype). An alternative definition emphasized the condition of continuous isolation and spoke of "genetical characteristics" that distinguished different groups. The geographical factor, a source of disagreement, was absent. The committee's mandate had been to define "how far particular races and populations are actually linked with particular cultures or culture elements," but the members could never agree on this question. Instead they appended seven individual definitions which reflected the various currents in the anthropology community.[39]

While the conflict between racists and non-racists was evident, the nonracist members of the committee also disagreed on method and content. Morant argued from a biometrician's perspective that biological knowledge was not sufficient for any practical application. He minimized the role of paleontology and archeology in favor

[37] The book was E. J. Bews, *Human Ecology* (London: Oxford University Press, 1935). Pitt-Rivers to Gates, Dec. 15, 1935. RRGP.
[38] G. E. Smith to Boas, Oct. 8, 1934; Sept. 26, 1934. FBP.   [39] *Race and Culture*, pp. 3–4.

of methods which are "essentially descriptive" and "do not presuppose any particular theory of individual or racial inheritance."[40]
This inexplicable definition of race and the overall political
impotency of scientists, was later regretted by Morant. Following
the outbreak of World War II, he expressed remorse that anthropologists had failed to oppose racism earlier.

Though Morant did not find an institutional niche for himself in
the post-war years, he certainly represented a respectable and viable
position during the thirties.[41] This illuminates two points: first that
it was still possible in England during the 1930s to be at the center of
scientific activity, to deal with inheritance and to reject genetics; and
second that there was no correlation between a progressive scientific
method and its application to social issues. Morant's biometric
method was leading to a dead end, but his conclusions were context
dependent and anti-racialist in content. Similarly, Elliot Smith's
only scientific instructive comment was that biologically the contemporary usage of "races" was the equivalent of Linnaeus'
"species." The rest was a rehearsal of his earlier diffusionism. Yet
Smith fought racism, both Nazi theories and the overtones of Arthur
Keith's "nationalism," until his death in 1937. The geographer and
anthropologist H. J. Fleure described the inadequacy of biological
or statistical methods in a language which discloses his anti-racialist
position only to a careful and attentive reader. While on other
occasions he was more direct as, for example, in a lecture to the
Royal Anthropological Institute, in the report he concluded that
"the averaging of whole populations regardless of these diversities of
strain or breed obscures important biological facts and gives results
which are sometimes too abstract to be of great value." This was not
quite the dynamite that could serve an egalitarianist political
campaign.[42]

J. B. S. Haldane and Raymond Firth criticized racism from what
might be considered the frontier of knowledge. Haldane argued that
any definition of race must include a reference to geographical
distribution as well as to human characters. Due to immigration, the
geographical aspect should relate to a certain past. Recognizing
obvious differences, Haldane focused on populations with overlapping characters. His insistence that biological, and therefore racial,

[40] G. M. Morant "Biometrician's View of Race in Man," in *Race and Culture*.
[41] On Morant's work see above, pp. 158–162.
[42] For Fleure's comments, see *Race and Culture*, pp. 6–8.

differences are due to genes was almost unique in the committee.
Firth approached the question from the perspective of a cultural
anthropologist. He minimized the influence of physical characters
on cultural achievements and rejected the assumed importance of
race. yet his anti-racist position can only be appreciated in its
historical context. In substance, Firth, like other anti-racist
members of the Committee, could have endorsed modern sociobiology, and conceded that "consideration of temperament" played a
part in the "acquisition of culture," although science has no way of
obtaining information "in substantiation of this general impression."[43] Despite their willingness to entertain racial conjectures,
their position elucidated the unscientific nature of such hypothesis.

Gates and Pitt-Rivers used the terminology of genetics to support
their idiosyncratic racial typologies, an approach which lent their
theories an appearance of scientific progressiveness and respectability. They differed with other members on two issues: firstly that
races did not mean geographical isolation, and secondly that racial
mixture was an evolutionary force which, in Gates's words, "produced many new races." Pitt-Rivers advocated his own "ethnogenics" to cover the combination of genetics with the "study of human
history in terms of changing race, population and culture." He
explicitly opposed Smith but accepted diffusionism and claimed
that the racial transfer of cultural elements by borrowing is a process
which involves selection and therefore implies inner capacity. These
scientific theories accentuated the racialist interpretations and
hence were compatible with Gates's and Pitt Rivers's political
alliances. They drew comfort from Germany, and from the German
anthropologist Eickenstedt, who also refrained from addressing the
geographical origin.[44] The growing political crisis of the 1930s was
not a congenial atmosphere for compromise, and the confrontation
became more fierce. The decision of the Race and Culture Committee to publish an unsatisfactory report was the only alternative to a
declaration of failure, which was inadvisable since an agreement
was needed for professional and political reasons. The small anthropological profession was suddenly given center stage in defining the
"truth" of the burning political question of race, an importance it
had never attained before. The benefits and publicity were tempt-
ing, as was the moral and political responsibility. While the
Committee failed to reach a consensual statement on race, the

[43] Firth's comments in *Race and Culture*.   [44] Pitt-Rivers to Gates, Dec. 15, 1935. RRGP.

pressure of international events made further attempts in other arenas inevitable.

One such instance was the joint session at the annual meeting of the British Association at Blackpool (1936) of the zoology and anthropology sections, which debated the definition of race. *Nature* supported the scientists' efforts to face "the exploitation of the race concept by politicians" and concluded that it "behoves all scientific workers ... to respond for the demand of the general public for guidance" in these matters. Perhaps more important, at the end of the article came a call for scientists to "relinquish" the scientific use of the term race because the politicians had "appropriated the term." In this it echoed Huxley's and Haddon's recently published *We Europeans*. *Nature*'s traditional emphasis on the objectivity of science and its role in guiding the public was being contradicted by political events. Though the magazine did not explicitly change its perceptions of the social relations of science, it implied that scientific terms were influenced and shaped by public opinion.[45] The public demand was for anthropology to define race scientifically and rename it. Most anthropologists followed this intellectual trend against racism and shifted the subject matter of their research from the biological to the cultural. For many the transformation preceded World War II, but the British scientific community followed the government's policy of appeasement, and prevented the shift against rigid racial typology and, by implication, against racism, from receiving formal approval.

WE EUROPEANS

Despite early hopes of reaching a professional consensus against racism, none materialized. The alternative venues were left to individual scientists who confronted racism by means of articles, symposia and at times petitions. Among the most important of this genre which helped undermine the scientific basis for racism was *We Europeans*, the title of which underscores its limited scope. The book was co-authored by Julian Huxley and Alfred C. Haddon, in collaboration with Carr-Saunders.[46] Further unofficial assistance was provided by Charles Seligman and Charles Singer. A publishing

45 "Genetics and Race," *Nature*, 137 (Dec. 12, 1936), pp. 998–999.
46 Julian S. Huxley and A. C. Haddon, *We Europeans, A Survey of 'Racial' Problems, With a Chapter on Europe Overseas, by A. M. Carr Saunders* (London: Jonathan Cape, 1935).

effort that predated the rise of Nazism, the book was a scientific statement, written in popular form, mainly by a biologist and an anthropologist in an explicit attempt to fight Nazi pseudo-scientific theories of race. The main achievement of *We Europeans* was its endeavor to combine biological and anthropological data in one volume in a serious application of advanced theories of genetics to a comprehensive study of ethnic groups. It aimed to refute the affinity between science and racism, a position which was too radical for the scientific community to adopt as a professional credo.

We Europeans was a popular and influential anti-racist statement. While the book put forward few new affirmative claims, the authors paid much attention to discrediting fallacious arguments and repeatedly stressed that there was "scientific ignorance on this fundamental subject," a polemical claim fifty years ago. This was hailed by the authors as a main conclusion of their survey of the European ethnic composition. While popular science often aims at the diffusion of knowledge, *We Europeans* highlighted the pervasive confusion among scientists and the general public on the concept of race.

The most important aspect of *We Europeans* was its anti-racist statements, a fact well reflected in the reviews. The authors argued that the scientific concept "race," as applied to humans, "has lost any sharpness of meaning. To-day it is hardly definable in scientific terms, except as an abstract concept." They did, however, leave the door open for the existence of races in the past and perhaps even in the future, but termed all these "hypothetical." Consequently the authors proposed a striking alternative of renouncing a racial groupings among human beings.

The scientific theory of *We Europeans* was eclectic and not altogether coherent. Its purpose was to formulate a scientific statement on the meaning of human races based on "the genetic differences between human groups." The authors concluded that compared with social factors, the biological factors were relatively unimportant. While biological knowledge might contribute to the debate, it could not elucidate the essence of race: "in the ultimate analysis the matter must be incapable of scientific determination since the decision as to what is a 'race' is a personal matter resting largely on subjective impressions."[47] It is perhaps not surprising that a study which suggested replacing *race* with *ethnic* also recognized the significance of subjectivity as a method of inquiry.

[47] *We Europeans*, pp. 7–8, 167.

If biology had insufficient data to define race, anthropology was considered wrong and outdated. Anthropologists were mainly engaged "in the collection of detailed evidence rather than in attack on the larger problems of ethnology ... the application of modern genetical theory to the problems of biology has still to make itself adequately felt in the domain of the anthropologist." The main theoretical failure was the inability to apply Mendelian theory to the classification of races, which led to inadequate empirical research: "in the absence of the genetic stimulus the field anthropologist has often failed to collect the most significant data or to present them in a manner susceptible to exact interpretation." The backward looking anthropologist belonged to a defunct "Darwinian era" when "the a priori idea of blending inheritance was in fashion," and groups had "well marked characteristics, and a small range of variation chiefly affecting quantitative characters." The antithesis of the unsophisticated anthropologist was the Mendelian geneticist, "knowing the facts of inheritance and the migratory habits of man," who expected groups to possess

a large range of variation, often concerned with striking characters of a qualitative nature as well as with quantitative ones; such groups can only be distinguished from each other by statistical methods. In such groups the *mean values* for characters, though still useful, no longer have the same theoretical importance. The *range of variation* of characters is of far greater practical importance, as is also the range of qualitatively different recombination-types. The two resultant 'racial' or ethnic concepts are fundamentally dissimilar.[48]

Compared with the anthropologist, even the biometricians were "of very great value," because their statistical approach guarded against imperfect generalization and inadequate data, a frequent scientific stumbling block for anthropologists. Disciplinary shifts made a revolution in the outlook on "race" possible. No longer was the "common ancestry, a single original stock ... the essential badge of a 'race'," rather it was replaced by a "probable number of common ancestors," which resulted in "a coefficient" of ancestry. This meant that popular and scientific perceptions of race were no longer similar: "The word 'race,' as applied scientifically to human groupings, has lost any sharpness of meaning." Frequency distribution and related mathematical concepts replaced any readily available definitions.[49]

[48] *We Europeans*, pp. 60, 104.   [49] *We Europeans*, pp. 61, 106–107, 160.

Additional scientific development which fed the new view of race was the increased recognition of the importance of the multiple genetical factors which molded every trait. The authors found it necessary to emphasize that not all genes have a large or clear-cut effect. They pointed to stature and weight, which in most animals is determined by a large group of genes each exerting a small effect, and capable of reinforcing each other's influence. Though this had been recognized among geneticists for two decades, its dissemination beyond the discipline was slow. This is a clear example of the time lag between a discovery and its adaption within a discipline and the long delay in its interdisciplinary applications. Conceptually the importance of polygenic inheritance was to refute the theory of blending, so closely associated with "race" and "blood."[50] Although biology was not very helpful in delineating heredity from environment, it enabled a refutation of the belief that "racial traits" or "national character" are "entirely or mainly of a permanent or genetic nature." The ultimate decision was political, and the authors chose to align themselves with Hogben, who in *Nature and Nurture* explicitly argued that environment and heredity did not contradict one another.[51]

This no-man's land, where theories in zoology and botany were extended to humankind, was the perfect setting for the infiltration of old cultural aversions, even in such an overtly egalitarian book as *We Europeans*. One such idea was that the "average genetic difference between different classes" fitted them for different tasks in society: on this hypothesis the lower stature of the working classes was adaptive, because "short types may be better suited to town life or factory conditions, and therefore be favoured in an urban-industrial civilization." Huxley continued to object to crosses between members of primary subspecies "on the ground that some ethnic groups possess a low average of innate intelligence," and upsetting the balance might lead to some disharmonies. In the twenties Huxley thought miscegenation could only produce negative results, but by 1935 he asserted that it might also produce "some exceptionally well-endowed types."[52] The most frequent confusion of scientific data with cultural biases occurred over the correlation between physical and mental characteristics, a point on which the authors admitted a universal scientific ignorance, though

[50] *We Europeans*, pp. 80, 21. [51] *We Europeans*, pp. 91, 103, 87, 91.
[52] *We Europeans*, pp. 89, 281.

"the main types of body-build and temperament recur in all ethnic groups, black, white, brown or yellow," and mental characters depended to a very high degree on the social environment.[53]

The most well known mental testings were intelligence tests which became especially popular in the United States, but less so in Britain. Despite Huxley's great enthusiasm for the intelligence tests during the twenties, they raised more objections during the thirties as the flaws in the first test were universally recognized. In the search for unlikely critics of the tests, *We Europeans* quoted E. A. Hooton, the American physical anthropologist who adhered to a formal racial typology but was an agnostic on the issue of comparing races according to intelligence tests.[54] Aiming to present their view as mainstream, the authors illuminated the 1930 retraction by Carl Brigham of his own interpretation of the results of the Army intelligence tests in World War I,[55] but they did not mention Boas – the most obvious egalitarian – even once.

The advocacy of subjective judgement and the refutation of racial typology promoted a new usage of the term "ethnic": one that projected an inability to classify human groups into objective categories. A new agenda was heralded, even if in a qualified and hesitant manner. Limiting themselves to the European population, the authors negated the existence of any pure race in the biological sense and proposed that the term "be dropped from the vocabulary of science."[56] As to the hypothetical sub-divisions among people around the world, these might be called primary races, but for the sake of conformity, the authors preferred subspecies. The conventional European sub-divisions should therefore be termed "*minor sub species*" (namely, Nordic, Euroasiatic and Mediterranean). In the same manner the anthropological term secondary race (a stabilized population, which betrays its mixed origin by a marked degree of variation) was substituted for "secondary subspecies." The authors did not deny the biological and anthropological nature of race and were committed to traditional ethnology, but they opposed its use on the grounds of the political implications. A pictorial quiz at the beginning of the book refuted the argument of racial typology, but at

[53] *We Europeans*, pp. 28, 103.
[54] E. A. Hooton, *Up from the Ape* (New York: Macmillan, 1931), p. 596, quoted in *We Europeans*, p. 122.
[55] *We Europeans*, pp. 124, 169, 259.   [56] *We Europeans*, p. 107.

certain points the text maintained a traditional approach to racial dissimilarity.[57]

The question of nationalism illuminated the distinction between politics and biology. Science was dressed in the liberal gown: "From a purely biological stand-point it might be a good thing to undertake mass crossing between say the British and the Bantu ... on account of the new genetic recombinations to be obtained." Yet it was judged inadvisable on social grounds. Thus they justified the restriction of immigration of Asian "races" to Australia and the United States. The advocacy of limiting immigration provided the prime example of the very danger the book tried to highlight: that of extending biological conjectures "to the domain of language, of morals, of culture, of art, of religion, without the necessary reservation that such principles cease to be axiomatic when applied elsewhere than in the biological field."[58]

The book's more traditional chapters described under the label of ethnic groups the three main varieties and numerous sub-divisions of the races of Europe. This was Haddon's contribution.[59] Though little had changed in the actual classification of races since Haddon's earlier publications, by 1935 in a new scientific context the old ethnology was integrated with biological and interdisciplinary theories into the political realm. This was Huxley's responsibility. Already in *The Races of Man* (1925) Haddon had expounded upon the problem of subjectivity and relativism in racial classification, suggesting that in time the definition of race would become even more doubtful. He pointed to the abstract character of race where generalizations "mask the real ethnic diversity" and "produce a fictitious appearance of uniformity" so that "it is very doubtful whether there are at the present time any races that can be termed 'pure'."[60] This skepticism is still more marked in *We Europeans*.

The disjunction between Haddon's cognitive recognition of the inability to classify a pure race and his acquiescence in cultural prejudices of race hierarchy led to contradictions in *The Races of Man*.

---

[57] *We Europeans*, pp. 107, 166, 27, 138, 110.

[58] *We Europeans*, pp. 282, 286, 144. This was the only remark for which the reviewer in *Nature* reproached the morals of the authors. Cedric Dover, "The Racial Myth," *Nature* (Nov. 1935), 736–737.

[59] Haddon to Gates, Feb. 23, 1937, marked 'confidential'. RRGP.

[60] Alfred C. Haddon, *The Races of Man And Their Distribution* (London: Milner & Company, 1909. 2nd edn New York: Macmillan and Co. 1925), p. 2.

Haddon quoted the biologist-eugenicist E. G. Conklin to disprove
the inheritance of acquired characteristics, though he was inclined
to believe in such hereditary mechanism. His skepticism as to the
equality of races was supported by conjecture; he argued "that
certain races are more static than others, and this may perhaps be
granted for what are termed the lower races."[61] Haddon admitted
that the theory of the inheritance of acquired characteristics had
been disproved by biologists, yet without it he could not explain
racial diversification. By 1925 Haddon was seventy years old and
though he recognized the biological advances and the importance of
Mendelian heredity, it is not surprising that he did not incorporate
"natural selection" into his explanation at the time when Darwinism was considered obsolete even by Huxley.

We Europeans suggested a replacement of Aryan or Latin races by
the term "mixed ethnic group." The new terminology in its own
way was dramatic and the review in Nature judged it to be "an
advance on Professor Boas's proposal to substitute 'populations' for
'race'."[62] By discrediting the scientific foundations of the concept of
race and thus undermining the term, the book stands an important
milestone in the evolution of non-racialist literature.

POLITICAL MANOEUVERS: WHO WROTE "WE EUROPEANS"?

Both the subject matter and the political context caused the authors
of We Europeans to mix their philosophy and ethics with their science
to a greater degree than is usual in a scientific monograph. But then
the surroundings of the enterprise were exceptional and so was its
execution. The circumstances of the writing of the book reveal a
great deal of the cultural milieu and the mechanism which transformed the scientific theories of race.

In his Memories, Huxley recalls that We Europeans was solicited by
the publishers Jonathan Cape, and that in addition to the collaboration of the coauthors, they received help from "an old friend," Dr.
Charles Singer, the prominent historian of science and medicine, in
whose house on the South Cornish coast the book was written, and
from the anthropologist Charles Seligman. The company spent
their days enjoying an early morning swim at a nearby cove, or
searching for "rare ferns and flowers," while the cosy evenings were

---

[61] Haddon, The Races of Man, pp. 156, 159.
[62] Cedric Dover, "The Racial Myth," Nature (Nov. 1935), 736–737.

devoted to talks on history, science and culture. *Kilmarth*, as the house was named, was gaining fame as "a focal point for scholars from many countries."[63] This was a pleasant setting for an anti-Nazi campaign.

When *We Europeans* was published, Ruggles Gates became its most outspoken critic and his correspondence illuminates the tension behind the scene. Haddon, by then eighty and a grand old man of the profession, was beyond reproach. Thus Gates directed his criticism at the liberal Huxley for the book's egalitarianism, and hoped to persuade Haddon to renounce his authorship. Huxley was the director of the enterprise and assumed after the publication the role of defender of the faith. In public lectures, debates and popular articles, he became an advocate for international cooperation to combat racism. Haddon left contradictory testimonies about his role in the enterprise as a whole. His position reflects the ambiguous way in which the old guard accepted advances in biology and the hesitant role it played in the transformation of anthropological theories of race. On a different level Haddon represented the mainstream attitude among English scientists who were unwilling to be involved in the political arena or to accept the scientist's responsibility to society.

Haddon's reply to Gates's criticism illuminates this ambivalence, and is worth a lengthy quotation:

> Many thanks for your letter. I read between the lines of your review of *We Europeans* and recognized that you were criticizing Huxley. My association with this enterprise dates back to 1932. I was rather rushed into it at the time by people behind the scenes – which was before Huxley had anything to do with it. I expressly stipulated that it was to be a dispassionate strictly scientific book – which then had no title.
>
> As a matter of fact I turned down some statements but I was powerless to alter the rather bitter controversial trend, though I did get some improvements effected in the more scientific portions. I have tried to withdraw from the concern, but was over-ruled.
>
> As I am a part author I have to be responsible for what was published – so Julian is technically right, but, as you appreciate, I am actually responsible for chapters VI & VII, my original draft of which was subjected to a certain amount of amendation.
>
> I have from the beginning been very sorry that I had anything to do with it, but ever since Julian took a hand in it he has been very pleased with it.[64]

[63] Huxley, *Memories* (London: Allen and Unwin, 1970), I, p. 216. E. A. Underwood, "Charles Joseph Singer," *Dictionary of National Biography* (1960).
[64] Haddon to Gates, Feb. 23, 1937, marked confidential. RRGP.

In this version Haddon is not merely embittered, but also conveys the impression that he was deceived, betrayed and perhaps even abused. It clearly suggests that he was a figurehead, whose reputation was utilized for political ends in a way and manner to which he opposed. A second version, written earlier, conveys the opposite impression; in fact it reflects what could be seen as an ordinary conclusion to such an enterprise. In a letter to Huxley, following some corrections to the text, Haddon wrote:

I am much relieved that the revision is now finished. I understand that you have seen and passed all Singer's and Seligman's matter and that you have not allowed them to put in discutable and polemic remarks – they are very bitter on the subject and might feel inclined to let themselves "go." I suppose I ought to see the final proof before it is set up. As I have mentioned before, you and I are technically and legally responsible and I for one don't want any discussion – acrimonious or otherwise – and I do not intend to be drawn into one – you, of course can do what you like or feel obliged to do.[65]

Haddon, aware that the book meant a new direction in his career and might draw him into public controversy, insisted from the very beginning that it was to be a purely scientific enterprise, despite the explicit political aim of fighting racism. At the age of eighty Haddon was reluctant to emerge from his retirement in Cambridge as a crusader, but he participated in the enterprise none the less. He was anxiously aware that the parts written by Seligman and Singer had to be monitored especially carefully. On September 15, returning the proofs, Haddon gave Singer due credit: "Singer has greatly improved the book, the few slips he has made are duly pointed out in the text," and was overall satisfied with the results:

I really am pleased with the book – it is much needed – no more so than in Germany – where it will be banned.[66]

In 1935, when reading the proofs, Haddon may have been pleased with the book, but changed his opinion eighteen months later. The duality of belonging to the mainstream while manifesting mild nonconformism always existed in Haddon's religious and secular life. He resisted confrontations; persistence and hard work were his trade marks, and they enabled him to achieve recognition for himself and for anthropology as an academic discipline. He was

[65] Haddon to Huxley, Aug. 9, 1935. JSHP, box 11.
[66] Haddon to Huxley, Sept. 15, 1935. JSHP, box 11.

moderately progressive, but not outspoken – a socialist sympathiser and a supporter of equal rights for women[67] (not of feminism), and he participated in the Race Congress of 1911 "on behalf of the [racially] oppressed."[68] In many respects Haddon was especially qualified to lend the credentials of traditional anthropology to the rejection of racial typology, but not to be its leader. This was left to scientists with "vested interests"; liberals, left wingers and Jews. Huxley was the liberal, Singer and Seligman were the Jews.

Charles Joseph Singer, born in 1876 to a well-off and scholarly family, had received the best possible education. His father was a classical and Hebrew scholar, who became the rabbi of the New West End Synagogue, where Charles Singer was brought up. His academic training included studies in medicine and zoology at University College London and at Magdalen College Oxford. Years later when he received an Honorary Doctorate in Science from Oxford in 1936, he had accomplished a unique triple, since he already held the two Doctorates in medicine and letters. At the start of his career, Singer practiced medicine and had some experience in a geographical expedition to Abyssinia. In 1910 he married Dorothea Waley Cohen, who had also studied the history of science and medicine, and together they had a prolific career marked by distinguished honors. During the thirties, Singer became deeply involved with the Society for the Protection of Science and Learning and with helping refugee scholars.

Charles Seligman was an eminent anthropologist ever since he had participated in the famous Torres Straits Expedition of 1898 with Haddon. Brenda Z. Salaman, who became Seligman's wife in 1905, had an anthropological career in her own right and during the thirties, due to her husband's deteriorating health, did much of his work herself. Both were also active on behalf of refugees from Germany, a concern shared by the other collaborators of *We Europeans*. In 1934 Seligman became a professor emeritus at the London School of Economics, but continued many of his other activities, including a visiting professorship at Yale in 1938.

When the initial plan for the book was drawn in 1932, the ostensible aim was to publish an anti-racist scientific monograph, with the emphasis on it being "strictly scientific." Haddon had

[67] A. H. Quiggin, *Haddon the Head Hunter* (Cambridge: Cambridge University Press, 1942,) pp. 110, 125–126, and passim.
[68] Haddon papers, 5406, pamphlets and letters to Haddon.

probably welcomed Huxley as he later became a coauthor. Haddon's early professional success was achieved with difficulty and owed much to Julian's grandfather, T. H. Huxley.[69] In addition, the expected royalties must have been a motivation for writing a popular book. Popular science was paying handsomely for a number of first rate English scientists, among whom Julian Huxley was both experienced and successful. *We Europeans* could therefore be seen as an enterprise motivated by sound science and humanistic ethics, in addition to anticipated financial rewards.

Because Seligman's Jewishness supposedly compromised his ability to write a scientific monograph on race, he devoted efforts to mobilize anti-racist sentiments within the anthropological community, of which his central role in *We Europeans* was a part. Seligman was even ready to recognize the advantage of the Race and Culture committee being appointed without any Jewish members to appear more impartial, as part of the general appeasement towards racists in a misconceived effort to gain their cooperation. He was not, however, discouraged by the various obstacles, and continued to be the driving force in objecting to any publicity of racist views.[70] At the time when the anthropological establishment was advancing carefully and very slowly in a non-racialist direction, *We Europeans* was a relatively straightforward anti-racist alternative. Amidst so much hesitation on the part of the Royal Anthropological Institute, and the professional controversy that ensued, Haddon might at times have regretted his bold step; Huxley was no anthropologist, and as a public figure might have been too much of an extrovert partner. Haddon had probably few regrets concerning the scientific aspects of the book, while its cultural and political context had more likely caused him some anxieties.

Reginald Ruggles Gates's opposition to *We Europeans* together with his role in the Race and Culture Committee highlighted the professional, personal, and scientific rivalry which forestalled any coordinated action by the scientific community. Yet despite the personal rivalry there was more scientific common ground between the parties and the antagonism was primarily political. The similarity consisted chiefly in the historical view of migration and the

---

[69] Quiggin, *Haddon the Head Hunter*, pp. 54, 79, 93–95.

[70] The evidence is limited, yet convincing. For example in arranging a talk on the topic of race at the Royal Anthropological Institute the response of the Seligmans was a major consideration. M. Tildesley to J. L. Myres March 9, 1935; Ms. Myres 121 fol 109–110, Bodleian Library. Also, Seligman to Gates, March 17, 1935; April 22, 1935. RRGP.

role of intermixture. Their main disagreement was a matter of direction; Gates objected to the amalgamation of races as presented in *We Europeans* and the limited division into "ethnic types," and preferred the taxonomy of species. Excluding the question of interfertility, which in Gates's definition of species is irrelevant, the typological disagreement was a matter of terminology, while the animosity was political. In *We Europeans* the major subdivisions in man are referred to as subspecies, which are further divided into primary races named major subspecies and other geographical groups (for example the tripartite European division into Nordic, Euroasiatic and Mediterranean) which are termed minor subspecies.[71] Both parties agreed that confusion resulted from speaking of every human aggregate as "a race." Gates chose to place the term in the middle of his hierarchy without defining its relation either to larger or smaller human aggregates. It was his claim that "races exist in all degrees of purity or mixture" and that "especially in modern times" migration "has produced many new races," which left the reader puzzled.[72] What is stable about race if it keeps changing? The authors of *We Europeans* chose to replace "race" with "type." All these verbal acrobatics would have made little sense had it not been for the political message. It was the emphasis on the contention that the existence of such "human subspecies is purely hypothetical" which turned the question of terminology into a scientific and ideological rift. Haddon and Huxley preferred the term ethnic group because it carried no moral commitment.

Singer elucidated the abstract dichotomies both philosophically and biologically. For him, type "is a mental image" and race is "an observed datum." He added: "I would therefore say that this or that group presents this or that type in a more or less [statistically] prominent degree. If this course were followed we should know how individual this or that group really was, and fantastic 'racial' claims could not be made."[73] The biological distinction was that "race must mean something in connexion with genotype, whereas type must mean something in connexion with phenotype".[74] Singer purposely left both definitions of race beyond the domain of science. Methodologically, however, his was still an antinomy leaving the door open to a positivist description of race. More telling was Singer's emotional response to the cultural stakes in the debate. He

[71] *We Europeans*, pp. 135–137.   [72] Gates, "The Conception of Race," in *Race and Culture*.
[73] Singer to Gates, Dec. 12, 1935, RRGP.   [74] Singer to Gates, Dec. 12, 1935, RRGP.

warned Gates against being branded a racist like Keith: "The
angels weep at the divorce of wisdom from learning and Keith's folly
disgraces his fame!" Racism was becoming disreputable, and in case
Gates should miss the point, Singer made it explicitly: "Keith is now
quoted and toasted in Germany as 'the man who has discovered the
organ of race antagonism deep down in the human brain'! Pause,
young man! Pause, while there is yet time! you too may be quoted
even as Keith! ... you might even become as famous as poor
Keith!"[75] It was Gates's fate that while he did not become as famous
as Keith, his renown was to stem from the very source against which
Singer had warned him.

Despite the challenge laid down by *We Europeans*, the scientific
community was too divided on substance and policy to present any
alternative for racist thinking. Outsiders were not aware of the
internal struggle among anthropologists on the definition of race,
which erupted for the first time during the International Congress of
Anthropological and Ethnological Sciences of 1934 in London. An
abortive attempt to reach an anti-racist agreement became the first
initiative to mobilize anthropologists during the 1930s. On July 30,
1934, the Congress assembled in London for its first meeting since
1912; the forum included 855 members from thirty-three countries.[76] It was an impressive display of professional vitality and
unity, in what turned out to be anthropology's most notable show
before World War II. The question of race, a central political issue,
played only a secondary role in the proceedings. During the formal
work of the sections, three lectures addressed the issue: Elliot Smith
in the section on physical anthropology, and at the plenary sessions
R. R. Marett and J. B. S. Haldane, who examined possible anthropological and biological approaches to race.

Behind the scene, the attempts to publish an anti-racist statement
proved futile. Little information apart from the official reports
reached the public, and it is no wonder that Franz Boas, who was
among the sponsors of the anti-racist effort, returned disappointed
to the United States and wrote to Elliot Smith in an attempt to
rescue the lost cause. Elliot Smith on the other hand, saw the
Congress as a success "even though the Council General prevented

[75] Singer to Gates, Dec. 12, 1935, RRGP.
[76] The "British Empire" delegates included additional representatives of twenty-one governments. *Congrès International des Sciences Anthropologiques et Ethnologiques* (Londres: Institut
Royal d'Anthropologie, 1934).

the submission to the Congress as a whole the resolution on the Aryan issue," because the "press ventilated that issue sufficiently."[77] Notwithstanding Smith's judgment, very little was actually published in the press, and *Nature* did not even note the manoeuvering for a resolution during the Congress. During those weeks in August, the issue of the responsibility of scientists to explain racial questions in a scientific manner was publicly highlighted, but the leaders of the profession failed to respond to the challenge.

In one of three lectures at the plenary session, Marett illuminated the difficulty faced by physical anthropologists in addressing the question of race in light of the developments in biological sciences. He had no doubt that specialized research on race must be conducted, but he acknowledged the scientific limitations and the need to rely on a biologist "who for his part has yet much to discover in the sphere of general genetics before he can attack the specifically human problem with any great chance of success. Meanwhile Physical Anthropology can at least try to be more thorough in supplying the geneticist, the ultimate interpreter of the race-principle in its scientific sense, with the necessary evidence."[78] Talking about the "senior branch" of anthropology, Marett complained that it was "a little slow in adopting the outlook of the new biology." His analogy of physical anthropology with an old man was not a mere metaphor, considering the age of many scholars present.[79] J. B. S. Haldane, the biologist who followed Marett, could offer little concrete help, but gave ample warning against the abuse of science in the name of racist theories.

In response to the growing pressure from intellectual peers on anthropologists to play their part in combating racism and the Nazi challenge to civilization, John Linton Myres, the Oxford classicist and the major representative of English anthropology in international diplomacy, wrote to Elliot Smith, the Chairman of the Race and Culture Committee, that anthropologists had "to refrain from public pronouncements till ... [they] had something [scientifically] positive to say." Anthropologists were asked by the old guard to

[77] The demand for developments regarding scientific evaluation of the question of race, coupled with the total lack of official response, turned Smith's provocative remarks at the section of physical anthropology into news, and that would explain his judgement. Smith to Boas, Sept. 25, 1934; Boas to G. E. Smith, Nov. 7, 1935. FBP.

[78] R. R. Marett, "The Growth and Tendency of Anthropological and Ethnological Studies," in *Congrès International des Sciences Anthropologiques et Ethnologiques*, p. 45.

[79] R. R. Marett, "The Growth and Tendency of Anthropological and Ethnological Studies," pp. 39–53.

refrain from public statements until they could declare what constituted race, and not only what race was not.[80] Myres believed that
the community should resist the temptation of publicity, and while
Elliot Smith certainly was not the one to shun public debate, the
politics of the profession forced the Race and Culture committee to
consider such demands which added to the constraints rendering
the committee's efforts futile.

THE AMERICAN SCENE

While the English Race and Culture Committee was debating
unsuccessfully, no organized action was taken by scientists in the
United States. An effort to change this was undertaken in September 1935, before the Nuremberg Laws were published, by Boas's
initiative to rally a new anti-racist campaign. As Boas indicated to
several Jewish leaders from whom he sought financial support for
his research efforts, this campaign was directed against a group of
scientists in England and the United States, as well as in Germany,
"who are of the opinion that racial descent and character are closely
correlated." While Boas was convinced, "as a scientist, that they
have not a shadow of proof for their contentions," they were,
unfortunately, sustained by "the whole modern development of
biology, in which heredity is considered as everything, and environment as nothing." The matter was further complicated by the fact
that, in trying to organize "an international organization for race
investigations," the names of biologists who were naturally proposed were "the very ones to be avoided because they are all
dogmatically wedded to the theory of fundamental race differences." In Germany they included Hans Gunther (Boas: "whom,
however, I do not consider a scientist"), Otto Reche, Walter
Scheidt, Theodor Mollison, "and many others"; in the United
States, there were E. M. East, Lothrop Stoddard, Charles Davenport, William Holmes, H. H. Newman and Raymond Pearl (the
only one "at all acceptable"); in England, conditions were "equally
difficult because the man whose name has the greatest weight, Sir
Arthur Keith, is also a race dogmatist."[81] The problem was that
while cultural anthropologists highlighted environmental factors,
traditional physical anthropologists were untouched by Boas's

---

[80] Myres to G. E. Smith, Oct. 23, 1934. JLMP.
[81] Boas to F. Warburg, Oct. 9, 1933; Boas to C. Adler, Dec. 20, 1933. FBP.

critique of racial typology,[82] and these were precisely the scholars who, on the basis of a subdisciplinary division of labor, were presumed qualified to speak authoritatively on race.

In order to circumvent the disciplinary division and engage a leading non-Jewish scientist, Boas solicited help from Livingstone Farrand, anthropologist and the President of Cornell University, who three decades earlier had cooperated with Boas in the critique of traditional assumptions regarding "the mind of primitive man." But despite Boas's offer to draft the statement and handle the correspondence, accepting any revisions Farrand might propose, or alternatively, to leave the matter entirely in Farrand's hands, his old friend declined, on the ground that as a rule petition "does no good in a time of inflamed opinion and often delays understanding rather than aids it."[83]

Boas next turned to Raymond Pearl of Johns Hopkins University. Boas was not aware of Pearl's private attitudes towards Jews or the "racial struggle," but what he knew was sufficient for him to suspect Pearl's position on race along the years. Yet Pearl was the most respected among the anthropologists who, to judge from his public statements, might conceivably have adopted an anti-racist position.[84] As the editor of *The Quarterly Review of Biology* and *Human Biology*, Pearl conducted relatively extensive research on human biology, but he declined Boas's request, citing book reviews he had written over the years describing "the philosophy of the Nordic enthusiasts" as "absurd," "unscientific," and "mischievous." His opposition to participate in the anti-racist campaign stemmed from a "strong aversion to round-robins by scientific men," particularly when they had to do with "political questions." These only resulted in "harm to the scientific men who sign them and through these men to science itself." In the present instance, such public pronouncement should come from "German anthropologists, because it is in their country that this mixture of pseudo-science and politics is making mischief."[85]

Having failed in his initial effort to rally cooperation in the United States, Boas solicited English support, since the "Americans are

[82] G. Stocking, *Race Culture and Evolution* (1968; Chicago: University of Chicago Press, 1982), pp. 161–194.
[83] Farrand to Boas, Sept. 13, 1935. Boas to Farrand, Sept. 12, 1935, FBP.
[84] On Pearl's racism, see above, chapter 4.
[85] Boas (on his reservation about Pearl) to C. Adler, Dec. 29, 1933. Pearl to Boas, Oct. 3, 1935. FBP. Also correspondence in RPP.

always very timid." He hoped through England to persuade
Americans to cooperate, and explored alliance with the French,
with the targeted audience in Germany.[86] Despite initial drawbacks
and disappointments, Boas did not give up, and his next attempt,
which produced perhaps the most surprising result, was directed at
Harvard's physical anthropologist Earnest Albert Hooton, who was
to prove the most cooperative anthropologist on the American
scene.

Hooton was one of the central figures of anthropology in the
United States. Hooton's approach to publicity was inconsistent and
somewhat unpredictable. While there is abundant evidence of his
reluctance to take part in, or contribute to public and political
discussions, he was a controversial figure. Though he occasionally
contributed to non-scientific periodicals, he usually refused solicitations by popular magazines including the *New Yorker*. His participation in the campaign against racism was therefore somewhat out
of character and illuminates his ambivalent cooperation later on.
His public exposure in the anti-racist campaign included speaking
engagements, and during the Second World War he even wrote a
script for a propaganda movie by MGM called "Does Nature Prefer
Blonds?"[87]

Hooton's ambiguous views on race and his cordial professional
relations with liberals, right-wing scientists and even with outright
racists, may have played a factor in Boas's hope that he would be
able to mobilize a broad coalition. Hooton maintained his ambivalence in the early forties when, for instance, he cooperated with
the National Association for the Advancement of Colored People
but at the same time sponsored Ruggles Gates and nominated

---

[86] Boas's request was very detailed, Boas to Haddon, Oct. 12, 1935; Oct. 24, 1935 (where he
attached a proposed statement). Boas also asked Haddon to concentrate on a similar
statement by English anthropologists, either presuming that the Race and Culture
Committee (which had begun a year earlier) failed, or perhaps attempting to sponsor an
alternative statement. Boas later wrote to G. E. Smith urging an English statement,
speculating that the Americans would join them; Nov. 7, 1935. FBP.

[87] Hooton became better known among the educated public during the 1930s, and Macmillan revised *Up from the Ape* not as a textbook but rather for "general trade." Macmillan
to Hooton, March 28, 1941, Hooton Papers (EAHP) box 1A. Hooton wondered whether
the revised edition should be more "sober and restrained," but the editor thought that it
was the "exuberance" which made the book "appeal to all classes of readers." (Sept. 29,
1943, EAHP box 1A) The revised edition was eventually published only after the war, by
which time Hooton perceived himself to be marginal in the community, and his
endorsement as "generally damning among 'social scientists.'" (Hooton to Mrs.
S. Glueck, June 26, 1945, EAHP box 1A).

Charles Davenport to the presidency of the American Association of Physical Anthropology. He declined to testify against an anti-lynching bill on the ground that it was against "my policy to appear in court or on any such occasion . . . because I am a scientist and not a legislative propagandist. I feel that as soon as I relax my rule and go in for this sort of thing, I will lose what little influence I may have as a scientist." But he had no hesitations to participate in the "Fourth National Conference on Race Betterment," organized by Davenport, where he delivered a "non-controversial" talk. He supported euthanasia in principle, but was reluctant to cooperate with the Euthanasia Society of America.[88]

Hooton's social views were never liberal, and he often displayed bigotry while claiming to strive for the truth. Though he denied the assertion that blacks were replacing whites in the United States, he spoke of the continuous "small infiltration of Negro blood into the White group." Highlighting the Jews' mental superiority and their contribution to society in an article aimed at combating racism, he also wrote of them as a determinate physical entity and embellished his article with pictures of blown-up noses.[89] In private, Hooton was more of a bigot. Writing to a stranger, he insisted on his very high esteem for Jews and the fact that he had "many friends, students and colleagues among them," yet hoped the Jews "could in some way strive to eradicate certain aggressive and other social character-istics which seem to me to account for some of their trouble." This view received a more explicit formulation in Hooton's refusal of Madison Grant's request to review *The Conquest of the Continent*: "I don't expect that I shall agree with you at every point, but you are probably aware that I have a basic sympathy for you in your opposition to the flooding of this country with alien scum."[90]

In retrospect, Boas's and Hooton's collaboration seems unlikely, but Boas tried and, for a time, Hooton acquiesced. Between October 1935 and February 1936 Hooton led the attempt to reach a

---

[88] National Association for the Advancement of Colored People, Wilkins to Hooton, June 3, 1944; Hooton to W. White, NAACP, Feb. 21, 1939. EAHP box 1B. On the National Conference on Race Betterment (and an honorarium of $100), correspondence with Davenport, July-Oct 1941 EAHP box 2B. On euthanasia, *New York Times*, April 25, 1941. R. L. Mitchell to Hooton, April 25, 1941. EAHP, Box 3DE.

[89] *Collier*, May 6, 1939. Boas replied to criticism of Hooton's article on the Jews: "Dr. Hooton misjudged the effect that this article might have. I feel reasonably certain that he thought he was doing a good thing." Boas to Lander, May 9, 1939. FBP.

[90] Hooton to Zendt, March 8, 1938. EAHP, box 1A; Hooton to Madison Grant, Nov. 3, 1933. EAHP.

consensus among leading anthropologists to define race scientifically. In doing so, he was at pains to indicate that the initiative was
in response to a request by "two of our best known and most
respected anthropologists" who were alarmed by anti-Semitic and
pro-Nazi propaganda and who "are actually of the opinion that
some grave consequences are likely to result from such propaganda
unless some effort is made to counteract it." He did not name the
anthropologists, later referred to as Boas and Shapiro, but left no
doubt about their identity. As to himself Hooton minimized his
involvement, claiming not to have "given any very deep thought to
this matter in so far as it affects present and future conditions in this
country." Yet he was willing to help "those who have been affected
directly or indirectly by the happenings in Germany during the past
few years." The timing for the statement was explained by a fear
that " within the next two weeks there will be issued from German
sources a sort of a general blast concerning their program of 'racial
hygiene'" and the proposed statement, "dispassionate and impartial," by American scientists should be ready for release at the same
time. Hooton expected the reaction to his request to be negative,
and lest anyone mistake his commitment to the issue, he added: "I
neither desire to urge physical anthropologists to subscribe to my
statements concerning race, nor have I any inclination whatsoever
to attempt to induce anyone against his will to enter into the field of
public propaganda." He failed miserably, and gave up. He did not
receive any substantial support, and the few endorsements he did
obtain were qualified in a way that made their publication impossible.[91]

Hooton's draft was addressed to seven anthropologists: Ales
Hrdlicka, C. H. Danforth (professor of anatomy at the medical
school, Stanford University), W. K. Gregory (curator of com-
parative anatomy at the American Museum of Natural History),
Raymond Pearl, Adolph Schultz (professor of physical anthropo-
logy at the medical school, Johns Hopkins University), Robert J.
Terry (professor of anatomy, Washington University), and
T. Wingate Todd (professor of anatomy and physiology at Western
Reserve University).[92]

The initial reports were encouraging; Tozzer, who taught archeology at Harvard and was close to Boas, wrote to him that Hooton's

[91] Hooton and Boas Correspondence, Oct. 1935–Feb. 1936, EAHP, Box 2ABC.
[92] Oct. 25, 1935. EAHP.

statement was a good one, and that even Hrdlicka, a long time professional antagonist of Boas, was willing to sign it. As it turned out, Hrdlicka was the only one to sign.[93] Pearl and Danforth declined outright, the latter suggesting that "the Jewish problem in this country is somewhat the responsibility of influential Jews themselves," who "because of their Jewish *radical* solidarity" were "over-anxious to retaliate on Germany through America."[94] The rest agreed in principle but requested major diverse revisions. A week after the first letter was sent, Hooton assessed the responses in his letter to Hrdlicka: "It may come down to a document signed only by you and by me." He turned out to be over-optimistic.[95]

Hooton submitted a second version which sought to incorporate the criticism of his fellow anthropologists. Hrdlicka tried to encourage him to continue despite the responses, commenting that "Boas should have submitted a draft of just what he had in mind." But the efforts were futile, and Hooton terminated his activity in early February.[96] He would continue to lend support to Boas in the following years, and his good intentions in this case should not be doubted. The disagreement among the individual anthropologists reflected a deep schism in the discipline, beyond personal contention. There was no consensus among physical anthropologists concerning methodology or subject matter; or on how to incorporate conclusions from allied disciplines, nor on how to measure and collect basic anthropometric data. They were unable to bridge scientific, professional or political differences, and the question of race belonged to all three categories.

From the twenties and into the late 1930s, the Committee for the Standardization of Anthropometrical Measurements had been working without success in the United States and Europe to bring order into the chaos of physical anthropology. The committee resulted from the recognition that the various measuring methods produced incomparable results; investigators who measured the same people obtained different results to a degree that made previous studies obsolete for comparative purpose. Measurements meant to convey "hard" objective data became so subjective that no

---

[93] Tozzer to Boas Nov. 2; Boas to Tozzer, Nov. 4, 1935. FBP.
[94] Danforth to Hooton, Nov. 4, 1935. EAHP.
[95] W. K. Gregory to Hooton, Oct. 28; R. J. Terry to Hooton, Oct. 31; Hooton to Hrdlicka, Nov. 2, 1935. AHP.
[96] Hrdlicka to Hooton, Nov. 7, 1935, Jan 20, 1936; Hooton to Hrdlicka, Jan. 15, 1936, Feb. 5, 1936. AHP.

two anthropologists could compare their work unless trained in the same school. Any synthesis of several studies was deceptive since it computed different measurements as though these were comparable. Though one could hardly imagine a worse professional crisis, it was only one of the difficulties faced by physical anthropologists. While they were busy with their own quibbles, their profession was losing its centrality and credentials to genetics, psychology, sociology and, nearer home, to cultural anthropology. Physical anthropology, more than proven wrong, was becoming irrelevant.

While Hooton gave up, Boas persisted. By March 1936 he wrote directly to a number of anthropologists sending a draft of his own, twice as long as Hooton's and more populist in tone. Hooton discouraged him, arguing that anthropologists were unwilling to cooperate not so much because they disagreed with a statement, but rather because they did not "wish to enter the arena of controversy and are unwilling to accept the responsibility of attaching their names to anything that may be interpreted as propaganda." Although Hooton was ready to sign Boas's statement, he predicted that it would face opposition "in many circles on the ground that you are an interested party," noting that Tozzer shared these views. Boas, who was consistently aware of the obstacles that his "Jewish descent" presented to such a role, had apparently decided to abandon the effort for a while.[97]

A coda to Hooton's leading role was his own "Plain Statement About Race" in *Science*, in which he argued that the "White Man's Burden" had been mainly one of hypocrisy, and with no more savage worlds left to conquer (save Ethiopia), "the White man has turned this same vicious argument to use against his own kind, committing more crimes in the name of race than have ever been perpetrated in the name of liberty." Hooton set forth his motivation for publishing the article:

I do not claim to speak in the name of all physical anthropologists, many of whom are either too wise or too timid to speak at all upon this subject, preferring to pursue their researches in academic seclusion, rather than cry their wares in the marketplace and run the risk of being pelted by the rabble. For myself, I prefer to be the target of rotten eggs, rather than to be suspected as a purveyor of that odoriferous commodity.[98]

---

[97] Boas to Hooton, March 24, 1936; March 31, 1936; Hooton to Boas, March 28; April 3, 1936. EAHP, box 2B.
[98] Hooton, "Plain Statement About Race," *Science*, 83, 2161 (1936), 511–513.

Hooton's participation in anti-racist politics was halfhearted, and lasted only until the late thirties. While he sustained his sympathies with the opposition to "the injustices which are perpetrated under the doctrine of racialism," his conservatism in politics and science mitigated his enthusiasm and he distanced himself from the anti-racist campaign. He criticized Boas's work publicly, referring polemically to an anti-racist booklet as a "propaganda;" Boas "takes a very extreme point of view on the subject of race, since he is a radical environmentalist and a Jew."[99]

During the war, anti-racism became a propaganda tool with which Hooton again felt more comfortable, advocating the dispersion of the German people among other states, so as to abolish the German menace from the world.[100] Yet, he rejected the argument of racial equality, which came from "these idealistic uplifting social scientists who think that race prejudice can be argued out of existence."[101] When confronted with his inconsistencies, and his claim that anthropologists could distinguish a race "with precision," his answer spotlighted the distortion of genetics as it had become incorporated into the old physical anthropology. In a populist manner, responding to a critique that he did not distinguish between genotype and phenotype, he exclaimed: "Of course, no one knows what a genotype is, or has ever seen one."[102]

Hooton's "abysmally low opinion of homo sapiens" buttressed his opposition to racist theories, since he recognized no superior – probably only inferior – races. His pessimism was translated into a theory of continuous degeneration during the last seven million years, since the time he believed the ape had climbed down from the

[99] This was despite the fact that Hooton actually worded most of that statement, yet he opposed the idea that "our lack of knowledge of the psychological correlates of racial physical characteristics justifies us in stating categorically that no such correlates exist . . . I am quite unwilling to conclude that race has no cultural significance whatsoever." Hooton to Waldrop, *Times Herald*, Washington, Sept. 18, 1939. EAHP, box 8.

[100] Oct. 1941 an article written for the *Jewish Advocate*, Boston. EAHP, box 2B.

[101] Hooton to R. L. Scaife, Feb. 20, 1945. EAHP, box 1B. Though he judged the ideals "admirable," he called for "more realism." Hooton to G. D. Henderson, April 10, 1945. EAHP, box 1B. He opposed "broad generalizations about the equality of races or the lack of racial differences when these are not based upon substantial evidence other than to make invidious distinctions in the matter of superiority and inferiority. I do not particularly like the little pamphlet of Benedict and Weltfish ("Races of Mankind"), since I think they have sacrificed science to well-meaning propaganda designed to overcome racial prejudices." But he considered individual differences "within races" more important than "any sort of average, composite, or hypothetical difference between groups as a whole." Hooton to J. W. Cantrell, Aug. 6, 1946, EAHP, box 1B.

[102] Hooton to J. Benjamin, March 23 and 30, 1943. EAHP, box 1B.

trees and began to walk upright. This could hardly have sustained a critique of racism. Thus, Hooton who became prominent for semi-popular writing and gave excellent technical training to students, supported both racists and anti-racists. In addition to helping Boas, he sponsored Gates and Davenport in the forties, but with much criticism of, and reservation about, the work of all three.[103] He participated in Boas's drive to reach a wide public through the media; he made sure Boas would know of his efforts and approve them.[104] But when Robert Yerkes wrote to Hooton with a "strong sense of gratitude ... for taking what you evidently consider a big risk of adverse criticism," he referred to the *Twilight of Man*, and to Hooton's racialist theories.[105]

American anthropologists as a group did not voice opposition to racism before 1938. This lack of public pronouncements was not inadvertent, neither was it for lack of trying by the anti-racists. Rather many anthropologists have maintained their beliefs, ideology, and science, which was closely concerted with political racism, while the public pressure to renounce such beliefs was as yet insufficient.

AN INTERNATIONAL INTERLUDE

Following the failures of the anti-racist campaign on the national levels in the spring of 1936 – both in Britain and the United States – the next initiative aiming at an international consensus came from Paris. The single most important factor in international diplomacy during the thirties was the mismatch between aggression and appeasement. The appeasement was well reflected in the lack of government involvement in combatting racism, which left the initiative solely in the hands of individuals. Among the first and most energetic anti-racist activists in Europe was Ignaz Zollschan.

---

[103] Hooton had spent almost two decades working on "Lombroso's long discredited 'criminal type,'" but little else. *New York Times*, editorial, Sept. 3, 1939, pg. 8. "The Proper Study of Man," Report on Le Gros Clark's lecture to the BAAS, which was never delivered, where he opposed Hooton. Hooton's writings displayed prejudice at the very time he was participating in the anti-racist campaign.

[104] Hooton to Boas, April 9, 1936. He spoke at a dinner given by the Foreign Language Information Service on "Statements about Race" at the suggestion of Boas and other anthropologists "who hoped for ... a wide publicity." When Hooton believed that this was not achieved, he asked to publish it in *Science*. Hooton to Lewis, May 6, 1936. EAHP, box 1B.

[105] Oct. 21, 1939. EAHP, box 1A.

As early as the 1920s he had visited New York to discuss with Louis Marshall, of the American Jewish Committee, and Franz Boas the possibility of creating an anthropological research center on racial questions in New York in order to discredit racism. Subsequently his activities touched upon each junction in the fight against racism, up to and including World War II. Yet his partners at each stage minimized his significance because he was assumed to be an interested party and lacked academic and formal political credentials.[106]

Zollschan's plan to establish an anthropological research center in New York failed, not least because Boas did not trust what he considered to be overly zealous Jewish nationalism.[107] Zollschan's plan included a position for himself, which no doubt made it difficult for the parties involved to evaluate whether the proposal was to be judged for its universal implications, or merely as a job request, but none the less in retrospect his memoranda suggest a unique insight. The 1926 proposal judged the theory of races to be "the basis of modern nationalism. It brings forth a kind of fixed historic conception and has become paramount for legislation and foreign policy. It may become the germ of future world-conception."[108] The New York center never materialized, and a question remains of whether Zollschan's insight referred only to the American anti-immigration laws of the twenties, against the background of which his proposal was written, or whether he was presenting with little success a fundamental perspective.

Against this background, it is not surprising therefore that following the Nazi seizure of power Zollschan was ready to rally whatever international influence he could to combat racism. Zolls-

---

[106] Much of the information concerning Zollschan's activities stems from his own long memoranda. Many of his achievements are corroborated by other sources. A few, however, seem empty arrogance, such as the claim that he declined an audience with Mussolini because the time allotted was too short, and could not be available in Rome for a longer interview with either Mussolini or the Pope on a different occasion. Zollschan's memos are to be found in the American Jewish Committee Archives at YIVO Institute in New York and in the FBP. Since these memos were primarily directed to people who were involved in the activities themselves, one presumes that the information in them was not altogether unfounded. Among the more detailed memos is Zollschan, "Bericht über die Vorarbeiten zur geplanten Rassen-Enquête," Typescript in AJC (also an English translation). See also A. Metraux, "Unesco and the Racial Problem," *International Social Science Bulletin*, 2 (1950), 385–386.

[107] Zollschan, "On the Importance of Comparative Anthropology in New York City," in FBP, submitted in 1926. Also L. Marshall to Boas, March 16, 1925. FBP.

[108] Zollschan, "On the Importance of Comparative Anthropology."

chan viewed Jewish nationalism, the meaning of race, combating anti-Semitism and race prejudice, as a cluster of questions that had to be addressed simultaneously. He argued that the philosophy of race was the basis of modern anti-Semitism, resulted in both doctrines spreading rapidly in many countries. Zollschan solicited help from a non too receptive Jewish community, but was somewhat more successful when he ventured into the international arena as a representative of Czechoslovakia and as a well-connected individual.

In 1933 Zollschan sought support for an international inquiry into the question of race. Undermining the scientific foundations of the racist ideology would create, in his view, the best antidote to the spread of racism. His first success was gaining support in Czechoslovakia, from the Academy of Science in Prague, as well as from both Eduard Benes, the Czech foreign minister and the next elected President, and Thomas Masaryk, the Czech President who later spoke favorably of Zollschan's plans to convene an international anthropological congress in order to prove the impossibility of distinguishing among races.[109] Following his success at home, Zollschan travelled to many countries in Europe. In Vienna he received the support of Professor Miklas, President of Austria, of Cardinal Innitzer, the Archbishop of Vienna and a past President of Vienna University who also introduced Zollschan to the Vatican, and of Oswald Redlich, the President of the Academy of Science in Vienna, as well as other scientists including Father Wilhelm Schmidt the ethnologist. In Rome he met Cardinal Pacelli, the Vatican State Secretary and the future Pope Pius XII. As a result, Zollschan circulated unofficial reports that the Vatican would support an anti-racist congress, one among his many other premature claims. He also received moral support in Holland and Sweden. Back in Vienna, he helped to set up a Society for Sociology and Anthropology of Jews, which became a center for his activity.[110] In both France and England, Zollschan's campaign overlapped with

[109] In December 1933 the Czech Academy decided to publish a volume on the scientific basis of the equality of races. The volume was published in Czech and was translated into German. J. Matiegka, *The Equality of European Races* (Circular, Dec. 22, 1933; also Boas to Matiegka, March 25, 1935. FBP). Masaryk supported an invitation of German scientists to such a congress. The "forum would then solve this problem independently of political doctrines." ("Masaryk on Racial Differences," translated from *Die Warheit*, May 18, 1934. FBP.)

[110] Zollschan to Boas, Jan. 4, 1936. FBP.

local efforts. There is no doubt that he was instrumental in pushing for a concrete international action, either an inquiry or a congress on racial questions, and in conveying to the local activists the message that similar international efforts were taking place. In Paris, his most prominent supporter was Edouard Herriot, the past Prime Minister and the President of the International Institute for Intellectual Cooperation.[111]

Armed with an introduction from Masaryk, Zollschan arrived in England early in March 1934 in the midst of attempts to set up a committee to discredit scientific racism. Zollschan's main contact in Britain was Seligman, and among others he was introduced by Haddon to Sir Gowland Hopkins, President of the Royal Society.[112] He spoke on March 20, 1934 at the Royal Anthropological Institute, and according to his own account "as a result [of the talk] the sections for "Human Biology" and for "Sociology" proposed to the Committee of the Institute to appoint a special Commission for the investigation of the problem outlined by me." Never one to minimize his own contributions, Zollschan later also took credit for the public anti-racist pronouncements of Sir Gowland Hopkins and Elliot Smith. He was not successful, however, in organizing support for his proposed international race congress. Whatever the relative input of Zollschan or other Institute members such as Seligman, the Race and Culture Committee was established a few weeks after Zollschan's call.[113] As part of the initial success, it seemed that Zollschan was able to persuade the Carnegie Endowment for World Peace to finance an international investigation, but due to the Depression the funds never became available.

Zollschan directed his efforts to the political scene in an attempt to receive the endorsement of an international organization, preferably the League of Nations. The few options such as the League for the Rights of Man or the P.E.N. Club failed at the initial stage since the question of race was too divisive. The best remaining vehicle was thought to be the International Institute for Intellectual Cooperation, which had its center in Paris. In principle Zollschan seems to have had the support of Masaryk and Benes, who provided

[111] "Bericht über die Vorarbeiten zur geplanten Rassen-Enquête."
[112] Zollschan to Waldman, Sept. 21. 1935. AJC.
[113] Zollschan to Boas, Jan. 4, 1936. FBP. Also "Bericht über die Vorarbeiten zur geplanten Rassen-Enquête."

him with letters of recommendation. But at certain points both Masaryk and Benes let him down. Masaryk adopted the appeasement line, implying that anti-Semitism was mostly a facade in Germany and claiming that the German government was seeking a way back into the European community and even into the League of Nations.[114]

In September 1934 Zollschan met Benes in Geneva twice and received official support for his proposed enquiry.[115] As a result, Zollschan felt confident that all parties involved supported his plan for an international investigation, and in his memo he exulted: "I am now formally authorized to declare, if not to the general public, at least to the circle of people who will eventually join me in the work, that the Race Enquiry has been resolved by those Powers with whom the decision rests." He expected that by January 1935 the investigation would be formalized, and would be over by the autumn. Among his supporters was Henri Bonnet, the director of the International Institute for Intellectual Co-operation, the proposed organizing institution. Yet the politics of organizing an investigation on the hotly-debated political topic in a divided international body were too complicated to be overcome. Zollschan, despite his celebration of what he viewed as a great success, recognized the potential conflict in any such endeavor between propaganda, which was the purpose of the enterprise, and keeping to scientific standards that would ascertain its credentials. The inquiry had to be conducted in such a manner, argued Zollschan "that its trend, its subject matter, its method, and its speed meet the interests of the promoting powers and that at the same time its impartial and objective results are such as will serve our purpose." These inherent contradictions were constantly encountered by the anti-racist camp.

Zollschan's euphoria during 1934 was premature: political devel-

---

[114] Masaryk wrote to Zollschan: "we must not be surprised if the League of Nations, with a view to the European situation would prefer to welcome Hitler himself in Geneva instead of an action directed against him. And in practice this would really be a better and quicker means of helping the Jews in Germany than any other." Masaryk was more encouraging about the scientific work than the political, but was surprised at Zollschan's failure to solicit funds from Jewish sources. "Is one to conclude that the Jews, who, as a rule, prove generous on similar occasions ... feel other grievances more acutely, or may they even be opposed to the discussion of this question?" His office advanced a small sum for expenses incurred by Zollschan. (Schiessl, Secretary to Masaryk, to Zollschan, July 25, 1934, in "Bericht über die Vorarbeiten zur geplanten Rassen-Enquête").

[115] Dec. 20, 1934 (letter of recommendation from Benes to Herriot on Zollschan's behalf). Also Zollschan to Edouard Herriot, Jan. 14, 1935 (memo which outlined his philosophy).

opments did not promote the success of the plan. Following the assassination of the Serbian King and the French Foreign Minister in October 1934 in Marseille, Benes forgot about Zollschan's initiative while being involved with the little Entente, and did not send his recommendations to the President of the International Institute for Intellectual Co-operation. In December Zollschan had another meeting with Benes, who gave him new letters to Herriot and Bonnet and promised further help. But while Zollschan was meeting Benes, he missed an opportunity in Paris, where on the very same day (December 19, 1934) the Executive Committee of the International Institute for Intellectual Co-operation was convening, instead of the following January. By the time Zollschan arrived to Paris (December 28, 1934) his letter of introduction had become obsolete because the report of his arrangement with Benes from Geneva did not arrive through Prague in time and did not come up for discussion by the Executive Committee, which meant that it could not come up for deliberation before the meeting of the General Assembly in December 1935. The proposal for international investigation thus came to a dead end.[116]

Zollschan's success in soliciting support from Jewish sources varied. Czechoslovakia's Jewry were the most helpful and supportive; America was too far away, and the limited support of the American Jewish Committee was directed in the immediate post-1933 period mostly through Boas, and did not reach Zollschan.[117] The English Board of Deputies declined any support, and the French Alliance Israélite were largely antagonistic, offering embarrassingly little help too late. The Race and Culture Committee also tried to solicit funds from Jewish sources with no success.

Boas had known Zollschan since 1912 and was always sceptical about his work, viewing him as too much of a Jewish nationalist: "My objection," wrote Boas to Einstein, "is that his whole attitude has been to set up the Jews as a particularly gifted and excellent group as over against other groups."[118] Boas conditioned his support on Zollschan's commitment to an objective investigation, a

---

[116] (April 28, 1935 Karlsbad – Report from Oct. 1, 1934 [six months] AJC–YIVO).

[117] American Jews were uninterested (specifically Warburg and Adler) in financing Zollschan's work. Boas to H. Schneiderman (AJC) June 26, 1934. A year later, when the Czech Academy's booklet against racism was published and Zollschan's plans showed tangible results, the American Jewish Committee became more receptive, but this did not materialize into financial support. H. Schneiderman to Boas, April 9, 1935. AJCP.

[118] Boas to Einstein, Oct. 31, 1935. FBP.

prerequisite which Zollschan himself seemed to have continuously advocated. It is probable that Boas, in his seventies, was still fighting old battles with Zollschan outdated by a decade or more, which further divided the anti-racist camp. Their substantive disagreements focused on the tactics to mobilize the scientists. Both agreed that it was difficult to induce individual anthropologists to participate in a concerted action. Boas's solution was to try and persuade the individual scientist. Zollschan, however, preferred not to solicit the help of individuals, but rather to cause a shift so that:

the intellectual public would require the scholars to give their opinion. Our task must be to find means and ways that such a public demand take place and become loud enough. Individual specialists have to prepare the material, individual personalities and interested institutions have to provide the means, writers have to create the public opinion, and political authorities have to act for the actualization of the whole.[119]

Zollschan was always asking for money, and almost always turned down. In one of his moments of frustration at the lack of Jewish response he angrily commented that it was not the business of Cardinal Pacelli, Masaryk, Herriot, and the English Clergy to organize on behalf of the Jews:

The enormous sums which would later be needed for charity cannot even be compared to the relatively small amounts needed by a preventive action.[120]

To replace Zollschan's defunct enquête, Bonnet proposed an alternative plan to investigate "the anthropological and ethnological foundations of Western Civilization," which would have to be approved by the executive committee.[121] The limitations of such research paralleled the politics of appeasement. The International Institute for Intellectual Co-operation was not a vigorous body, and the strong hope of bringing the Germans back to the League of Nations meant that nobody was going to provoke Germany. None the less, Zollschan was up in arms to rally support for the new program. After getting Herriot's approval for the new inquiry he

[119] Zollschan to Boas, Jan. 4, 1936. FBP (emphasis in original).
[120] Zollschan to Boas, Jan 4, 1936. FBP.
[121] "The Anthropological and Ethnological Sciences the the Study of Civilization," excerpt of document C.A.47 – 1935, League of Nations, International Institute for Intellectual Co-operation. Report of the Director of the International Commission of Intellectual Cooperation to the council of the Institute, 1935, pp. 39–40. Also Zollschan April 28, 1935 Karlsbad – Report from Oct. 1, 1934 (six months). AJC.

had to convince the other members of the executive committee. These included, beside Herriot, the President of the committee, Gilbert Murray of Oxford, Rocco, Rector of Rome University and a confidant of Mussolini, Castillejo of Madrid, a left-winger and a supporter of the plan, and de Reynold of Freiburg in Switzerland, a conservative representative.

Zollschan proceeded to meet Rocco and developed preliminary contacts with the Church in Rome. Through connections with the Dominicans who ran the Catholic University of Lille, he received a recommendation to the General of the Dominican Order in Rome, Père Gillet, who introduced him to de Reynold and arranged an audience with Pacelli, the Vatican State Secretary. The Church was supportive which led Zollschan to exaggerate his success. Zollschan was able to solicit support from other organizations such as the "Friends of Europe" headed by Ronnie Smith, and affiliated with the Society of Friends and the "Royal Institute of International Affairs" led by Arnold Toynbee, but these culminated his diplomatic efforts.[122] Zollschan had to retreat to Karlsbad and wait for developments, while appeasement came to dominate diplomacy. Fifteen years later, the United Nations Educational, Scientific and Cultural Organization, which replaced the International Institute for Intellectual Co-operation, would pick up and publish its statement on race, which resembled very much Zollschan's original intentions.[123] The next effort Zollschan participated in was the Paris Congress in 1937.

THE PARIS CONGRESS

In 1936 the French Groupe D'Étude et D'Information "Races et Racisme" had initiated an international congress on race to take place in Paris. Concurrently the International Population Congress presided by Adolphe Landry was being organized in Paris by a French National Committee in cooperation with the fourth general assembly of the International Union for the Scientific Investigation of Population Problem. The subject matters of the two proposed gatherings were intertwined and the "Races et Racisme" group joined the more prestigious Population Congress. "Races et

---

[122] Zollschan April 28, 1935 Karlsbad – Report from Oct. 1, 1934.
[123] A. Métraux, "Unesco and the Racial Problem," *International Social Science Bulletin*, 2 (1950), 384–390.

Racisme" was a Parisian organization formed to fight German armament and propaganda of Nordic superiority, judged to be a different facade of the Nazi threat. The group published a newsletter, *Races et Racisme*, on the spread of racist doctrines in various countries to warn the public against pseudo-scientific theories. The group included Professor Célestin Bouglé, Director at the École Normale Supérieure; Professor Edmond Vermeil, Director of the Institute of German Studies at the Sorbonne; the historian Georges Lefèbvre and the anthropologists Lucien Lévy-Bruhl and Paul Rivet.[124]

The Congress heard between 200 and 300 papers in five sections, and was mainly concerned with the danger of population decline in Europe, predicted to amount to forty million people in the next generation. This provided a favorable background to the German and Italian reports on policies to halt population decline and on race improvement. The distinction between racial and population questions paralleled the dichotomy between qualitative and quantitative studies and many issues belonged to both. The race questions, however, were dealt with in the Congress at a separate section on Biometry, Biotypology, and Heredity.

Ostensibly, the Congress was strictly scientific and the organizing committee was rigid enough in its interpretation of "scientific" as to decline a communication on the relation between Germans and Jews, recommended by Boas, as too sociological and not scientific enough.[125] That the organizing committee included Durkheim's intellectual heirs only added irony to the decision. On the other hand the attitude towards the German delegation was lenient.

Financial sponsorship came from among others the American Jewish Committee, which had a strong preference for non-Jews among anthropologists. Even Boas had to defend his own credentials and subject matter: "So far as I am concerned I think my Jewish descent would not make any difference for a Congress of this kind, particularly since what has to be said are purely objective observations." Despite everything Boas remained idealistic and naïve to his last days.[126] The Promethean struggle to gain objectivity was waged even though everyone knew, or should have

124 Report by "Groupe d'étude et d'information 'Races et Racisme' on the International Congress of Population July 29th–August 1st 1937." Copy in FBP. Also *Nature*, 140 (1937), 458, 471–472.
125 Landry to Boas, May 25, 1937; June 28, 1937. FBP.
126 Boas–Wallach correspondence, May 1937. FBP.

expected, that the debate was to become an arena for the fight over the validity of racism; after all this was the purpose of the anti-racist organizers.[127] The rationale of inviting the Germans in the first place was the belief that in order to delegitimize racism the racists' consent was needed. This could best be achieved if the German representatives would be confronted with the scientific facts in an international gathering and would then have to publicly recognize the merit of egalitarianism. Probably the boycott against Germany following World War I, to which liberals like Boas had objected, inhibited the organizers from resorting to exclusion. Past experience was somewhat misleading in creating the illusion of possible success. In 1934 at the International Anthropological Congress, Elliot Smith's criticism of the Nazi racist theories had apparently caught the Germans off guard, and although they had an official representation, they did not respond.[128] This the Germans were apparently determined to avoid at the Paris Congress and their aggressive response surprised the organizers.

The German professors present at the section included among others Ruedin, the Director of the Kaiser Wilhelm Institute, Verschauer from Frankfurt, Burgoerfer, the Director of the Office of Statistics of the Reich, and Hellpach from Heidelberg, in addition to "a whole small army of German Doctors and reporters" who heated the atmosphere by cheers and loud clapping in response to German reports on "Nordisation." This, according to the organizers, encountered a solid resistance on the part of French and foreign scholars, which the official memorandum of the Congress by the group "Races et Racisme" emphasized as satisfactory in opposing Hitler's science. The media coverage of the Congress was not extensive and did not describe any political upheaval among the participants.[129]

The results of the Congress were discouraging. Racism was left

[127] Copy of unsigned letter [Vanikof] to M. Waldman, June 3, 1937, from Paris. FBP.

[128] Zollschan, "Bericht über die Vorarbeiten zur geplanten Rassen-Enquête."

[129] The *New York Times* reported on the Congress (July 30, 1937, 4:5; August 1, 1937, 32:1) but refrained from mentioning any conflict. The paper commended Dr. Thurnwald of Berlin University for stating that scientists are never objective, but did not mention that Thurnwald's advocacy of subjectivity was part of his rebuttal of Zollschan's plan for an international inquiry and included a differentiation between German and Jewish logic. *Nature*'s (140 [1937], 458, 471–472) relatively extensive report ignored the general national clash between Germans and other scientists. It did mention the stormy debate on "Eugenics of the Mentally Defective," which involved a German call for sterilization of all hereditary diseased.

undefeated; its supporters became noisier. The organizers' earlier
hopes that a prearranged program and the numerous scholars from
various countries would "affirm on the occasion ... the absurdity of
certain doctrines" and overwhelm "the ten German scholars," who
were expected to use the tribune of the Congress as an opportunity
for "spreading racial propaganda," were dashed.[130] Boas was
disappointed especially in light of his judgement that the Germans
had succeeded in swamping the Congress. In response, the organizing group "Races et Racisme" held a Banquet at the restaurant
Lape'ruse, under the chairmanship of Paul Rivet at which the group
instituted itself as the "Committee for the Initiative of International
Action Against Racist Doctrines." The participants hoped that
national committees would be formed in each country to study the
race issue scientifically and that they would try to influence leading
institutions to organize an international investigation under the
auspices of either a European government or the League of Nations
to culminate in a Universal Race Congress at the 1939 Chicago
World Fair.

THE POPULATION COMMITTEE

Inclined to put great faith in the power of scientific research, and by
now with little hope left in the willingness of scientists to speak out
strongly in public, Boas returned to the United States from the Paris
congress resolved to devote much energy to the establishment of a
local scientific committee on race problems. Upon his return, he
asked Frederick Osborn to become a co-sponsor for an American
effort to counter race propaganda by organizing a research group to
act as a national steering committee. Although Osborn had declined
his earlier requests, by 1937 he became more receptive as a result of
both the changing political atmosphere and of reforms he initiated
within the eugenics movement; he therefore agreed. As to the
content of the proposed research, Boas emphasized the German
menace, while Osborn believed an attempt to treat the subject
scientifically was still possible in the United States, whereas in
Europe the political situation made it hopeless.[131]

Frederick Osborn was critical of anthropologists' overemphasis
on human origins, and their lack of interest in the evolution of

[130] Copy of unsigned letter [Vanikof] to M. Waldman, June 3, 1937, from Paris. FBP.
[131] Osborn–Boas correspondence, Sept. 1937–1939. FBP; FOP.

mankind. His approach was to study population trends, especially "differential reproduction," and he hoped that "it may be possible to work out research in fields which add to our knowledge of what is happening to the human race today." His criticism was directed at the futility of anthropological classification. No "satisfactory classification of physical types" could exist, he argued, unless "we could relate them to various socially useful characteristics, such as relative immunity to disease, or balanced personalities or superior intellectual capacities." Osborn joined Boas in the enterprise with a focus on population studies and hoped to coordinate a research program on demography and the state of contemporary races.[132] Osborn's emphasis on "population" as opposed to "race" was part of his attempt to portray the eugenics movement as scientifically and socially progressive.

The American Committee's first aim was to organize administrative matters and fundraising, while the research program was to be decentralized. Its comprehensiveness depended on a delicate balance of conflicting interests, left at the initial stage to the individual investigator. The original invitations to join the American Committee, signed by Boas and Osborn, went to the same people with whom Boas had cooperated earlier: Leslie C. Dunn (genetics), Gardner Murphy, Otto Klineberg (psychology), T. Wingate Todd (anatomy), Franz Kallman (genetics and psychiatry), Robert M. MacIver (sociology) and F. A. Hooton and Harry L. Shapiro (anthropology.) Hooton hoped the Division of Anthropology and Psychology of the National Research Council would handle the project. Soured by his failure to mobilize the anthropologists a year earlier, Hooton advocated the initiation of the program through official channels; otherwise, the touchy anthropologists were unlikely to lend their support. Although Hooton was reluctant to take an active part, he assured Boas of his support, and entrusted Shapiro at the American Museum of Natural History with the task of representing him. Boas's experience taught him that apathy of individual scientists may be more conducive to attaining their support than leaving the matter in the hands of the Division, which would result in "much talk and no action." To entrust the investigation to scientific organizations such as the American Association of Physical Anthropologists, the American Anthropological Association or the various psychological

132 Osborn to Hooton, Nov. 4, 1937, EAHP box 3DE.

and genetic groups would have been too cumbersome. Yet the committee agreed to approach the Social Science Research Council, the National Research Council and various other national organizations. This, as Boas expected, met with little success.[133]

Some of the other members also took only a nominal part in the committee's work. L. C. Dunn offered substitutes. Todd could not afford the time to come to New York "to discuss even so compelling and urgent a problem."[134] Despite the initial reluctance, Boas was optimistic. He had eleven non-refusals and urged his European counterparts to do their share in the organization of the proposed congress on population. The committee added as members the sociologists Donald Young (despite Osborn's opposition) and Robert Lynd, and at the request of Osborn, the psychologist Barbara Burks. The term race was avoided, choosing as title Klineberg's proposal "Studies in the Determination of Population Qualities by Genetic and Environmental Factors," replacing the earlier title "Characteristics of Races."[135] The research program integrated the biological, psychological and sociological points of view. It was divided into the study of the "inbreeding in city and rural communities" as it influenced family lines, the "crossing of various lines of descent," and the process of selection in "internal migration."[136]

Despite his early skepticism, Osborn became very active and suggested numerous research proposals. He justified adding Barbara Burks to the committee based on her acclaimed study on foster children in California, published in 1927. She had continued

[133] Hooton to Boas, Oct. 30, 1937; Boas to Hooton, Nov. 4, 1937; Boas to Kallman, Nov. 15, 1937. FBP.

[134] As a replacement for himself, Dunn suggested E. C. MacDowell, of the Department of Genetics at the Carnegie Institution, Cold Spring Harbor, who had a similar background to Dunn and whose "general views on racial questions are also similar," or Walter Landauer of Storrs, Connecticut, who was interested in the organization of a section on race at the International Congress of Genetics which was to be held in Moscow (later cancelled) and was experienced in these matters. Dunn to Boas Oct. 28, 1937. Todd was sympathetic enough to draw up a research program that included the influence of early training on the subconscious, and the effect of subclinical variants of health (nutrition). Todd to Boas, Nov. 4, 1937, Jan. 4, 1938. FBP.

[135] Boas was especially worried about sponsorship and financial backing, an aspect that was assigned to Sir Robert Mond. On the European efforts see Boas to Mond, Nov. 15, 1937. Also to Paul Rivet. The two coordinated the efforts in England and France respectively. On Boas's proposed draft, see Osborn to Boas, Nov. 15, 1937. FBP.

[136] Boas to Hooton, February 21, 1938. FBP. Hooton turned out to be the least cooperative member of the committee, since he was absorbed in the publication of his two books on criminality.

with similar work and at E. B. Wilson's recommendation was engaged at Cold Spring Harbor by Merriam in 1936. Burks's case is particularly interesting, because it points both to the continuity of the old eugenics and the delicate task of coalition-building in the formation of the committee. Burks's studies in the twenties were conducted under the guidance of Lewis Terman at Stanford, and emphasized the heredity factor in intelligence, quantifying the impact of environment to merely seventeen percent. Her efforts to select a socially homogeneous group illustrated the response of the hereditarian school to the criticism directed against the I.Q. tests of the early twenties, yet her "environmental approach" was overshadowed by factors of heredity. Her critics included Otto Klineberg, Boas's student and colleague, whose role in the committee was to study the psychology of Blacks by examining selective migration, delinquency, intelligence, and equal opportunity. Burks partially accommodated herself to the new ideas in terminology and gave greater emphasis to environmental factors.[137] On June 2, 1938 the committee approved the various proposals. Osborn was especially unhappy about Kallman's work, judging Kallman to be over confident in "the finality of his work," and hoped the group would have control over the final conclusions before they were published. Kallman for his part raised objections to the research done by Burks. Boas was not very happy with either of them, although Kallman's views were closer to Boas's, who recognized that cooperation depended on such "political" compromises.[138]

Osborn represented the new face of eugenics, which despite its transformation preserved significant aspects of its old character.[139] His participation in the work of the committee was instrumental in

---

[137] Osborn to Boas, Dec. 13, 1937. Also Burks to Boas Dec 23, 1937, following a meeting between them. Her studies in the twenties resembled Davenport and Steggerda's study of Jamaica which was published in 1929. Also Klineberg to Boas, Jan 12, 1938. See H. Cravens, *The Triumph of Evolution* (Philadelphia: University of Pennsylvania Press, 1978), pp. 258–259, and D. Kevles, *In The Name of Eugenics* (New York: Knopf, 1985), pp. 140–141.

[138] Osborn to Boas, June 7, 1938, Sept. 8. Boas had helped Kallman organize the research. Boas to Osborn, April 10, 1939. Boas to Kallman, Feb. 21, 1938. Kallman to Boas Oct. 26, 1938. Also Murphy to Boas, June 13, 1938. Boas accepted Burks's work following her change of terminology. Boas to Burks, Nov. 2, 1938. When the Carnegie stopped supporting Boas's work in 1941, he asked Burks to find a place for one of his researchers. Nov. 28, 1940. FBP.

[139] For the persistence of the bigoted movement into the 1970s see Martin Barker, *The New Racism. Conservatives and the Ideology of the Tribe* (Frederick, Maryland: University Publications of America, 1982).

raising financial support and achieving legitimacy in circles Boas could not have approached otherwise. Part of the price was the inclusion of Burks as a member of the group. If the coalition proved successful, Osborn could claim part of the credit. A trustee of the Carnegie, Osborn represented the interests of the committee to the Foundation. The Carnegie Foundation, which had begun to support Boas's own research in 1935, continued with annual installments of $2,000 up to 1941, and turned out to be the population committee's only source of funding. This reflected a major shift in American science. The Carnegie's support of Boas's anti-racialist studies symbolized the shift away from Davenport's studies, which the foundation had financed earlier.

Boas and Osborn cooperated in cementing the coalition. Part of Boas's concern was that if his own project was approved while others were not, the whole enterprise would be judged as an exercise in personal financing.[140] The belief that the growing interest in racial questions might bring new sources of support for anthropological research was an additional motive for some to participate in the concerted work. In the tight financial situation of the discipline, no one could decline such a prospect. Rockefeller funding, once the major source of finance for anthropology, was waning, and the discipline was on the verge of bankruptcy.[141]

OUT OF THE CLOSET

Historians often judge the position of authors on various issues by their publications. For instance, an anti-racist volume which was published in the late 1930s would conventionally be considered a reaction to Nazism, and alternatively a lack of such publications implies compliancy. In the absence of additional information this becomes the only approach, but one must be aware of its possible shortcoming. Though political developments were crucial to the publication and reception of this literature, other considerations also played a role. These included the authors' previous book on the

[140] Boas wrote to Osborn that he would like to receive $1,500 for his studies, but that his first priority was Shapiro. Boas to Osborn, April 10, 1939. When Boas's project was approved and Shapiro's was not, Boas included him in the project. Boas to Kappel, June 12, 1939. Also "Studies in the Determination of Population Qualities by Genetic and Environmental Factors" – financed by the Carnegie Institute, April 39, $6,000 to Kallman and $4,500 to Boas (Boas to Schneiderman, May 8, 1939. AJC.)

[141] One example was Hooton who hoped to receive assistance to his laboratory. Hooton to Boas, Dec. 29, 1937. FBP.

market, the cost of revising an old edition and its impact on the price of the new edition and royalties, the number of unsold copies of the previous edition, the date of publication in relation to the beginning of the college year, and the ability to raise a subsidy when the book was not expected to be widely sold. All resulted in delays ranging from months to years, and sometimes decades. Articles suffered a similar fate when authors were asked to contribute an arbitrary sum, decided upon by the editor or the publisher, towards the cost of publishing.

The examination of some of the important anti-racist publications of the thirties, such background knowledge is indispensable. Boas's *The Mind of Primitive Man*, first issued in 1911, argued that there was no fundamental difference between the thinking of primitive and civilized man. Reprinted several times before finally being revised in 1938, the book was an important anti-racist statement, but the new edition was more than a decade overdue in Boas's opinion, who was very annoyed with Macmillan for issuing unauthorized reprints. The volume *General Anthropology* (1938), with Boas as editor and contributor, was also a venture that took years to complete.[142] It was clear at the time, and has since been reconfirmed, that Ruth Benedict's *Race: Science and Politics* was initiated by Boas. Her political participation was that of a disciple who accepted the responsibility of dealing with issues which are dear to her mentor, as she did when she collaborated with the American Committee for Democracy and Intellectual Freedom. Boas was closely associated with the writing of *Race*, though Benedict wrote it in California on her sabbatical. He read every word and corrected much, especially in the sections on biology and physical anthropology. Benedict had no desire to play a role on the political scene: she did her part as a member of the Boas group.[143] Benedict appended anti-racist statements and resolutions of the American Anthropological Association, the executive council of the Society for Psychological Study of Social Issues, a subgroup of the

[142] For example see Boas to the Author's League of America, May 29, 1934, on the mishandling of his affairs by Macmillan and more so by W. W. Norton; Boas to Macmillan, Dec. 4, 1934; Macmillan to Boas, July 3, 1936; D. C. Heath and Co. to Boas, March 15, 1928; The Viking Press to Boas, Aug. 12, 1931; Boas to Huebsch, The Viking Press, March 21, 1935. FBP.

[143] Benedict, *Race: Science and Politics*. Benedict acknowledged her limited qualifications especially on a discussion such as on mutation, she said it was "pared to the bone, but then I've pared down all the genetics," see Benedict to Boas, Feb. 16, 1940 as well as Jan. 18 & 29, and Feb. 5, 1940. FBP.

American Psychological Association, and the "biologists' manifesto" at the International Genetics Congress in Edinburgh. Her intent was to convey a sense of agreement in the scientific community. This type of network gave an albeit exaggerated impression of an increased anti-racist atmosphere. During the war, it became easier to denounce racism, which became a synonym of the enemy – Nazism. Anthropologists continued to oppose racism, and on one occasion the American Association of Physical Anthropologists protested that "Jim Crow" blood banks in the American Army bore "an embarrassing resemblance" to practices "based on the Nazi theory of race."[144]

Contrary to public memory which relies greatly on Benedict's testimony, the American scientific community – even if moving since late 1938 towards anti-racism had not reached this position before the outbreak of the war. This becomes evident upon differentiating between the American scientific community according to geographical regions: New York, the rest of the East Coast, and the remainder of the country. Within the first constituency, the balance had shifted by and large in favor of anti-racism even at an earlier period; the old generation was still lingering but was overtaken by events. Scientists along the East Coast were accepting New York's leadership and consenting to an anti-racist facade, but many were a long way from abandoning internalized attitudes. In the rest of the country, scholars, excluding migrants from the East, were learning slowly about the efforts of the New York scientists and intellectuals to awaken the country to the changing world.

James McKeen Cattell displayed the ambivalence of New York's older generation of scientists. A prominent psychologist, a member and president of various scientific societies, Cattell was the editor and owner of a number of scientific journals of which the most important were, from 1894, *Science* (publication of the American Association for the Advancement of Science), from 1900, the *Scientific Monthly*, and from 1915, *School and Society*. His impact on what was perceived to be the scientific community's opinion is unquestionable. Cattell had a very clear policy concerning what should be published in *Science*, and for a long time this excluded anti-racist statements. Boas and Cattell were both seventy-five

---

[144] June 1942, the Committee on Racial Relations of the American Association of Physical Anthropologists protested to the American Red Cross. The members of the committee were Greulich, Shapiro, W. K. Gregory, and Weidenreich.

years old and had been acquainted for at least four decades, since Boas had joined the anthropology department at Columbia, headed by Cattell. It would be difficult, and not quite to the point, to explain the complicated relations between the two men, which pose many questions, but it is instructive to recount two major episodes. The first goes back to the period of World War I, when Cattell was fired from Columbia in 1917, ostensibly for supporting the deferment of the draft for students, but in reality for his opposition to the war. Cattell was not the only one to oppose the war, but he used Columbia's stationery to convey his protest to members of Congress. The affair shook the faculty and Cattell received widespread support, from among others, Boas and Dewey, who were members of the Cattell Committee. James Harvey Robinson and Charles Beard resigned from the University and joined the newly established New School for Social Research.[145] The affair certainly influenced Cattell's future political attitude, and the fact that he had to pay the highest price for a political stand he shared with many others (especially Boas) made his approach more cautious. This is surely part of the explanation of *Science*'s position under Cattell's ownership and editorial direction. This attitude was already evident in 1919, when Cattell refused to publish Boas's denunciation of three anthropologists who had spied for the United States in Mexico while supposedly conducting research. When *The Nation* published the story, it became the "Boas Affair." The denunciation of Boas by the Washington Anthropological Society, which was adopted in a shorter and milder form by the American Anthropological Association, was published by Cattell. But in 1936 Boas was able to solicit from Cattell a general statement of sympathy with the anti-racist position and Cattell promised "to cooperate in any feasible way in making the situation known in this country and in Germany itself." These promises turned out to be empty words when Cattell declined speaking engagements and later when *Science* refused to publish anti-fascist articles.[146]

Boas achieved the first broad-based participation of scientists and

[145] Cattell took his case to court, and it was finally settled privately; Columbia avoided publicity, and Cattell won a complete victory. Among others see M. M. Sokal, "Science and James McKeen Cattell, 1894–1945," *Science*, 209 (1980) 43–52; Cravens, p. 112; Alexander Lesser, "Franz Boas," in Sydel Silverman (ed.), *Totems and Teachers: Perspectives in the History of Anthropology* (New York: Columbia University Press, 1981), pp. 14–15, and Boas correspondence with Cattell, JMCP, FBP.

[146] Correspondence Boas–Cattell, June 8 and 13; Sept. 3 and 9, 1936; Dec 23, 1938; April 14, 1939; June 1, 1940; JMCP, box 5.

reached a wide audience with the American Committee for Democracy and Intellectual Freedom. On April 30. 1938 the British Journal *Nature* published an article by the German Nobel prize physicist, Johannes Stark, entitled "The Pragmatic and Dogmatic Spirit in Physics." Stark presented "the official racialism of the Nazis to divide physicists into good, i.e., nontheoretical and Jewish." The article received considerable notice in the American press, and Boas sought to use the opportunity "to get American scientists to take a plain stand against the race nonsense and the general suppression of free thought."[147] Working with a Columbia graduate student named M. I. Finkelstein, with whom he had become acquainted in the course of his own involvement in other political issues (notably, support for the Republican side in the Spanish Civil war), Boas launched a campaign to circulate a counterstatement which became known as the "Scientists' Manifesto."[148]

The document drew on a resolution passed at the preceding annual meeting of the American Association for the Advancement of Science asserting that "science is wholly independent of national boundaries and races and creeds, and can flourish only where there is peace and intellectual freedom." Because of Stark's insistence on race, the "Scientists' Manifesto" could go beyond the A. A. A. S. resolution and explicitly condemn the "official racialism of the Nazis." It pointed out that not all the scientists attacked by Stark were Jewish and that "the racial theories which [Stark] advocates have been demolished time and again."[149]

With an initial grant of $750 from the American Jewish Committee, a campaign was conducted during the summer to gain the support of prominent scientists. Following the organization of an informal sponsoring committee which included forty-eight outstanding scientists, 12,000 copies of a national anti-racist statement were circulated to scientists in universities and research institutes. An energetic campaign conducted by Finkelstein helped reach a reply rate of about 10 to 12 per cent, ten times the expected rate of commercial advertisers on circular letters and as high as the Federal government's compulsory questionnaires. The responses represented "every major college and many smaller ones as well as many

---

[147] Boas to E. G. Conklin, June 14, 1938; to Hooton, June 14, 1938. FBP.
[148] Boas to S. Wallach, Oct. 31, 1938. FBP.
[149] Boas to Hooton, June 14, 1938. FBP.

laboratories (industrial and otherwise) and government departments." Many of the respondents had written individual letters expressing a "feeling of isolation in their bitterness against the Fascist menace," which was partially broken down through generating discussion on campuses. The organizers concluded that they "have tapped a powerful but latent anti-Fascist sentiment."[150]

On December 10, the "Scientists' Manifesto" was released at a news conference with 1,284 signatures including three Nobel laureates and 64 members of the National Academy of Sciences.[151] The publication of the statement was followed by a concerted columnists' coverage. The list of signatories was impressive. For the first time a large body of American scientists condemned "pseudo-scientific racialism."[152] Boas hoped to capitalize on the success and planned to send similar statements "one to educators ... and journalists, and one for people in the humanities and social sciences." Another pamphlet "Scientists Take Sides" was to be published in 50,000 copies, targeted at "social sciences courses in hundreds of schools." Organizations across campuses were to be set up to emulate the University Federation for Democracy and Intellectual Freedom at Columbia, coordinated by a national committee. The financial burden was minimal. The first circular had cost $700 and much of the work was done by volunteers; while the extensive program was estimated to cost $4,500. Mobilizing public opinion was within reach, as yet limited to scientists but not to the scientific institutions as representative bodies. When Edward Sapir, then the President of the American Anthropological Association, asked Boas about the possibility of having "important scientific bodies" like the American Association of University Professors, the National Academy of Sciences, the American Association for the Advancement of Science and the American Philosophical Society, issue a joint statement against the German anti-Jewish policy, Boas reiterated his doubts about a possible "official expression from any outstanding scientific bodies" while he drew great encouragement from the individual response among scientists. For the same reason, Boas continued to object to Zollschan's "enquête" as political and therefore untenable. Scientific work and politics

[150] "Report on Progress of Public Statement of Scientists in Condemnation of Nazis." FBP.
[151] *New York Times*, Dec. 11, 1938. p. 50.
[152] Boas to Cattell n.d., attached to Cattell answer Dec. 23, 1938. JMCP, box 5. W. C. Mitchell to Boas, June 30, 1938. FBP.

must be kept separate; the former "acts slowly, but is our only hope."[153]

During the second half of December Boas seems to have reconsidered the tactics of the anti-racist campaign. He wrote to Cattell asking that the American Association for the Advancement of Science would endorse the "manifesto," and would encourage affiliated societies to follow. Now that "mass expression" by scientists against racism had been achieved, Boas sought to "strengthen the case very much" by having "the societies formally endorse the manifesto." The executive committee of the American Association for the Advancement of Science judged it inadvisable to approve the "manifesto" on behalf of the association as a whole, since the opinions of the members might be divided, but following its Ottawa meeting, limited access to the Association's mailing list was given to the American Committee for Democracy and Intellectual Freedom. In its own way this limited cooperation was an important step in the uphill struggle.[154] Yet no scientific society ever endorsed the manifesto. As J. B. Conant, President of Harvard, reminded Boas, the ivory tower continued to provide an excuse for not being involved in public affairs.[155]

Three of the four "resolutions and manifestoes of scientist" reproduced in Benedict's anti-racist book were published in this context.[156] The first, and the most elaborate, was a news release issued on December 19, by twelve members of the executive council of the Society for Psychological Study of Social Issues. The second, much shorter, presented by Boas and passed at the meeting of the American Association of University Professors on December 28, protested against totalitarian persecution of teachers "on account of

[153] Sapir to Boas, Nov. 29th; Boas to Sapir Nov. 29, 1938. Boas to Zollschan, Dec. 6, 1938. FBP.
[154] Boas to Cattell n.d., attached to Cattell's answer Dec. 23, 1938, JMCP; box 5. *Science* refused to publish a press release of the American Committee for Democracy and Intellectual Freedom against attempts by various groups to remove textbooks from American public schools. Cattell replied he could not publish the statement because "It seems best ... to confine *Science* to its proper field of the advancement of the natural and exact sciences, and not to take up here economic, social, and political problems on which the opinions of scientific men are divided." Cattell was quick to add that his own sympathies were with such efforts, "but this may be due to the emotions, rather than to scientific evidence." Boas to Cattell n.d. [May?] 1940.
[155] "I have adhered strictly to a policy against making public commitments of any sort," he wrote to Boas on the eve of the Kristallnacht, Oct. 31, 1938. Conant belonged to the most influential group in deciding science policy under F. D. Roosevelt's administration.
[156] Benedict, *Race*, pp. 195–199.

their race, religion, or political ideals."[157] The third was presented at the meeting of the American Anthropological Association.

The difficulty of reaching agreement in this group is suggested by an eye-witness:

The question of a resolution against Nazi classification of race came up. Sapir proposed the resolution. Thereafter the whole meeting split. On one side were most of the people; on the other side was a poor little group which included you [Alexander Lesser], me [Gene Weltfish] May Edel and Gladys Reichard. We voted for this resolution. All the rest of the gang rose up and voted against it, on the grounds that Germany was a friendly power. Thereafter Sapir, with his fine sense of humor, said, "this resolution was proposed by E. A. Hooton of Harvard." Everyone thought they were voting against a resolution proposed by Boas."[158]

Hooton's original draft was drawn up at Sapir's request. The version included a denunciation of "so-called anthropology in Germany"; an assertion of positive scientific knowledge regarding the physical variations of race; and a denial of scientific support to its psychological or cultural connections. All were rejected.[159] The next meeting was chaired by Father John Cooper, of Catholic University, and the motion drafted by Hooton was read by Fay Cooper Cole of Chicago. It was passed unanimously. Boas was quoted as saying that the Association was "very rightly" following the lead of the "scientists' manifesto." A similar resolution was presented by Ashley Montagu at the Philadelphia meeting of the physical anthropologists, but was referred to a committee which never acted on it.[160] The full impact of the shift was to be felt during the war and in its aftermath in the UNESCO statements, in which Montagu played a major role.

The statement's noncommittal attitude on the issue of race differences was secondary. By its very publication, the anthropologists' declared themselves to be against racism, which further propaganda could utilize according to the writer's purposes to impress upon the public a supposed consensus among scientists. The legacy of these resolutions is illuminated when compared with the English failure to publish even such a diluted statement. It could

---

[157] Himstead to Boas, Dec. 20, 1938. FBP.
[158] Alexander Lesser, "Franz Boas," in Silverman (ed.), *Totems and Teachers*, p. 30.
[159] Hooton to Selzer, Secretary of A. A. A., Dec. 21, 1938. EAHP Box 2ABC.
[160] In April 1940, after the war began, W. W. Howells asked Hooton what would be done about the matter. Hooton responded: "Not only has the horse been stolen, but the barn has been burned."

be argued that had the English tried in the late thirties they probably would have succeeded, but their earlier experience at the Race and Culture Committee was apparently enough of a discouragement. As propaganda tools, the declarations were meaningful, if late, achievements. Nothing was more powerful than an official sanction, and Boas was finally able to implement Zollschan's tactics.[161] Three years before, in defending his pet plan for an "enquête" of scientists into the race problem, Zollschan had suggested to Boas that in order to cause a shift it was necessary that "the intellectual public would require the scholars to give their opinion."[162] Despite their disagreements, in a way Boas realized Zollschans plan; he organized research through the population committee to address the substantive questions and mobilized the critically important group of "intellectuals" through the "scientists' manifesto." Taking advantage of Stark's linkage of race with scientific freedom, Boas was able to mobilize a sizeable group on an uncontroversial subject (scientific freedom), and include the politically divisive topic of race. This was as close as the "intellectual public" came to be represented in the debate; this was a wider group than specialists on race, but smaller than an amorphous "American public," whose attitude was yet to change.

[161] Boas found it difficult to reach the pages of the *New York Times* with his "radical" propaganda. It was much easier for the paper to rely on the resolution of the A. A. A., when it cited "Schools Rebuked on Racial Errors: Professor Boas, Chairman of the American Committee for Democracy and Intellectual Freedom headed a study of 166 textbooks of which two out of three misuse the term and 20% teach what amounts to Nazi doctrines about superior and inferior races." This was followed by a description of the broad educational campaign, and names of supporters. *New York Times*, June 17, 1939, 16:8.

[162] Zollschan to Boas, Jan. 4, 1936. FBP.

Epilogue

"No Scientific Basis for Race Bias Found by World Panel of Experts" announced the *New York Times* on July 18, 1950. The story described a report issued by UNESCO which "provided evidence that there was no scientific justification for race discrimination." The headline implied that scientists had finally reached an egalitarian consensus on the concept of race. While this was not to be, the anti-racist campaign had come to fruition and the public message was that science repudiated conventional bigotry. The UNESCO's statement, however, rekindled the controversy over the definition of race. The Statement presented four premises, three of which were generally accepted: that mental capacities of all races are similar; that no evidence for biological deterioration as a result of hybridization existed; that there was no correlation between national or religious groups and any race. But it was the fourth claim, that "race was less a biological fact than a social myth," which had old opponents up in arms.[1]

The 1950 declaration was the first in an on going series of UNESCO's statements on the concept of race, and it displayed the environmental determinism at its peak. The reversal in the scientific credo on race since the early 1920s had been completed. The study heralded its conclusions as representing the "most modern views of biologists, geneticists, psychologists, sociologists and anthropologists," not an easy task even in the emotional anti-racism of the postwar period. The scientific community's responses were mixed. Some opposed the environmental essence of the declaration, others its tone and the absolute denial of a biological concept of race. Most criticism was aimed at the statement that "biological studies lend support to the ethic of universal brotherhood, for man is born with drives towards co-operation." This target was relatively safe, since

[1] *New York Times*, July 18, 1950. p. 1.

341

it could not be supported by any scientific data, and the backlash necessitated a revised statement within a year. A second UNESCO statement was consequently published in June 1951, acknowledging that the powerful criticism represented for some "a victory for racism and the defeat of a naïve humanitarianism."[2] The polarity between racists (those pre-war racialists) and egalitarians remained, but the substance of the debate has dramatically changed. Any hereditarian explanation of social or cultural characteristics or ability was prone to be classified as racist. Naturalism and biological reductionism were generally viewed with suspicion, an attitude which has remained to the present, as the heated debates of sociobiology since the mid seventies illustrate.

Comparing the UNESCO's statement, which claimed to represent most scientists in the varied social and natural disciplines, with the difficulties encountered by scientists who attempted to publish anti-racist declarations in the pre-war years elucidates the revolution in the concept of race. UNESCO picked up where its predecessor, the International Institute of Intellectual Co-operation, had failed fifteen years earlier. The pre-war efforts had been abandoned so as not to antagonize Hitler, and had never reached even the level of a committee of experts.[3] By 1950, while no consensus had been reached, racism had been refuted. Scientists who were involved in the pre-war years with the anti-racist campaign, such as Julian Huxley, J. B. S. Haldane, L. C. Dunn, and Otto Klineberg, were leaders in the new enterprise. These and other commentators had earlier participated in anti-racist publications, such as the "Geneticists' Manifesto,"[4] and some were becoming still more active in the post-war years.

UNESCO's statement provides only one illustration of the shift between the end of World War I and 1950 which saw biological explanations replaced by cultural analysis. Rigid views of hierarchies among human groups largely yielded to relativism and indeterminism. The minority of academics who dissented from the new convention protested against a surrender to "cultural determi-

---

[2] Unesco, *The Race Concept, The Race Question in Modern Science* (Paris: Unesco, 1952), p. 7.

[3] A. Metraux, "Unesco and the Racial Problem," *International Social Science Bulletin*, 2 (1950), 384–390.

[4] "Social Biology and Population Improvement," *Nature* 144 (1939), 521. Diane Paul, "Eugenics and the Left;" William Provine, "Geneticists and Race," *American Zoologist*, 26 (1986), 857–887. The main actor in the post-war years was Ashley Montagu, who published extensively on the subject.

nism." But the revolution spread to a constituency far wider than universities or intellectuals. Perhaps the single most celebrated case where the new scientific view influenced political formulations came in Brown v. the Board of Education, the successful anti-segregation case in the United States. The Civil Rights movement expressed socio-political grievances and challenged the intellectual legitimacy of the racist tradition, among others by appealing to science, the only arbiter in a relativist world. Science became the supreme purveyor of truth for American society overcoming traditional particularism – religious or otherwise – particularly in the aftermath of the Scopes Trial, against the teaching of evolution (1924). Science could be challenged only on metaphysical questions or if the scientific community itself propounded conflicting theories. During the interwar years, laymen and scientists alike increasingly contested scientific and traditional race prejudice, until the balance had tipped in favor of egalitarianism during the thirties within the discipline, and reached the public thereafter.

A main conclusion of this study is that political beliefs had a greater impact in attitudes toward race than did scientific commitments. Ostensibly, scientists' attitudes toward race were based on scientific theories in biology or anthropology. However, this was not the case; political implications were more important than the scientists admitted. Any hereditarian theory, for example, could support various race theories; and vice versa, a race theory could be justified by several biological explanations. Therefore, scientists' positions on race could not be predicted from their research or the progressiveness of their science. Similarly, the spectrum of anti-racist activity, conveyed primarily in political terms, varied greatly and had no direct affinity to the scientists' views on race. Whether a person held racist or egalitarian views did not determine the participation level in campaigns against racism. Rarely could scientists be classified as coherent progressives or reactionaries and ordinarily they supported theories and opinions which fell into both categories.

The social diversification of the scientific community has been an important factor in the redefinition of the race concept. Members of the "inferior" groups were coming to play a growing role in the scientific community, and to assert their political interests. Immigrants, women and Jews, created new spaces and provided necessary data to refute claims of their own "inferior" qualities. The biological significance of race as a social explanation declined as the heredity – environment debate subsided. The general socio-economic circumstances enhanced this trend during the 1920s. Prosperity and immigration restriction in the United States eased Yankee xenophobia. The Great Depression furthered the belief in biological equality. Massive new poverty made it painfully real that destitution was not caused by a biological flaw. The Depression undermined the confidence of the middle classes, and unsettled the eugenic belief in heredity. The lesson was shared in Britain, and in both countries was accentuated during the 1930s by the rise of Nazism and the polarization between right and left.

Anti-Nazi sentiments led to the refutation of racism because sufficient preconditions supportive of an anti-racist position existed. One way to evaluate the relative impact of Nazism, is to speculate on the possible fortunes of theories of race in science had the Nazis not come to power. Drawing on the tendencies in the pre-1933 years – on the rise in the professional heterogeneity, the growing sophistication in the substance of heredity, and the reaction to earlier exaggeration by racists – it seems that the trend would have conceivably led to a mild and gradual decline of racist theories in science. It is, however, difficult to envision a total rejection of biological theories, or the dominance of cultural determinism in the way it occurred after the war. The indecisiveness as regards the two approaches – biological and cultural – might have remained. A slightly different interpretation would emphasize more the potential egalitarianism which regardless of Nazism would have led to a similar refutation of racism. As shown above, the biological school was on the retreat. It produced no meaningful new studies or theories, and most of its supporters belonged to the older generation. Even the more sophisticated scientists – such as Ronald Fisher – who belonged to the biological school, did so mostly along the old discarded dichotomy of nature versus nurture. The shift was evident even among the most rigid hereditarians who began to study the impact of the environment and thus agreed to the egalitarian's demarcation of the discourse which led to a growing discrepancy between the racist data and theories. Davenport's study of *Race Crossing in Jamaica* exemplified the hereditarians' failure, and his critics were quick to point to the incongruity between his data and conclusions. Biologists proclaimed their inability to apply studies of drosophila to questions of human heredity in any clear and simple way, explicitly showing that questions of culture or mental abilities lay outside the biologists' domain. Against the growing agnosticism of biologists, social scientists had a professional interest in furthering the social interpretation at the expense of biological theories. Consequently, psychologists began to concede a greater role to the environment in the determination of mental performance; physical anthropologists began to discover that their own methodological shortcomings were responsible for the discipline's imbroglio, while other anthropologists and ethnologists were becoming environmentalists, studying culture and society. Sociologists by and large – since the late twenties – ignored biological variables as irrelevant. Institutionally, too, the scientific community was coming under the tutelage of the environmental schools. It is thus not inconceivable that these developments, which were in full swing by 1933, would have followed the egalitarian path, just as happened after the rise of Nazism.

An important qualification should be added. Despite the likelihood that a new scientific consensus would have evolved even if Nazism did not come into power, the historical fact remains: the opposition to Nazism shaped in a dramatic fashion the refutation of racism as a legitimate intellectual stance. Politics mobilized many respectable intellectuals and scientists, who showed their eagerness to participate in the political discourse – and even more so, disclosed commitment and initiative. Whatever the political commitments of the various individuals, these were nurtured during the thirties by the clear and immediate danger of ideological polarization. The new scientific consensus was achieved largely as a result of interdisciplinary cooperation which enhanced the egalitarian argument. This cooperation succeeded through the mobilization of scientists involved in questions which ordinarily were not related to their field of study. Biologists such as J. B. S. Haldane or Lancelot Hogben wrote extensively on racial questions, not because it was their speciality, but rather in order to refute simplistic affinities of culture to Mendelism. This also motivated Leslie Dunn who became by default the American expert on human heredity.[5] In this respect the uniqueness of Nazism underscored the immanent wickedness of racism, crystallizing the dichotomy between respectable bigotry within middle class circles and the evilness of the enemy. Once

---

[5] Leslie C. Dunn and Teodosius Dobzhansky, *Heredity, Race, and Society* (New York: New American Library, 1946; 4th edn 1972).

racism was rejected, the edifice of prejudice was shaken. The need for a cognitive coherence confronted conventional bigotry, and the growing political involvement by intellectuals induced scientists – especially those who were socially involved and politically motivated – to commit themselves to the egalitarian cause. The source of the egalitarian conviction lay outside of scientific discourse, but its details and elucidation were worked out by the specialists in the various disciplines, in accordance with methodological and disciplinary requirements.

Bibliography

Allen, Garland E. "Genetics, Eugenics, and Class Struggle." *Genetics*, 79 (1975), 29–54.
"Genetics, Eugenics and Society: Internalists and Externalists in Contemporary History of Science." *Social Studies of Science*, 6 (1976), 105–122.
"The Misuse of Biological Hierarchies: The American Eugenics Movement, 1900–1940." *History and Philosophy of the Life Sciences*, 5 (1984), 105–128.
"The Eugenics Record Office, Cold Spring Harbor, 1910–1940." *Osiris*, 2nd ser. 2 (1985).
"The Role of Experts in Scientific Controversy," in H. Tristram Engelhardt and Arthur L. Caplan (eds.), *Scientific Controversies: Case Studies in the Resolution and Closure of Disputes in Science and Technology.* Cambridge: Cambridge University Press, 1987.
Asad, Talal, ed. *Anthropology and the Colonial Encounter.* London: Ithaca Press, 1973.
Bajema, Carl Jay, ed. *Eugenics Then and Now.* Stroudsburg, PA., 1976.
Baker, John R. *Julian Huxley Scientist and World Citizen, 1887–1975.* A biographical memoir. With a bibliography compiled by Jens-Peter Green. Paris: UNESCO Press, 1980.
Race. London: Oxford University Press, 1974.
Bannister, Robert C. *Social Darwinism: Science and Myth in British – American Social Thought.* Philadelphia: Temple University Press, 1979.
Banton, Michael. *The Idea of Race.* London: Tavistock Publications, 1977.
Racial and Ethnic Competition. Comparative Ethnic and Race Relations Series. Cambridge: Cambridge University Press, 1983.
Racial Theories. Cambridge: Cambridge University Press, 1987.
Barker, Martin. *The New Racism. Conservatives and the Ideology of the Tribe.* Frederick, Maryland: University Publications of America, 1982.
Barnouw, Victor. *Culture and Personality.* Homewood, IL: Dorsey Press, 1963.
Barzun, Jacques. *Race: A Study in Modern Superstition.* New York: Harcourt, Brace and Company, 1937.
Bateson, Mary Catherine. *With A Daughter's Eye.* New York: Washington Square Press, 1984.

Baur, Erwin; Fischer, Eugen, and Lenz, Fritz. *Menschliche Erblichkeitslehre*, Munich: 1923. Translated *Human Heredity*, New York: Eden and Cedar Paul, 1931.
Beddoe, John. "Anthropological History of Europe" (1891), in Count (ed.), *This Is Race*, pp. 162–170.
  The Races of Britain: A Contribution to the Anthropology of Western Europe. Bristol: Arrowsmith, 1885.
  "Colour and Race." Huxley Memorial Lecture, 1905. *Journal, Royal Anthropological Institute of Great Britain and Ireland*, pp. 219–250.
Bellomy, Donald C. " 'Social Darwinism' Revisited." *Perspectives in American History*, n.s. 1 (1984), 1–129.
Ben-David, Joseph. *The Scientists' Role in Society*. With a new introduction. Chicago: The University of Chicago Press, 1971, 1984.
Benedict, Ruth. *Race: Science and Politics*. 1940; 2nd ed. New York: Viking Press, 1943.
  "Franz Boas as an Ethnologist." *American Anthropologist*, 45 (1943), Memoir no. 61, by A.L. Kroeber *et al*. Menasha, Wisconsin: American Anthropological Association.
  "Obituary of Franz Boas." *Science*, 47 (1943), 60.
  Patterns of Culture. 1934; with a new preface by Margaret Mead. Boston: Houghton Mifflin, 1959.
Bennett, J.H., ed. *The Collected Papers of R.A. Fisher*. 5 vols, Adelaide, 1971–74. [*RAFCP*]
  Natural Selection, Heredity and Eugenics. New York: Oxford University Press, 1983.
Bews, J.W. *Human Ecology*. London: Oxford University Press, 1935.
Biddiss, Michael D. *Father of Racist Ideology: The Social and Political Thought of Count Gobineau*. New York: Waybright & Talley, 1970.
Biddiss, Michael D., ed. "The Universal Race Congress of 1911." *Race*, 13 (1971), 37–46.
  The Images of Races. Leicester: Leicester University Press, 1979.
Blacker, Carlos P. *Eugenics, Galton and After*. Cambridge: Harvard University Press, 1952.
Block, N.J., and Dworkin, Gerald, eds. *The IQ Controversy. Critical Readings*. New York: Pantheon Books, 1976.
Blumenbach, Johann Friedrich. "On the Natural Variety of Mankind" (1775), in *Anthropological Treatise*. Trans. T. Bendyshe. London: Anthropological Society, 1865.
Boardman J. "Myres, Sir John Linton." *Dictionary of National Biography, 1951–1960*. pp. 762–763.
Boas, Franz. "The Study of Geography." *Science*, 9 (1887), 137–41. Reprinted in Boas, *Race, Language and Culture*.
  "Human Faculty as Determined by Race." *Proceedings of the American Association for the Advancement of Science*, 43 (1894), 301–327.
  "The Mind of Primitive Man." *Science*, 12, 321 (1901), 281–289.

"Heredity in Head Form." *American Anthropologist*, 5 (July-September 1903), 530–538.

Changes in the Bodily Form of Descendants of Immigrants. Washington DC: Senate Document 208, 61st Congress, 2nd Session, 1911.

The Mind of Primitive Man. New York: Macmillan, 1911. Revised edition 1938. With a new foreword by Melville J. Herskovits, New York: The Free Press, 1965.

"Changes in the Bodily Form of Descendants of Immigrants." *American Anthropologist*, 14, 3 (1912), 530–562.

"New Evidence in Regard to the Instability of Human Types." *Proceedings of The National Academy of Sciences*, 2 (December 1916), 713–718.

"Scientists as Spies." *Nation*, 109, 2,842 (1919), 797.

"The Great Melting Pot and Its Problem." *New York Times Book Review* (February 6, 1921), 3.

"The Question of Racial Purity." *American Mercury*, 3, 10 (October 1924), 163–169.

"This Nordic Nonsense." *Forum* (October 1925), 501–511.

"Fallacies of Racial Inferiority." *Current History*, 25 (1927), 676–682.

"Changes in Immigrants." *The National Research Council Division of Anthropology and Psychology Conference on Racial Differences*. Washington DC, February 25 and 26. 1928.

Materials for the Study of Inheritance in Man. New York: Columbia University Press, 1928.

"Race and Progress." Presidential Address, American Association for the Advancement of Science, *Science*, 74 (1931), 1–8. Reprinted in Boas, *Race Language and Culture*.

"The Effects of American Environment on Immigrants and Their Descendants." *Science*, 83 (1936), 490.

"Race." *The Encyclopaedia of the Social Sciences*. Edited by Edwin Seligman and Alvin Johnson. New York: Macmillan, 1937. XIII, pp. 25–35.

"Genetic and Environmental Factors in Anthropology." *The Teaching Biologist*, 9, 2 (1939), 17–20.

Race, Language, and Culture. New York: MacMillan, 1940.

Bowler, Peter J. *Evolution, The History of an Idea*. Berkeley: California University Press, 1984.

Theories of Human Evolution. A Century of Debate, 1844–1944. Baltimore: Johns Hopkins University Press, 1986.

The Non-Darwinian Revolution. Baltimore: Johns Hopkins University Press, 1988.

Box, Joan Fisher. *R.A. Fisher: The Life of A Scientist*. New York: John Wiley and Sons, 1978.

Boyd, W.C. *Genetics and The Races of Man*. Oxford: Blackwell Press, 1950.

Brace, C. Loring. "The Roots of the Race Concept in American Physical Anthropology," in Frank Spencer (ed.), *A History of American Physical Anthropology*. New York: Academic Press, 1982, pp. 11–29.

Braun, Heywood and Britt, George. *Christians Only: A Study in Prejudice*. New York: The Vanguard Press, 1931.

Brigham, Carl C. *A Study of American Intelligence*. Princeton: Princeton University Press, 1922, 1928. New York: Kraus Reprint Co., 1975.

Burks, Barbara S. "The Relative Influence of Nature and Nurture Upon Mental Development." 27th yearbook N.S.E.E. I, pp. 219–316.

Burks, Barbara S., and Tolman, R.S. "Is Mental Resemblance Related To Physical Resemblance in Sibling Pairs?" *Journal of Genetic Psychology*, 40 (1932), 3–15.

Burrow, J.W. *Evolution and Society: A Case Study in Victorian Social Theory*. Cambridge: Cambridge University Press, 1966.

Campbell, J.A. "Some Sources of the Humanism of H.J. Fleure." *Research Papers, School of Geography, Oxford University*, 1972.

Caplan, Arthur L., ed. *The Sociobiology Debate: Readings on Ethical and Scientific Issues*. New York: Harper & Row, 1978.

Carr-Saunders, A.M. *The Population Problem*. London: Oxford University Press, 1922.

Population. London: Oxford University Press, 1925.

Cassidy, Robert. *Margaret Mead. A Voice for the Century*. New York: Universe Books, 1982.

Castle, William E. *Genetics and Eugenics*. 1916; Cambridge, MA: Harvard University Press, 1921.

"Race Mixture and Physical Disharmonies." *Science*, 71 (1930), 604–60.

Cattell, Raymond B. *The Fight For Our National Intelligence*. London: P.S. King and Son, 1937.

Chase, Allen. *The Legacy of Malthus*. New York: Knopf, 1980.

Childe, V. Gordon. *The Dawn*. New York: Knopf, 1925, 6th edn 1958.

The Aryans: A Study of Indo-European Origins. London: Kegan Paul, 1926.

The Bronze Age. New York: Macmillan, 1930.

"Is Prehistory Practical?" *Antiquity*, 7 (1933), 410–418.

"Races People and Cultures in Prehistoric Europe." *History*, 18 (1933), 193–203.

What Happened in History. Harmondsworth: Penguin, 1942.

Clark, W.E. Le Gros. "Scope and Limitations of Physical Anthropology." Presidential Address to Section H (Anthropology) of the British Association, Dundee, September 1939. *Nature*, 144 (1939), 804–807.

"Keith, Sir Arthur." *Dictionary of National Biography* (1951–1960), pp. 565–566.

Clark, Ronald. *The Life and Work of J.B.S. Haldane*. London: Northumberland Press, 1968.

Cobb, M.W. "The Physical Constitution of the American Negro." *Journal of Negro Education*, 31 (1934), 340–385.

Cole, F.C. "The Concept of Race in the Light of Franz Boas' Studies of Head Forms Among Immigrants," in Stuart A. Rice (ed.), *Methods in Social Science*. Chicago: Chicago University Press, 1931, pp. 582–585.

Congrès International des Sciences Anthropologiques et Ethnologiques. *Compte-rendu de la première Session, Londres.* Londres: Institut Royal d'Anthropologie, 1934.

Compte-rendu de la deuxième Session, Copenhague 1938. Copenhague: Einmar Munksgaard, 1939.

Conklin, E.G. *Heredity and Environment.* Princeton: Princeton University Press, 1922.

Cook, Paul B. *Academicians in Government. From Roosevelt to Roosevelt.* New York: Garland Publishing, 1982.

Coon, Carlton Stevens. *The Races of Europe.* New York: Macmillan, 1939. *The Origins of Races.* London: Jonathan Cape, 1963.

Count, Earl W., ed. *This Is Race. An Anthology Selected From the International Literature on Races of Man.* New York: Schuman, 1950.

Cravens, Hamilton. *The Triumph of Evolution. American Scientists and the Heredity–Environment Controversy, 1900–1941.* Philadelphia; University of Pennsylvania Press, 1978.

Crew, F.A.E. "Reginald Crundall Punnett." *Dictionary of Scientific Biography.* New York: Scribner's, 1975, XI, 211–212.

Daniel, Glyn. "Elliot Smith, Egypt and Diffusionism," in Zuckerman (ed.), *The Concepts of Human Evolution.*

Darnell, Regna. "The Professionalization of American Anthropology." *Social Science Information,* 10 (1971), 83–103.

Dart, R.A. "A Tribute to Reginald Ruggles Gates 1882–1962." Reprint. *The Mankind Quarterly,* 7, 1 (1966).

Davenport, Charles B. *Heredity in Relation to Eugenics.* New York: Henry Holt and Co, 1911. Arno Press and the New York Times reprint edition, 1972.

"Euthenics and Eugenics." *The Popular Science Monthly,* 78, 2 (1911), 16.

"Heredity, Culpability, Praiseworthiness, Punishment and Reward." *Heredity,* 83, 3 (1913), 33–39.

"The Effect of Race Intermingling." *Proceedings of the American Philosophical Society,* 65 (1917), 364–368.

"On Utilizing the Facts of Juvenile Promise and Family History in Awarding Naval Commissions to Untried Men." *Proceeding of the National Academy of Sciences,* 3 (1917), 404–409.

"Research In Eugenics." *Science,* 54 (October 28, 1921), 397.

"Measurement of Men." Read before American Association for the Advancement of Science, Section H (Anthropology), Dec. 29, 1926. *American Journal of Physical Anthropology,* 10, 1 (1926), 68.

"The Skin Colors of the Races of Mankind." *Natural History,* 26, 1 (1926), 44–49.

"Dr. Storr's Facial Type of the Feebleminded." *Journal of Mental Deficiency,* 68, 4 (April 1944), 339–343.

Davenport, Charles B., and Allen, G. "Family Studies on Mongoloid Dwarfs." Address at the 49th Annual Session of the American

Association for the Study of Feeble Minded, *Journal of Psycho-Asthenics*, 29 (1925).

Davenport, Charles B., and Steggerda, M. *Race Crossing in Jamaica.* Washington, DC: Carnegie Institution of Washington, 1929.

Dawson, Warren R., ed. *Sir Grafton Elliot Smith, A Biographical Record by His Colleagues.* London: Jonathan Cape, 1938.

Degler, Carl. "Slavery and the Genesis of American Race Prejudice." *Comparative Studies in Society and History*, 2 (October 1959), 49–66 (July 1960), 488–495.

Neither Black nor White. Slavery and Race Relations in Brazil and the United States. Wisconsin: The University of Wisconsin Press, 1986.

Deniker, J. *The Races of Man: An Outline of Anthropology and Ethnology.* London: Scott, 1900.

Dixon, Ronald B. *The Racial History of Man.* New York: Scribner's Sons, 1923.

"What is A Jew." *Nation*, February 21, 1923.

Dobzhansky, Theodosius. "Leslie Clearance Dunn." *Biographical Memoirs of the National Academy of Science*, 49 (1978) 79–104.

Dover, Cedric. "The Racial Myth." *Nature* 136 (November 1935), 736–737.

Dronamraju, K.R., ed. *Haldane and Modern Biology.* Baltimore: Johns Hopkins University Press, 1968.

Du Bois, Cora. *Lowie's Selected Papers in Anthropology.* Berkeley: University of California Press, 1960.

Dunn, Leslie C. "Some Results of Race Mixture in Hawaii." *Eugenics, Genetics and the Family*, 2 (1923), 109–124.

"An Anthropometric Study of Hawaiians of Pure and Mixed Blood." *Papers of the Peabody Museum, American Archaeology and Ethnology* (Cambridge: Harvard University), 11, 3 (1928), 89–211.

Race and Biology. Paris: Unesco, 1951.

A Short History of Genetics. New York: McGraw-Hill, 1965.

"William Ernest Castle, 1867–1962." *Biographical Memoirs of the National Academy of Sciences*, 38 (1965), 43–44.

Dunn, Leslie C. and Dobzhansky, Theodosius. *Heredity Race, and Society.* New York: New American Library, 1946; fourth edn 1972.

Dupree, A. Hunter. *Asa Gray.* Cambridge, MA: Harvard University Press, 1959.

Durkheim, Emile. *The Division of Labor in Society.* 1893. Introduction by Lewis Coser, translated by W.D. Halls. New York: The Free Press, 1984.

The Rules of Sociological Method. 1895. Translated by W.D. Halls, edited with introduction by Steven Lukes. New York: Free Press, 1982.

East, Edward. "Population." *Scientific Monthly*, 10 (1920), 603–624.

Mankind at the Crossroad. New York: Charles Scribner's Sons, 1923.

"Civilization at the Crossways." *Birth Control Review*, 7 (1923), 328–332.

Heredity and Human Affairs. New York: Charles Scribner's and Sons, 1929.

Biology in Human Affairs. New York: McGraw-Hill and Co., 1931.

Elkin, A.P., and Macintosh, A.W.G., ed. *Grafton Elliot Smith. The Man and His Work.* Sydney: Sydney University Press.

Evans-Pritchard, Edward. *The Nuer. A Description of the Modes of Individual and Political Institutions of a Nilotic People.* Oxford: Clarendon Press, 1940; Oxford University Press, 1971.

A History of Anthropological Thought. London: Farber and Farber, 1981.

Evans-Pritchard, Edward, Firth, Raymond, Malinowski, Bronislaw, and Isaac Schapera. *Essays Presented to C.G. Seligman.* London: Kegan Paul, 1934.

Farrall, Lyndsay A. "Controversy and Conflict in Science: A Case Study – The English Biometric School and Mendel's Laws." *Social Studies of Science,* 5 (1975), 269–301.

Firth, Raymond. *Human Types.* London: Nelson and Sons, 1938.

"Bronislaw Malinowski" in Sydel Silverman (ed.), *Totems and Teachers; Perspectives in the History of Anthropology.* New York: Columbia University Press, 1981.

Firth, Raymond, ed. *Man and Culture: An Evaluation of the Work of Bronislaw Malinowski.* London: Routledge & Kegan Paul, 1957.

"Seligman's Contributions to Oceanic Anthropology." *Oceania,* 45, 4 (June 1975), 272–282.

Fisher, Ronald A. "Some Hopes of A Eugenist." Read before the Eugenics Education Society, October 2nd, 1913. *Eugenics Review,* 5 (1914), 309–315. In *RAFCP,* I, p. 80.

"Positive Eugenics.". *Eugenics Review,* 9 (1917), 206–212. In *RAFCP,* I, p. 131.

"The Causes of Human Variability." *Eugenics Review,* 10 (1918), 213–220, In *RAFCP,* I, p. 176.

"The Correlation Between Relations on the Supposition of Mendelian Inheritance." *Transactions of the Royal Society of Edinburgh,* 52 (1918), 339–433.

"The Biological Effects of Family Allowances." In *RAFCP,* II, pp. 554–58. [See Bennett, J.H.]

"The Renaissance of Darwinism." *RAFCP,* IV, pp. 616–620.

"Review of *Inbreeding and Outbreeding* by E.M. East and D.F. Jones." *Eugenics Review,* 12 (1920), 116–119. In *RAFCP,* I, pp. 202–204.

"Contribution to a Discussion on the Inheritance of Mental Qualities Good and Bad." *Eugenics Review,* 14 (1922), 210–213, In *RAFCP,* I, pp. 452–454.

"The Evolution of Conscience in Civilised Communities (In special relation to Sexual Vices)." Paper read at the International Eugenics Congress 1921. In *Eugenics Review,* 14 (1922), 190–192, In *RAFCP,* I, p. 448.

"The Elimination of Mental Defect." *Eugenics Review,* 16 (1924), 114–116.

"Eugenics: Can It Solve the Problem of Decay of Civilizations?" *Eugenics Review*, 18 (1926), 128–136. In *RAFCP*, II, p. 113

"Modern Eugenics – Being A Review of *The Need For Eugenics Reform* by Leonard Darwin." *Science Progress*, 21 (1926), 130–136. In *RAFCP*, II, p. 122.

"Biometry and Evolution." *Nature*, 126 (August 16, 1930), 246–247.

"Family Allowances – In the Contemporary Economic Situation." *Eugenics Review*, 24 (1932), 87–95. In *RAFCP*, II, p. 74.

The Social Selection of Human fertility. The Herbert Spencer Lecture. Oxford: Clarendon Press, 1932. In *RAFCP*, II, p. 66.

"The Coefficient of Racial Likeness' and the Future of Craniometry." *JRAI*, 66 (1936), 57–63.

Fisher, Ronald A., and Taylor G.A. "Scandinavian Influence in Scottish Ethnology." *Nature*, 145 (1940), 590. In *RAFCP*, IV, pp. 319–321.

Fleming, R.M. "Anthropological Studies of Children." *Eugenics Review*, 18 (1926), 294–301.

"Human Hybrids: racial crosses in various parts of the world." *Eugenics Review*, 21, 4 (1930), 257–263.

"Physical Heredity in Human Hybrids." *Annals of Eugenics*, 9, 1 (1939), 55–81.

Fletcher, M.E. *Report on an Investigation into the Colour Problem in Liverpool and Other Ports.* With a Foreword by Prof. P.M. Roxby. Liverpool: The Liverpool Association for the Welfare of Half-Caste Children, 1930.

Fleure, Herbert John. "On the Artistic Side of Science." *The Dragon*, 27 (1905). Reprint.

The Treaty Settlement of Europe. London: Oxford University Press, 1921.

"Review of Dixon's *The Racial History of Man.*" *Man*, 23, 87 (September 1923), 142.

The Races of England and Wales: A Survey of Recent Research. London: Benn Brothers, 1923.

"The Regional Balance of Racial Evolution." *Address Section H. British Association for the Advancement of Science*, Oxford, Pamphlet, 1926.

The Races of Mankind. New York: Doubleday, Drogan, 1928.

"The Nordic Myth: A Critic of Current Racial Theories." *Eugenics Review*, 22 (1930), 117–121.

"Racial Distribution in the Light of Archaeology." Reprint. *The Bulletin of the John Rylands Library* 17, 2 (1933).

"Racial Evolution and Archaeology," Huxley Memorial Lecture. *JRAI* 67 (1937). Reprint.

"Race and Its Meaning in Europe.". Reprint. *The Bulletin of the John Rylands Library*, 24, 2 (1940).

"Alfred Cort Haddon. 1855–1940." *Obituary Notices of the Royal Society*, (1940), 449–465.

"The English Heritage: Its Study and Demonstration." *Man*, 55 (August 1955), 120.

Fortes, Meyer, "Charles Gabriel Seligman, 1873–1940." *Man*, 41 (1941), 1–6.

"Seligman, C.G." *International Encyclopedia of the Social Sciences*. New York: Crowell Collier and Macmillan, 1968.

Foucault, Michael. *Power/Knowledge: Selected Interviews and Other Writings 1972–1977*. Edited by Colin Gordon. New York: Pantheon Books, 1980.

Fraser Roberts, J.A. "Reginald Ruggles Gates 1882–1962." *Biographical Memoirs of the Royal Society*, 10 (1964), 82–106.

Fredrickson, G.M. *The Black Image in the White Mind: The Debate on Afro-American Character and Destiny, 1817–1914*. New York: Harper & Row, 1971.

Freed, Stanley A., and Freed, Ruth S. "Clark Wissler and the Development of Anthropology in the United States." *American Anthropologist*, 85 (1983), 800–825.

Friedman, John Block. *The Monstrous Races in Medieval Art and Thought*. Cambridge, MA: Harvard University Press, 1981.

Froggart, P. and Nevin, N.C. "The 'Law of Ancestral Heredity' and the Mendelian Ancestrian Controversy in England, 1889–1906." *Journal of Medical Genetics*, 8 (1971), 1–36.

"The 'Law of Ancestral Heredity': Its Influence on the Early Development of Human Genetics." *History of Science*, 10 (1971), 1–27.

Fryer, Peter. *Staying Power. The History of Black People in Britain*. London: Pluto, 1984.

Garnett, A. "Herbert John Fleure." *Biographical Memoirs of the Royal Society*, 16 (1970), 253–278.

Gasman, David. *The Scientific Origins of National Socialism: Social Darwinism and the German Monist League*. New York: American Elsevier, 1971.

Gates, Ruggles R. *Heredity and Eugenics*. London: Constable, 1923.

"Mendelian Heredity and Racial differences." *JRAI*, 55 (1925), 468–482.

"A Pedigree Study of Amerindian Crosses in Canada." *JRAI*, 58 (1928), 511–532.

Heredity in Man. 1928; New York: Macmillan, 1931.

"Genetics and Race." *Man*, 37 (1937): 28–38.

"The Species Concept in the Light of Cytology and Genetics." *American Naturalist*, 72 (1938), 340–349.

"Inheritance of Racial and Sub-Racial Traits." Rome Congress 1961, vol 1. of Proceedings of the Second International Congress of Human Genetics. Rome: Institute G. Mendel, 1963, p. 369.

"Geneticists' Manifesto at the International Congress of Genetics in Edinburgh." *Journal of Heredity*, 30 (1939), 371–374.

Gilson, John C. "Geoffrey Mackay Morant." *Dictionary of National Biography 1960–1970*.

Gobineau, Arthur de. *The Inequality of Human Races.* 1853. New York: Howard Fertig, 1967.

Goddard, Henry H. *Feeble-mindeness: Its Causes and Consequences.* New York: Macmillan, 1914; Arno Press, 1973.

Goldschmidt, Walter, ed. *The Anthropology of Franz Boas.* American Anthropological Association, 62, 5 (1959), Pt. 2, Memoir 89.

Goldschmidt, Walter, ed. *The Uses of Anthropology.* American Anthropological Association, special publication No. 11. Washington: American Anthropological Association, 1979.

Gossett, Thomas F. *Race, The History of an Idea in America.* New York: Schocken Books, 1963, 1965.

Gould, Stephen J. *Ontogeny and Phylogeny*, Cambridge MA: Belknap Press of Harvard University Press, 1977.

The Panda's Thumb. New York: W.W. Norton, 1980.

The Mismeasure of Man. New York: W.W. Norton, 1982.

Grant, Madison. *The Passing of the Great Race: Or the Racial History of European History.* New York: Scribner's, 1916.

Green, Sally. *Prehistorian: A Biography of V. Gordon Childe.* Bradford-on-Avon: Moonraker Press, 1981.

Greenwood, Davydd J. *The Taming of Evolution. The Persistence of Non-Evolutionary Views in the Study of Humans.* Ithaca: Cornell University Press, 1984.

Haddon, Alfred C. "The Ethnography of British New Guinea." *Science Progress*, 2, 8 (October 1894), 82–95; 2, 9 (October 1894), 226–248.

The Study of Man. New York: G.P. Putnam's Sons, 1898.

Head Hunters. Black, White, and Brown. London: Methuen and Co., 1901.

The Races of Man and Their Distribution. London: Milner & Company, 1909. 2nd edn. New York: Macmillan and Co. 1925.

Environment and Cultural Progress Among Primitive Peoples. Pamphlet. The Herbertson Memorial Lecture, London, October 26, 1927.

"Appreciation of C.G. Seligman." In *Essays in Honour of C.G. Seligman,* edited by Evans Pritchard et al. 1934.

Haddon, Alfred C., ed. *Reports of the Cambridge Anthropological Expedition to the Torres Straits,* 6 vols. Cambridge: Cambridge University Press, 1901–1935.

Haldane, J.B.S. *Daedalus or Science and the Future.* New York: E.P. Dutton, 1924.

Possible Worlds and Other Papers. New York and London: Harper & Brothers, 1928.

Science and Human Life. New York and London: Harper & Brothers, 1933.

"Anthropology and Human Biology." Congrès International des Sciences Anthropologiques et Ethnologiques. *Compte-rendu de la première Session, Londres.* Londres: Institut Royal d'Anthropologie, 1934, pp. 53–64.

"A Day in the Life of A Magician." In *My Friend, Mr Leakey*. London: Cresset Press, 1937.

Heredity and Politics. New York: W.W. Norton, 1938.

The Marxist Philosophy and the Sciences. London: Allen and Unwin, 1938.

Haller, Mark H. *Eugenics, Hereditarian Attitudes in American Thought*. 1963; New Brunswick: Rutgers University Press, 1984.

Halliday, R.J. "Social Darwinism: A Definition." *Victorian Studies*, 14 (1970–71), 389–405.

Hammond, Dorothy, and Jablow, Alta. *The Africa That Never Was: Four Centuries of British Writing About Africa*. New York: Twayne Publishers, 1970.

Harnad, Steven. "Montagu, Ashley." *International Encyclopedia of the Social Sciences. Biographical Supplement*, 18 (1979), 536.

Harris, Harry. "Lionel Sharples Penrose." *Biographical Memoirs of Fellows of the Royal Society* 19 (1973): 521–561.

Harris, Jose. *William Beveridge: A Biography*. Oxford: Clarendon Press, 1977.

Harris, Marvin. *Patterns of Race in The Americas*. New York: Walker and Company, 1964.

The Rise of Anthropological Theory: A History of Theories of Culture. New York: Thomas Y. Crowell, 1968.

Hassenchal, Frances J. *Harry H. Laughlin, "Expert Eugenics Agent" for the U.S. House of Representatives Committee on Immigration and Naturalization, 1921 to 1931*. Ann Arbor: University Microfilm, 1971.

Henderson L.J. "Raymond Pearl." *American Philosophical Society Yearbook*, 1940.

Herder, Johann. *Outlines of a Philosophy of the History of Man*. trans. T. Churchill. Riga, 1784; London, J. Johnson, 1803.

Herrnstein, Richard J. and Wilson, J.Q. *Crime and Human Nature*. New York: Simon and Schuster, 1985.

Herskovits, Melville J. *American Negro. A Study in Racial Crossing*. New York: Knopf, 1928.

The Anthropometry of the American Negro. New York: Columbia University Press, 1930.

"The New World Negro as an Anthropological Problem." Summary of a communication presented 3rd February 1931, *Man*, 31 (1931).

"Charles Gabriel Seligman." *American Anthropologist*, 43 (1941), 437–439.

The Myth of the Negro Past. New York: Harper & Brothers, 1941.

Man and His Works. The Science of Cultural Anthropology. New York: Alfred Knopf, 1949.

Franz Boas: The Science of Man in the Making. New York: Scribner's, 1953.

"Freudian Mechanism in Primitive Negro Psychology," E.E. Evans-Pritchard *et al.* (eds.), in *Essays presented to C.G. Seligman*.

"Franz Boas as Physical Anthropologist." American Anthropological Association, *Franz Boas, 1858–1942*, pp. 39–51.

Herskovits, Melville J. and Willey, M.M. "A Note on the psychology of Servitude." *Journal of Social Forces*, 1 (1923), 228–234.

"Psychology and Culture." *Psychological Bulletin*, 24 (1927), 253–283.

Higham, John. *Strangers in the Land: Patterns of American Nativism, 1860–1925.* New Brunswick, NJ: Rutgers University Press, 1955.

Hirschfeld, Magnus. *Racism.* Translated and edited by Eden and Cedar Paul. London: Victor Gollancz, 1938. Reissued Port Washington, NY: Kennikat Press, 1973.

Hofstadter, Richard. *Social Darwinism in American Thought, 1860–1915.* Philadelphia: University of Pennsylvania Press, 1944.

Hogben, Lancelot. "The Concept of Race." In *Genetic Principles in Medicine and Social Sciences*, by L. Hogben, pp. 122–144.

Genetic Principles in Medicine and Social Sciences. London: Wiliams & Norgate, 1931.

Nature and Nurture. New York: W.W. Norton, 1933.

Retreat From Reason. New York: Random House, 1937.

Dangerous Thoughts. London: George Allen & Unwin, 1939.

Hooton, Earnest Albert. "Race Mixture in the United States." *Pacific Review*, 2 (1921), 116–127.

"Methods of Racial Analysis." *Science*, 63, 1,621 (1926), 75–81.

"Progress in the Study of Race Mixtures with Special Reference to Work Carried on at Harvard University." *Proceedings of the American Philosophical Society*, 65 (1926), 312–325.

"Radcliffe Investigates Race Mixture." *Harvard Alumni Bulletin*, April 3, 1930, Reprint.

Up from the Ape. New York: Allen and Unwin, 1931. Revised edn Macmillan, 1949.

"Preliminary Remarks on the Anthropology of the American criminal." *Proceedings of the American Philosophical Society*, 71, 6 (1932), 349–355.

"Plain Statement About Race." *Science*, 83, 2,161 (1936), 511–513.

"What is an American?" Reprint. *American Journal of Physical Anthropology* (1936).

Apes, Men, and Morons. New York: G.P. Putnam's Sons, 1937.

American Criminal. Cambridge: Harvard University Press, 1939.

Twilight of Man. New York: G.P. Putnam's Sons, 1939.

Crime and the Man. Cambridge: Harvard University Press, 1939.

"Why the Jews Grow Stronger." *Collier*, May 6, 1939.

Howard, Jane. *Margaret Mead, A Life.* New York: Simon and Schuster, 1984.

Howells, W.W. "Boas as Statistician," in Goldschmidt (ed.), *The Anthropology of Franz Boas*, pp. 112–116.

Hrdlicka, Ales. *Old Americans.* Baltimore: Williams and Wilkins, 1925.

"Human Races," in E.V. Cowdry (ed.), *Human Biology and Racial Welfare.*

Huizer, Gerrit, and Mannheim, Bruce, eds. *The Politics of Anthropology. From*

Colonialism and Sexism Toward a View from Below. Paris: Mouton Publishers, 1979.

Hutchinson, E.P. *Legislative History of American Immigration Policy. 1798–1965.* Philadelphia; University of Pennsylvania Press,,1981.

Huxley, Julian Sorel. "The Negro Minds." Typescript, 1918. JSHP, Box 58:6.

"Eugenics and Eugenists." *The Athenaeum,* Dec. 1920, 895. JSHP.

"America Revisited. III. The Negro Problem." *The Spectator,* November 29, 1924, 821.

"America Revisited. V. 'The Quota'." *The Spectator,* December 20, 1924, 980–982.

"Nature and Nurture." *The New Leader,* February 29, 1924. JSHP.

"Norman Lockyer Lecture." November 23, 1926, British Science Guild, in *Nature* (Dec 1926), 884–5.

"Eugenics and Heredity." Letter to the Editor, *The New Statesman.* 1924. Reprint in JSHP.

Essays in Popular Science. New York: Knopf, 1927.

"The Influence of Heredity." *The Times,* April 2, 1930. JSHP.

"The Problem of the Unfit." Letter to the Editor" *The Times,* September 26, 1930. JSHP.

Africa View. New York: Harper & Brothers, 1931.

"The Vital Importance of Eugenics – Letter to the Editor." *Harpers Monthly,* 163 (1931) , 325. JSHP.

"Why Is The White Man In Africa?" *Fortnightly Review* (January 1932), 65.

Man Stands Alone. New York: Harper & Brothers, 1940.

Evolution, The Modern Synthesis. London: Allen & Unwin, 1942.

Memories. 2 vols. London: Allen and Unwin, 1970–1973.

Huxley, Julian Sorel and Haddon, Alfred C. *We Europeans, A Survey of 'Racial' Problems, With a Chapter on Europe Overseas by A.M. Carr-Saunders.* London: Jonathan Cape, 1935.

Huxley, T.H. "Ethics and Evolution" (1893), in *Evolution and Ethics and Other Essays* (London: Macmillan, 1894), 1–45.

Jennings, Herbert S. "On the Advantages of Growing Old." *Johns Hopkins Alumni Magazine,* 10, 4 (1922) 241–251.

"Undesirable Aliens." *The Survey,* 51 (December 15, 1923), 309–312, 364.

"The Relative Number of European-Born Defectives from the Chief Sources of European Migration and the Effect of a Change in the Basis of Admission From the Census of 1910 to That of 1890." *Hearing before the Committee on Immigration and Naturalization, House of Representatives, 68th Congress, 1st Session, January 1924.* Washington, pp. 512–18.

"Proportions of defectives from the Northwest and from the Southeast of Europe," *Science,* 59 (March 14, 1924), 256–258.

Prometheus, or Biology and the Advancement of Man. London: Kegan Paul, 1925.

"Diverse Doctrines of Evolution, Their Relation to the Practice of Science and Life." *Science*, 65, 1,672 (1927), 19–26.

Genetics and The Results of Racial Intermingling and Intermarriage. Notes for lecture delivered to International Conference at Baltimore, December 1, 1928. 4pp. HSJP.

The Biological Basis of Human Nature. New York: W.W. Norton, 1930.

The Universe and Life. New Haven: Yale University Press, 1933.

Genetic Variations in Relation to Evolution. A Critical Inquiry into the Observed Types of Inherited Variation, in Relation to Evolutionary Change. Princeton: Princeton University Press, 1935.

Genetics. New York: W.W. Norton, 1935.

"The Inheritance of Acquired Characteristics." Pamphlet, Tozzer Library, Peabody Museum, Harvard University.

"Raymond Pearl." *National Academy of Sciences, Biographical Memoirs*, 22 (1943), 292–347.

Jennings, Herbert S. et al. *Scientific Aspects of The Race Problem*. Washington DC: The Catholic University of America Press, London: Longmans, Green and Co., 1941.

Jones, Greta. *Social Darwinism and English Thought: The Interaction Between Biological and Social Theory*. New Jersey: Humanities Press, 1980.

"Eugenics and Social Policy Between the Wars." *The Historical Journal*, 25 (1982), 717–728.

Keith, Sir Arthur. *Nationality and Race From an Anthropologist's Point of View*. Oxford: Humphrey Milford, Oxford University Press, 1919.

"The Evolution of the Human Races in Light of the Hormone Theory." Reprint. *The Johns Hopkins Hospital Bulletin*, 33 (1922), 196–201.

"Phrenological Studies of the Skull and Brain of Sir Thomas Browne of Norwich." *The Henderson Trust Lectures*, No. III, May 9, 1924. London: Oliver and Boyd, 1924.

"The Evolution of the Human Races." Huxley Memorial Lecture. *JRAI*, 58 (1928), 305–321.

Ethnos, or the Problem of Race. London: K. Paul, 1931.

An Autobiography. London: Watts & Co., 1950.

"The Evolution of Human Races, Past and Present," in G. Elliot Smith et al., *Early Man, His Origin, Development and Culture*.

Kevles, Daniel J. "Testing the Army's Intelligence: Psychology and the Military in World War I." *Journal of American History* 55 (1968): 565–581.

"Into Hostile Political Camps': The Reorganization of International Science in World War I," *Isis*, 62 (1971), 47–60.

The Physicists. New York: Vintage Books, 1971.

In The Name of Eugenics. Genetics and the Uses of Human Heredity. New York: Knopf, 1985.

Klineberg, Otto. "An Experimental Study of Speed and Other Factors in 'Racial' Differences." *Archives of Psychology*, 93 (Jan. 1928).

"A Study of Psychological Differences Between 'Racial' and National Groups in Europe." *Archives of Psychology*, edited by R. S. Woodworth, no. 132, New York, 1931.

Negro Intelligence and Selective Migration. 1935. Reprint Westport, Conn.: Greenwood Press, 1974.

Race Differences. New York: Harper & Brothers, 1935.

"32 Social Scientists Testify against Segregation." *UNESCO Courier*, 6 (1954), 24.

"Mental Testing of Racial and National Groups," in Herbert S. Jennings *et al.* (eds), *Scientific Aspects of The Race Problem*.

"Otto Klineberg," in *A History of Psychology in Autobiography*, 6 (1974), 163–182.

"Tests of Negro Intelligence," in Otto Klineberg (ed.) *Characteristics of the American Negro*, pp. 23–96.

Klineberg, Otto, ed. *Characteristics of the American Negro*. New York: Harpers, 1944.

Kluckhohn, Clyde K. *Ruth Fulton Benedict. A Memorial*. New York: Viking Fund, 1949.

"Earnest Albert Hooton." Reprint. *Year Book of the American Philosophical Society*, (1955), 418–422.

Kroeber, Alfred L. "The Morals of the Uncivilized People." *American Anthropologist*, 12, 3 (1910), 437–447.

"Inheritance by Magic." Reprint. *American Anthropologist*, 18, 1 (1916).

"The Superorganic." *American Anthropologist*, 19 (1917), 163–213. Reprinted in Kroeber, *The Nature of Culture*.

"Heredity, Environment and Civilization." *American Museum Journal*, 18 (1918), 351–359.

"Observations on the Anthropology of Hawaii." *American Anthropologist*, 23, 2 (1921), 129–137.

Anthropology. New York: Harcourt Brace and Jovanovich, 1923.

"The So-Called Social Science." *Journal of Social Philosophy*, 1 (1936), 317–340.

"Structure, Function and Pattern in Biology and Anthropology." *The Scientific Monthly*, 56, 2 (1943), 105–113.

The Nature of Culture. Chicago: The University of Chicago Press, 1952.

"The Place of Boas in Anthropology." *American Anthropologist*, 58 (1956), 151–159.

Kroeber, Alfred L. *et al.* "Franz Boas. 1858–1942." *American Anthropologist*, 45 (1943), memoir no. 61. Menasha, Wisconsin: American Anthropological Association.

Kroeber, Theodora. *Alfred Kroeber: A Personal Configuration*. Berkeley, CA: University of California Press, 1970.

Krogman, W. M. "Fifty Years of Physical Anthropology: The Men, The Material, The Concepts, The Methods." *Annual Review of Anthropology*, 5 (1976), 1–14.

Kuhn, Thomas. *The Structure of Scientific Revolutions.* 2nd edn. Chicago: Chicago University Press, 1970.

Kuklik, Henrika. "The Sins of the Fathers: British Anthropology and African Colonial Administration." *Res. Soc. Knowl. Art.*, 1 (1978), 919–933.

———— "Tribal Exemplars: Images of Political Authority in British Anthropology, 1885–1945," in George W. Stocking (ed.), *Functionalism Historicized*, pp. 59–82.

Kuper, Adam, ed. *The Social Anthropology of Radcliffe Brown.* London: Routledge & Kegan Paul, 1977.

Kuper, Hilda. "Function, History, Biography: Reflections on Fifty Years in the British Anthropological Tradition," in George W. Stocking (ed.), *Functionalism Historicized*, pp. 192–213.

Kuper, L. "Political Change in Plural Societies: Problems of Racial Pluralism." *International Social Science Journal*, 23 (1971).

Kuttner, Robert E., ed. *Race and Modern Science.* New York: Social Science Press, 1967.

Kuznick, Peter J. *Beyond the Laboratory: Scientists as Political Activists on 1930s America.* Chicago: Chicago University Press, 1987.

Lander, Joyce, ed. *The Death of White Sociology.* New York: Vintage Books, 1973.

Langham, Ian. *The Building of British Social Anthropology: W. H. R. Rivers and His Cambridge Disciples in the Development of Kinship Studies, 1898–1931.* Dordrecht: Reidel, 1981.

Leach, E. R. "The Epistemological Background to Malinowski's Empiricism," in Raymond Firth (ed.), *Man and Culture.*

LeFanu, W. "Keith, Arthur." *Dictionary of Scientific Biography.* New York: Scribner's, 1970–1980, VIII, pp. 278–279.

Lesser, Alexander. "Franz Boas," in Sydel Silverman (ed.), *Totems and Teachers*, pp. 1–31.

Lieberman, Leonard. "The Debate Over Race: A Study in the Sociology of Knowledge." *Phylon*, 29, 2 (1968), 127–141.

Lieberman, Leonard, and Reynolds, Larry T. "The Debate Over Race Revisited: An Empirical Investigation." *Phylon*, 39, 4 (December 1978).

Lipset, Seymour Martin, and Reisman, David. *Education and Politics at Harvard.* New York: McGraw-Hill, 1975.

Little, K. L. *Negroes in Britain. A Study of Racial Relations in English Society.* London: Kegan Paul, Trench, Trubner, 1948.

Locke, A. ed. *The New Negro: An Interpretation*, New York: A and C Boni, 1925.

Lorimer, Frank, and Osborn, Frederick. *Dynamics of Population. Social and Biological Significance of Changing Birth Rates in the United States.* New York: Macmillan, 1934.

Lowie, Robert H. "Psychology, Anthropology and Race." *American Anthropologist*, 25 (1923), 291–303.

"Evolution in Cultural Anthropology: A Reply to Leslie White." *American Anthropologist*, 47 (1946), 223–233.

"Professor White and 'Anti-evolutionist' Schools." *Southwestern Journal of Anthropology*, 2 (1946), 240 241.

"Franz Boas." *Biographical Memoirs of the National Academy of Science*, 24 (1947), 303–322.

Social Organization. New York: Rinehart, 1948.

Ethnologist: A Personal Record. Berkeley, CA: University of California Press, 1959.

Ludmerer, Kenneth M. *Genetics and the American Society. A Historical Appraisal*. Baltimore: Johns Hopkins University Press, 1972.

McDougall, William. *Is America Safe For Democracy?* New York: Scribner's, 1921.

MacDowell, E. Carleton. "Charles Benedict Davenport, 1866–1944: A Study of Conflicting Influences". *Bios*, 17 (1946), 3–50.

MacKenzie, Donald A. "Eugenics in Britain." *Social Studies of Science*, 6 (1976), 499–532.

Statistics in Britain, 1865–1930. The Social Construction of Scientific Knowledge. Edinburgh: Edinburgh University Press, 1981.

McNairn, B. *The Method and Theory of V. Gordon Childe: Economic Social and Cultural Interpretations of Prehistory*. Edinburgh: Edinburgh University Press, 1980.

Malinowski, Bronislaw. *Argonauts of the Western Pacific*. New York: Dutton, 1922.

Crime and Custom in Savage Society. London: Kegan Paul, 1926.

Sex and Repression in Savage Society. New York: Harcourt, Brace & Company, 1927.

The Sexual Life of Savages in North Western Melanesia. London: Routledge, 1929.

Coral Gardens and their Magic. 2 vols. London: Allen & Unwin, 1935.

The Scientific Theory of Culture. Chapel Hill: University of North Carolina Press, 1944.

The Dynamics of Cultural Change. An Inquiry into Race Relations in Africa. Edited, with a new introduction by Phyllis M. Kaberry. New Haven: Yale University Press, 1945.

Magic, Science and Religion and Other Essays. Selected, with an introduction by Raymond Firth. Boston: Beacon Press, 1948.

A Diary in the Strict Sense of the Term. New York: Harcourt, 1967.

Manning, Kenneth R. *Black Apollo of Science. The Life of Ernest Everett Just*. New York: Oxford University Press, 1983.

Marett, Robert Ranulph. *The Diffusion of Culture*. The Frazer Lecture in Social Anthropology. Cambridge: Cambridge University Press, 1927.

Man in the Making. An Introduction to Anthropology. London: Ernst Benn, 1927.

Head, Heart & Hands in Human Evolution. London: Hutchinson's Scientific Books, 1935.

"Charity and the Struggle for Existence." The Huxley Memorial Lecture for 1939. *JRAI*, 69 (1939), 137–149.

A Jerseyman at Oxford. London: Oxford University Press, 1941.

"The Growth and Tendency of Anthropological and Ethnological Studies," in *Congrès International de Sciences Anthropologiques et Ethnologiques*, pp. 39–53.

Mather, Kenneth. "Review of Penrose's Outline of Human Genetics." *Heredity*, 14, 1&2 (February 1960), 215–216.

May, Roy and Cohen, Robin. "The Interaction Between Race and Colonialism: A Case Study of the Liverpool Race Riots of 1919." *Race and Class*, 16 (1974–5).

Maynard Smith, J. "John Burdon Sanderson Haldane." *Dictionary of National Biography*, 1961–1970.

Mayr, Ernst. *The Growth of Biological Thought. Diversity, Evolution and Inheritance.* Cambridge, MA: Harvard University Press, 1982.

Mayr, Ernst and Provine, William B., eds. *The Evolutionary Synthesis: Perspectives on the Unification of Biology.* Cambridge: Harvard University Press, 1980.

Mead, Margaret. *Coming of Age in Samoa. A Psychological Study of Primitive Youth for Western Civilisation.* New York: William Morrow, 1927.

Growing Up in New Guinea. A Comparative Study of Primitive Education. New York: William Morrow, 1930.

An Anthropologist at Work. Writings of Ruth Benedict. Boston: Houghton Mifflin Company, 1959.

"Apprenticeship Under Boas," in Walter Goldschmidt (ed.), *The Anthropology of Franz Boas*, pp. 29–45.

Blackberry Winter. My Early Years. New York: William Morrow, 1972.

Ruth Benedict. New York: Columbia University Press, 1974.

Letters From the Field 1925–1975. New York: Harper & Row, 1977.

Mead, Margaret, ed. *Cooperation and Competition Among Primitive Peoples.* New York: McGraw-Hill, 1937. Revised edition Boston: Beacon Press, 1961.

Mehler, Barry A. "The New Eugenics: Academic Racism in the US Today." *Sage*, 9, 4 (1984), 13–23.

A History of the American Eugenics' Society, 1921–1940, Ph.D. dissertation, University of Illinois, Urbana-Champaign, 1988.

Merriam, Alan. "Herskovits – Obituary." *American Anthropologist*, 66 (1964), 83–109.

Merton, Robert K. "The Perspective of Insiders and Outsiders," in *The Sociology of Science.* Chicago: Chicago University Press, 1973.

Métraux, A. "Unesco and the Racial Problem," *International Social Science Bulletin*, 2 (1950), 384–390.

Miller, Roland. *The Piltdown Men.* London: Gollanz, 1972.

Modell, Judith Schachter. *Ruth Benedict, Pattern of a Life*. Philadelphia: University of Pennsylvania Press, 1983.

Montagu, Ashley M. F. *Man's Most Dangerous Myth: The Fallacy of Race*. With a foreword by Aldous Huxley. New York: Columbia University Press, 1942. Fifth edn, New York: Oxford University Press, 1974.

Statement on Race. Third edn, London: Oxford University Press, 1972.

Montagu, Ashley M. F., ed. *Race and IQ*. New York: Oxford University Press, 1975.

Morant, Geoffrey Mackay. "A Contribution to the Physical Anthropology of the Swat and Hunza Valleys Based on Records Collected by Sir Aurel Stein." *JRAI*, 66 (1936), 19–42.

"Biometrician's View of Race in Man." In *Race and Culture*, Royal Anthropological Institute.

"Racial Theories and International Relations." *JRAI*, 69 (1939), 151–162.

The Races of Central Europe. London: Allen and Unwin, 1939.

Morant, Geoffrey Mackay and Samson, Otto. "An Examination of Investigations By Dr. Maurice Fishberg and Professor Franz Boas Dealing with Measurements of Jews in New York." *Biometrika*, 28 (1936), 1–31.

Morant, Geoffrey Mackay, Tildesley, M. L., and Dudley Buxton, L. H. "The International Committee for Standardization of the Technique of Physical Anthropology – A General Statement of Aims and Methods." *Man*, 34, 109 (June 1934), 83–86.

Murphy, Robert F. *Robert H. Lowie*. New York: Columbia University Press, 1972.

Myrdal, Gunnar. *An 'American Dilemma.' The Negro Problem and Modern Democracy*. 2 vols. New York: Harper & Brothers, 1944.

Myres, John Linton. "The Influence of Anthropology on the Course of Political Science." *Nature*, 81 (1909), 379–84.

The Influence of Politics on the Course of Political Science. Berkeley: University of California Press, 1916.

"Correlation of Mental and Physical Characteristics in Man: Being a summary of the opening address in a discussion which took place in Section H, at the meeting of the British Association at Hull in September, 1922." *JRAI*, 23 (1923), 116–9.

Norton, Bernard J. "The Biometric Defense of Darwinsim." *Journal of the History of Biology*, 6 (1973), 283–316.

"Biology and Philosophy: The Methodological Foundations of Biometry." *Journal of the History of Biology*, 8 (1975), 85–93.

"Karl Pearson and Statistics: The Social Origins of Scientific Innovation." *Social Studies of Science*, 8 (1978), 3–34.

Osborn, Frederick. *Preface to Eugenics*. 1940. Rev. edn, New York: Harper & Brothers, 1951.

Osborn, Frederick and Bajema, Carl Jay. "The Eugenics Hypothesis," in

Carl Jay Bajema (ed.), *Eugenics Then and Now*. Stroudsburg, PA. 1976, pp. 283–291.

Paul, Diane. "Eugenics and the Left." *Journal of the History of Ideas*, 45 (1984), 567–590.

"The 'Real Menace' of the Feebleminded: Scientists and Sterilization, 1917–1930." Typescript.

Peake, Harold. "The Study of Prehistoric Times." The Huxley Memorial Lecture for 1940, *JRAI*, 70 (1940).

Pearl, Raymond. "Breeding Better Men." *World's Work*, 15 (1908), 9824.

"The Influence of Alcohol on Duration of Life." *Proceedings of the National Academy of Sciences*, 10, 6 (1924), 231–237.

"The Racial Effect of Alcohol." Reprint. *Eugenics Review*, April 1924.

"The Biology of Superiority." *American Mercury*, 12 (November 1927), 257–266.

"The Weight of the Negro Brain." *Science*, 80 (1934), 431–434.

"On Biological Principles Affecting Populations: Humans and Others." *American Naturalist*, 71, 732 (1937), 50–68.

Pearson, Karl. *The Grammar of Science*. London: Scott, 1892.

"On the Inheritance of the Mental and Moral Characters in Man, and Its Comparison With the Inheritance of the Physical Characters." *JRAI*, 33 (1903), 179–237.

"The Science of Man: Its Needs and Prospects." Reprint. *The Smithsonian Report 1921*, pp. 423–441.

"The Problems of Anthropology." *Scientific Monthly*, 2 (1929), 451–458.

"On a New Theory of Progressive Evolution." *Annals of Eugenics*, 4 (1930), 1–40.

"On Jewish-Gentile Relationships." *Biometrika*, 28 (1936), 32–33.

Pearson, Karl and Moul, Margaret. "The Problem of Alien Immigration into Great Britain Illustrated by an Examination of Russian and Polish Jewish Children." *Annals of Eugenics*, 1 (1925), 5–127; 2 (1926), 111–244, 290–317; 3 (1927), 1–70, 201–264.

Penniman, T. K. *A Hundred Years of Anthropology*. London: Duckworth, 1935.

Penrose, Lionel S. "A Study in the Inheritance of Intelligence. The Analysis of 100 Families Containing Subcultural Mental Defectives." Reprint. *The British Journal of Psychology*, 22 (1933).

Mental Defect. London: Sidgwick & Jackson, 1933.

The Influence of Heredity on Disease. London: Lewis & Co., 1934.

The Biology of Mental Defect. 1949. Rev. edn, London: Sidgwick and Jackson, 1954.

Pirie, N. W. "John Burdon Sanderson Haldane." *Biographical Memoirs of Fellows of the Royal Society*, 12 (1966), 219–249.

Poliakov, Leon. *The Aryan Myth: A History of Racist and Nationalist Ideas in Europe*. Translated by Edmund Howard. New York: New American Library, 1971.

Popenoe, Paul, and Gosney, E. S. *Twenty-Eight Years of Sterilization in California*. Pasadena, CA: The Human Betterment Foundation, 1938.

Provine, William B. *The Origins of Population Genetics.* Chicago: Chicago University Press, 1971.
"Geneticists and Race." *American Zoologist,* 26 (1986), 857–887.
Punnett, Reginald C. *Mendelism.* 1905; New York: Wiltshire Book, 1909.
"Eliminating Feeblemindedness." *Journal of Heredity,* 8 (1917), 464–465.
"Genetics, Mathematics, and Natural Selection." *Nature,* 126 (October 18, 1930), 595–597.
Purcell, Edward A. *The Crisis of Democratic Theory: Scientific Naturalism and the Problem of Value.* Lexington: University of Kentucky Press, 1973.
Quiggin. A. Hingston. *Haddon, The Head Hunter.* Cambridge: Cambridge University Press, 1942.
Richards, Audrey. "Culture in Malinowski's Work," in Firth (ed.), *Man and Culture.*
Radcliffe-Brown, Alfred Reginald. "The Methods of Ethnology and Social Anthropology." *South African Journal of Science,* 20 (1923), 124–147.
"The Present Position of Anthropological Studies." A Presidential address to Section H of the British Association for the Advancement of Science, 1931. In Radcliffe-Brown, *Method in Social Anthropology.*
A Natural Science of Society. Glenco, The Free Press, 1948, 1957.
Method in Social Anthropology. Edited by M. N. Srinivas, Chicago: University of Chicago Press, 1958.
Reinders, Robert C. "Racism on the Left: E. D. Morel and the 'Black Horror' on the Rhine." *International Review of Social History,* 13 (1968).
Rich, Paul B. *Race and Empire in British Politics.* Cambridge: Cambridge University Press, 1986.
Ripley, William Z. *The Races of Europe: A Sociological Study.* London: Kegan Paul, 1900.
Rivers, W. H. R. "The Unity of Anthropology." *Nature,* 109 (1922), 323–324.
Rivers, W. H. R. *et al.* eds. *Reports Upon the Present Condition and Future Needs of the Science of Anthropology.* Washington: Carnegie Institution of Washington, 1913.
Rosenberg, Charles E. *No Other Gods: On Science and American Social Thought.* Baltimore: Johns Hopkins University Press, 1976.
Royal Anthropological Institute and the Institute of Sociology. *Race and Culture.* London: Le Play House and Royal Anthropological Institute, n.d. (1936).
Schroeder-Gudehus, Brigitte. "Challenge to Transitional Loyalties: International Scientific Organization After First World War." *Science Studies,* 3 (1973), 93–118.
Schultz, A. H. "Ales Hrdlicka, 1869–1943." *National Academy of Sciences Biographical Memoirs,* 23[1945].
Schwesinger, Gladys C. *Heredity and Environment.* Edited by Frederick Osborn. New York: MacMillan, 1933.
Searle, Geoffrey R. *Eugenics and Politics in Britain 1900–1914.* Leyden: Noordhoff International Publishers, 1976.

"Eugenics and Class," in Charles Webster (ed.), *Biology, Medicine and Society* pp. 217–242.

"Eugenics and Politics in the 1930s." *Annals of Science*, 36 (1979), 159–179.

Seligman, Charles G. "Anthropology and Psychology. A Study of Some Points of Contact." *JRAI*, 54 (1924).

Races of Africa. London: The Home University Library, 1930. 4th edn Oxford: Oxford University Press, 1966. Reprint 1979.

"Anthropological Perspective and Psychological Theory." The Huxley Memorial Lecture for 1932. *JRAI*, 62 (1932), 193–228.

Egypt and Negro Africa. A Study in Divine Kinship. London: George Routledge and Sons, 1934.

"Patterns of Culture, A Symposium between the British Psychological Society (Medical Section) and the Royal Anthropological Institute." 27 May 1936. *Man*, 36 (1936) 113–114.

Seligman, Charles G; Ginsberg, Morris; and Mair, Ramsay. *Psychology and Modern Problems*. Edited with an introduction by J. A. Hadfield. London: Longmans, Green & Co., 1936.

Seligman, Herbert J. *Race Against Man*. New York: Van Rees Press, 1939.

Shils, Edward. *The Intellectuals and the Powers*. Chicago: The University of Chicago Press, 1972.

"Center and Periphery" in *The Constitution of Society*. Chicago: The University of Chicago Press, 1982, 93–109.

Silverman, Sydel, ed. *Totems and Teachers: Perspectives in the History of Anthropology*. New York: Columbia University Press, 1981.

Simpson, George E. *Melville J. Herskovits*. New York: Columbia University Press, 1973.

Slobodin, Richard. *W. H. R. Rivers*. New York: Columbia University Press, 1978.

Smith, Grafton Elliot. "The Influence of Racial Admixture in Egypt." *Eugenics Review*, 7 (1915), 163–183.

The Evolution of Man: Essays. New York: Milford, Oxford University Press, 1924.

Human History. New York: Norton, 1929.

The Diffusion of Culture. London: Watts, 1933.

"Chairman's Address. Section A. Anatomy and Physical Anthropology." In *Congrès International des Sciences Anthropologiques et Ethnologiques*, Londres: Institut Royal d'Anthropologie, 1934. pp. 65–68. JLMP.

"Problems of Race." *Eugenics Review*, 60, 1, (1968), 25–31.

Smith, Grafton Elliot et al. *Early Man, His Origin, Development and Culture*. London: Ernest Benn, 1931.

Smith, Marian W. "Boas's 'Natural History' Approach to Field Method," in Walter Goldschmidt (ed.), *The Anthropology of Franz Boas*, pp. 46–60.

Sokal, M. M. "Science and James McKeen Cattell, 1894–1945." *Science*, 209 (1980), 43–52.

Solomon, Barbara M. *Ancestors and Immigrants*. Cambridge: Harvard University Press, 1956.

Soloway, Richard A. *Demography and Degeneration. Eugenics and the Declining Birthrate in Twentieth-Century Britain*. Chapel Hill: The University of North Carolina Press, 1990.

Sonneborn, Tracy M. "Herbert Spencer Jennings, April 8, 1868- April 14, 1947." *Biographical Memoirs of the National Academy of Sciences*, 47 (1975), 143–223.

Sorokin, Pitrim. *Contemporary Sociological Theories*. New York: Harper Brothers, 1928.

Spencer, Frank, ed. *A History of American Physical Anthropology, 1930–1980*. New York: Academic Press, 1981.

Spiro, Melford E. *Oedipus in the Trobriands*. Chicago: The University of Chicago Press, 1982.

Steggerda, Morris. "Charles Benedict Davenport (1866–1944); The Man and His Contributions to Physical Anthropology." *AJPA* n.s. 2, (1944), 167–185.

Stepan, Nancy. *The Idea of Race in Science: Great Britain 1800–1960*. Hamden, Conn: Archon Books, 1982.

Steward, Julian H. *Alfred Kroeber*. New York: Columbia University Press, 1973.

Stocking, George W. Jr. *Race, Culture and Evolution in the History of Anthropology*. Chicago: University of Chicago Press, (1968) 1982.

"From Chronology to Ethnology: James Cowles Prichard and British Anthropology, 1800–1850." In *Researches into the Physical History of Man*, by J. C. Prichard Chicago, 1973, pp. ix–cx.

"Anthropology as Kulturkampf: Science and Politics in the Career of Franz Boas." In *The Uses of Anthropology*, edited by Walter Goldschmidt, American Anthropological Association, special publication No. 11. Washington: American Anthropological Association, 1979, pp. 33–50.

"Radcliffe-Brown and British Social Anthropology." In *Functionalism Historicized*, edited by George W. Stocking Jr., pp. 131–191.

Stocking, George W. Jr. ed. *The Shaping of American Anthropology 1883–1911: A Franz Boas Reader*. New York: Basic Books, 1974.

Functionalism Historicized. Essays on British Social Anthropology. History of Anthropology, vol. 2, Madison: University of Wisconsin Press, 1984.

Objects and Others. Essays on Museums and Material Culture. History of Anthropology, vol. 3, Madison: University of Wisconsin Press, 1984.

Stoddard, Lothrop. *The Rising Tide of Color Against White World Supremacy*. Introduction by Madison Grant. New York: Scribner's Sons, 1920.

Szacki, Jerzy. *History of Sociological Thought*. Westport, Conn: Greenwood Press, 1979.

Tanner, J. M. "Boas' Contribution to Knowledge of Human Growth and

Form," in Goldschmidt (ed.), *The Anthropology of Franz Boas*, pp. 76–111.

Tildesley, M. L. "Measurement of Head Length and Breadth: The Systems of Broca, Topinard, Monaco Agreement, British Association, Martin," *Man* 38 (1938), 102–104.

Tildesley, M. L. "Racial Anthropometry: A Plan to Obtain International Uniformity of Method," *JRAI*, 58 (1928), 351–361.

Topinard, P. *Anthropology*. London: Chapman and Hall, 1878.

Toulmin, Stephen. "Can Science and Ethics be Reconnected?" *Hastings Center Report* 9 (June 1979), 27–34.

"How We Can Recontruct the Sciences with the Foundation of Ethics?" in Engelhardt Jr and Callahan (eds.), *Knowing and Valuing: The Search for Common Roots*. Hastings-on Hudson, N.Y.: Hastings Center, 1980

Tozzer, Alfred. *An Anthropometric Study of Hawaiians of Pure and Mixed Blood.* Cambridge, MA: Harvard University, Peabody Museum, 1928.

Trigger, Bruce G. *Gordon Childe: Revolutions in Archaeology*. New York: Columbia University Press, 1980.

Underwood, E. A. "Charles Joseph Singer." *Dictionary of National Biography*, 1960.

United Nations Educational Science and Cultural Organization. *The Race Concept: Results of An Inquiry*. Paris: UNESCO, 1952.

U.S. Congress. *Hearing Before The House Committee on Immigration and Naturalization*. 68th Congress, 1st Session, Washington: Government Printing Office, 1924.

Urry, James. "Englishmen, Celts and Iberians: The Ethnographic Survey of the United Kingdom, 1892–1899," in Stocking Jr. (ed.), *Functionalism Historicized*, pp. 83–105.

De Vos, George, and Romanucci-Ross, Lola. *Ethnic Identity, Cultural Continuities and Change*. 1975. Chicago: University of Chicago Press, 1982.

Weiss, Sheila Faith. "Race Hygiene and the rational management of national efficience: Wilhelm Schallmayer and the origins of German eugenics, 1980–1920." Ph.D. dissertation, Johns Hopkins University, 1983.

"Willhelm Schallmayer and the Logic of German Eugenics." *Isis*, 77 (March 1986), 33–46.

Wells, George Philip. "Lancelot Hogben." *Biographical Memoirs of Fellows of the Royal Society*, 24 (1978), 183–221.

Wells, H. G., Huxley, Julian Sorel, and Wells, George Philip. *Science of Life*. 3 Vols. London: The Amalgamated Press, 1929.

Werskey, Gary. *The Visible College*. London: Allen Lane, 1978.

White, Leslie A. "Diffusion Versus Evolution: An Anti-Evolutionist Fallacy." *American Anthropologist*, 47 (1945), 339–56.

"Evolutionism in Cultural Anthropology: A Rejoinder." *American Anthropologist*, 49 (1947), 400–411.

The Science of Culture. New York: Grove Press, 1949.

"The Ethnography and Ethnology of Franz Boas." *Bulletin of the Texas Memorial Museum*, 6 (April 1963). Reprint.

Wilson, J. T. "G. E. Smith." *Obituary Notices of Fellows of the Royal Society* (1938), 323–333.

Wissler, Clark. *Man and Culture*. New York: Thomas Y. Crowell, 1923.

Wolf, Eric R. "Alfred L. Kroeber," in Silverman (ed.), *Totems and Teachers*, pp. 35–64.

Wright, Sewall. Contributions to Genetics," in K. R. Dronamraju (ed.), *Haldane and Modern Biology*. Baltimore: Johns Hopkins University Press, 1968.

Yerkes, Robert M. ed., *Psychological Examining in the United States Army*, Memoirs of the National Academy of Sciences, no. 15. Washington: National Academy of Sciences, 1921.

Zuckerman, Solly. *The Social Life of Monkeys and Apes*. London: Kegan Paul, 1932. Reissue, with a Postscript, 1981.

From Apes to Warlords. London: Hamish Hamilton, 1978.

Zuckerman, Solly, ed. *The Concepts of Human Evolution*. London: The Zoological Society of London, 1973.

Index

medicine, 187, 260–266, 329
  blood groups, 233 *see also* genetics
  public health, 187
Mencken, H. L., 130, 210
Mendelism, 71, 72, 75, 77, 82, 85, 87n, 92,
  101, 117, 137, 143–151 passim, 152,
  154, 170, 171–172, 182, 186, 213, 220,
  234, 302 *see also* genetics, biometrics
Mental Deficiency Committee, 186, 265
Merriam, John Campbell, 68, 69n, 84n,
  113n, 272, 273, 331
mesocephalic index *see* race theory, head
  shape
Métraux, A., 325n, 342n
Mond, Sir Robert, 330n
Mollison, Theodor, 310
Montagu, Ashley, 3n, 16n, 97, 339, 342n
Morant, Geoffrey, 105, 158–162, 260,
  293–294
  political/professional activity, 159, 289
  critique of Boas, 161
Morel, Edmond Dean, 24–25
Morgan, L. H., 87n, 274
Morgan, T. H., 7n, 149, 197
Muller, H. J., 197, 233, 237
Murphy, Gardner, 329
Murray Islanders, 20, 28
Murray, Gilbert, 281, 324
Mussolini, B., 324
Myres, Charles S., 24
Myres, John Linton, 34–36, 286
  professional activity, 34, 289–290
  political/intellectual activity, 36, 309–310
  on theories of race, 35–36

National Academy of Sciences, 282, 337
National Association for the Advancement
  of Colored People (NAACP), 312
National Research Council, 84n, 112,
  113–4, 115, 211, 329, 330
naturalism *see* biological determinism,
  racism
natural selection, 103, 138, 183, 187
Nature (on race), 287–288, 296, 309, 327n
Nazism, 1, 2, 31, 54, 55, 161, 218, 249, 327,
  336
  response to, 1, 66, 107, 269, 279,
  281–285, 318–329, 334
  in Britain, 31, 107, 162, 232, 245, 247,
  250, 256, 258, 259–260, 285 passim
  in USA, 275, 280–285, 310–318 passim,
  332–340
  see also Germany
New Negro Movement, 118, 148
New School of Social Research, 96, 115,
  128, 335

New Guinea, 20
New York, 9, 67, 68, 70, 80, 93, 94, 96
New York Zoological Society, 69
Newman, H. H., 310
Nilsson-Ehle, H., 146

Osborn, Frederick, 168, 197n, 199n,
  272–276, 283n, 328–332
Osborn, Henry Fairfield, 67, 68, 96, 272, 275
Oxford, 20, 25, 26, 31, 34–37, 122, 139, 185

Pacelli, Cardinal, 320, 324, 325
Pacific Islands, 119, 122, 129, 132–133
paleontology, 17, 19, 21, 38, 67, 294
Paris, 318, 321, 323, 325–328
Parsons, Elsie Clews, 95, 115
Peake, H. J. E., 69n
Pearl, Raymond, 68, 142, 144, 177, 204,
  209, 210–220, 310, 311
  background, 210–211
  professional activity, 210–211, 212, 218,
  219, 314, 315
  on eugenic theories, 211–213
  on racism, 210, 213–219
Pearson, Egon S., 157
Pearson, Karl, 49n, 82n, 138, 139, 141–142,
  151–159, 160, 161, 209, 220, 222, 234,
  270
  background, 151–153
  political/intellectual activity, 151–152
  on theories of race, 152, 154–159
  critique of Boas, 161
  critique of Davenport, 166
  see also biometrics
Penrose, Lionel, 72, 150, 162, 177, 209, 228,
  260–266, 268
  background, 261–262
  on science, 262–266
  on theories of race, 262n, 265–266
Perry, W. J., 41n, 44n, 45
pessimism, 41, 47, 59, 62, 71, 102, 109, 156,
  182 *see also* civilization, race
  theory-human nature
phrenology, 52
physical anthropology, 4, 15, 16, 18, 19, 28,
  42, 44, 52, 67, 76, 83, 86, 95–118, 123,
  137, 159–161, 174, 309, 311, 329, 345
  standardization of techniques in, 159,
  315–316
  see also anatomy, paleontology, primates
physiology, 44, 85
Piltdown Affair, 21, 38, 42–43, 52
Pitt-Rivers, Captain George H. L. F., 244,
  288, 289, 291 passim, 295
Poffenberger, A. T., 283
polygeny, 15, 17, 35–36